English as a Lingua Franca: Attitude and Identity

GW00771333

Published in this series

English as a Lingua Franca:
Attitude and Identity

JENNIFER JENKINS

OXFORD
UNIVERSITY PRESS

OXFORD
UNIVERSITY PRESS

Great Clarendon Street, Oxford OX2 6DP

Oxford University Press is a department of the University of Oxford.
It furthers the University's objective of excellence in research, scholarship,
and education by publishing worldwide in

Oxford New York

Auckland Cape Town Dar es Salaam Hong Kong Karachi
Kuala Lumpur Madrid Melbourne Mexico City Nairobi
New Delhi Shanghai Taipei Toronto

With offices in

Argentina Austria Brazil Chile Czech Republic France Greece
Guatemala Hungary Italy Japan Poland Portugal Singapore
South Korea Switzerland Thailand Turkey Ukraine Vietnam

OXFORD and OXFORD ENGLISH are registered trade marks of
Oxford University Press in the UK and in certain other countries

© Oxford University Press 2007

The moral rights of the author have been asserted

Database right Oxford University Press (maker)

First published 2007
2011 2010 2009 2008 2007
10 9 8 7 6 5 4 3 2 1

No unauthorized photocopying

All rights reserved. No part of this publication may be reproduced,
stored in a retrieval system, or transmitted, in any form or by any means,
without the prior permission in writing of Oxford University Press,
or as expressly permitted by law, or under terms agreed with the appropriate
reprographics rights organization. Enquiries concerning reproduction outside
the scope of the above should be sent to the ELT Rights Department, Oxford
University Press, at the address above

You must not circulate this book in any other binding or cover
and you must impose this same condition on any acquirer

Any websites referred to in this publication are in the public domain and
their addresses are provided by Oxford University Press for information only.
Oxford University Press disclaims any responsibility for the content

ISBN: 978 0 19 442237 6

Printed in Spain by Unigraf S.L.

Dedicated to the memory of Sara García Peralta
dear friend and colleague
1947–2004

Contents

Acknowledgements

In writing this book, I have benefited from the generosity of numerous people, who have contributed their time and expertise in various ways. First of all, I would like to thank the 363 people around the world who completed the questionnaire that forms the basis of the discussion in Chapter 6. Many of them not only provided the information requested, but went way beyond the 'call of duty' by discussing—sometimes at considerable length—the issues that the questions raised for them. The questionnaires could not have reached the respondents in the first place without help, sometimes extensive, from a number of people in the participating countries. In this respect, I am indebted to Veronica Colwell, Annike Denke, Beth Erling, Sara Hannam, Frauke Intemann, Jing Jin, Tomoko Miki, Yuka Kakihara, Kumiko Murata, Tarja Nikula, Zaina Abdulla Nunes, Stuart Perrin, Mila Plá, Dolores Ramírez, Edna Sung, Robin Walker, Magdalena Wrembel, and Melissa Yu.

I would also like to thank the authors of the three written texts that are analysed and discussed in Chapter 5. I am well aware that these authors will not sympathize with my critique of their work, but hope they will understand that what I say concerns the claims made in the texts, and not the people who made them. My thanks, too, to all the interview participants who provided such detailed insights into their English-speaking and English-teaching lives. They cannot be named here, but will recognize in Chapter 7 the extent of their contribution.

A number of colleagues at King's College London provided advice on data collection and analysis, and in this regard, I would especially like to thank Constant Leung, Gabriella Rundblad, and Christopher Tribble. I have also gained a great deal from discussions of ELF with my research students, particularly Alessia Cogo, Martin Dewey, Toshie Mimatsu, Sumathi Renganathan, and Ayako Suzuki. My thanks, too, to my current Head of Department, Jonathan Osborne, for smoothing the path to the sabbatical leave that made writing the book a possibility in the first place.

In the wider world, Barbara Seidlhofer contributed to the book on many levels, providing both inspiration and information in equal and copious measure. I was also able to sharpen my thinking about ELF in all kinds of ways as a result of discussions with colleagues including Suresh Canagarajah, David Deterding, Alan Firth, Adrian Holliday, Juliane House, Anna Mauranen, Robert Phillipson, Robin Walker, and Peter Trudgill, while Vicky Hollett provided helpful information about developments in Business English.

x *Acknowledgements*

At OUP, Cristina Whitecross has been a constant source of encouragement, support, and patience throughout, while Julia Sallabank played an important role in the early phase of the book and Simon Murison-Bowie in the final phase. Above all, I would like to note my profound gratitude to Henry Widdowson, who painstakingly and sensitively commented on the original manuscript, the revision, and re-revision, and gave more generously of his time and wisdom than any author has the right to expect.

Finally, on a personal note, as I write I am about to take up a post at the University of Southampton, and am looking forward to developing ELF in a major way in an environment where this field will thrive. Such an environment of course owes much to the influence of the late Christopher Brumfit and his interest in and enthusiasm for the study of English as an International Language.

The author and publisher are grateful to those who have given permission to reproduce the following extracts and adaptations of copyright material:

p.12 Görlach, M. 2002. 'Global English' in *Still More Englishes*, pp12–13. Amsterdam: John Benjamins. With kind permission of John Benjamins Publishing Company, Amsterdam/Philadelphia www.benjamins.com

p.19 Phillipson, R. 2007. 'English, no longer a foreign language in Europe?' in J. Cummins and C. Davison (eds.). *The International Handbook of English Language Teaching*. Vol. 1. Norwell, Mass.: Springer. With kind permission of Springer Science and Business Media.

p.46 Hammersley, M. and P. Atkinson. 1983. *Ethnography: Principles in Practice*, pp142–3. London: Tavistock.

p.130 and p.211 mark-up conventions of the VOICE project. See http://www.univie.ac.at/voice/voice.php?page=transcription_general_information

p.130 and p.211 Niedzielski, N. A. and D. R. Preston. 2000/2003. *Folk Linguistics*. Berlin and New York: Mouton de Gruyter.

p.191 Wiegand, P. 1994. Map of the world from *The Oxford Infant Atlas Workbook*. © Oxford University Press.

p.202 Omoniyi, T. and G. White (eds.). 2006. 'Introduction' in *The Sociolinguistics of Identity*. London: Continuum.

p.229–30 Tribble, C. 2003. *Looking at ELT*. London: British Council.

p.243–4 Coleman, J. A. 2006. 'English-medium teaching in European higher education' in *Language Teaching* 39:1–14. Cambridge: Cambridge University Press.

p.250 Cauldwell, R. T. 2002. *Streaming Speech*.CD-Rom, Speechinaction. 2006 http://www.speechinaction.net/SPARC_ELF.htm

Although every effort has been made to trace and contact copyright holders before publication, this has not been possible in some cases. We apologize for any apparent infringement of copyright and if notified, the publisher will be pleased to rectify any errors or omissions at the earliest opportunity.

Preface

In essence this is a book about language change and the responses it elicits among speakers of a language. Its specific focus is English as a Lingua Franca (ELF), and in particular, though not exclusively, ELF accents. The concept of ELF is discussed extensively in Chapter 1, but for the moment, suffice it to say that ELF and EIL (English as an International Language) are one and the same phenomenon, and that both refer to lingua franca uses of English primarily among its non-mother tongue speakers. The term ELF has recently become the favoured one for reasons that are explained in Chapter 1. By contrast, at the time I wrote my first book on the subject, *The Phonology of English as an International Language*, few people had heard of ELF,[1] and for that reason, I chose then to use the term EIL. (See Jenkins 2000: 11.)

Despite the switch from 'EIL' to 'ELF', this book is in some ways a sequel to the 2000 book. In fact one of my reasons for embarking on the new book was the controversy that the previous one had elicited. I have therefore explored in depth, and with an emphasis on L2 English users' perspectives, the many, varied, and often contradictory or polarized responses to the changes that are currently being identified and described as ELF innovations, as well as the misinterpretations and misconceptions that characterize many of these responses.

It is often observed that English has become a global language, and that the majority of its non-native speakers (NNSs) use it as a lingua franca among themselves rather than as a 'foreign' language to communicate with its NSs. However, this development has not so far had much impact on English language attitudes, let alone English language teaching: users of English, NNS and NS, teacher, learner, applied linguist, world English scholar, and general public alike, are finding it difficult to make the conceptual leap needed in order to allow ELF a legitimate place alongside the Englishes of the inner and outer circles,[2] even at the descriptive level. For despite the fact that ELF, like any other instance of language change, is an entirely natural phenomenon, and attempts to arrest language change entirely unnatural, ELF is often not viewed in this way. Again, although ELF innovations could be said to reflect the identities of its lingua franca speakers, the identity issue is by no means as clear-cut as this suggests, and is affected in critical ways by language attitudes.

The aim of this book, then, is to explore the reasons for concerns about ELF. Regardless of the case for change in principle, it is essential to consider how it appears to those who will be most affected—in this case primarily

English language teachers and, by association, their learners—and to consider carefully and critically their alternative arguments and attitudes. By bringing these to the surface, ELF researchers will be in a much better position to evaluate the feasibility and validity of ELF as a potential provider of norms for English language teaching, rather than as an interesting new phenomenon that will remain the stuff of corpus description. In order to investigate these arguments and attitudes, I have analysed ELT and applied linguistics texts (spoken and written) from a content analytical perspective (Chapter 2) and discourse analytical perspective (Chapter 5), carried out a large-scale questionnaire study in expanding circle countries (Chapter 6), and conducted in-depth interviews with NNS teachers of English (Chapter 7).

It is my hope that the research findings in this book, in so far as they reveal the language attitudes, beliefs, ideologies, and identity conflicts that underlie many of the negative responses to ELF, will contribute towards a reappraisal that will enable ELF, one day perhaps, to be offered as a pedagogic alternative to (but not necessarily a replacement for) traditional EFL.

Notes

1 At the time I was conducting my earlier research on ELF accents (1989–1995), a small number of scholars in mainland Europe were also researching and writing about lingua franca uses of English (for example, Firth 1990, 1996; Meierkord 1996), using terms such as 'lingua franca English' and 'non-native/non-native speaker discourse'. In the majority of cases, however, they were not talking about ELF in the sense in which it is conceived in this book and understood by most current ELF researchers. Firth's interest (1990, 1996) for example, was in demonstrating how English may be used successfully in lingua franca communication *despite* 'deficiencies' such as 'unidiomaticity' when compared with English native speaker use. ELF research proper investigates the phenomenon *in its own right* and not by comparison with an ENL baseline.

2 This is a reference to Kachru's three-circle model of English according to which the inner circle consists of the countries where English is spoken as a native language; the outer circle of the countries which were colonized by native English speakers and where English is spoken as part of a multilingual repertoire; and the expanding circle of the countries where English is learnt and spoken but does not serve institutional purposes. (See, for example, Kachru 1985.)

I

ELF: what it is and what it is thought to be

This chapter introduces the themes of the book and sets the scene for all that follows. As its title suggests, it is divided into two main parts. The first (and longer) takes up and develops the initial explanation of ELF provided in the Preface, as well as considering a range of orientations towards it. The second part examines a number of typical misinterpretations and misconceptions about ELF in general and ELF accents in particular.

What is ELF?

ELF stands for English as a Lingua Franca. Let us first consider what is meant by the term 'lingua franca'. In essence, a lingua franca is a contact language used among people who do not share a first language, and is commonly understood to mean a second (or subsequent) language of its speakers. According to Knapp and Meierkord, '[i]n its original sense, the term "lingua franca" referred to a variety that was spoken along the South-Eastern coast of the Mediterranean between appr. the 15th and the 19th century' (2002: 9). Although earlier languages had performed lingua franca roles, this was the first variety to be explicitly labelled as such, while alternative terms have included 'contact language', 'auxiliary language', 'trade language', and 'trade jargon' (see Samarin 1987). This first lingua franca was 'a pidgin, probably based on some Italian dialects in its earliest history, and included elements from Spanish, French, Portuguese, Arabic, Turkish, Greek and Persian' (Knapp and Meierkord, ibid.). Its plurilinguistic composition, then, clearly exemplifies an intrinsic and key feature of lingua francas: their hybrid nature.

Turning specifically to *English* as a Lingua Franca, however, an immediate problem needs to be resolved *vis-à-vis* the traditional definition of a lingua franca and native speakers (NSs) of English. The historical lingua franca had no NSs, and this could be taken to imply that NSs of ENL (English as a Native Language) should be excluded from the definition of ELF. Because of the international spread of English that has been growing apace since the latter part of the 20th century (a situation recognized as unprecedented for any other language hitherto), English is frequently the mutual language of choice in settings such as conferences, business meetings, and political gatherings. The difficulty here is that such interactions may include NSs of English as well as its NNSs, even though the former are generally in the minority.[1] Some scholars nevertheless prefer to stay with a 'pure' interpretation of a lingua franca. Firth, for example, describes it as:

> a 'contact language' between persons who share neither a common native tongue nor a common (national) culture, and for whom English is the chosen *foreign* language of communication.
> (1996: 240; emphasis in original)

However, as I pointed out in the Preface, Firth was not at that time referring to ELF as it is now conceived, i.e. as an emerging English that exists in its *own right* and which is being described in its *own terms* rather than by comparison with ENL. Instead, he was talking about a 'foreign' language that happens to be English, and the ways in which successful communication is achieved in spite of its speakers' errors (as compared with the native language). If ELF is conceived as a foreign language in this way, then, by definition, none of its speakers can be native speakers of the language.

Like Firth, though not for the same reason, House defines ELF interactions as being 'between members of two or more different linguacultures in English, *for none of whom English is the mother tongue*' (1999: 74; emphasis added). Others differentiate between ELF and English as an International Language (EIL), the former excluding NSs and the latter including them. However, this distinction has become less frequent of late, perhaps because it runs the risk of causing confusion. Meanwhile, some scholars use EIL as a blanket term for all uses of English involving NNSs worldwide regardless of whether they are interacting with other NNSs or with NSs (for example, Llurda 2004), while still others use EIL to refer more specifically to NNS–NNS communication (for example, McKay 2002).

On the other hand, while arguing that the conceptualization of ELF must be separated from a 'nativeness criterion', Seidlhofer considers that 'it has to be remembered that ELF interactions often also include interlocutors from the Inner and Outer Circles' (2004: 211–12). In other words, according to her interpretation, ELF is not limited to members of the expanding circle, and those who also speak English intranationally, whether they come from an inner or outer circle country, are not excluded from ELF communication. Or, to put it another way, ELF does not stop being ELF if inner or outer circle members happen to be present. Seidlhofer's only proviso is that empirical work on describing ELF should not involve too many NS informants. This is because they would confound the data with non-ELF forms and make it more difficult to identity emerging ELF norms, i.e. to find out 'whether and in what ways ELF interactions are actually *sui generis*' (House ibid.). NSs, then, are to a large extent excluded from ELF corpus research (VOICE, for example, allows only up to ten per cent of NSs of English in any specific speech event)[2] and perhaps, for the same reason, this should also apply to speakers of established (nativized) outer circle Englishes.[3] My own position on the NS-ELF question and the one taken throughout this book, is very much in line with Seidlhofer's. That is, ELF does not exclude NSs of English, but they are not included in data collection, and when they take part in ELF interactions, they do not represent a linguistic reference point.

Terminology

This leads to the reasons for preferring 'ELF' to any of the other terms currently in circulation, an issue that is less trivial than it might initially appear. As was mentioned in the Preface, at the time when I first employed the term 'ELF', it was also in use, if not extensively, among scholars in mainland Europe. On the other hand, both the term and—to a considerable extent—the concept it represents, appeared to be unknown to applied linguists and ELT professionals almost elsewhere else. This was still largely the situation a few years later when I explained my decision to stay with EIL:

> ... it remains to be seen whether ELF ultimately catches on. In the meantime, I will for present purposes restrict its use to describing the core of pronunciation features that I identify ... as a model for international English phonology—the 'Lingua Franca Core', and will continue to use the more widely-acknowledged EIL.
> (Jenkins 2000: 11)

Since then, however, change has occurred rapidly. The concept of expanding circle English (by whatever name) as involving communication predominantly among NNSs rather than between NSs and NNSs, has become widely known, if not necessarily widely approved. During the same period, the term ELF itself has figured prominently in a number of publications by ELF researchers (for example, Knapp and Meierkord 2002; Mauranen 2003; Seidlhofer 2004) and in their conference papers (for example, House 2004; Jenkins 2004; Seidlhofer 2002; Seidlhofer and Jenkins 2003). As a result, the term has finally begun to be employed (usually in preference to EIL) in publications by academics who are not themselves engaged in ELF research (for example, Phillipson 2003), and has even been accorded sufficient status to merit an entry (by Gnutzmann) in a recent encyclopedia of language teaching and learning (Byram 2004: 357–8).[4]

ELF has a number of advantages that are not shared by other terms such as EIL, International English, Global English and the like. To repeat what I said a few years ago:

> ELF emphasizes the role of English in communication between speakers from different L1s, i.e. the primary reason for learning English today; it suggests the idea of community as opposed to alienness; it emphasizes that people have something in common rather than their differences; it

implies that 'mixing' languages is acceptable ... and thus that there is nothing inherently wrong in retaining certain characteristics of the L1, such as accent; finally, the Latin name symbolically removes the ownership of English from the Anglos both to no one and, in effect, to everyone. (Jenkins 2000: 11)

Last, but by no means least, as Seidlhofer (2004) points out, ELF is preferred not so much 'because most lingua franca definitions restrict it to communication among nonnative users as such, but because it best signals that it is these nonnative users that provide the strongest momentum for the development of the language in its global uses' (p. 212). That is, ELF more than any of the alternatives implies that it is NNSs rather than NSs who are at the forefront of innovation and change in lingua franca English, an issue which will be taken up later in this chapter.

In addition to these benefits, ELF is more likely than its most frequent alternative, EIL, to discourage some of the kinds of misconception that are discussed in the second part of the chapter. One such misconception seems, according to Seidlhofer (op. cit.), to have been brought about by the use of 'International English' as 'a shorthand for EIL'. This, she argues, 'is misleading in that it suggests that there is one clearly distinguishable, codified and unitary variety called *International English*, which is certainly not the case' (p. 210; emphasis in original). In addition, the use of this term is also ambiguous in that it is used to describe an entirely different communicative situation: the English of countries where it is the first language of the majority (the inner circle) and/or of countries where it is an official second language (the outer circle). In other words, it is used to describe an entirely different linguacultural context from that which obtains for ELF communication. Others use it to mean merely the international circulation of an NS variety of English, for example, City & Guilds Pitman 'International English Qualifications' in 'International ESOL' and 'International Spoken ESOL'. Meanwhile, the terms 'English as a global language' or 'Global English' are not only vague as regards what type of communication they represent, but also imply—wrongly—that English is spoken by everyone around the globe, whereas statistics suggest that around a quarter of the world's population speak English fluently or competently (Crystal 2003: 6).

To summarize, then, ELF is the preferred term[5] for a relatively new manifestation of English which is very different in concept from both English as a Second Language (ESL)—the label frequently given to outer circle Englishes, and English as a Foreign Language (EFL)—the traditional, if to a great extent anachronistic, label for English in the expanding circle. Unlike ESL varieties, it is not primarily a local or contact language *within* national groups but *between* them. And unlike EFL, whose goal is in reality ENL (English as a Native Language), it is not primarily a language of communication between its NSs and NNSs, but among its NNSs.

Orientations to the concept of ELF

Characterized thus, ELF would seem to be an entirely logical and natural development arising out of new language contact situations in expanding circle contexts as a result of the changing role of English. This is very much how Brutt-Griffler sees it:

> One of the processes within the internationalization of English is what I call *transculturation*: the process by which varieties of World English increasingly become multicultural media within pluralistic communities. ... Transculturation is the process of transcending monoculturalism in language both within the world econocultural system and also within the varieties of World English. There is an interplay of forces in which these varieties influence one another and so each variety becomes itself more and more multicultural.
> (2002: 177–8; emphasis in original)

Brutt-Griffler contrasts what she sees as a natural development with the traditional orientation to English in international contexts, in which '... the "nonnative" user is situated along an interlanguage continuum, with the "native speaker" ... as the point of reference' (op. cit.: 179). According to this position, authority is 'granted' to the privileged speech community and it is assumed that 'the non-mother tongue user/learner seeks affiliation in the community of native speakers ... . Disguised as a relationship between individual English speakers', this is a uni-directional relationship in which 'the "native speaker" community is held to affect the "nonnative" without itself being affected'. (op. cit.: 179–80)

Similarly, in his chapter 'Teaching English as a world language', Brumfit (2001) points out how '[t]he major advances in sociolinguistic research over the past half-century indicate clearly the extent to which languages are shaped by their use' (p. 116). He then points out:

> Statistically native speakers are in a minority for language use, and thus in practice for language change, for language maintenance, and for the ideologies and beliefs associated with the language—at least in so far as non-native speakers use the language for a wide range of public and personal needs.
> (ibid.)

Brumfit adds that 'if a substantial number of non-native speakers did come to see themselves as a single group with major shared interests, the impact on the international language would be considerable' (ibid.). Meanwhile, Melchers and Shaw (2003) describe expanding circle English as currently 'exonorma-tive' but add that it may be in the process of becoming independent:

> one can imagine two stages, one in which features of different varieties are mixed to create a norm, and the second in which regional expanding-

circle Englishes develop which have unique features due to their own
substrates, etc., like the outer-circle varieties.
(p. 186)

Or, as De Swaan (2001) says, more directly and politically, quoting Bourdieu,
'*Il faut désangliciser l'Anglais*'. De Swaan adds that 'Europeans might develop
their own variety, the way Indians did, for example' and that '[n]ative speakers of other European languages 'trained in English at the language academies
of the Union, could become authoritative editors and judges of style for an
emerging European English' (p. 192). Such a group (or groups) as Brumfit
describes and De Swaan implies is believed by many ELF researchers, to exist
already, at least in embryonic form, and to be growing both in number and in
strength of conviction. One of the purposes of the research underpinning this
book is, indeed, to explore the extent of expanding circle speakers' identification with ELF speech communities at both global and local (for example,
European, SE Asian) levels.

Widdowson approaches the situation from a very similar perspective,
although for him it is not hypothetical in the way that it is for Brumfit, De
Swaan, and Melchers and Shaw. Instead, he contends that the linguistic
process is already under way, and that the critical issue is the need for the
results of this process to be legitimized. His much-quoted 1994 article on the
ownership of English was among the first (if not *the* first)[6] to point out the
implications of the increasing international use of English. He then developed
his argument in another well-known article (1997) in which he contrasted the
phenomena of language distribution and language spread, arguing that they
are in conflict with one another:

> Distribution denies spread. So you can think of English as an adopted
> international language, and then you will conceive of it as a stabilized and
> standardized code leased out on a global scale, and controlled by the
> inventors, not entirely unlike the franchise for Pizza Hut and Kentucky
> Fried Chicken. Distribution of essentially the same produce for customers
> worldwide. English the *lingua franca*, the franchise language. There are
> no doubt people who think in these conveniently commercial terms, and
> if English as an international language were indeed like this, there would
> be cause for concern. But it is not. It spreads, and as it does it gets adapted
> as the virtual language gets actualized in diverse ways, becomes subject to
> local constraints and controls.
> (p. 140; emphasis in original)

Widdowson repeats and extends his claims in two chapters of a later book
(2003), one on 'The ownership of English' (based on Widdowson 1994a),
and another on 'English as an international language' (based on Widdowson
1997). And as evidence of his conviction of the importance and pedagogic
relevance of international developments in English, he adds a final chapter
to Howatt's second edition of *The History of English Language Teaching*
(Howatt with Widdowson 2004), 'A perspective on recent trends'. Here he

points out the arguments in favour of lingua franca English as well as counter-
ing some of the misconceptions that have arisen:

> With the lingua franca proposals, there is no suggestion that any reduc-
> tion should be imposed, but that *the modified forms of the language
> which are actually in use should be recognized as a legitimate develop-
> ment* of English as an international means of communication. The
> functional range of the language is not thereby restricted, but on the
> contrary enhanced, for it enables its users to express themselves more
> freely without having to conform to norms which represent the socio-
> cultural identity of other people.
> (p. 361; emphasis added)

An interesting expression of this positive orientation towards ELF is that of
Lowenberg. In 2000, he was still claiming that it was reasonable for expanding (as opposed to outer) circle learners to be tested against NS norms. For
although he criticized as 'faulty' the assumption 'held by many of the qualified professionals who construct and administer tests of English proficiency,
particularly tests of English as an *international* language, such as TOEIC'
that 'native-speaker varieties of English still provide the norms which all of
the world's non-native speakers ... attempt to follow, even when no native
speakers are involved', he added that '[t]his assumption may still be accurate
in settings where English is used primarily as a foreign language with few
intranational functions, such as Japan, Egypt, and Spain', as contrasted with
the nativized Englishes of the outer circle (2000: 81; emphasis added). Thus
he argued, paradoxically, that tests of English as an International Language
should continue to defer to NS norms in the case of the very people who speak
English as an International Language the most.

Lowenberg seems to have changed his position as regards expanding
circle Englishes shortly afterwards. In an article in which he discusses the
assessment of proficiency in the expanding circle, he echoes his earlier discussion by pointing out that 'the prevailing wisdom ... has long been that the
appropriate norms for Standard English usage around the world are those
that are accepted and followed by educated native speakers of English', but
that '[c]onsiderable research in recent years ... has demonstrated that this
assumption is no longer valid in Kachru's (1985) Outer Circle countries,[7]
where English ... is widely used by large numbers of non-native speakers as
a second, often official, language in a broad range of *intra*national domains'
(2002: 431; emphasis in original). However, he then goes on to argue that
'change is occurring just as dynamically in the Expanding Circle as in the
Outer Circle' and that 'developers of proficiency tests in English as a world
language will have to be ever more cognizant of this change' (p. 435).

However, scholars who recognize the legitimacy of ELF are at present in
a fairly small minority among linguists (even, surprisingly, sociolinguistics
and applied linguists). ELF appears not to be seen in a positive light by large
numbers of NSs and NNSs alike, including members of the expanding circle

themselves, who for various reasons continue to support the traditional orientation to English in international contexts. It could perhaps be predicted that many NSs, especially those involved in the ELT profession, would feel uneasy when faced with what amounts to a loss of linguistic 'control' in respect of the largest group of L2 users of English (between 500 million and 1,000 million as compared with 320–380 million in the inner circle and 300–500 million in the outer circle, according to Crystal 2003: 61). Their responses to ELF vary. For example, taking a rather more simplistic view of the numbers than does Brumfit (above), Trudgill, dismisses the ELF claim by dispensing with the figures as an irrelevant diversion: 'The vast majority of native speakers will use English for something close to 100 per cent of all interactions, while for the average non-native [he seems to be referring to expanding circle use] the figure will be very much lower than that indeed. It is safe to assume that there is still very much more native than non-native English usage' (2005: 78). How Trudgill can be so sure of his 'facts' without citing any empirical evidence is not at all clear.[8]

Later in the same article, Trudgill takes issue with Widdowson's claim that as far as EIL is concerned 'how English develops in the world is no business whatever of native speakers ... they have no say in the matter, no right to intervene or pass judgement' (1994a: 385). Trudgill responds by insisting that 'some of us have an *obligation*, when asked, to ignore Widdowson's attempt to censor us' (op. cit.: 86; emphasis in original), and goes on to say 'it is not entirely clear to me what exactly 'ownership' of a language can mean' (op. cit.: 87). This is an unconvincing admission from a sociolinguist and Trudgill evidently realizes this, as he swiftly modifies his point by adding 'even if native speakers do not "own" English, there is an important sense in which it *stems from them*, especially historically and *resides in them*' (ibid.: emphasis added). His point is, of course, entirely true of English as a *Native Language*—the English varieties used in the inner circle countries. But from an ELF perspective his comments reveal precisely the sense of ownership of English that he affects not to understand: NSs spoke (a variety of) English first and thus, he believes, they have some sort of proprietorial claim to the language wherever, whenever and whoever speaks it 1,500 years later, regardless of the fact that it was ENL and not ELF that was spoken by those early NSs. This is in stark contrast to Brutt-Griffler, who dismisses the privileging of the English varieties of NS speech communities on the basis of their greater age as an essentially political criterion (2002: 179), and argues that 'English as a national language is only the source of world language, not the world language itself. And it must more and more be reduced to merely one variety of World English among many' (op. cit.: 181). Trudgill also ignores the whole issue of language contact, both past and present, and the phenomenon of accommodation. In fact he does not mention the latter in his article (other than in relation to his own capacity to accommodate to NNSs of English), although it has been shown to be a critical feature of ELF interactions, particularly at the level of pronunciation (Jenkins 2000: Chapter 7).

Another NS who does not appreciate the notion of ELF norms is Quirk, although this is perhaps less surprising in a grammarian than in a sociolinguist. Almost twenty years ago, Quirk argued that speakers in the Expanding Circle (he described them as 'EFL speakers') 'live in countries requiring English for what we may broadly call "external" purposes: contact with people from other countries, either through the spoken or written word, for such purposes as trade and scientific advance' (1985: 1). For these speakers, Quirk argues that standardness is a crucial concept, and that 'regarding the term "standard" as fit only for quotation marks is a *trahison des clerks*' (p. 5). He goes on to claim that 'the relatively narrow range of purposes for which the non-native needs to use English (even in ESL countries) is arguably well catered for by a single monochrome standard form that looks as good on paper as it sounds in speech' (p. 6). He has in mind, of course, the *native speaker* 'monochrome standard form'—ignoring the fact that no such thing exists and that it is notoriously difficult to pin down standard English even within a single country. (See the various articles in Bex and Watts 1999 for a range of detailed discussions of this issue.) Whatever this standard is, however, Quirk is convinced that it is 'both understood and respected in every corner of the globe where any knowledge of any variety of English exists' (ibid.). This myth, as I will demonstrate later, is a common folk belief even among English language teachers. Not surprisingly, Quirk produces no evidence to support the claim.

Quirk takes the argument in favour of a single 'standard' still further a few years later, in an article which precipitated what has since become known as the '*English Today* debate'. In a paper delivered to the Japanese Association of Language Teachers (JALT) in Tokyo in 1988 and subsequently published in the journal *English Today*, he describes support for NNS varieties of English (whether outer or expanding circle, and whether by academics or language teachers) as 'liberation linguistics' and 'half-baked quackery'. He warns his mainly-Japanese audience that

> [t]he implications of this, if hard-working Japanese teachers took such advice seriously, are quite horrendous. Students, 'liberally' permitted to think their 'new variety' of English was acceptable, would be defenceless before the harsher but more realistic judgment of those with authority to employ or promote them. They have in effect been denied the command of Standard English.
> (1990: 9–10)

Quirk goes on to say that if he 'were a foreign student in Tokyo[9] or Madrid to be taught English, [he] would feel cheated by such a tolerant pluralism' (p. 10). Paradoxically this is because he would want to acquire English 'because of its power as an instrument of *international* communication' (ibid.; emphasis added), as though EIL (or ESL for that matter) was merely a question of distributing NS varieties of English on the international market. (On this point, see above (p.6), and Widdowson 1997.) Quirk then compounds his error by complaining that the same kind of 'equivocation' does not happen in the case of other languages such as French, German, Russian, or Chinese, completely missing the point that they are learnt primarily as foreign languages for communication with their NSs, rather than as lingua francas primarily for communication among their NNSs.

Quirk's lack of sympathy with the concept of ELF is perhaps to some extent understandable if not acceptable. He was, after all, making his points several years ago at a time when far less had been said or written on the subject and little ELF research had been carried out. Nevertheless, the attitude he expresses towards expanding circle varieties still prevails,[10] as can be seen from the above discussion of Trudgill's very recent article, which is not yet published as I write. Indeed, a similar position is taken by Bruthiaux (2003) who, in his reconsideration of Kachru's three circle model, explores—if generally in a more measured manner and tone than either Quirk or Trudgill—the issue of ELF varieties. On the one hand he concedes that 'the increase in transnational communication across Europe has led to a well-documented claim for variety status to be accorded to English used as a lingua franca (or "ELF") by second language speakers among themselves' (p. 168). But on the other hand, he plays the same numbers game as Trudgill in arguing that 'the domain of such language use remains restricted to specialized transactions (business negotiations, industrial cooperation, tourism, etc.) by a relatively small number of speakers, and broader variety-creating conditions remain largely absent' (ibid.).

Thus, while Bruthiaux concedes that 'there may be a marginal case for speaking of "Dutch English" or "Norwegian English"' (i.e. small countries where a relatively high proportion of the population engage in transnational communication in English), he is convinced that 'the kind of English occasionally heard in Brazil or China constitutes English with Brazilian or Chinese characteristics, not "Brazilian English" or "Chinese English"' (pp. 168–9). Here he seems to be missing the point about the *inter*national nature of ELF communication and that it is therefore not relevant to ELF to talk about 'the kind of English heard in Brazil or China' (if as seems likely, by this he means interaction among Brazilians in Brazil and among the Chinese in China). English is not at present an *intra*national lingua franca in either country and it is unsurprising if it is spoken only 'occasionally' among the inhabitants of two countries where most of the population are able to speak, respectively, Portuguese and Putonghua among themselves. Further, unlike the 'well-documented claim for variety status' of ELF researchers to which Bruthiaux refers, he himself produces no empirical evidence to support any of his own claims; so once again one could be forgiven for asking: how does he know?

Negative orientations to ELF are not confined to NS scholars, however. Resistance to the acceptance of its legitimacy can be found among scholars from both the outer and expanding circles. Kachru's pioneering work on outer circle Englishes has led to the recognition of at least some of these varieties (for example, Indian English and Singapore English), and Kachru was the first to respond on their behalf to Quirk's (1990) article in *English Today*. In his response he takes great exception to the latter's denigrating of outer circle Englishes, and labels Quirk's approach to these varieties 'deficit linguistics'. Nevertheless, Kachru does not extend his criticisms of Quirk's attitude to expanding circle Englishes, which elsewhere he himself designates 'norm-dependent' and 'exonormative' (1985: 17). On the contrary, he strongly rejects Quirk's lumping together of the Englishes of these two circles,[11] precisely because he does not regard them as having equal rights: 'there is a widely recognized and justified sociolinguistic and pedagogical distinction between ESL and EFL' which, he claims, Quirk ignores (1991: 5). In other words, because the expanding circle Englishes (unlike the outer circle Englishes) do not have a substantial number of country-internal functions (if any), Kachru does not recognize the legitimacy of ELF varieties.

Although the same applies to Kachru as to Quirk in terms of the lack of information available about ELF in the early 1990s, to my knowledge Kachru, like Quirk, has not substantially altered his position *vis-à-vis* the expanding circle since then. For example, in a book entitled *World Englishes 2000*, he states: '[t]he norm-dependent varieties are used in the Expanding Circle (for example, Korea, Iran, Saudi Arabia). The norms are essentially external (American or British)' (1997b: 221), while in the same book, he argues that the expanding circle's Asian members such as Japan should look more to the Asian outer circle varieties for their norms and identity and less to those of the inner circle (Kachru 1997a).

Kachru's position on ELF, then, seems not to recognize that far from posing a threat to the nativized Englishes of the outer circle, it actually protects them. For, as Seidlhofer observes in relation to inner circle Englishes—but precisely the same applies to outer circle Englishes—'the option of distinguishing ELF from ENL [English as a Native Language] is likely to be beneficial in that it leaves varieties of native English intact for all the functions that only a first language can perform' (2004: 229; and see also Seidlhofer 2003a: 11). In addition, by cutting across all three circles in respect of users, ELF makes it clear that outer (and inner) circle English speakers are not excluded from ELF. The only challenge for them—as for expanding circle speakers—is to accept that they will need to adjust their legitimate local variety for *inter*national, but not *intra*national, use in order to be better understood in international communication.

Even among academics who are themselves members of the expanding circle, it is not difficult to find negative responses to ELF among those who hold a particular admiration for NS varieties of English. Görlach is a case in point. In 1999 he had come to the conclusion that there was no justification to talk of ELF varieties (for which he uses the term 'EFL) 'because the diglossia which is so characteristic of ESL countries has not arisen so far, the native languages and English being kept distinct, with sloppy interferences often stigmatized' (p. 14). A few years later, Görlach's position has become more entrenched:

> The demand for English will continue and possibly increase, which means that more and more people will acquire broken, deficient forms of English which are adequate to the extent that they permit the communicational functions they were learnt for .... However, the incomplete acquisition reflected in such instances will never become the basis for a linguistic norm, which is, and has always been, based on the consent of the learned and guided by the accepted written norm, which has remained surprisingly homogeneous around the globe .... There is no danger of such deviant uses 'polluting' the standards of native speakers even if they become a minority in the global anglophone community. IE [International English] will not be corrupted by such uses.
> (2002: 12–13 cited in Seidlhofer 2004: 228)

What is surprising is that scholarly opposition to ELF seems to be based not so much on rational argument as on irrational prejudice. These references by Görlach to pollution and corruption echo remarks made two years earlier by the unscholarly Derwent May in an article that appeared in *The Times* newspaper in March 2000 (p. 4):

> there is something sinister about these pools of corrupt English lying about in the world. They are not just unpleasant for English people to encounter—and indeed for foreigners who care about speaking pure English. One also feels that they could grow and spread and eventually invade good English itself. They are like pools of language disease.

In fact the only real difference between Görlach's and May's positions as expressed in Görlach 2002 and May 2000 is that the former is confident that the ELF 'disease' will not ultimately pollute 'proper' English while the latter fears that it will.

I will return to these and other critiques of ELF and discuss their implications in some detail in the next chapter, where I consider the phenomenon of standard language ideology. One further issue that needs raising at this point, however, is that of prestige. Davies brings this up in his discussion of standard English. Agreeing with Quirk, he argues that '[p]restige ... is not even-handed and it is indeed a *trahison des clercs* for applied linguists to advocate a new or emerging or politically motivated variety of English as the standard of choice where it does not have the imprimatur of speech community acceptance' (1999: 184–5). This is, of course, rather similar to Honey's (1997) 'language is power' argument. In a nutshell it is saying 'if you can't beat 'em, join 'em'. In other words, rather than try to counter prejudice, one should comply with it on pragmatic grounds: in recognizing the emergence of non-standard forms we would, in effect, be promoting a kind of ('bad') English that will disadvantage its speakers.

Regardless of what I and others personally think of this argument, it would be foolish indeed for me to ignore it, as it evidently resonates with so many of the ELF speakers who took part in my research (and the research of others), as well as being voiced in a number of NNS publications. To quote just one example, from Scheuer, a Polish phonetician writing on the subject of ELF pronunciation: 'Advising learners of English to disregard the unfriendly response their pronunciation provokes, simply because this response is not politically correct, means preparing them for functioning in an ideal, rather than real, world' (2005: 126).

Quirk himself takes his original argument a stage further, condemning those who would advocate one standard for themselves and a different ('lower') one for others:

> ... the *clercs* themselves are careful to couch even their most sceptical remarks about standard language in precisely the standard language about which they are being sceptical. Disdain of élitism is a comfortable exercise for those who are themselves securely among the élite.
> (1985: 6)

Again, Scheuer makes the same point and in so doing, turns the ELF argument on its head. She appears to accuse ELF promoters of some kind of conspiracy to hold NNSs of English back: 'LFC (Lingua Franca Core)-like approaches ... are about teaching foreigners only enough English—pronunciation-wise—to let them survive within the EIL community (i.e. be intelligible and get the message across), but those foreigners are then not taken seriously in professional exchanges, and often come across as unintelligent ... ' (ibid.). And once again, such fears must be addressed rather than dismissed out of hand, although unless the legitimacy argument can be made sufficiently convincingly, it seems unlikely that any of the above ELF sceptics will change their minds. It is to the arguments in favour of accepting ELF as legitimate English that we now turn.

ELF as legitimate English

Much discussion has focused on the issue of what determines a legitimate new variety of English. Platt, Weber, and Ho begin their book on the Englishes of the outer circle with the question '[w]hen is something a learner's error and when is it part of a new language system?' (1984: vii). As far as outer circle English varieties are concerned, agreement has more or less been reached over the years in all but name. (They are variously referred to as indigenized Englishes, institutionalized Englishes, nativized Englishes, New Englishes among others.) For Platt, Weber, and Lian, the criteria on which they can be identified are: their use in the educational system as both subject and medium of instruction; their development in an area where an NS variety is not the majority language; their use for a range of functions among its speakers and writers; and evidence that they have become 'nativized' by developing local features at grammatical, lexical, pragmatic, and phonological/phonetic levels (op. cit.: 2). They also make the important observation (p. 6) that many of these Englishes have a high status in the region where they are used.

Writing specifically about English in SE Asia, Llamzon (1983, in Bolton 2003: 5–6) also provides a set of criteria by which to identify new varieties of English. These fall into four groupings: ecological features, historical features, sociolinguistic features, and cultural features. Of these, the first two groups of criteria could also be applied to ELF, in that the ecological features include code-mixing and borrowing from the local language, while the historical features relate to the recency of both the new varieties' development from the dominant variety and of descriptions of them. On the other hand, the sociolinguistic features, which relate to the use of new varieties in more private domains (with family and friends, for example) would need adapting to give weight to the international character of ELF (which is not by any means to say that it is not used as a lingua franca among friends). As for the cultural features, which relate to the existence of a local literature in English, it is too soon to say, although it seems entirely reasonable that there will ultimately be ELF literature, that is, literature which makes use of the frequent and systematic features identified in ELF corpora, along with local features which are found not to affect mutual intelligibility in ELF.[12]

To Llamzon's four groups of criteria, Bolton (op. cit.) adds a further three: linguistic, attitudinal, and political. These, together with Llamzon's, need to be satisfied, he believes, 'in order to achieve recognition as a legitimate new or World English' (p. 46). All three may one day apply to ELF. The first, 'the identification of sets of distinctive linguistic items typically associated with a new variety', he points out, 'is a central feature of the discussion of ... varieties [of English] around the world' (ibid.). As far as attitudinal factors are concerned, Bolton argues, it is important to assess the speech community's acceptance of the new English: in particular, the extent to which it is felt to express their identity or to be merely a collection of errors. This is a critical issue for ELF, and something which we will consider in several chapters of this book. Bolton's political features relate to recognition of the variety by governments, educational institutions, and other official bodies, and again, this is an important issue for ELF.

Butler (1997: 106) also provides a set of criteria for determining a variety of World English: 'a standard and recognizable pattern of pronunciation handed down from one generation to another ... particular words and phrases which spring up usually to express key features of the physical and social environment and which are peculiar to the variety ... a history—a sense that this variety of English is the way it is because of the history of the language community ... a literature written without apology in that variety of English ... reference works—dictionaries and style guides—which show that people in the language community look to themselves, not to some outside authority, to decide what is right and wrong in terms of how they speak and write their English'. Again, with slight adjustments to the criteria in order to embrace its international character, it could be predicted that ELF will eventually fit all these criteria.

Finally, Bamgboṣe (1998: 3–5) provides a checklist of five factors which can be used to decide whether an innovation has the status of a norm. These are:

- demographic, in other words, how many and which speakers use the innovation?
- geographical, i.e. how widespread is it?
- codification, in the sense of appearing in written form in grammars, dictionaries and the like;
- authoritative, meaning that it needs to be sanctioned by examination bodies, teachers, publishing houses and so on; and
- acceptability, which Bamgboṣe describes as 'the ultimate test of an innovation' (p. 4).

Of the five factors, Bamgboṣe singles out codification and acceptability as the two most important because 'without them, innovations will continue to be labeled as errors' (ibid.). This applies every bit as much to ELF as it did (and in some cases still does) for the outer circle varieties of World Englishes on which Bamgboṣe focuses. And it underlines the point already made in this book that it is critical to the future of ELF for its corpus linguists to provide detailed descriptions as quickly as possible.

Returning to Platt *et al.*'s question with which this section began, readers will realize that as far as expanding circle Englishes are concerned, applied linguists and ELT professionals (let alone the general public) are a considerable way from reaching a consensus, with many of the latter groups as confident in their characterizations of ELF as broken English, intermediate English, and the like as ELF researchers are convinced that it is not. In a passage that has considerable relevance to the ELF debate, Trudgill (2002) sums up the prevailing attitude towards the applications of the findings of sociolinguistic research as follows:

> ... people working in sociolinguistics are, sadly, familiar enough with the phenomenon of lay people ignoring what they have to say about linguistic variation and linguistic diversity. Much more regrettable, however, and much more disturbing, is the lack of awareness on the part of some of our non-sociolinguistic colleagues within general linguistics about these issues.
> (p. 3)

And he goes on to criticize

> ... pronouncements by linguists—and here I am concerned in particular about European linguists, including in some cases sociolinguists—which signal a woeful ignorance on their part about linguistic variability, the value of linguistic diversity, and the preservation of languages and dialects, as well as *an unwillingness to fight for linguistically democratic and egalitarian issues* ...
> (ibid.: emphasis added)

Somewhat surprisingly, in the final chapter of the book for which this was (part of) the introduction, Trudgill argues in favour of the continued use of RP as the pedagogic model for NNSs of English, saying '[m]y own response to the question "why teach RP?" is "why not?". After all, we have to teach something' (p. 172). He subsequently followed this with the article discussed above (pp. 8–9), in which he heavily criticizes the concept of ELF accents (i.e. Trudgill 2005).

It seems, then, that even a sociolinguist of Trudgill's (usual) frame of mind does not consider ELF to be a 'linguistically democratic and egalitarian issue' which merits his support. And if some sociolinguists are unable to see ELF as a natural linguistic development borne of language contact and change, it is not surprising that many 'non-sociolinguistic' linguists, including most SLA researchers, phoneticians, and grammarians, are unwilling to treat it seriously. In fact ELF, unlike any other type of English or language issue that I can think of, has succeeded in uniting these very disparate groups of linguists in a single perspective—one of 'deficit linguistics' (Kachru 1991) towards ELF. Still less surprising is it, then, that the majority of English language teachers remain unconvinced of the wisdom of an ELF approach to teaching and unable to make the necessary conceptual shift. It seems that we are back where we started this chapter: with the political issues raised by Brutt-Griffler (2002), and the fact that linguistic legitimacy is determined largely by political criteria which give or deny status to the variety in question and which, in turn, influence people's attitudes towards it and the extent to which they wish to identify with it. Also worth pointing out in this regard is the role played by authority. That is, when influential figures such as Quirk and Trudgill are dismissive of a particular perspective, they influence a lot of others to be so too.

Mufwene's (1997, 2001) discussion of 'the legitimate and illegitimate offspring of English' has an interesting bearing on this negative orientation towards ELF. Mufwene is referring here to the Englishes of the outer circle and creoles, but the same, I believe, applies to ELF except that 'racial' should be substituted with 'non-native':

> ... the naming practice of new Englishes has to do more with the racial identity of those who speak them than with how these varieties developed and the extent of their structural deviations. It has little to do with how mutually intelligible they are.
> (2001: 107)

Mufwene goes on to demonstrate that the so-called 'native' Englishes (including Old English, Middle English, and Hiberno-English) can be a lot less intelligible (even to NSs) than the so-called 'non-native' Englishes. But what is really at stake, he contends, is not the intelligibility of the English variety. Rather, it is the kind of contact involved in its evolution, with contact involving African languages being particularly 'illegitimate'. Citing McMahon (1994) in his support, Mufwene argues that it has thus been possible to label certain Englishes as illegitimate by invoking the concept of their '"unnatural" or "nonordinary" developments' (p. 118). This is an issue to which we will return later in the chapter. For now, suffice it to say that Mufwene's objections to such orientations to outer circle Englishes can be extended to orientations to ELF, whose contact situations are, likewise, regarded by many as 'unnatural'. For example, the supposedly 'unnatural' fact that ELF speakers use English less than NSs is considered a reason to deny ELF varieties legitimacy. (See for example, Trudgill's point above, p. 8). Yet it seems more than a little odd to consider ELF unnatural and nonordinary given both its widespread use across peoples and functions, and the fact that, as McMahon (1994: 200) points out, 'bilingualism necessarily means linguistic contact' (whether limited or stable bilingualism), and linguistic contact means language change.

To sum up, ELF innovations are, I believe, as entitled to recognition as any other, be they innovations in the development of American English, Indian English, Singapore English, or whatever. The fact that ELF varieties are used internationally rather than intranationally and are born of international contact among their NNSs does not negate the creative processes involved: one cannot be selective about what counts as language contact and what does not. It is unacceptable to label creativity as 'L1 transfer' (or, more pejoratively, 'L1 interference') on the grounds that it results from contact between an individual's L2 English and their L1, or from contact between L2 English speakers who have different L1s. Indeed, as Lowenberg (2002) demonstrates, the kinds of processes involved in the innovations emerging from ELF contact not only have much in common with those involved in contact and change in inner and outer circle Englishes, but also result in some very similar language forms, such as uncountable nouns becoming countable (for example, 'informations', 'advices', 'staffs'). As Lowenberg concludes, language change is occurring dynamically in the expanding circle, and sooner or later, this will have to be acknowledged. To return to Widdowson's (1997) point about English spreading and adapting to suit its new uses as an international lingua franca, rather than being distributed and adopted unchanged to suit its old uses as a native language, the logical conclusion can only be that ELF is an entirely natural phenomenon, while attempts to hold it back and arrest its development are entirely unnatural.

ELF and World Englishes

In concluding the discussion of what ELF is, I believe it is important to point out that ELF is not only an entirely natural development and thus worthy of recognition as a legitimate branch of modern English, but that it also sits more comfortably within a World Englishes framework than the alternatives, such as World Standard Spoken English (Crystal 2003), International English (Görlach 1990), and World Standard English (McArthur 1998). The problem with all these is that they promote a unitary and essentially monolithic model based on idealized NS norms, with little scope for either local NNS variation or NNS-led innovation at the international level (and see Chapter 2 pp. 38 ff.). Bolton considers that the terms 'World English' and 'global English' refer to 'the idealised norm of an increasingly internationally propagated and internationally intelligible variety of the language, increasingly associated with the American print and electronic media' (2003: 4). Indeed, this seems to be precisely the outcome that Crystal has in mind at the spoken level: 'US English does seem likely to be the most influential in the development of WSSE [World Standard Spoken English]' even if, he concedes, 'there is no reason for L2 features not to become part of WSSE' (2003: 188). As was explained in the previous section, however, Crystal's version of events is the exact opposite of what ELF researchers believe to be happening. That is, NNSs are leading the changes in ELF, not being 'allowed' to introduce the odd feature or two. To paraphrase Crystal's words: 'L2 English does seem likely to be the most influential in the development of ELF', although 'there is no reason for L1 features not to become part of ELF'.

Phillipson (in press) includes ELF in his description of a 'World Englishes paradigm', which he contrasts with a 'Global English paradigm' (and in which he places WSSE). The latter paradigm assumes NS norms for NNS English, favours subtractive English learning (which by definition includes an accent-reduction approach to pronunciation), and has a preference for the NS teacher of English (whether monolingual or not). On the other hand, the former assumes NNS norms for NNS Englishes, favours additive learning (thus including an accent-addition approach), and favours bilingual, bicultural teachers of English (whether NNS or NS). Parts of Phillipson's table are reproduced below (see Table 1.1 on page 19), as they demonstrate so clearly the respects in which ELF is in tune with the plurilinguistic nature of a World Englishes paradigm, where other perspectives on international developments in English are not. They also serve as a timely reminder that an international lingua franca cannot divorce itself from the world's linguistic situation, and that ELF researchers (and speakers) should never lose sight of the importance of all languages as well as all varieties of English, or they will run the risk of being 'seen as introducing a form of neo-standardization in the guise of a universal pedagogical solution for L2 speakers of English' (Rubdy and Saraceni 2006: 14).

What ELF is thought to be

Having established what ELF is and presented a number of orientations towards it, I turn now to the matter of what ELF is not, but is often wrongly thought to be. The negative attitudes towards ELF discussed above are born primarily of a distaste for the notion of English varieties being developed 'legitimately' by NNSs of English from the expanding circle. Nevertheless, in the main, the notion itself appears to have been understood by these scholars, even if ELF researchers might regard their responses to it as 'half-baked

Global English paradigm	World Englishes paradigm
Assimilationist	Celebrates and supports diversity
Monolingual orientation	Multilingual, multi-dialectal
'International' English assumes US/UK norms	'International': a cross-national linguistic common core
World Standard Spoken English	English as a Lingua Franca
Anglo-American linguistic norms	Local linguistic norms, regional and national
Exonormative English	Endonormative Englishes
Target norm the 'native speaker'	Target norm the good ESL user
Teachers can be monolingual	Bilingual and bicultural teachers

Table 1.1 Phillipson's Global English and World Englishes Paradigms (taken from Phillipson in press)

quackery' (Seidlhofer 2005a). On the other hand, the attitudes discussed below are the result of partial or complete misunderstanding of the notion. In the first section that follows, I examine a number of misinterpretations of ELF in general, and then a number of misinterpretations of ELF pronunciation specifically. The chapter concludes by looking at typical recent reactions to my ELF pronunciation proposals (the Lingua Franca Core) by teachers, and considering the misconceptions involved along with the difficulties for teachers in trying to come to terms with the concept of ELF when faced with so much published misinterpretation and scepticism.

Misinterpretations of ELF

One misconception, which I touched on briefly in the earlier discussion, is that ELF is monocentric, i.e. that the goal of ELF is to establish a single lingua franca norm to which all users should conform. It has been a matter of considerable surprise to its researchers that ELF could be so seriously misunderstood in this respect. For example, the call for papers for Rubdy and Saraceni (2006) portrayed ELF (which they call EIL) as a notion which does not acknowledge 'the polymorphous nature of the English language worldwide', which prescribes 'either a reduced or extended form of standard English ... a monolithic [model]', that 'denies tolerance for diversity and appropriacy of use in specific sociolinguistic contexts', and 'from this point of view, [which] might conceivably be seen as introducing a form of neo-standardization in the guise of a pedagogical solution for L2 speakers of English'. This was of great concern to Seidlhofer and me (who had both been invited to contribute to the volume), and in an effort to set the record straight, we each focused our contribution to the Rubdy and Saraceni volume on correcting the editors' misrepresentation of ELF researchers' position on the diversity of world Englishes.[13] In a paper entitled 'English as a lingua franca in the expanding circle: What it isn't', Seidlhofer (2006) identifies five major misconceptions inherent in the accusations, which are summarized here:

- *Misconception 1: ELF research ignores the polymorphous nature of the English language worldwide.* In this section of her paper, Seidlhofer points out that by collecting ELF corpora, scholars are actually contributing to the diversity of Englishes rather than ignoring it. The problem is, she argues, that the diversity which ELF scholars describe tends to pass unnoticed because expanding circle diversity is not widely accepted as having validity.
- *Misconception 2: ELF work denies tolerance for diversity and appropriacy of use in specific sociolinguistic contexts.* Here, Seidlhofer explains the distinction between core and non-core. She points out that while the core areas are indeed norms to be conformed to (although determined by NNS rather than NS communication needs), the non-core features are free for (NNS) regional variation, thus 'allowing the speakers' identities to 'shine through' while still ensuring mutual intelligibility' (p. 43).
- *Misconception 3: ELF description aims at the accurate application of a set of prescribed rules.* Here, Seidlhofer explains that prescription is precisely what ELF research is calling into question. Instead, it is offering learners alternatives to the prescriptive (NS-based) rules of the kind so admired by supporters of standard language ideology. She also points out that ELF research is by its nature descriptive, and that ELF researchers are not attempting to pre-empt local pedagogic decisions.
- *Misconception 4: ELF researchers are suggesting that there should be one monolithic variety.* In this section, Seidlhofer points out that there is not a single variety called 'ELF', and that while common processes are emerging from the data—as can be expected in any language contact situation—there is plenty of scope for and evidence of local variation. (See Misconception 2 on 'non-core' features.)
- *Misconception 5: ELF researchers suggest that ELF should be taught to all non-native speakers.* Seidlhofer explains here that it is precisely because EFL and ELF are such different conceptualizations of English that it would be ludicrous to suggest teaching ELF to all, and that only learners themselves can decide which one they need. Instead she argues in favour of the more sensible notion of raising all English learners' awareness of the global roles of English, and of the effort that everyone needs to make to achieve successful global communication.

In my own paper (Jenkins 2006b), I demonstrate how it is possible to promote international intelligibility and show respect for diversity across Englishes at one and the same time. Because my focus is specifically on accents, the points made in my paper are discussed when I deal with misinterpretations of the ELF pronunciation proposals in the next section of the chapter.

Another frequent misinterpretation of ELF arises from a misunderstanding of language contact. As Mufwene (1997, 2001) argues, it is a commonly-held belief that the English of NSs has a single identifiable 'parent' and a linear development from Old English to the present day without being 'contaminated' by other languages on the way. These Englishes are therefore considered 'legitimate'. On the other hand, English creoles and the indigenized Englishes of the outer circle, it is widely believed, have been 'infected' by large-scale contact with Asian and African languages and are therefore regarded as the 'illegitimate offspring of English'. This is patently absurd, and has arisen, Mufwene suggests, because '[w]e have typically downplayed the role of contact in the case of "native" Englishes but have routinely invoked it in the case not only of creoles but also of indigenized Englishes' (2001: 107).

Although Mufwene is talking specifically about outer circle Englishes and English creoles, the beliefs he describes are identical with those currently held in relation to ELF varieties. In other words, any noticeable outcome of contact between an ELF speaker's L1 and their L2 English (i.e. where NS English and ELF differ) is labelled an 'L1 transfer error' rather than a legitimate ELF variant resulting from innovation, regardless of how systematically and frequently it is produced and how easily it is understood by ELF listeners. This, in turn, leads to the misconception that the speakers who provide ELF researchers with their data must have a low level of proficiency rather than being successful and proficient speakers of ELF varieties. The root of the problem is the difficulty many people have in grasping the point that errors in ELF are not determined by reference to ENL norms, and therefore that ELF proficiency should not be judged in relation to the English of its NSs.[14] The same is also true of the outcome of contact between ELF speakers from different L1s. This completely disregards the role of accommodation in the normal processes of language change for, as Mufwene points out, '[t]he agency of change lies definitely within the behaviour of individual speakers, and causation partly in the mutual accommodations they make to each other while they are more intent on communicating effectively than on preserving ideolectal, dialectal, or language boundaries' (op. cit.: 24). Surprisingly, accommodation has been largely ignored by traditional SLA researchers and ELT professionals, despite its major roles in both communication and language change. Any attempt to accommodate which results in a non-NS form, no matter how intelligible it is to the listener concerned, continues to be regarded as an 'error'. As was demonstrated in some detail in Jenkins (2000: Chapter 7), however, accommodation strategies are critical to the intelligibility of English in international communication.

A further misinterpretation of ELF is that it patronizes learners. This will be discussed in greater detail in Chapter 8, as it is an accusation which tends to be made by institutions such as examination boards and others who have a particular interest in promoting NS English (for example, corpus linguists engaged in the collection of NS English or learner English corpora). Nevertheless, it is essential to point out here that there is no intention among ELF researchers to patronize learners by telling them that they do not need to learn native-like English. Far from it: ELF is a matter of learner choice. As far as ELF researchers are concerned, it is entirely for learners to decide what kind of English they want to learn, be it EFL (in effect ENL) for communication with NSs, an ESL (outer circle) variety, or an ELF variety for international communication (for example, China English, Spanish English, Japanese English, etc.)—or, indeed, more than one of these. In this way, ELF increases rather than decreases the available choices, while it is the insistence on conformity to NS norms (British and American English as the default models throughout the expanding circle) that restricts them. ELF researchers merely suggest that learners should be put in a position to make an *informed* choice by means of having their awareness raised of the sociolinguistic, sociopsychological, and sociopolitical issues involved.

A final misinterpretation of ELF research concerns its links with pedagogy. Mukherjee and Rohrbach (2006: 210), for example, refer erroneously to the 'English-as-a-lingua-franca teaching model' when no such thing exists. While corpus linguists who collect corpora of NS English (so-called 'real' English) tend to have few qualms about transferring their descriptions swiftly into pedagogic materials, ELF researchers are more tentative, believing, in line with Widdowson that '[l]anguage teaching cannot simply be based on descriptive facts ... .These are "factors" to be considered, of course, but not facts to be uncritically incorporated into prescriptions' (1991: 20). At all but the level of pronunciation, there is general agreement among ELF researchers not only that it would be premature to make detailed pedagogic recommendations but also that such decisions are for those who are themselves involved in the teaching of English and in materials design, rather than for those who collect and analyse the data. At present, they restrict themselves to 'attempting a broad outline of likely consequences of an orientation towards teaching ELF' (Seidlhofer 2004: 226), and making suggestions as to what is not necessary to teach for ELF communication, rather prescribing what *should* be taught. (See Jenkins 2004.) As far as pronunciation is concerned, because the core features for ELF intelligibility have been identified (although they still need validating by means of replications of the research before they can be considered definitive), it has been possible to make a number of initial suggestions for the teaching of pronunciation, but as is clear in the section which follows, these too have been misinterpreted.

Misinterpretations of the ELF pronunciation proposals

As I mentioned in the Preface, one of my main motivations in researching and writing this book was to explore the reasons for the controversy caused by my earlier book, *The Phonology of English as an International Language* (2000), in which I had presented my pronunciation proposals, the Lingua Franca Core (LFC). The aim of the original ELF pronunciation research was primarily to identify those segmental and suprasegmental features that obstruct the intelligibility of pronunciation in ELF (but not EFL or ENL) interaction when pronounced with L1 influence. My intention was both to find a means of promoting mutual pronunciation intelligibility in ELF communication, and to encourage acceptance of those pronunciation features that are regularly and systematically pronounced 'incorrectly', and found not to impede intelligibility for an NNS listener. My argument was that as far as ELF is concerned, these so-called 'errors' should be considered legitimate features of the speaker's regional (NNS) English accent, thus putting NNS accents on an equal footing with regional NS accents. This, in turn, I argued, would resolve any conflict between the need for international intelligibility and the apparent desire of many NNSs to project their L1 identity in their L2 English (see for example, McKay 2002; Dalton-Puffer *et al.* 1997) by extending to NNS English speakers the same right to express their geographical origins in their English as has always been enjoyed by NS English speakers.

The LFC was based on extensive miscommunication data gathered over several years and in a range of ELF settings, social as well as educational. All breakdowns in communication, gathered in both field notes and recordings, were analysed—often by the NNS participants as well as the researcher—in order to identify those that had been caused by pronunciation. In this way, it was possible to distinguish between L1-influenced pronunciation features that did and did not obstruct successful communication among NNSs of English from a wide range of different L1s. Those that caused problems were assigned to the ELF pronunciation core, the LFC, while those that did not were designated non-core. Table 1.2 summarizes the main core features for ELF communication (on the right-hand side) as compared and contrasted with those features that are typically considered necessary for EFL communication (in the middle column), i.e. where the listener is assumed to be an NS of English.

	EFL target Traditional syllabus	ELF target Lingua Franca Core
1 The consonantal inventory	• all sounds close RP/GA • RP non-rhotic /r/ GA rhotic /r/ • RP intervocalic [t] GA intervocalic [ɾ]	• all sounds except /θ/, /ð/ but approximations of all others acceptable • rhotic /r/ only • intervocalic [t] only
2 Phonetic requirements	• rarely specified	• aspiration after /p/, /t/, /k/ • appropriate vowel length before fortis/lenis consonants
3 Consonant clusters	• all word positions	• word initially, word medially
4 Vowel quantity	• long-short contrast	• long-short contrast
5 Tonic (nuclear) stress	• important	• critical

Table 1.2 EFL and ELF pronunciation targets: core features (adapted from Jenkins 2002: 99)

The features in the ELF column on the right-hand side of Table 1.2, then, are those that, according to my empirical data, are important for intelligible pronunciation when English is used as a lingua franca among its NNSs. On the other hand, many features that have traditionally been regarded as essential for intelligible English pronunciation were found in the research not to be necessary for intelligible pronunciation in ELF communication. These non-core items are listed below in Table 1.3, again comparing and contrasting them with the pronunciation features to be found in an EFL syllabus.

	EFL target Traditional syllabus	ELF target Lingua Franca Core
1 Vowel quality	• close to RP or GA	• L2 (consistent) regional qualities
2 Weak forms	• essential	• unhelpful to intelligibility
3 Features of connected speech	• all	• inconsequential and may be unhelpful
4 Stress-timed rhythm	• important	• unnecessary
5 Word stress	• critical	• can reduce flexibility/ unteachable
6 Pitch movement	• essential for indicating attitudes and grammar	• unnecessary/ unteachable

Table 1.3 EFL and ELF pronunciation targets: The non-core features (adapted from Jenkins 2002: 99)

Where NNS pronunciation differed from NS production in the case of these non-core features, I argued, the resulting forms should be regarded as features of NNS accent varieties rather than pronunciation errors for ELF communication. This would mean that for learners who wished to make ELF rather than EFL their target, it would no longer be necessary to spend classroom time on the non-core items for production, but only to learn them receptively, so that these learners would still be able to understand NSs of English should the need arise. I also made a case for developing learners' accommodation skills so that they would be in a better position to adjust their pronunciation in accordance with the needs of specific interlocutors. So, for example, while a French and Italian interlocutor would not cause intelligibility problems for one another if they elided the first sound in the words 'head' and 'house', they would require the /h/ in their accent repertoires, as well as the skill to notice the need for it, in interactions with ELF speakers from many other L1s.

This approach, combining the use of core features and accommodation, along with locally pronounced non-core features and a receptive understanding of the ways they are produced by NSs of English would, I believed, resolve the intelligibility-identity conflict by enabling NNSs to express both their L1 identity and membership of the international ELF community, while remaining intelligible to their ELF interlocutors, and still able to understand ENL accents. At a practical level, it would mean that pronunciation teaching would become more relevant for those learners who intended to be ELF users (i.e. to communicate primarily with other NNSs of English rather than NSs), as classroom time could be focused on the LFC items, while the non-core items would be relegated to activities to promote reception only.

Responses to the 2000 book have tended to be polarized. At one extreme are those who have welcomed the proposals more or less unconditionally, and have gone about adapting the LFC for use in their own teaching contexts. (See, for example, Walker 2001a on using the LFC in Spain.) At the other extreme are the much larger number who take exception to the book's call to legitimize expanding circle English accents along the lines of outer circle accents, and its proposal of a core of features (the LFC) to be used as and when required to ensure mutually intelligible pronunciation in lingua franca interactions. Their reactions, however, are characterized by misinterpretations of the proposals, some of which we now consider.

One frequent misinterpretation of the Lingua Franca Core (LFC) is that it is a model for imitation. This is not at all the case. It is, rather, a core of pronunciation features which occur in successful NNS–NNS communication and whose absence leads to miscommunication.[15] The features of an NS accent (Received Pronunciation or General American) that do not appear in the core—i.e. the 'non-core' items—represent areas free for NNS variation. In other words, when L1 transfer occurs in any of the latter areas, they can be considered variants of an ELF accent (for example, Italian English, Korean English) rather than pronunciation errors. The model, then, is not the LFC but the local teacher whose accent incorporates both the core features and the local version of the non-core items. One commentator, Gupta (2006) even likens the LFC to 'Quirk's notion of a "common core"' (2006: 96), whereas the differences between Quirk's notion and thinking behind the LFC are far greater than any superficial similarities.

Related to the latter misinterpretation is the mistaken belief, even among those who speak of the LFC approvingly (for example, Llurda 2004) that it is a single variety or, worse, that the LFC proposal involves adherence to an unadaptable and unchanging model. For example, Savignon (2003: 72) responds to Yano's (2003) recommendation of the LFC as follows: 'Current efforts to establish (and promote?) universal norms should be viewed with suspicion. A norm adapted yesterday in the business community of the European Union may or may not be appropriate in the transactions tomorrow in Singapore or Argentina'. Here Savignon misses the point about the LFC. For not only are the core features identified by NNS intelligibility requirements and the non-core features dictated entirely by speaker choice (rather than by conformity to a universal NS norm such as General American), but the accommodation element of the ELF proposals mean that a speaker in Europe or Singapore or Argentina is entirely free to adjust even the core features if this suits local communication needs. The point of the LFC is that the pronunciation norms in any given interaction are determined by ELF users themselves.

However, it is this very suggestion that NNSs should have input into the determining of their pronunciation norms, and that we need to distinguish between *EFL errors* and *ELF variants*, which some phoneticians seem to find the most difficult to grasp. For example, in the abstract of his paper for a phonetics conference held in Poznan in 2003, the British phonetician Wells argued that '[t]he Jenkins LFC permits deviations from existing standard practice—for example, the substitution of [t] or [s] for [θ] or inappropriate word stress—that evoke the worst negative stereotypes'. The Polish phonetician and pronunciation materials writer, Sobkowiak, made similar points in his own paper (published as Sobkowiak 2005), and was particularly exercised by my (2000: 101) suggestion that the optimum teacher and pronunciation model for ELF 'is often a bilingual English speaker who shares her students' L1'.

Another misconception of the LFC is that it is being prescribed for all learners of English. Harris (2002: 6), for example, asserts that '[t]he English as a Lingua Franca (ELF) movement has claimed ownership of English for foreign language (FL) users (Jenkins 2002)[16] and suggested that standard NS varieties should be ousted from both classroom and public examination. Instead, they propose that FL varieties should form the basis of a new lingua franca'. (See also Kellogg's 2002 response, Harris's 2003 reply to him, and Kellogg's 2003 reply to his reply.) This is no more true of pronunciation than it is of any other linguistic level, as was explained in the previous section. As I have argued elsewhere in respect of ELF accents (though the same argument holds for all linguistic levels): 'it will be important not to patronise those learners who, having heard the arguments, still wish to work towards the goal of a native speaker accent, by telling them they have no need to do so' (Jenkins 2002: 101).[17] Those learners who will be communicating mainly with NSs and wish their accents to blend in, as well as those learners who wish to aim for a near-native goal for personal reasons, will probably find a traditional EFL pronunciation target more appropriate for their purposes. On the other hand, those who will be communicating mainly with other NNSs may find an ELF target as described in the Lingua Franca Core more useful—or at least may find it unnecessary to spend time on acquiring the non-core features. (See pp. 23–4 above for a summary of the core and non-core features.) To my knowledge there has been no attempt by researchers to *prescribe* ELF to any learners of English, nor am I aware of any intention to do so in the future.

One final misinterpretation which needs to be mentioned here relates to my claim in *The Phonology of English as an International Language* that '[t]he LFC ... drastically simplifies the pedagogic task by removing from the syllabus many time-consuming items which are either unteachable or irrelevant for EIL' (p. 160). This claim has been interpreted wrongly to mean that pronunciation teaching will become 'easier' for all and, indeed, that this was the starting point of my original EIL research. Far from it. The starting point, as is made abundantly clear in Jenkins (2000) was the goal of promoting mutual intelligibility in NNS–NNS communication. I anticipated (correctly, as it turned out), that the effect would be the potential to reduce the complexity of pronunciation syllabuses in the sense of removing from them a range of items that did not contribute to such intelligibility. (See, for example, Walker 2001a, 2001b, for the way in which the LFC thus simplifies the pronunciation syllabus for Spanish learners of English.) With the removal from the syllabus of items such as nineteen of the twenty RP vowel and diphthong qualities, this was a likely outcome.[18] In addition, I argued that 'unteachable' items could be removed from the ELF pronunciation syllabus (i.e. those items which cannot be learnt by means of classroom teaching), particularly when it emerged from the empirical data that these, in the main, are not necessary as safeguards of NNS–NNS intelligibility. Again, this meant the removal of features such as pitch movements to signify attitudes, since these depend very much on the specifics of context and on speaker characteristics, and are therefore ungeneralizable. This is not to say I was claiming that unteachable = unlearnable. In fact I made a point of arguing that an item that appears to be unteachable in the classroom (because it does not provide the appropriate conditions for acquisition) may subsequently be acquired *outside* the classroom, given sufficient exposure and motivation.

   What the LFC does, then, is reduce the number of pronunciation features to be learnt for those who opt for an ELF pronunciation syllabus, and thus reduce the *size* of the task, while increasing teachability. What it does not do, nor did it set out to do, is claim that the items within the core are necessarily 'easy' to learn, 'easier' than those items in the 'non-core' category, or identically 'easy' for all learners regardless of their L1. And yet 'simplification' of the task is regularly misinterpreted as meaning that the items which remain for learning are 'easier' *per se*, rather than being both the subset necessary for intelligibility and teachable. So, for example, Szpyra-Kozlowska devotes an entire article (2003, 2005)[19] to demonstrating that some of the non-core features are easy for Polish learners while some of the core features are difficult. She concludes that for Poles, the LFC is 'no simplification of this task at all' (2003: 207), without any reference to the overarching purpose of the LFC, the promotion of NNS–NNS intelligibility. One is left wondering whether such writers entirely understand the concept of ELF, or even that of 'teachability'. After all, many features of an L2 are 'difficult' while being ultimately teachable, and there is no reason to expect the LFC's items to be an exception to this. We return to the problem of misinterpretations of ELF in Chapters 5 and 6, where they will be seen to link closely with attitudes towards ELF in general and ELF accents in particular. Bailey (1991: 97) quotes lines from the poem *Musophilis* by Daniel (1599) to demonstrate that 'the idea that English had a destiny beyond Britain has an extensive lineage':

And who in time knowes wither we may vent
The treasure of our tongue, to what strange shores
This gaine of our best glories shal be sent,
T'inrich vnknowing Nations with our stores?
Which worlds in th'yet vnformed Occident
May come refin'd with th'accents that are ours.

What is particularly noticeable here (apart from the inevitable triumphalist tone—despite the fact that, as Bailey (ibid.) points out, '[a]t the time they were composed, Daniel's speculations were pure patriotic pipe dream')—is the attitude towards English accents which is expressed in the final line. Not much seems to have changed during the intervening four centuries as far as accent attitudes are concerned (although the accents themselves have changed dramatically). As is demonstrated in the chapters below, NS accents are still considered by many to be every bit as 'refin'd' as they were in 1599, while NNS accents—in the eyes of many, NS and NNS, linguist, language teacher, and general public alike—are at best less valued and at worst stigmatized. In the next chapter, we explore the standard language ideology that engenders and supports such attitudes, and consider the extent to which it undermines the concept of ELF and thus leads to the kinds of reactions and misinterpretations described in this chapter.

Notes

1 Back in 1991, Beneke estimated that 80 per cent of interactions involving NNSs of English did not involve any NSs. Other researchers have had similar findings. For example, Firth investigated the interactions of two Danish international trading companies, and found both that most of their international communications were conducted in English, and that most of these communications 'exclusively involve[d] nonnative speakers' (1996: 241).

2 VOICE, the Vienna-Oxford International Corpus of English, currently being compiled at the University of Vienna, is a computer-readable corpus of spoken ELF interactions among speakers from a wide range of first language backgrounds in various professional, educational and informal settings. See http://www.univie.ac.at/voice/voice.php?page=what_is_voice and for two qualitative studies of ELF that draw on VOICE see Breiteneder (2005) and Pitzl (2005).

3 In fact I take the view that speakers of nativized Englishes such as Indian English and Singapore English are not NNSs of English but NSs of, for example, Indian English or Singapore English, who have a linguistic repertoire which includes English and at least one other language (though nowadays there are occasional instances of outer circle *monolingual* English speakers). Nevertheless, I realize that this view may not be shared by the majority of English users.

4 However Eoyang (1999) dislikes the term 'lingua franca' because to him it implies linguistic impurity. In this, he ignores the critical role of language contact in ELF's (and any natural language's) development. Kachru (2005), too, dislikes the term 'lingua franca', but this is because he interprets it in its original restricted meaning. (See the beginning of this chapter.) He also fears that it is being used as a cover term for all NNS uses of English (i.e. intra- as well as inter-national) and for this, he prefers 'World Englishes' (p. 216). ELF researchers should take heed of Kachru's concerns and recognize the sensitivity of issues relating to the outer circle. In particular, they should be careful to avoid seeming either to exclude outer circle speakers from international communication in English or to imply that outer circle Englishes are interlanguages.

5 Somewhat surprisingly, McArthur (2004) omits any mention of ELF from his discussion of labels for 'English at large' (p. 3), and focuses exclusively on 'world English', 'international English', and 'global English'. This contrasts with two other journals, which both feature ELF: *ELT Journal* in its 'Key Concepts' column (Seidlhofer, in volume 59/4 p. 339), and *IATEFL Issues*—now renamed *IATEFL Voices*—in its new column 'The ABC of ELT' (Jenkins, in volume 182: 9).

6 Kachru (1997a: 85) quotes Widdowson approvingly and refers to him as 'the guru from the Inner Circle'.

7 Lowenberg cites Jenkins 2000 in his list of publications which present research findings in relation to outer circle norms. This is a mistake, however: my 2000 book is concerned exclusively with *expanding* circle norms.

8 In fact this is not the first time that Trudgill has made a numerical claim based on relatively flimsy empirical evidence. For, as he freely admits, the 3 per cent figure for speakers of RP in Britain which he was responsible for popularizing, was not in fact rigorously researched, but resulted from generalization based on a small sample of British-English speakers living in Norwich, supplemented by guesswork (Trudgill 2002:171–2).

9 Quirk seems here to be describing Japanese and Spanish learners of English as 'foreign' in their own countries, as though 'foreign' equates with being an NNS of English. (See Seidlhofer 2005a.)

10 And as Seidlhofer (2005a) points out, Quirk himself must have held the same views at least up to 1995, when his 1990 paper was reprinted in his 1995 collection, *Grammatical and Lexical Variance in English*.

11 Regardless of expanding circle considerations, it is absurd for Quirk to claim that he is unaware of the existence of any instutionalized NNS Eng-lishes, and to label long-recognized outer circle Englishes such as Indian English and Nigerian English 'performance varieties' (1990: 6).

12 These two types of features correspond to the core and non-core features identified for ELF pronunciation. (See Jenkins 2000: Chapter 5.)

13 It has to be pointed out that a number of major misconceptions about ELF remain in the editors' introduction to the (2006) volume, particularly

in their continued misrepresentation of ELF as 'reducing or restricting variation' (p. 11), as 'a monomodel' (ibid.), as an attempt to impose 'a single model or template on the diverse contexts in which English is taught worldwide' (p. 12) and the like. They argue that 'the validity of the EIL/ELF proposal will probably depend upon whether or not it chooses to embrace a polymodel approach to the teaching of English or a monolithic one' (p. 13), completely failing to grasp (despite Seidlhofer's and my attempts, ironically in the same volume, to demonstrate otherwise) that ELF is not in any sense a monolithic approach to the teaching of English. It is almost as if, having given their volume the subtitle 'Global rules, global roles', they were determined to present ELF/EIL as the 'global rules' half, in line with their original prejudices rather than in line with the emerging evidence. The same kinds of misconception about ELF characterize several other contributions to the volume, for example those of Gupta (2006), and Tomlinson (2006) (and see Chapter 5 below for an analysis of Prodromou's contribution).

14   This is not to suggest that all ELF speakers are proficient. ELF has its own cline of proficiency, with some speakers being highly proficient while '[o]thers are still learners, and yet others have ceased learning some way short of expert (ELF) level' (Jenkins 2006c: 141). The point is that ELF proficiency levels are not determined by the degree of closeness to ENL norms.

15   Even here, the situation is not clear-cut because, as was pointed out in Jenkins (2000), interlocutors from different L1s may share alternative ways of pronouncing core features, so will be mutually intelligible if they continue to use these variants when communicating with each other.

16   This is an article specifically about the LFC.

17   Oddly, Harris seems to have overlooked this point in making his claims about the content of my 2002 article.

18   This does not mean, as Tomlinson (2006) seems mistakenly to believe, that the LFC is 'a restricted code of Core Lingua Franca features' (p. 141). The point is that each expanding circle accent would have its own legitimate pronunciation norms (modelled optimally by a proficient NNS of English from the L1 in question), and would include in its repertoire the (definitive) core features to be used as required.

19   These are in essence the same article, the second being a slightly extended version of the first.

2
ELF and standard language ideology

The previous chapter provided evidence of the extent of negative orientations towards the notion of ELF among teachers, linguists (including grammarians, applied linguists, and even some sociolinguists), and the general public. As was demonstrated, such perspectives are often built on shaky foundations involving serious misinterpretations of ELF that may, themselves, be the result of strongly held ideological positions and/or sociolinguistic naïvety. There is, for example, the 'English first' argument: the assumption that because the native language had an earlier place in the chronological development of the English language it is somehow more suitable than other varieties for use as an international lingua franca several centuries later. Yet 'first' is not necessarily 'best', especially when 'first' changes over time (Old English, Middle English, Early Modern English, etc.) and is not even easily definable within our own period, as evidenced by current debates as to what standard British and American English actually are. (See, for example, Bex and Watts 1999.) Again, there is the 'language is power' claim of Quirk and Honey, with its simplistic assumption that there is 'an inherently powerful standard version of the language, the learning of which can act as a panacea for all sorts of other social ills ... coupled with a sociological naïvety that learning a standard version of the language will bring about social and economic advantage' (Pennycook 2001: 48).

In this chapter, we look in more detail at the kinds of standard language ideology that underpin the negative orientations to ELF presented in Chapter 1. This, in turn, acts as a prelude to the studies reported in Chapters 5, 6, and 7. Although it is not possible to attribute the perceptions expressed by the teacher participants in these studies directly to the prevailing NS English ideology in much of the ELT and applied linguistics literature, there are strong indications in my findings that such a causal link exists. This is not in itself surprising, for as this chapter demonstrates, ELT practitioners[1] are constantly being presented with a standard language ideology that pervades the vast majority of publications available to them. And thus, the notion of ELF, too, is being undermined in their eyes, sometimes explicitly, more often by implication. The cumulative effect is that long after the end of the colonial period and in regions of the world which were never colonized in the first place, NS norms continue to 'colonise the minds' (Tsuda 1997) of non-native English speakers, leading to assumptions of NS linguistic superiority and often, with them, feelings of linguistic insecurity. (See Chapter 7.) This, in turn, results in the kinds of NNS teacher attitudes reported in Chapters 5 and 6, as well as the identity conflicts that emerge in the data reported in Chapter 7, and a self-deprecating acquiescence in the ELT gatekeeping practices (in teaching, testing, and teacher education) which are discussed in Chapter 8.

The purpose of this chapter, then, is to demonstrate how standard language ideology informs various kinds of published material available to teachers of English, and to make explicit the (often hidden) assumptions and values which underpin these materials, and to consider the possible overt or subliminal influences they may exert on their readers' attitudes to the language and its teaching.

The first part of the chapter is a discussion of standard language ideology and anti-ELF sentiment in the writings of linguists. In the second part of the chapter, I move on to consider some ELT 'documents' by taking a semi-ethnographic approach to analysing four issues each of three professional ELT periodicals: *EL Gazette*, the *Guardian Weekly* 'Learning English' supplement, and *IATEFL Issues*. All are published in the UK but widely read in many countries around the world by both NNS and NS teachers. Later in the book (Chapter 8), I show how standard language ideology of the kind discussed here is linked with gatekeeping practices in SLA research, English language testing, ELT materials, and teacher education.

Standard NS English language ideology in linguistics

In Chapter 1, I discussed the position taken by a number of linguists, such as the grammarian Quirk and the sociolinguist Trudgill, that NNSs from the expanding circle are best served by a single variety of English lexicogrammar and pronunciation, and that for historical reasons (among others), this should be based on an NS standard variety. Inevitably, as was clear from their writings, those who hold such positions are opposed to the notion of ELF lexicogrammar, pronunciation, and the like, and not in the least afraid to say so. Others who may agree with their sentiments are less direct. Indeed, as this chapter demonstrates, one way of disparaging ELF is simply to ignore it; another is to belittle its researchers' efforts, or to question the feasibility of the research endeavour, while avoiding open disagreement with the ELF notion in principle. More effective in holding ELF at a distance among ELT practitioners, though, is the way standard (NS) language ideology (without specific mention of ELF) permeates, albeit sometimes unintentionally, the various texts typically read by those who teach and learn English. It may be implicit (for example, in terms of unstated assumptions or in what is left unsaid), or explicit (for example, by linking the acquisition of nativelike English to success in life). Examples of these tactics, whether witting or unwitting, and both NS- and NNS-initiated, are provided in this and the two sections which follow.

Language ideology is, of course, a well-critiqued phenomenon. (See for example, Blommaert 1999; Irvine and Gal 2000; J. Milroy 2001; Woolard 1992.) In terms of English, it is prominent in discussions of so-called 'standard English', its sociopolitical basis, its influence in inner and outer circle education systems, its role in promoting social and racial discrimination, and the like. (See, for instance, Bex and Watts 1999; Bonfiglio 2002; Cameron 1995; Crowley 2003; Holborow 1999; Lippi-Green 1994, 1997.) L. Milroy defines the term 'standard language ideology' as characterizing

> a particular set of beliefs about language .... [which] are typically held by populations of economically developed nations where processes of standardisation have operated over a considerable time to produce an abstract set of norms—lexical, grammatical and ... phonological—popularly described as constituting a standard language.
> (1999: 173)

She points out the importance of this historical dimension 'for an understanding of how ideologies work since, typically, they are historically deep-rooted and thoroughly naturalized—hence their resistance to analysis or argument' (2004: 167). ELF speakers are deeply affected by the standard language ideology that has resulted from these historical processes by virtue of the fact that their Englishes are (still) designated as 'performance' varieties that should look to Britain or North America for their norms. The significance of standard language ideology to ELF is highlighted in Garrett *et al.*'s observation that:

> In sociolinguistics *language ideology* is emerging as an important concept for understanding the politics of language in multilingual situations, such as in relation to immigration and social inclusion/exclusion generally .... and indeed as a politically more sensitive backdrop to any investigation of language variation and change ...
> (2003: 11; emphasis in original)

The authors go on to point out that '[l]anguage ideology is coming to be seen as a key part of the 'ethnoscapes' ... in which language codes and varieties function' (ibid.). In this regard, the ELF context—while larger and less wieldy—bears a strong similarity to the one in which Garrett *et al.* conducted their own empirical investigations, i.e. contemporary Wales. Indeed, to the extent that speakers from both contexts of enquiry have been and still are subject to 'the politics of language in multilingual situations', and especially to the prevailing ideology of the superiority of standard English over all other varieties of English, NS or NNS, they share a considerable degree of overlap. As an illustration, while the Welsh teenagers in Garrett *et al.*'s data do not regard Received Pronunciation as '*our* voice', they still see it as 'the voice of success in Wales' (p. 217), thus articulating a duality rooted in standard language ideology which is also characteristic of the NNSs who provided the ELF interview data reported below in Chapter 7 below.

Success is also linked to the English language (though not in the simplistic manner of Quirk and Honey), in an article by the poet and scholar Thumboo (2003), in which he discusses attitudes to 'globalised English'. Although he does not mention standard NS English explicitly, it is implicit in many of his references, such as to the monolingualism of those that English benefits the most, to prestige, to 'the belief in an innate superiority' (p. 237) which, as Thumboo observes, exists today as it did in colonial times, and to 'old hegemonies dressed in acronyms':

> Then the Word begot TEFL, TESOL
> And TG, ways of discourse, meta-fiction,
> Streams of specialists whose disciples
> Hypothesized, quarrelled, exported heresies.
> (Thumboo 1993, quoted in Thumboo 2003: 235)

Economic success for many of those engaged in the TEFL (Teaching English as a Foreign Language) and TESOL (Teaching English to Speakers of Other Languages) enterprises has, of course, long been assured. For, as Thumboo points out '[i]ts expansion into every corner of the world, into every instrument of mass media that required language, made English an asset to be exploited to generate considerable visible and invisible exports: selling education, publishing, manpower export ...' (p. 236). With such a strong profit motive, the desire to retain the status quo—and this means promoting not only English, but also a particular kind of English—is unlikely to recede. It should come as no surprise, then, that ELT documents reveal that '[c]ertain attitudes from a super-power past, especially in matters concerning English, the real jewel in the British crown, persist far into her post-colonial life' (ibid.).

The desire to preserve the English 'asset' for its historical 'owners' is inevitably bound up with the kinds of standard language ideology that are the subject of this chapter. Bolton (2003: 200) discusses what he calls 'three sets of interlocking ideologies' in relation to Hong Kong English: the 'falling standards myth', the 'monolingual myth', and the 'invisibility myth'. While the second is specific to Hong Kong (which is mistakenly said to be mono-lingual in Cantonese) and certain other countries, including England (where, typically, the large number of community languages passes unnoticed by non-sociolinguists), the first and third ideologies also apply to the countries of the expanding circle.

The 'falling standards myth' is based on nostalgia: in Hong Kong's case, 'a peculiar variety of neo-colonial nostalgia' for the English of a mythical 'golden age' within the colonial period (Bolton op. cit.: 111); in the expand-ing circle countries' case a nostalgia for the decades of the twentieth century when English in the ELF countries was unequivocally assumed to be a foreign language (for communication with its NSs) rather than a lingua franca, when 'correct' English was standard NS English, and when expanding circle norms (perhaps 'developments' is a better word) were automatically equated with low standards. This stance can be seen, for example, when Medgyes (1999: 185) describes 'International English' (by which he means EIL/ELF) as 'merely an idealization, an amalgam of beliefs and assumptions about rules and norms to which certain people adhere with varying degrees of success' and goes on to agree with 'Lewis's (1995) sarcastic remark that International English is a mere euphemism for, or a politically correct equivalent of, Intermediate English'. It can be seen again when Prodromou (2003: 12) describes a 'Successful User of English' or 'SUE' (i.e. a proficient NNS of English) as having 'a virtually flawless command of grammar and vocabulary', by which he means 'flawless' in relation to NS norms. Thus they deny the possibility of the existence and potential emergence of ELF norms and, in essence, subscribe to the deficit approach to NNS English (Kachru 1991), according to which any lexicogrammatical difference from an NS variant is by definition an error.

For many, then, ELF represents a decline in standards just as, for them, any departure from *the standard* necessarily represents a decline in *standards*. And this 'falling standards' perspective overlaps with the 'invisibility myth', which for Hong Kong refers to the claim that there is no such variety as Hong Kong English (Bolton op. cit.: 200) and for the expanding circle to the claim that there is no such variety as ELF. In both Hong Kong and the expanding circle countries, the assumption underlying this myth is that speakers do not use English with each other, but only (if infrequently) with its NSs, and that on those rare occasions when they speak English, their target is to approximate a standard NS variety (including an NS accent). This ignores the extent to which English has become a part of the daily lives of its NNSs in both Hong Kong and many countries of the expanding circle. It also indicates a failure to appreciate how far code-switching and code-mixing have become the norm among their English-knowing bilinguals and how these are, in turn, contributing to the emergence of local English norms appropriate to the local communication context. A further factor which is not appreciated by advocates of the falling standards and invisibility myths is, as Ammon (2003) observes that, in acquiring English, its NNSs pay greater attention to the language than do its NSs, which enables them to shape it into a form more appropriate for a practicable lingua franca than the form created by its NSs.

Local conditions and purposes—in other words, local context—call, then, for adaptation. Yet despite its importance to language learning and use, context is a concept that, as Baumgardner and Brown (2003) point out, has so far been largely ignored in theory development with regard to ELT in the expanding circle. These scholars link the neglect of context to a monolingual ideology which promotes the English norms of inner circle speakers both because these are seen as somehow more 'correct', and because promoting these norms leads to the sorts of economic reward mentioned above (for example, the profits to be made from 'centre'-produced English-only text books). Obviously these two phenomena are closely related—as they have been since the first days of English colonization—although it is not entirely clear whether one is the cart and one the horse—and if so, which is which.

Learners of English in the expanding circle are nevertheless entitled to choice in relation to appropriateness for context. As Baumgardner and Brown argue, '[c]lients have the right to pick the variety they want for their programs' (p. 249), and 'it is the needs of the local context and not the alleged superiority of the model that should inform their pedagogical choices' (ibid.). This means, *vis-à-vis* ELF, that if they wish to identify and be identified with a local ELF variety, that is their decision. Equally, it is up to them to decide whether they prefer to learn an inner (or outer) circle English. The critical point is that the decision should be made by those directly involved, according to their perceived needs and, crucially, on the basis of sound information concerning sociolinguistic variation and the socio-psychological issues involved in learning a second—and in this case, specifically an international—language. (See Jenkins 2000: Chapter 8.)

Unfortunately, at present, the lack of theory development to which Baumgardner and Brown refer is hindering the process of *informed* learner choice in the expanding circle. For if the only information learners typically receive about ELF is pejorative, they are highly unlikely to nominate an NNS variety as their target for learning. The strategy of denigrating NNS English thus represents a highly effective means of gatekeeping. According to Kachru, there are three major groups of English language gatekeeper: 'the protectors of the canon; the ELT enterprise ... ; and professional networks of various types' (1997b: 229). He describes them as having a range of motives, national interests, and agendas, and of the three considers the ELT enterprise to be the most influential. But what they all have in common, as will be demonstrated in the following sections of this chapter, is the promotion in the expanding circle of particular kinds of exonormative English and the demotion of endonormative Englishes. In other words, they all subscribe to the deficit view described above, according to which any NNS difference from NS norms signifies an interlanguage error rather than an ELF variant, while maintaining that the only appropriate variety is one that is imported from a distant inner circle context of use.[2]

Various 'commonsense' reasons are routinely given as to why standard NS English is to be favoured over other varieties. For instance, as Niedzielski and Preston demonstrate, 'many find the standard variety to be the only embodiment of rule-governed behavior' (2003: 311). The other side of the coin is the claim that non-standard varieties lack rules, and that variation from the standard is, in L. Milroy's words 'an undesirable deviation from a uniquely correct form'—a view 'widely and tenaciously held by people of all ages, intellectual levels, political persuasions and social statuses' (1999: 175). This is evidently all the more so when the non-standard variety in question is also a non-native one. It no doubt accounts in part for the stigmatizing and proscription of ELF lexicogrammatical features such as the all-purpose question tag, 'isn't it?' and the dropping of 3rd person singular -s in the present tense (see Seidlhofer, 2004: 220 for further examples), despite the fact that such variants occur systematically and frequently in ELF interactions, and are therefore likely to be (shown to be) rule-governed once more descriptions become available.

Another 'commonsense' view is often aired in discussions about identity in L2 English. For example, one of the reasons Preisler (1999) puts forward to justify his favouring of NS norms for learners in the expanding circle is that standard English is simply not an issue affecting NNS learners' social or individual identities. He is thus advocating that learners should endeavour to master for lingua franca use those forms of English which Seidlhofer (2005b: 71) refers to as 'native speaker 'shibboleths' that indicate membership of a very specific, confined native-speaker community' but which do not play a communicatively important role in lingua franca interactions. By claiming that identity is not an issue for ELF speakers (apparently without asking them), Preisler would thus deny learners both the right to choose a local ELF variety as their goal, and the possibility—if they made this choice—of replacing the 'shibboleth' NS English identity markers with features which would perform the same identity function for their own community. As will become clear in Chapter 7, the ELF identity issue is far from simple, and certainly not the non-issue that some, whether themselves NNSs of English like Preisler and Görlach, or NSs like Quirk and Trudgill, seem to consider it to be.

Anti-ELF sentiment in the writings of linguists

Those linguists who appear to be motivated by support for standard NS English language ideology to disparage ELF[3] employ three main 'techniques': they ignore it altogether in places where they might be expected to refer to it; they marginalize it by discussing it dismissively or over-briefly; and they disparage it directly. For the rest of this section, we will look at what has been said by some of the linguists whose writings fall into these three categories.

An example of one who ignores ELF completely is Crystal. The first edition of his book *English as a Global Language* (EGL) was published in 1997. It subsequently received some heavy criticism. (See, for example, Holborow 1999; Pennycook 2001; Phillipson 1999.) The second edition (2003) seems therefore to have been motivated by a desire not only to take account of developments in the swiftly-changing World Englishes scene, but also to respond to some of the criticisms levelled at the first edition. However, the updating element, at least as far as ELF is concerned is surprisingly lacking, given that the expanding circle has arguably seen the most extensive and far-reaching developments in the English language in the period between 1997 and 2003 and that these developments have been well-documented in the world Englishes and applied linguistics literature. This, coupled with the fact that Crystal is himself a prolific reader and writer in the field of world

Englishes[4], leads me to assume that the omission of ELF was neither the result of ignorance nor inadvertent.

The subject index of EGL contains several references to 'lingua franca', but none to English as a Lingua Franca/ELF or English as an International Language/EIL. By way of contrast, there are two entries for 'Euro English', which Crystal describes as a 'novel variety' of English which emerges 'when Germans, French, Greeks and others come into contact, each using English with its own pattern of *interference* from the mother tongue' (p. 182; emphasis added), and is an example of those expanding circle territories which 'may be bending English to suit their purposes' (p. 185). This phenomenon, 'a natural process of accommodation which in due course could lead to new standardized forms' (p. 182), is nevertheless 'so recent that it is difficult to make predictions with much confidence' (p. 183). This is undoubtedly true, and yet there have been research findings over the past decade (in ELF lexicogrammar, phonology, and pragmatics), particularly in mainland Europe and SE Asia, which are generating hypotheses and providing indications of how ELF varieties are developing independently of Anglo-American norms and how their speakers' interactions are becoming *sui generis*. In the almost 70 pages of the book's final chapter, 'The future of global English', readers might have expected, among the extensive discussion of inner and outer circle Englishes and World Standard Spoken English (WSSE[5]), at least some mention of this work. Crystal's follow-up to his first edition thus contrasts with another follow-up book: Graddol's *English Next* (2006), which, while not giving consideration to ELF as a major development in the spread of English, nevertheless gives coverage to lingua franca uses of English and includes a section specifically on ELF.

The author index of EGL likewise contains no references to any of the several researchers who have been engaged in ELF research over the past decade or more, despite the fact that they have already provided empirical evidence in respect of two of the phenomena about which Crystal offers predictions (substitutions of the voiced and voiceless 'th' sounds, and NS idiomatic language). On the other hand, there are several references to the scholars Görlach and McArthur, who appear to share Crystal's vision of the emergence of a monolithic English variety for international use (Crystal's 'WSSE'). Indeed, Görlach not only supports the concept of a single world English for international communication, but is emphatically against a pluricentric approach to the development of expanding circle Englishes. (See p. 11–12 above). Crystal is less appalled by the idea of ELF variants, and sees 'no reason for L2 features not to become a part of WSSE' (p. 188). However, there is little sense here of ELF being self-determining and independent of Anglo-American English: ELF features (insofar as Crystal discusses such NNS 'interference') are merely 'permitted' to contribute to a single world variety in whose development 'US English does seem likely to be the most influential' (ibid.).

Whereas Crystal makes no mention of ELF (or EIL) and ELF research, Melchers and Shaw at least acknowledge its existence in their book, *World*

Englishes which, like the second edition of EGL, was published in 2003. Here, it is more a question of balance as the authors themselves observe in their preface, in an admission of commendable honesty: 'We have tried not to present an explicit political stance in our book, and we have tried to make the implicit one as egalitarian and inclusive as possible, but we recognize that we are prisoners of our prejudices and hope that readers can see past them' (pp. ix–x). They continue: 'although we have found all varieties rich and fascinating, it is inevitable that our personal knowledge and experience is not evenly distributed. Our base in Europe and Sweden in particular shows through here and there' (p. x). All the more surprising, then, that the emerging ELF varieties of Europe are barely touched on at all, apart from a brief discussion of the role of English in the international organizations of the EU.

Overall, the book has 197 pages of text, of which the first 40 are concerned with the historical spread of English and with types of variation and classification; the next 80 or so deal with inner circle Englishes, followed by approximately 50 pages which cover the outer circle. The expanding circle is then dealt with somewhat cursorily in 15 pages. Evidently the authors do not find ELF varieties as 'rich and fascinating' as all the others. The imbalance is also reflected, though slightly differently, in the recordings on the CD-ROM which accompanies the book. Of the seventeen speakers, the majority (eleven) are from inner circle countries, with a bias towards the UK), one is from St Lucia in the West Indies (although English is his first language), two from the outer circle, and three (including one of the authors) from the expanding circle. The Englishes of all three types of user, ENL, ESL, and EIL are thus covered, as the authors claim, but very unequally. And despite their claims to be 'liberals' in terms of the ownership of English and target for learning (p. 193), Melchers and Shaw appear to be heavily influenced by some of the more linguistically (and politically?) conservative commentators on world Englishes such as Crystal, Trudgill, and Wells. (Indeed, the latter two are among those thanked in the acknowledgements for their support and help.)

To be fair to the authors, research into ELF is in its infancy relative to research on the Englishes of the other two circles. And although they say fairly little on the subject (especially when one considers the vast number of English speakers in the expanding circle), they do at least refer to ELF, and make a clear distinction between an 'independent "international" colloquial English' that may in time develop its own norms, and the 'nonstandard "mistakes"' that its features are still thought to be. They also refer to ELF researchers (for example, James, Modiano, and Seidlhofer) and some of their findings, including one of the most—if not *the* most—important ELF research projects, Seidlhofer's ELF corpus, VOICE (Vienna-Oxford International Corpus of English).[6] They are also among the very few commentators who understand that the aim of my ELF pronunciation proposals (Jenkins 2000) 'is a common core, not uniformity' (ibid.).

McArthur is another scholar who marginalizes ELF, both in his *Oxford Guide to World English* (2002) and in an article two years later in the journal

English Today, which he edits.[7] In the former, he at least has an entry for EIL, and mentions ELF in the body of the text, as the superordinate for the term 'Euro-English'. Like Crystal (who has several entries in the index), he sees Euro-English as 'likely to be influenced by both American and British [English], increasingly with American English predominating' (p. 160). His comment that 'Euro-English is not however by any means homogeneous .... at the *present time*' (p. 160; emphasis added) suggests that he endorses Crystal's prediction of a WSSE based on American English.[8] The suggestion is in fact confirmed in McArthur 1998, where he presents his own (1987) 'Circle of World English' at the centre of which is 'World Standard English' (1998: 97). Nevertheless, McArthur does, like Melchers and Shaw (and unlike Crystal), refer briefly to ELF research, in relation to a group of short articles under the heading 'Euro-English' written for *English Today* (Jenkins, Modiano, and Seidlhofer 2001).

Moving on to those who directly attack the notion of ELF, I will begin with Preisler, whose view of identity I mentioned above. Given that he does not consider identity to be an issue in L2 English, Preisler not surprisingly discusses learners' choice of variety as one between British and American English, in contrast to the point made (above) by Baumgardner and Brown that learners should have the right to pick the variety they want, untroubled by considerations of the perceived 'superiority' of particular models. Indeed, Preisler even describes as 'political correctness' the notion that 'a concept of Standard English associated, in particular, with the standards of Britain and North America challenges the autonomy of the other Englishes of the world' (1999: 263). His reasoning is that '[s]uch political correctness fails to distinguish between the functions of *an international variety*. The form of English taught in an EFL country should be determined only by the degree in which it will enable non-native speakers to cope with *the linguistic aspects of internationalisation* as it affects their own lives' (ibid.; emphasis added). Preisler thus assumes, oddly and without evidence, that a native variety of English will best enable NNSs to communicate in English internationally when—as he himself points out—they are most likely to interact with other NNSs rather than with NSs.

When he addresses the issue of ELF directly, Preisler demonstrates more clearly the extent to which his position on NNS English is grounded in standard language ideology: 'if EFL is based on models such as these, English as a lingua franca may become *even more pidginised than it already is*' (op. cit.: 265; emphasis added) and goes on to argue that '[i]f English is learned simply as a lingua franca—i.e. if the teaching of English is not firmly rooted in the cultural context of native speakers—there is a danger that *it will become unidiomatic*' (ibid.; emphasis added). In other words, according to Preisler, NNS English—where it differs from that of speakers of standard NS English—is both pidginized and unidiomatic. He is not able to contemplate the possibility of ELF varieties emerging through contact situations, or the fact (as demonstrated by empirical research) that these tend to be more appropriate and intelligible in lingua franca settings, and that NS idiomaticity is irrelevant or counterproductive. This perspective is all the more surprising since it appears in a collected edition (Bex and Watts 1999), which sets out to critique standard English and whose subtitle is 'The widening debate'. Others who have taken the third approach and explicitly disparaged the concept of ELF from a standard language ideological perspective include presenters of conference papers (for example, Cullen 2005; MacKenzie 2002); writers of journal articles and book chapters, (for example, Harris 2002, 2003; Kuo 2006; Rosewarne 2003; and several contributions to Dziubalska-Kołaczyk and Przedlecka 2005; and to Rubdy and Saraceni 2006); and even (mainly anonymous) customer reviewers of Jenkins (2000) on the Amazon website.

I will briefly look here at a selection of the anti-ELF positions in order to reveal the standard NS English ideology in which they are grounded, starting with a paper given by MacKenzie at a seminar on 'English as a Lingua Franca in Europe' during the sixth ESSE[9] conference held in Strasbourg in 2002. The title of his paper revealed his scepticism : 'Language teaching and the uses of the *so-called* English as a Lingua Franca' (emphasis added), and indeed, his abstract, circulated in advance of the seminar, made the point that his would be 'a somewhat sceptical contribution'.

In a nutshell, MacKenzie's presentation was based on two premises:
- firstly, that there is no such entity as ELF, 'but rather a variety of local versions of English, each influenced, as one would expect, by the grammar and vocabulary of the local language or languages'
- secondly, that 'an extensive ELF (or, more modestly, 'European non-native English') corpus would be a valuable resource for linguists and language teachers' merely because 'it might reveal which lexical phrases non-native speakers have been taught, or acquired, but which native speakers tend not to use'.

In the paper (whose main purpose was to attack two previously published papers, Seidlhofer 2001a and 2001b), these two points were developed in arguments which made clear his belief in the superiority of NS English and its 'correctness' in relation to NNS varieties; in the importance of learners acquiring 'real' English (in the sense of the fixed and semi-fixed lexical phrases which characterize NS English use); and in the irrelevance of NNS identity issues. He even argued that NS models are needed 'to permit [learners of English in higher education] to participate usefully in the spheres of science, technology, commerce, etc. that their presence at university suggests they wish to enter'. Thus, he neatly contradicted his own claim that English for science is 'scientific English' based on 'scientific English norms' rather than 'native speaker norms', and that teaching it is about 'empowerment' rather than 'exerting power and domination'.

MacKenzie's position in essence, then, is more or less identical with that of Preisler, Quirk, and the like. It is also shared by those who advocate the selection in language courses of the 'real' (i.e. NS) English that is recorded in corpus descriptions. While the latter are keen to argue in favour of learner choice and against the 'imposing' on learners of ELF forms identified in ELF corpora, they do not appear to have the same problem with the NS forms identified in NS corpora. Thus, contemporary ELT course books and speaking skills materials present copious examples of forms used in everyday conversation between NSs, without any consideration of their appropriateness for learners' communication contexts. (See Widdowson 1991; Seidlhofer 2003b: Section 2.) Underpinning the promotion of 'real' English is the same standard NS English ideology as that of all the other authors cited in this section. A good example is the published debate (an *ELT Journal* 'Point and counterpoint') between Carter and G. Cook (Carter 1998; G. Cook 1998; and see also the similar debate between Prodromou and Carter/McCarthy: McCarthy and Carter 1995; Prodromou 1996a, 1996b: Carter and McCarthy 1996). While Carter acknowledges that a large proportion of spoken interaction takes place among NNSs, he nevertheless argues that it is patronizing to remove the NS cultural/idiomatic references from coursebooks. His reason is that 'learners seem to want to know what real English is and are generally fascinated by the culturally-embedded use of language of native speakers' (1998: 50), 'real' in his view thus equating beyond doubt with 'native'. He goes on to argue that denying this (NS) 'real English' to learners condemns them to a life of transaction in English rather than one of genuine interaction in which they can 'build relationships, express attitudes and affect, evaluate, and comment, and make the propositional content of a message more person-oriented' (ibid.), as though these things cannot be done without the use of the forms of ENL. Carter then echoes MacKenzie (see above) in both argument and word, by concluding that 'there are issues of power and *empowerment* at stake here' (ibid.; emphasis added), adding that 'it would be clearly disempowering, and once again patronizing to teachers and learners, to say that we can ignore a lot of these informal and interactive meanings, because one outcome would be to deprive the learner of pedagogic, linguistic, and cultural choices' (p. 51). Here, then, we have the issue of choice, which, as I pointed out above, is not generally seen as relevant when mooted in relation to ELF as opposed to EFL. On the contrary, to offer the alternative of ELF is apparently to *remove* choice. Carter is thus presenting another version of the 'language is power' argument of Quirk, Honey *et al.*, albeit in terms of informal spoken NS English rather than formal standard NS English. This moves Cook in his reply to conclude that '[s]uch corpus-driven pedagogy is a vain attempt to resuscitate a patriarchal attitude to ELT' (1998: 62).

The Carter/Cook debate appeared in a widely-read publication for teachers of English and Carter's comments, supported by copious corpus data, *pace* Cook's objections, would undoubtedly have reinforced teachers' beliefs in the 'rightness' of the prevailing ideology of 'NS = best'. The overall effect on teachers of the widespread promotion of standard (and 'real') English language ideology, of the kind discussed in this section, will be considered in Chapter 8. Clearly, though, so much favouring of NS English and denigrating of forms that differ from those of NSs is affecting teachers' attitudes towards 'good' and even 'appropriate' English. The result is that they are often convinced that the English spoken in ELF contexts should, paradoxically, be ENL. Thus, it seems that despite all the ELF research activity, little has changed in terms of language attitudes. And as will be seen in the discussion of my data in Chapter 7, this is an attitude that was voiced repeatedly by the proficient non-native English speakers who participated in the interviews.

Readers may have noticed the absence among the anti-ELF positions outlined above of contributions from North American linguists. This does not by any means signify that US and Canadian linguists are pro-ELF. It is merely an indication that the interests of the majority tend to be directed more towards theoretical and practical issues relating to the teaching of ESL and EFL within their own national boundaries than towards those relating to ELF/EIL in the world at large. This is perhaps the reason why Mauro E. Mujica, the chairman of US English (the largest organization campaigning for English to be made the USA's official language), looked to David Crystal, a British linguist, when he wanted to sponsor a book explaining to his members the reasons for the global status of English (Crystal 1997, now in its second edition, 2003). For while a small number of American linguists are favourably disposed to the notion of ELF (such as Berns, for example 1995; Levis, for example 2006, Lowenberg, for example 2002; and McKay, for example 2002), the majority of American applied linguists and ESL/EFL teachers appear not to be aware of ELF/EIL at all—or if so, only dimly, and my own experience of introducing the concept to audiences at the annual TESOL convention in North America has, on the whole, been a negative one. For although TESOL is advanced in terms of its concerns with human rights in general and the rights of NNS teachers specifically (for example, there is a Non-native English Speakers in TESOL Caucus), and has even recently invited a European to talk about ELF in a plenary address at its annual convention,[10] little of this is reflected in the taken-for-granted English norms of the bulk of ESL/EFL literature produced by American authors, TESOL publications included. So, for example, while issues such as inequalities faced by NNS teachers, and the importance of intercultural awareness in the English classroom, are regularly aired in TESOL's quarterly magazine, *Essential Teacher*, standard NS American English is never called into question, and continues to reign supreme.

One further phenomenon of interest in relation to standard language ideology is the recent publication in the UK of a number of non-specialist books all advocating a highly prescriptive normative approach to English, including Lynne Truss's *Eats, Shoots and Leaves* on punctuation (a best seller in the UK), Vivian Cook's *Accomodating Brocolli in the Cemetary* on spelling, and John Humphreys's *The Mangling and Manipulation of the English Language* on grammar. At much the same time, several general interest books have been published on the history of the English language, such as the third and updated edition of McCrum *et al.*'s (2002) *The Story of English*, Crystal's (2004b) *The Stories of English*, and Bragg's (2003) *The Adventure of English*. It is curious that there should be such a perceived public interest in the history of the

English language and its norms in this particular time. One possible explanation is that these books, along with the others in the same two 'genres', are indicative of a desire (conscious or not) to assert the inner circle's historical 'ownership' of English and 'superior' linguistic expertise and knowledge of the language at a time when the numerical balance of its speakers is shifting so dramatically in favour of NNSs. And as Garrett (2001: 629) observes, 'there is room to speculate as to whether, historically, comment on language has tended to increase in quantity and anxiety at times of comparative change'.

While the intended audience for these books is presumably an NS English one, they are likely to be gaining the attention of L2 teachers, learners, and users of English. This being so, it is also likely that collectively the books will contribute to the existing linguistic insecurity of NNSs of English by reinforcing their attitudes *vis-à-vis* 'good' (i.e. standard NS) English. For, taking us back to where this chapter began, the discourse involved in the perpetuation of standard language ideology, as Baumgardner and Brown point out (citing Escobar 1995), 'promotes a type of subjectivity by which individuals who are not users of Inner Circle varieties of English see themselves as unequal users of English. They define their strengths as English language users with respect to Inner Circle speakers and come up short' (2003: 245). Whether the standard language ideology of the inner circle and its admirers will ultimately prevail, and ELF speakers will continue to see themselves as 'unequal users of English' way into the future, is far from clear at the time of writing.

Standard language ideology in the ELT press

Even if standard NS English language ideology and anti-ELF sentiment were restricted to the kinds of academic text that formed the bulk of the discussion in the previous section, it would still exert a powerful influence on many NNS and NS teachers of English and on their sense of NNSs as 'unequal users of English'. But the problem goes much further, for the ideology seems to be deeply ingrained in the communal ELT psyche and to infuse much of the day-to-day literature available to teachers, whether or not this is the intention. Indeed, I would go so far as to say that any text that does not actively promote NNS varieties is likely, to a greater or lesser extent, to be promoting NS norms and their users. In other words, the vast majority of texts, whether in professional newspapers, journals and websites, teaching and testing materials, and the like, are promoting NS English (usually standard British or American) as the ideal and, by default, NS teachers (and those NNSs who 'achieve' nativelike competence) as having the greatest knowledge of English and highest level of expertise in using and teaching it.

To demonstrate the extent to which the same kind of standard language ideology that was identified in the academic literature discussed above is reflected in the ELT literature, I turn now to an analysis of some of the materials which teachers typically read and use. In this section[11] the focus is on three ELT periodicals, *EL Gazette*, the *Guardian Weekly* 'Learning English' supplement, and *IATEFL Issues*. These were selected primarily because of the size of their readerships in terms of both their numbers of subscribers/readers and the international nature of their circulation:

- *EL Gazette (ELG)*, a monthly subscription-based newspaper which has a minimum print run of 7,000 copies which translates into a readership of 49,000 per issue, and is distributed in over 100 countries. Its readers are pre-service and in-service teachers, academic managers, school owners, academics, and publishers.

- The *Guardian Weekly*, and hence its monthly 'Learning English' supplement (*GWLE*), claims to be one of the world's best selling weekly newspapers. It has a circulation figure of almost 90,000 per issue, which translates into a total readership of just over 300,000. It is printed in London, Sydney, and Montreal, and sold primarily in Africa, Asia, Australasia/the Pacific, Europe, the Middle East, North America, and South/Central America.

- *IATEFL Issues (II)* is the bi-monthly newsletter of the UK-based IATEFL (International Association of Teachers of English as a Foreign Language), which sees its role as '[l]inking, developing and supporting English Language Teaching professionals worldwide'.[12] The association has a membership of 3,600 of which approximately two-thirds are based outside the UK in over 100 countries. The newsletter is sent to all members, both individual and institutional, as well as to libraries and ELT institutions, and is also distributed at international conferences. Thus, as with the other two publications, its readership is considerably higher than its circulation figure.[13]

By examining all three of these widely distributed ELT publications of different kinds (*ELG*, a free-standing professional newspaper; *GWLE*, a section of a mainstream newspaper; and *II*, an association's newsletter) I hope to demonstrate representativeness. And in order to avoid the charge of being selective, I decided to look at the four most recent issues of each publication that had been circulated at the time I was writing this chapter, regardless of how well they supported my case (i.e. September, October, November and December 2004 in the case of *EL Gazette* and the *Guardian Weekly* 'Learning English' supplement, and August/September 2004, and October/November 2004 in the case of *IATEFL Issues*). By focusing on the most recent issues, I am also able to claim that any standard NS English language ideology identified is still very much in force.

Two further points need making before I start the analysis itself. Firstly, it is not in any sense my intention to mount a gratuitous attack on these three publications. All three have numerous positive features and perform an invaluable service to their many readers around the world. They have not been singled out as being particularly 'guilty' of reflecting standard language ideology and in so far as they do so, they are unlikely to be any more 'guilty' (and possibly a good deal less so) than other similar publications. They were selected entirely on account of the number and spread of their respective readerships and their own claims to be widely representative.[14] Secondly, I am not in any way implying that the reflection of standard language ideology found within their pages is a deliberate ploy: I doubt that their editors and journalists are even aware of much of it. My aim in analysing these publications is simply to establish how ingrained the ideology is within some of the main disseminators of information to ELT professionals as a prelude to considering its role in NNS teachers' attitudes towards ELF in Chapters 6 and 7.

For the purpose of focusing the analysis, I have made use of Hammersley and Atkinson's 'Ethnographic questions about texts' that are shown in full in Table 2.1:

---

1   How are texts written?
2   How are they read?
3   Who writes them?
4   Who reads them?
5   For what purposes?
6   On what occasions?
7   With what outcome?
8   What is recorded?
9   What is omitted?
10   What is taken for granted?
11   What does the writer seem to take for granted about the reader?
12   What do readers need to know in order to make sense of them?

Table 2.1 Ethnographic questions about texts (Hammersley and Atkinson 1983: 142–3)[15]

All twelve questions would no doubt have yielded insightful findings in relation to the materials being analysed. The demands of space meant, however, that I had to be highly selective, and for this reason my analysis focuses on the two most relevant questions for the purpose in hand: 'What is recorded?' and 'What is omitted?' The sheer number and size of the various texts being analysed (ten items each extending to several pages, or twelve items if each double issue of *II* is counted as two) also means that my analysis cannot involve as close attention to detail as is typical of ethnographic approaches to texts and will, of necessity be relatively sketchy. The overall aim of the analysis is, nevertheless, to demonstrate the extent to which standard language ideology, an NS bias, and (by default) an anti-ELF stance are conveyed by these three widely-distributed publications; this applies to both the quality and quantity of their content in, for example, the number and kind of their advertisements for courses for teachers and ELT qualifications/examinations, teaching activities, book reviews and the like. In other words, my intention is to explore how far standard NS English norms are being promoted both explicitly and implicitly, and conversely, how far NNS manifestations of English are being ignored or even characterized as deficient, whether overtly or by omission.

Analysis of three ELT periodicals

We turn now to look more closely at the three sets of publications.[16] After a brief commentary on the first three categories shown in Table 2.2—i.e. adverts for courses, adverts for examinations, and adverts for books/book reviews—the more detailed focus is on the main articles and the activities for teachers in each individual publication. For whereas it could be argued that the number and kind of adverts for courses, examinations, teaching qualifications, books, and even book reviews depend to a great extent on what is sent to these periodicals by examination boards, teaching institutions, and publishers,[17] the same cannot be said of features, articles, or teaching activities, where there is much greater scope for journalistic freedom. In these articles and activities, the periodicals could, if they wished, opt to promote NNSs and NNS forms of English. By doing so, they would create an effective counter-balance to the impression of NS expertise and NS English correctness caused by the sheer number of adverts promoting these. As will be seen, however, *IATEFL Issues* to some extent apart, they reinforce the effect of the adverts by using the services of NS experts to provide the majority of their articles and teaching activities, and by referring almost exclusively to NS forms of English both in practice and in any theoretical discussion.

In the discussion that follows, the terms 'NS' and 'NNS' signify that the items in question present either an NS or NNS perspective on the topic, and/or represent the interests of an NS or NNS institution, examination board or publisher, and/or assume an NS or NNS variety of English. However, 'NS' does not assume that the items were authored by NSs, nor 'NNS' that they were authored by NNSs. It is entirely a matter of perspective. For example, the book which features in the one NNS-designated book review in *II* was written by an NS (Brumfit), while several of the NS-designated articles (in *II*) were written by NNSs. The categorization of the articles, however, is less straightforward and objective than it is for the adverts. As before, by 'NS' I do not mean that an article was necessarily written by an NS of English (although in most cases they in fact are); nor, by 'NNS', do I mean that it is written by an NNS of English. In each case, it is a question of focus and perspective: whether the author, NNS or NS, is in some way focusing on, deferring to, or implicitly assuming, an 'NS-as-expert' stance and/or a standard NS English language ideology (in particular, the assumption that 'correct', 'good', or 'appropriate' English is that of an NS variety), or whether the author is explicitly focusing on, promoting or implicitly accepting NNS Englishes and/or expertise and/or multilingualism. Having said this, I realize that not everyone will agree with my categorizations and that it is in the very nature of this kind of exercise that it must remain to some extent subjective. I am aware, too, of my personal bias in favour of ELF, and its potential to affect my decision-making. I believe, nevertheless, that the kinds of evidence offered in support of my categorizations provide reasonable justification for my choices.

	EL Gazette	Guardian Weekly 'Learning English'	IATEFL Issues
Course adverts mainly for teacher education, also for ELT	NS: 108 NNS: 1 (Berlitz, Malta)	NS: 37 NNS: 0	NS: 8 NNS: 0
Exam board adverts for ELT exams and teaching qualifications	NS: 14 NNS: 0	NS: 3 NNS: 0	NS: 2 NNS: 0
Book/teaching materials adverts and reviews	NS: 59 NNS: 0	NS: 2 NNS: 0	NS: 11 NNS: 1
Articles	NS: 46 NNS: 6 Neutral: 3	NS: 12 NNS: 5 Neutral: 1 Ambiguous: 2	NS: 14 NNS: 5 Neutral: 1
Teaching activities and advice	NS: 8 NNS: 0	NS: 14 NNS: 0	NS: 1 NNS: 0

Table 2.2 Summary of the analysis of three ELT periodicals

Advertisements

Starting with adverts for courses, these are predominantly masters programmes as well as other levels of (mainly postgraduate) teacher education, and much less frequently, courses for learners of English for Academic Purposes and general English. Of *ELG*'s 109 adverts, only one is for a non-inner circle institution, and as this is a Berlitz language school (in Malta), it is unlikely to be promoting anything other than an NS perspective and norms. *GWLE* and *II* have no adverts for courses in non-inner circle institutions. A similar situation obtains for ELT examinations and teaching qualifications. Across the issues of all three periodicals, adverts for examinations and teaching qualifications are exclusively NS exam boards (British and North American). In *ELG*'s case, each issue averages three or four (mostly large or very large) adverts for examination boards, with not a single one advertising an NNS exam board.[18] The impression given is that the kind of English 'opening doors across the world' is still very much an NS variety.

Moving on to books, again all the publishers' adverts (several of which occupy whole pages in *ELG* and *II*) are for books, ELT materials, and reference works written by NSs, while no advertised or reviewed book is written (or reviewed) by an NNS. And as far as I am able to tell, every book advertised or reviewed promotes, or at least assumes, an NS of English, while none promotes or assumes an NNS.[19]

Thus, going back to the two ethnographic questions, it would be true to say that what is recorded across the three categories of adverts is overwhelmingly an NS perspective on the English language and English teaching expertise, while what is omitted is overwhelmingly an NNS perspective. The cumulative picture presented by these dozens of adverts for NS-authored and -published books, NS-devised qualifications, and NS-led educational programmes in the absence of anything comparable advertising NNS expertise, is one of a taken-for-granted view of 'the NS-as-expert'. Whether this feeds subliminally into NNS and NS beliefs about each other's roles and English varieties, or whether readers are in fact aware of the perspective being presented is largely immaterial in terms of the effect on their attitudes. (See Chapter 8 for further discussion of these issues.)

Articles and teaching activities

Moving on to the main part of the analysis, attention is focused on the question of what is recorded and what is omitted in the articles and teaching activities/advice in the three publications. Starting with *ELG*,[20] I identified 46 articles as reflecting an NS perspective and six reflecting an NNS one (although most of the latter were written by NSs of English rather than a speaker of the L2 English concerned, and in standard British English rather than the speaker's local variety). Three items were designated 'neutral' as I could not detect any bias whatsoever.[21] Four of the six items designated 'NNS' appear in the November 2004 issue. These are:

- 'Multilingual, multinational' (Business English supplement, p. V)
- 'Natives not the answer says China ...' (p. 3)
- 'IB [International Baccalaureate] for beginners' (p. 13)
- 'International understanding' (p. 14)

The fifth and sixth items appeared in the December 2004 issue:

- 'Indian English will dominate says Crystal' (p. 3)
- 'ICWE [International Conferences, Workshops and Exhibitions] report' (p. 9)

However, even these six NNS-designated articles do not offer an exclusively NNS perspective on the issue in hand. For example, 'Multilingual, multinational', an article on the need to learn languages other than English, obtains its report on the markets for four European languages (Spanish, French, German and Italian) in the respective country, entirely from 'one major multinational provider, International House'. It seems that NNSs are not even allowed to supply the information on the teaching of their own L1s in their own countries. Meanwhile, the article on the International Baccalaureate (IB), makes specific references to the IB only in the UK, to Cambridge ESOL examinations as guides to proficiency levels, and, despite its stressing of the importance of encouraging multilingualism, focuses on the teaching of English. (In fairness, the latter was its purpose.) Again, the article 'International understanding', focuses not on understanding borne of mutual acceptance of linguacultural variation, but on one international school in Israel run by an NS of English from the UK, and issues to do with the teaching of English by immersion. It ends by reporting the NS school director's belief that 'where language becomes a vehicle for the sharing of ideas then seeds of understanding are sown'. As English is the language in question here, and the only target language discussed in the article, the implication is that not only do NSs provide the world with its most important language, but that English and international understanding are in some way intrinsically bound together.

The remaining three NNS-designated items, the second, fifth, and sixth in the above list, represent a clear NNS perspective. For example, the second item presents the case against untrained NS teachers of English in China from various NNS points of view, along with the argument that while English is useful, Chinese should come first. The fifth item in the list, which seems to be based on a longer article in *GWLE*, presents Crystal's view that Indian English is likely to become the most widely spoken variety of English in the world. In *ELG*, the perspective is unambiguously NNS, whereas this is not entirely the case in the longer *GWLE* version, which is discussed below.

Of the 46 articles identified as having an NS perspective, some focus exclusively on the UK and/or NS teachers such as UK language schools, UK-based qualifications (for example, DELTA),[22] UK-based masters and doctoral programmes, and the like. Others may look beyond the UK, but only in order for an NS teacher to give other NS teachers advice on how to obtain work in particular countries (for example, Spain, the Czech Republic, Korea), and information on how to survive once there. Even those articles which feature the teaching of English in another country still have a strong NS bias. For example, an article on Taiwan, 'Taiwan turns professional', in the Business English supplement (November 2004, p. I), refers mainly to NS institutions as the 'global providers' supplying the increased demand for high quality Business English courses. Wall Street Institute and the British Council, for instance, are described as having recently entered the market, the former 'to take advantage of the increasing demand for *better quality service*', and the latter to deliver services 'to the *top end* of the market' (emphasis added). There is little mention of local Taiwanese providers, and no comparable high quality 'tag' attached to them.

Moving on to *GWLE*, the balance favours NSs slightly less, and NNSs slightly more, with twelve articles designated 'NS', five designated 'NNS', two 'ambiguous' and one 'neutral'. The NNS designated items are:

- 'Which English do you want?' (September, p. 3)
- 'Working out the right way not to worry' (September, p. 6)
- 'Finding out how English scores on the pitch' (September, p. 7)
- 'Will the monoglot ever understand' (October, p. 7)
- 'France falls behind in English' (November, p. 3)

The first item, and the one which presents the most extreme case from an NNS perspective (although the author is in fact an NS), is Tomlinson's article arguing that it is up to NNSs to decide 'what varieties of English they want to learn; what they want to be able to do in English; what they don't want to be able to do in English; how they want to learn English; how they don't want to learn English; what type of materials they want to use; what type of materials they don't want to use; how they want to be assessed and how they don't want to be assessed'. He even questions whether he is 'being arrogant in asserting this', asking '[i]sn't the logical conclusion of my position that it is non-native learners of English who need to decide what it is that they need to decide?' This article stands out not only because it argues the NNS case more strongly than any other across all four months of all three publications, but also because it is surrounded by articles, teaching activities, and advertisements for NS-run courses, which so patently do not offer NNS teachers (and therefore their learners) the opportunity to decide for themselves between NS and NNS norms, teaching/assessment methods, materials, and so on, but assume instead that they will want to follow in NSs' footsteps.

The second item on the list (and the only one of the five actually authored by NNSs) is a shortened version of an article which had recently appeared in *ELT Journal* (58/3, July 2004). Written with Japanese learners particularly in mind, it reports the authors' research carried out at two Japanese universities to investigate Japanese language learners' strategies in coping with anxiety. Although the authors do not enter into any discussion of the type of English to be taught or the methods used to teach it, their (Japanese) learner-centred approach is very different in kind from the NS assumptions which typically underpin advice given to learners (even when accompanied by claims of 'learner-centredness'). The third item is not quite so straightforwardly NNS. For although it questions the relevance of the way English is taught in Australia to learners from East Timor, and despite the influence of Pennycook (who is quoted at length), the article does not develop its pro-NNS theme very much. And like some of the NNS-designated items in *ELG*, it also shifts occasionally towards a more NS stance (for example, in discussing the problem—presumably for NSs—in finding teaching jobs or coping as managers with limited training). The fourth article, written by the director of CILT, the national centre for languages in Britain, problematizes the monolingual perspective of NSs of English arising from the spread of ELF. While not criticizing the spread of English as a global lingua franca, she argues against NS English speakers' monolingualism and presents the case for plurilingualism in order that individuals are able to participate fully in a global society. This is, of course, entirely in accord with an ELF perspective. Indeed, the monolingual NS English attitude of expecting others to make all the (language learning) effort presents one of the greatest obstacles to the recognition and acceptance of NNS English varieties.

On the other hand, some of the NS-designated articles not only adopt an NS perspective on English language/learning, but unashamedly focus on NS interests, thus reinforcing the effect of the many advertisements for NS courses. In this regard there are, for example, articles discussing issues such as the recruitment of international students in inner circle countries (for example, 'Signs of slower international enrolments fail to scare the ELT "canary"' (September, p. 7). Again, there is an article promoting the work and

ELT 'expertise' of the British Council ('Defending a reputation for quality', September, p. 1). No attempt is made to disguise the Council's central aim of promoting British education ('courses skills and products'—and hence British English). Even the admission that countries such as India are developing the capacity to teach English without help from outside NSs is followed immediately by the comment that 'there are no plans to expand capacity in India' because 'if you go over a certain size, quality is called into question' whereas the British Council are 'only interested in maintaining and improving the standard of the service we deliver to people'. The implication seems to be that the English teaching being offered by Indians for Indians, because of the higher numbers involved, is of a lower standard than that being offered by the British Council.

In a similar vein, the NS-designated articles include advice offered by NS experts based on assumptions of the rightness of NS speech styles. For example, 'Untying the culturally tongue-tied' (October, p. 7), advises teachers on ways of preparing for speaking exams students who come from cultures which 'use silence in more calculated ways than *most English speakers*' for speaking exams (emphasis added). No evidence is offered to support this numerical claim, while nowhere in the article is there any suggestion that it is the exams themselves which may need adjusting to take account of cultural difference. Instead, the learners themselves are described as 'reticent' and 'culturally tongue-tied'. Ironically, this item appears immediately below the item on NS monolingualism discussed in the previous paragraph, in which this very point about arrogance towards other cultures is made.

The most extreme example of an NS perspective among the articles is 'Village living nurtures English' (December, p. 1), an account of an 'English immersion village' in South Korea. Here, most of the teaching is carried out by NSs, and 'good' English, learnt by immersion, is assumed to be NS English. Although the writer mentions that in addition to 'native teachers', English Village also recruits 'teachers proficient in English from as far away as Poland', he does not consider the possibility that such NNS teachers might in fact be more appropriate than NS teachers for Korean learners of English. And as Polish teachers of English (the only NNS group specifically mentioned) tend to have a strong preference for NS English and close approximation to its norms (see Jenkins 2005b), the implication is that the minority of NNS teachers share the standard NS language ideology of the NS teachers. The writer also claims that 'English Village goes out of its way to avoid connections with US symbols, stressing English as a "global language" separate from the politics of one nation'. Yet, judging from the range of activities conducted in English (checking into a hotel, shopping, banking, ordering food, and so on), NS cultural rules are being taught together with the language, while the implication of the language written on the blackboard in the photograph alongside the article is that the culture and language being taught are very much those of North America, if not specifically of the US.

Finally, the ambiguous and neutral items: the neutral item is an article on recent research investigating dyslexia across languages (October, p. 3). The two ambiguous items are 'A window opens on world classrooms' (October, p. 3), and 'Subcontinent raises its voice' (November, pp. 1–2). In the first, Max de Lotbinière, the editor of *GWLE*, discusses a new CD-ROM, *Looking at Teachers*, produced by Christopher Tribble (2003) for the British Council. (See Chapter 7 for samples from the interviews.) The CD-ROM contains interviews with teachers and photographs of classes in action across eight countries in which Tribble had been working as a teacher trainer over the previous two years (China, Georgia, Poland, Tunisia, Ethiopia, Senegal, Sri Lanka, and Britain). As Tribble points out, the CD-ROM not only allows 'mother-tongue teachers to see the different conditions that teachers work in' and to hear from teachers in their own voice, but it could be 'the first time that many trainee teachers will be able to hear and compare non-native or lingua-franca English being spoken by users from diverse world regions'. One of the benefits of the CD-ROM, then, is that it demonstrates to NS teachers that teaching takes place successfully in settings very different from their own.

On the other hand, the teaching methods taking place successfully are presumably NS-led methods; for, as Tribble himself says, despite teaching taking place in very large classes in China, for example, 'the teacher is still successfully using communicative methods', as though these imported methods are the only acceptable way to teach English. It seems that it is the different conditions in which teachers work rather than their different approaches to teaching that are the focus of the CD-ROM, which is perhaps unsurprising in view of the fact that it was sponsored by the British Council. Also less satisfactory is Tribble's claim that '[t]he language offers them [the teachers] an extension of their identity, in a way that no other teaching subject can', and that through their 'emotional engagement with the language' they are 'changed as a person'. Identity is, of course, a very complicated issue, and one that will be considered in detail later in this book. The assumption that learning an L2 (the subject here being English rather than any L2) should by definition alter the learner's identity and change them as a person sits uncomfortably with the notion of ELF.

The second ambiguous article in *GWLE* is Crystal's article on Indian English, the longer version of the short item which appeared in *ELG*—see above. In the article, Crystal points out that Indian English now has many more speakers than NS varieties of English have, and discusses the implications for the future of English. The ambiguity of perspective lies not in the facts and figures, but in some of the assumptions that are implicit in certain comments. For example, Crystal asks '[w]hat status will this rapidly growing English dialect have in the eyes of the rest of the world?' (p. 2), as though Indian English is a dialect without its own standard forms. Later, in arguing that Indian English is more likely than China English to become the world's 'linguistic superpower', one of the points he makes in its support is the fact that 'British people are familiar with (British dialects of) Indian English as a result of several generations of immigration'. The implication here is that the world's main variety of English must be one with which the British feel comfortable. Again, as Crystal's fact-finding visit to India, on which this article draws, was sponsored by the British Council, this is again perhaps not surprising.

Finally, we turn to the articles in *II*. Of the three publications under consideration, this one is similar to *GWLE* in terms of the percentage of articles which promote an NNS approach to English and/or its teaching in some way. And had the December 2004–January 2005 issue arrived a couple of weeks earlier, I would have been able to include an article specifically on ELF (in the new 'ABC of ELT' column) which provides a parallel, in terms of the strength of its NNS perspective, with the Tomlinson article in *GWLE* discussed above. *II* also includes more articles written by NNSs themselves than do either of the other two publications, although as I pointed out earlier, this is not necessarily indicative of an NNS perspective. Five articles are designated 'NNS', 14 'NS', and one 'neutral (Robin Walker's article, 'Good ELT practice', October–November, pp. 5–6 in which he makes an analogy between the doctor–patient and teacher–learner relationships).

The five articles designated 'NNS' are:

- 'The Communicative Approach is never the problem' (Deepti Gupti, August–September, p. 2)
- 'Notes for a trainee' (Franca Schiavo-O'Connell, August–September, p. 6)
- 'Working week: A week in the life of an IATEFL member' (Gyögyi Végh, August–September, p. 13)
- 'Assessing bilingual language programmes' (Maria Martinez Lirola, October–November, p. 4)
- 'What makes a good teacher?' (Nicola Martin, October–November, p. 8)

The first of these is an article discussing how the communicative approach (CA) has finally come to India, but on local terms. Gupti concludes that 'a healthy dose of scepticism in looking at imported methodological answers and an awareness of the differences that characterise the NEM [non-English medium] classroom are two essential components of the FL [foreign language]-NEM teacher's perspective. The CA experience in India is reason enough to make this an FL-NEM teaching maxim'. The third article is an account of a working week in the life of a Hungarian secondary school teacher of English. It is designated 'NNS' not because the teacher is by definition describing an NNS perspective on teaching (i.e. her own), but because her teaching includes discussions of identity, of perceptions of one's own culture, and of stereotyping. However, other aspects of her teaching and training are less sympathetic to an NNS English point of view. She talks, for example, of teaching her students English songs and literature and about British culture (the British Parliament).

The fourth item, the article on bilingual programmes (in this case for immigrants in the US), presents a much more clearly defined NNS perspective in its discussion of respect for cultural diversity. The aim of such programmes is 'to make the acquisition of English easier, while maintaining the maternal language and culture, in this case Spanish'. Although diversity in English is not explicitly mentioned, it is only a short step from the latter aim to recognizing and accepting the influence of the mother tongue on English, in other words, the acceptance of ELF. This is also implicit in the writer's conclusion that 'it is essential that the teacher understand the English language learner not as one who does not speak English well, but as one who has been raised in the context of a different culture. The teacher needs to understand the student's background, recognize the learning strengths and potential available to the student through the home language, and be sensitive to the similarities and differences that may exist'. A similar concern with the acceptance of cultural diversity arises in the final item on the list, although again linguistic diversity is not specifically mentioned, let alone problematized. The article nevertheless refers to variables such as 'students' cultural expectations', 'accepted/expected teaching methods within a country', and 'an understanding of the students' learning history', rather then advising on ways of imposing NS methods.

The 'NS' items are so designated for a range of reasons. In some cases they focus overtly on the NS as expert. For example, in her 'Report on the 38th International IATEFL Conference' (August–September, p. 21), Nicole Tavares refers to having her awareness raised of different modes of teacher training in different countries, but refers only to NS 'experts' in her list of 'prominent ELT figures' (Harmer, McCarthy, Swan, Rinvolucri, and Underhill) and describes how 'they model *good* teaching' (emphasis added), as though the same could not be said of NNS figures. As these figures are all closely associated with British norms and most of them also with British teaching methods,[23] the implication is that she considers these superior to NNS norms and methods. Other articles focus specifically on NS teaching methods such as task-based learning, or recommend NS-based materials; there is in each issue, for example, an article recommending predominantly NS sources of online reference materials. The remainder do not promote as overt an NS perspective on English as those found in EGL and *GWLE*, but together create an overall impression that NSs are somehow in the ascendancy: their names appear more frequently; their institutions seem to be the most respected; their English is evidently regarded as the best; and so on.

The impression created by the articles is compounded by the teaching activities across two of the three publications, *ELG* and *GWLE*. Starting again with *ELG*, each issue except October contains a number of photocopiable teaching activities and tips. In the September issues there are three half-page activity sections, two in the 'EL examinations supplement' ('You don't need to be an expert', p. III, offering tips for teaching Business English, and 'Fashion victims', p. V, an exam practice activity for Cambridge First Certificate), and one in the main section ('Talking up a storm', p. 9, offering tips for discussion classes). The November issue has half a page of tips, 'Put English into business', in the EL business English section (p. IV) advising on how to make tasks stimulating, and a full page activity on the 'EL eap' page (main section, p. 9) on festivals. The December issue has five general English activities spread across two-and-a-half pages, all on the theme of Christmas.

Where the designer of an activity is named, it is, in every case, an NS. This would not, in itself, be an issue were it not for the fact that the majority of these activities and tips either explicitly or implicitly focus on NS linguistic and, in some cases, NS cultural norms. The only exception to this is provided by two of the Business English activities which, typical of the more intercultural interests of the genre, tend to use more neutral language (with no NS idiomaticity at all), to avoid NS cultural reference, and to incorporate much greater scope for what learners themselves bring to the activity. Of the remainder, several focus overtly on NS idiomatic language and NS culture. For example, 'Fashion victims?' is a questionnaire about British youth culture, while all five activities in the December issue involve a very NS English approach to Christmas, along with much idiomatic language. (This includes, surprisingly, the Christmas activity on Business English.) Another activity, 'Talking up a storm', while less NS-biased in its content, nevertheless includes a considerable amount of NS idiomaticity in its wording, and 'Putting it together', which purports to be a brainstorming activity in preparation for writing an essay on a festival in the student's own country focuses almost entirely on North America's Thanksgiving Day.

Turning to *GWLE*, there are 'classroom materials and exercises' in each of the four issues, filling a single page in September, and a double page spread in the following three months. In each issue there is a reading comprehension, a column containing 'class tips' which, we are told, is '[b]rought to you by Macmillan Education's community resource site for teachers, onestopenglish.com' and which offers '[s]olutions for English Teaching' (see, for example, September, p. 5), and a 'Talking pictures' activity (except September.) From October onwards there is also a new regular column, 'Word search', in which Chris Tribble (whose British Council-sponsored CD-ROM was discussed above on pp. 56–7) is taking 'a fresh look at the way words and language are used in the *Guardian Weekly*—and offering teaching ideas that can be used for activities and discussions' (October, p. 5). There is also a column, 'New teachers' (except September), in which John Hughes, 'a teacher, teacher trainer and author of *Lessons in Your Rucksack* (Modern English Publishing, £14.95)' offers advice to fledgling teachers and also invites them to email their queries to him, to be answered in future issues.

The topics of the four reading comprehensions are: British research into anxiety in sheep (September, p. 5); matchmaking in an Irish bar (October, p. 4); a project in Graz, Austria to improve health by laughter (November, p. 4); and the threat to London's Chinatown from a new business development (December, p. 2). Although there is not much more NS than NNS cultural content and reference in most of these articles, they contain a lot of NS idiomatic language. On the other hand, the 'Talking pictures' are all heavily NS in their cultural reference, with the focus on the US presidential candidate, John Kerry (October, p. 5); Princess Diana (November, p. 5); and fox hunting (December, p. 3). Although the 'Word search' column includes cultural references to NNSs as well as NSs, the words selected and explored inevitably reflect an NS perspective in the main, given that the words themselves are taken from a British newspaper (the *Guardian*)[24] in the first place. Meanwhile, *GWLE* puts Scrivener and Hughes, two NS teacher trainers and materials writers, in the position of experts, apparently forgetting that the ELT community for whom it claims to be 'essential reading' (front page) also has NNS experts. Scrivener's columns include a lot of idiomatic language and even activities to teach NS idioms, while the advice in Hughes's columns projects a largely NS style of methodology (for example, in references to complimenting learners, discouraging their use of the L1, and the like).

The activities in the *II* sample are more difficult to assess as Chaz Pugliese's one-page column, 'Activities for busy teachers', does not appear in the August–September issue. Judging from the four activities in the October–November issue (p. 14)[25], however, the emphasis is on making suggestions rather than providing detailed advice, and leaving teachers to decide how to interpret them locally. Pugliese also invites teachers to send him activities which have worked for them so that they can be shared with others, and he is also careful to point out the origins of activities where these are known. For example, after describing a 'lipogram' activity which he learnt from another teacher, he informs readers that the technique in fact dates back to ancient Greece (where they were used by Tryphiodorus) and has also been used in modern times by the French writer, Georges Perec and others in the Ouvroir de Littérature movement. Thus, the activities in *II* stand apart from those of the other two publications in many respects. Even here, though, we find NS idiomatic language (for example, 'weed out the mistakes', 'power walking'). And while the activities are culturally neutral and can be easily adapted to local interests, at the linguistic level there is no suggestion that anything other than NS English norms could provide an acceptable target.

The overall impression created by the teaching activities, then (if sometimes by default) is that the language on which teachers should be focusing is standard NS English along with NS idioms and collocations. To a greater or lesser extent (*ELG*'s Business English activities and *II*'s activities apart), there is also an implicit assumption that NS cultural content forms an important aspect of English teaching. In most cases (again, *II* apart), the message conveyed is of the NS as the exclusive provider of teaching expertise and, thus, the NNS as the receiver of expertise. This is, in a sense, inevitable if the linguaculture being promoted is that of NSs rather than those of ELF speakers. And as Widdowson (2003: 152) argues, the dominant pedagogy being presented in these (and most other) teaching activities is not only that of NSs of English, but also monolingual, despite the fact that 'the dominant majority of teachers are more bilingually inclined' (Whitney 2005: 72, Note 6).

The larger picture

Returning to our two ethnographic questions as to what is recorded and what is omitted, the picture which emerges across all the analysed issues of these three periodicals is undoubtedly one in which the NS dominates. NNS English countries emerge as places where NSs of English go to teach, NS countries as places that NNSs go to learn, and where experts and authoritative publications originate. This is particularly clear in the case of advertisements. Advertisements for postgraduate courses offering to enhance teachers' knowledge and expertise have, almost without exception, been placed by inner circle institutions (largely British, North American, and Australian). The same is true of publishers' adverts for books and other published materials, and also of book reviews. Likewise, the majority of articles (and *ELG*'s and *GWLE*'s activities) have an NS bias. That is, they focus on NS English and/or are written by NSs or, less often, by NNSs who tend to show an explicit or implicit preference for NS norms, and who in many cases are working in an inner circle country or for a British Council institution elsewhere. Meanwhile, the few items focusing exclusively on NNSs tend to be relegated to brief news sections and snippets, while there is almost nothing (by NNSs or NSs) promoting NNS English or NNS cultural norms. The standard NS language ideology of the academic literature discussed in the first half of this chapter is thus clearly reflected in the periodicals for teachers considered in the second half. And as is demonstrated in Chapter 8, it exists in a wide range of other ELT publications and processes, where (wittingly or unwittingly) it performs similar gatekeeping functions.

To counter the possible objection that the same ideology would not be found in comparable ELT literature emanating from expanding circle contexts themselves, I also looked at a selection of locally-produced publications, including periodicals of BRAZ-TESOL, GRETA,[26] KATE,[27] MELTA,[28] TESOL-Greece, TESOL-Italy and TESOL-Spain (although in many cases these organizations are affiliates of one of the two larger international 'umbrella' organizations: TESOL or IATEFL). The indications are that with a very few exceptions[29] the opposite is in fact the case, and that these periodicals reflect standard NS English language ideology and a view of the 'NS-as-expert' even more strongly than the publications originating from inner circle countries. For instance, the conference reports of these locally-produced publications regularly feature as the conference highlight a presentation of some visiting NS 'expert' rather than their own speakers' presentations. The fact that some of this can be explained by a relationship between the local organizations and IATEFL or 'North American' TESOL does not in any way make it acceptable. It seems that the sheer weight of the NS ideology being communicated to NNS teachers around the world on a regular basis is convincing many of them (along with NS teachers, should they need convincing) that 'good' English is NS English, and that its most important experts are NSs in terms of both the language itself and by a somewhat curious and tenuous link, its teaching.[30] Much of this may take place below the level of consciousness for, as Holliday (2005: 10) observes, 'native speakerism is so deep in the way in which we think about TESOL that people are standardly unaware of its presence and its impact'. This in turn, goes a considerable way to explain NNSs' admiration for NS norms, their deficit view of their own NNS Englishes (which they see as characterized by errors rather than local NNS variants), and their sense of linguistic insecurity, all of which inevitably reduce their receptivity to the notion of ELF.

Having painted this somewhat negative picture, it is only fair to concede that in the present circumstances, the attitudes expressed in the three news-periodicals analysed above, as well as in the other periodicals to which I have referred, are understandable, since there is, as yet, no practical alternative. If the whole ELT industry—textbooks, teacher education, examinations, and the like—is based on NS standard norms, and success or failure depends on conformity to these norms, it is hardly surprising that dissent is rare. So while there needs to be a change in attitude, this is understandably difficult to bring about. And in this respect, there is an important distinction between scholars such as Trudgill and Quirk, who are in a position to change their attitude but are prevented from doing so for ideological reasons, and those who are not in a position to change attitude because they are, in effect, the victims of an ideology that is imposed upon them.

As Tucker points out, 'discrimination on the basis of language is one of the few types of discrimination that is seemingly still tolerated by many members of present society' (2003: 246). And as Lippi-Green (1997) demonstrates, language-based discrimination is particularly evident at the level of accent, the level that seems to elicit the most negative views of non-native Englishes from both NSs and NNSs themselves. L. Milroy observes that '[a] major instantiation of American language ideology ... presents itself overwhelmingly as a negative and sometimes demonstrably irrational attitude to languages other than English, and by association to English spoken with a "foreign" accent' (1999: 179). The same, I believe, holds true of other NS English groups including British, while accent is frequently the item that NNSs single out when they criticize their own or others' NNS English. In Chapters 5 and 6, we look at some new research that demonstrates the extent to which standard NS English language ideology may be affecting NNSs' attitudes to and beliefs about their own Englishes and, particularly, their accents, and then in Chapter 7 relate these attitudes and beliefs to the issue of ELF identity. But first, we move on, in the next chapter, to explore previous research into language attitudes in general and ELF attitudes specifically.

Notes

1 Throughout the book I tend to use the terms 'ELT' and 'TESOL' interchangeably. However, in this chapter, I have used the term 'ELT' throughout. This is because 'TESOL' is more closely connected than 'ELT', in many people's perceptions, with the teaching of English to learners of EAL (English as an Additional Language) in the UK and ESL (English as a Second Language) in North America, whereas my concern in this chapter is with English teaching/learning specifically in expanding circle countries. This is by no means intended to imply that the same sorts of ideology problems do not afflict EAL and ESL.

2 It is important to clarify that when people promote NS English norms, they generally have in mind the norms of a small sub-group of English speakers, i.e speakers of so-called 'educated standard English', and not the norms of all English NSs. (See Trudgill 1999.) Their position contrasts with that of sociolinguists, who regard all NS varieties as legitimate, and who prize and study the non-conformities of non-standard NS Englishes (but who nevertheless dismiss the non-conformities of *non*-native speakers).

3 I include here both those who favour a standard inner circle variety and those who promote a monolithic world standard based essentially on an NS variety.

4 In the year following the 2nd edition of EGL, Crystal published two further books on the development of the English language: *The Language Revolution* (Cambridge: Polity Press) and *The Stories of English* (London: Penguin). Like EGL, these books also neglect to mention ELF/EIL research.

5 Crystal elsewhere refers to this as 'International Standard Spoken English' (for example, 2004a: 39).

6 This was a timely position of the authors to take in view of the fact that the *Oxford Advanced Learner's Dictionary* 7th edition was about to include a page on ELF for the first time, both explaining the phenomenon and illustrating it with examples from VOICE.

7 McArthur's article discusses the terms 'World English', 'International English' and 'global English'. ELF is not mentioned at all (but see Erling's 2005 reply in which she refers favourably to the term and concept), while EIL shares 'International English' with other (non-lingua franca) interpretations of the term. In fact ELF gets fairly short shrift in *English Today* generally.

8 Canagarajah (1999: 180) responds to Crystal's concept of American-influenced WSSE with the observation that ' Crystal is apparently not troubled by the linguistic inequalities set up by his proposal, the hegemony of the center Englishes through the "standard", and the ways in which WSSE can provide ideological and economic advantages to center communities'.

9 European Society for the Study of English.

10 At the 39th Annual Convention in 2005, one of the plenary addresses was given by the German applied linguist, Juliane House, whose talk was entitled 'Teaching and Learning English as an International Lingua Franca'.

11 Evidence of standard NS English language ideology in a wider range of ELT materials is provided in Chapter 8 along with a consideration of its gatekeeping effects on the teaching and learning of English.

12 Taken from IATEFL's letter head, November 2004.

13 I chose *IATEFL Issues* (now *IATEFL Voices*) rather than *Essential Teacher*, the equivalent publication of IATEFL's American counterpart, TESOL (Teachers of English to Speakers of Other Languages). This is because *TESOL Matters*, the predecessor of *Essential Teacher*, ceased publication shortly before I began my analysis, which meant that insufficient issues of the latter were available at the time. Even if this had not been the case, however, I may still have chosen *IATEFL Issues* rather than *Essential Teacher*. Although this may seem an odd comment in terms of the two organizations' relative membership figures (TESOL has approximately 13,500 members), despite the fact that its website describes it as 'A global education association', around 80 per cent of its members are based in the US; and while its members range across 126 countries, the majority have only a small handful, in most cases less than ten. This, in turn, means that TESOL's principal interest is in English teaching within the context of North America rather than the wider world. Meanwhile, unlike IATEFL, members of the regional TESOL affiliates (for example, BRAZ-TESOL, TESOL-Italy etc.) are not members of the 'worldwide' (i.e. North-American-based) TESOL Association.

14 *ELG*'s subheading is 'English language journal opening doors across the world'; *GWLE*'s front page says 'Essential reading for the English language teaching community'; and *II*'s front cover describes it as 'Linking, developing and supporting English language teaching professionals worldwide'.

15 Hammersley and Atkinson's 1983 list appeared in prose and was later presented in this tabular form by Silverman (2001: 129). In their second edition (1995), Hammersley and Atkinson provide the same prose list of questions except that they omit item no.10, 'What is taken for granted?' (p. 173). This seems a pity, at least for ELF research, as this question has the potential to yield important insights into the mindsets of those who write about the teaching and use of English in lingua franca contexts.

16 News items are not considered except in a very few cases where items which appear on 'news' pages are more typical of articles. Although it would be of interest to examine the extent, if any, of NS bias in what is reported (and how), space did not permit me to include everything, and I decided that for the purposes of revealing standard language ideology, news items would be less fruitful than articles, activities, and adverts.

17 This is, of course, indicative of the ideological position of the institutions and publishing houses concerned—a point that is taken up in Chapter 7.

18 The lack of adverts for NNS examination boards is not surprising given that NNS-run examinations tend to operate on a local rather than global scale, and are therefore unlikely to be advertised in periodicals with so wide a distribution.

19 The assumption is that in these three categories—courses, examinations, and teaching materials—an NNS can only be concerned with English as it is locally learnt, and that the only way to generalize beyond the local is to focus on the NS standard. The underlying problem is that at present there is no choice when it comes to providing for learners beyond their *local* English needs: there is only the NS standard to offer. This situation can only change if and when the principle of ELF is established.

20 Whereas all adverts and teaching activities were counted regardless of their size, in the case of articles, only those of at least an eighth of a page in *ELG* (which is A3 in size) and *GWLE* (which is almost A3), and a quarter of a page in *II* (which is A4) are included in the count. However, it is not possible to discuss each article individually within the space permitted, and only a small number of articles (whether NNS- or NS-designated, neutral, or ambiguous) are considered in any detail.

21 Of these three, one was on neuroscience (October, p. 13), the second on research in support of Chomsky's theories (November, p. 12), and the third on the European Council of International Schools (November, p. 13).

22 Diploma in English Language Teaching to Adults.

23 Rinvolucri is an exception as far as teaching methods are concerned, as his methods have always been idiosyncratic; meanwhile, both Rinvolucri and Underhill have developed a recent interest in the issue of NNS English varieties (although to my knowledge they have not published materials that put this into practice).

24 *Guardian Weekly* is a compilation of selected items from that week's *The Guardian*.

25 I also looked at the same item in the December–January issue, where the impression given by the August–September issue is confirmed. In fact the former contains two activities, one by a Polish and the other by a Belgian teacher of English.

26 Granada English Teachers' Association.

27 Korean Association of Teachers of English.

28 Munich English Language Teachers' Association.

29 Examples of such rare exceptions are two articles in the September–October 2003 issue of the *TESOL-Italy Newsletter* (Vol.XIII, No.4): Enrico Grazzi's 'Which English? Whose English?' and Franca Ricci Stephenson's 'Food for thought'.

30 There is a double fallacy here: firstly, that NS English is the only English; and secondly, that NSs of English are uniquely capable of teaching—and

writing about teaching—this. It is, of course, possible to hold the first view but not the second, and there is a vibrant literature demonstrating that NNS teachers may have greater declarative knowledge of the NS standard than do NS teachers, whose knowledge is sometimes largely procedural. NNS teachers, for this and other reasons, may thus be better qualified as instructors of English even if not necessarily as informants (Widdowson 1994b; and see, for example, Braine (ed.) 1999; Brutt-Griffler and Samimy 2001; Kamhi-Stein (ed.) 2004; Nemtchinova 2005; Seidlhofer 1999, among many others). However, this is not the main point that I have been making in this chapter. Regardless of whether or not NNS teachers know English better in the declarative sense, it is the extent to which they still defer to an NS perspective on both the language and its teaching that interests me, along with the part played in this phenomenon by the prevailing NS ideology. And as was seen above in the NS orientations towards English/English teaching of the articles written by NNS teachers, they reinforce the NS perspective in their own writings, and in turn contribute to the ideology that has influenced them.

3

Language attitudes

Chapter 1 provided a taste of prevailing attitudes towards non-standard English(es) among both the academic community (for example, Görlach 1999, 2002; Quirk 1990, 1995) and the lay population (for example, May 2000), and towards ELF specifically (for example, Trudgill 2005). I went on, in Chapter 2, to draw links between negative attitudes towards ELF and standard language ideology. But as Seidlhofer (2004) points out, 'the important issue of attitudes towards ELF by researchers, teachers, learners and the public at large has only begun to be addressed' (p. 229). This state of affairs is a serious omission given what is known about the effects of language on social judgements (Giles and Billings 2004) and the vast number of ELF speakers who may be at the receiving end of prejudice based on the language they use.

In contrast to the vast literature (academic and pedagogic) that disseminates knowledge about standard English varieties and directly or indirectly disparages ELF varieties, little has been written about the attitudes towards ELF which such literature both reveals and perpetuates. This state of affairs in turn creates the false impression that standard varieties are self-evidently superior, and ELF varieties self-evidently inferior. What seems self-evident to me, by contrast, is that there is an urgent need for ELF both to be explored in relation to the many existing findings of language attitudes research, and to be the subject of new, ELF-specific language attitudes studies. I undertake this kind of exploration in Chapters 5 and 6, where my principal aim is to demonstrate empirically how the prevailing native speaker standard English language ideology in ELT and applied linguistics may be affecting NNS teachers' attitudes, beliefs, and feelings about their own and other NNSs' English accents, and how this can lead to linguistic insecurity and the kind of ambivalent ELF identities that are then revealed in Chapter 7. But first, because of its relevance to the study of ELF attitudes, we consider in this chapter the burgeoning socio-psychological literature in the field of language attitudes research, initially general and secondly accent-related, and in

Chapter 4, go on to look at some of the small number of ELF accent attitudes studies that have been carried out to date.

General research findings

The beginnings

As Giles and Billings (2004) point out, language attitudes research dates back to a study in the 1930s (Pear 1931) in which BBC radio listeners were asked to supply personality profiles of voices from a range of British dialects. Further research was unable to demonstrate any convincing match between listeners' ratings of vocal features and actual personality. By contrast, other studies found substantial agreement among listener raters in terms of stereotypical character traits associated with voices (see Giles and Billings op. cit.; Giles and Powesland 1975), and since 1960, there has been 'an explosion of research ... showing that people can express definite and consistent attitudes towards speakers who use particular styles of speaking' (Giles and Billings op. cit.: 188). In this respect, the pioneering work of Lambert and his colleagues within the 'speaker evaluation paradigm' using the matched guise technique (see, for example, Lambert *et al.* 1960) has been particularly influential.

Since that time, the matched guise technique (MGT) has been the standard social-psychological method used in studying how people evaluate social groups on the basis of their linguistic varieties. In the classic model of MGT, respondents listen to a series of recorded speech samples of the same text read aloud, and rate on scales the speaker of each sample for qualities such as intelligence, ambition, friendliness, honesty, and generosity. In so far as the respondents answer questions and are aware that their attitudes are being studied, this could be considered a direct method. However, the MGT is in reality indirect because 'the respondents are deceived into thinking that the researchers are investigating attitudes other than those that they are actually researching' (Garrett *et al.* 2003: 17).

In the classic MGT, the respondents are in fact led to believe that each speech sample is the voice of a different speaker, whereas each one is the same speaker under different 'guises' (i.e. using different speech styles, particularly accents). This means that any variation in the informants' evaluations of the speech samples must be the result of the stereotypes that they associate with the linguistic cues. To put it another way, the informants are not, as they believe, judging the individual speakers, but the speakers' language varieties (for example, accents). Their judgements, in turn, provide evidence of their social evaluation of those language varieties, that is, of all members of the social group who 'speak like that'. The MGT continues to this day to be used in language attitudes research of this kind, but as a result of misgivings over the original research design, especially the deception of informants, modified versions have also been developed. For example, in the verbal guise technique (VGT), although the respondents still believe they are rating people rather than language, the speech samples are provided by authentic speakers of each variety rather than one speaker using different guises.[1]

Also dating from around the same time as Lambert's work is Wolff's classic study (1959) of the phenomenon of non-reciprocal intelligibility. Wolff found that although the languages spoken by two communities in the Niger Delta, the Nembe and the Kalabari, were linguistically so similar that they could be considered dialects of a single language, the communities themselves did not both see them in this light. While the economically poor and politically powerless Nembe said they could understand the speech of the Kalabari, the prosperous and politically powerful Kalabari claimed to find the Nembe's speech unintelligible. Wolff came to conclusions about the link between attitude and intelligibility in interlingual communication that have relevance to the study of ELF communication some half a century later. In particular, he noted that '[l]inguistic comparability, although it may play a limiting factor or boosting role, is not a decisive factor', that 'a great variety of factors and circumstances come into play', and that 'when intelligibility is on-reciprocal, the language or dialect spoken by the culturally dominant group … seems to be the preferred medium for interlingual communication' (p. 39). ELF communication contexts are, of course, somewhat different from that of the Nembe and Kalabari in the 1950s. Nevertheless, the effect of attitude on (claims of) intelligibility that Wolff was the first to identify is one that undoubtedly has implications for ELF, particularly in relation to accents. Although it represents a classic beginning in the establishing of links between language attitudes and intelligibility, somewhat surprisingly Wolff's work is rarely cited in the relevant social psychology literature (for example, it is not referenced in Giles and Coupland 1991), in the relevant intelligibility literature (for example, it is not mentioned in Smith 1992),[2] or indeed in the more recent literature on intelligibility in ELF contexts (see Chapter 4 below).

Later work

By contrast, as I observed above, the work of Lambert and his disciples has been extremely influential. Indeed, it is described as having initiated an 'empirical avalanche' (Giles and Coupland 1991: 37), a 'frenzy of language attitudes studies' (Preston 2002: 41), and an 'empirical explosion of research' (Giles and Billings 2004: 191). Of the publications that followed, the appearance in 1982 of a volume edited by Ryan and Giles seems to have been a particularly important landmark. In fact it could be said that this volume both marked the beginning of a more programmatic approach towards language attitudes research within the social psychology community, and initiated an interest in the subject of language attitudes among those engaged in communication-based research outside it. For the collection was published at a time when 'language and communication [held] at the most a peripheral status within the discipline [of social psychology]' (ibid.: vii). The editors' intention was that their edited collection would lead to greater interdisciplinarity, and would 'permit the development of a wide ranging theory of language attitudes which can more directly focus on social planning and policy issues' (Giles and Ryan 1982: 223). In particular, they hoped that social psychologists would thenceforth have a greater understanding of the role of language variables in determining attitude formation and change, that sociolinguists would be more aware of 'the complexities and consequences of attitude, inference and identification processes which cognitively mediate speech' (ibid.), and that language planners would appreciate the crucial source language attitude research could offer them in policy formulation.

Among the articles in the 1982 volume are several themes that could usefully inform any discussion of attitudes towards ELF. For example, in their agenda-setting opening chapter, Ryan *et al.* point out the (still) often-unrecognized link between language variation and power:

> In every society the differential power of particular social groups is reflected in language variation and in attitudes towards those variations. Typically, the dominant group promotes its patterns of language use as the model required for social advancement; and use of a lower prestige language, dialect, or accent by minority group members reduces their opportunities for success in the society as a whole. Minority group members are often faced with difficult decisions regarding whether to gain social mobility by adopting the language patterns of the dominant group or to maintain their group identity by retaining their native speech style.
>
> (p. 1)

What is particularly interesting here is that by contrast with the kinds of situation Ryan *et al.* have in mind, as far as ELF is concerned, the *dominant* group (educated NSs of British and American English) is also the de facto *minority* group, while NNS ELF speakers are the overwhelming majority. And yet such attitudes towards NNS varieties continue to prevail, and—as will be seen in the ELF research reported below—'nativelike' English, particularly in terms of accent, is still frequently considered a prerequisite for success.

The theme of power is also explored in relation to the sociology of deviance. St. Clair demonstrates how language variation and change that is led by the socially powerful is regarded as prestigious and to be emulated, while that led by the non-powerful, however much the change is a natural linguistic development, is regarded as deviant and not to be emulated. This point resonates loudly with ELF researchers, whose corpora are beginning to reveal manifold ways in which ELF variants differ from NS English, but which are widely considered—by both NNSs and NSs—to be deviant and inappropriate for imitation. Meanwhile, Street and Hopper demonstrate the complexity of the language evaluation process, and the way in which a speech style similar to one's own may be favourably or unfavourably received depending on the prestige of the style, the degree of ethnic pride of subordinate groups, the speech context, and the amount and type of perceived adjustment (or accommodation). Again, there are important links with ELF in all these respects. For example, my own research into ELF identity reported in Chapter 7 reveals that ELF speakers from some backgrounds appear to have greater pride than others in their ethnic/national/L1 identity; and notwithstanding the fact that all ELF varieties are regarded as being non-prestigious, ELF speakers emerge from my research into ELF attitudes (reported in Chapter 6) as perceiving a clear hierarchy of ELF varieties (and, particularly, accents) in terms of their relative prestige.

Other ELF-salient chapters in the 1982 volume include that of Edwards (Chapter 2), who highlights the social basis of language attitudes, the stereotyping involved in accent evaluations, and the role that teachers could play in helping people overcome negative evaluations of their language variety made by both others and themselves. Specifically, he considers three possible bases of evaluations of language varieties: that they 'may reflect intrinsic linguistic inferiorities/superiorities, intrinsic aesthetic differences or social convention' (p. 21). He goes on to explain why the first two possibilities are untenable and concludes that 'language varieties, although clearly differing from one another, cannot reasonably be described in terms like 'better' or 'worse', 'correct' or 'incorrect' ... . Similarly, aesthetic judgements made of language varieties do not appear to be based upon any inherent qualities of pleasantness and unpleasantness' (ibid.).[3] Thus, observes Edwards, the studies leave us with the suggestion that 'judgements of the quality and prestige of language varieties are dependent upon a knowledge of the social connotations which they possess for those familiar with them' (ibid.). In the case of ELF (and L2 Englishes in general), the social connotations attached by NSs of English to their own NS varieties seem to be applied irrelevantly (by both NSs and NNSs themselves) as the 'default connotations' to NNS varieties in ELF communication contexts. In this respect, Edwards makes the crucial point *vis-à-vis* the spread of English that '[w]e should ... bear in mind, generally, the position of English as a world language when considering linguistic attitudes. A language of great scope, dominance and prestige will obviously evoke attitudes different from those related to 'smaller' languages' (p. 32). This is, of course, an empirical question that ELF researchers are currently exploring.

In the closing chapter of their 1982 volume, the editors Giles and Ryan revisit both power and identity. Reiterating St. Clair's point that socially dominant groups ensure by various means that their norms are '*the* norms for speaking properly' (p. 208), they go on to point out how identity factors may mediate in the acquisition of these norms: '[s]uch is the fundamental importance of speech characteristics for one's sense of group identity that many individuals have negative attitudes about acquiring the dominant group's prestige code and as a result may fail to become proficient in it' (ibid.). It is often said that ELF speakers who learn English beyond (approximately) the age of puberty 'fail' to acquire native-like English, especially accents, merely because they have passed the 'critical period' for such acquisition. (See, for example, Scovel, 1998.) This explanation, however, ignores the potential for group identity to have a role in the process. For whether at a conscious or subconscious level, it seems from much of the research on attitudes to non-native English accents, that L1 identity plays a key intervening role, and prevents the acquisition of the accent (invariably RP or GA) that the ELF speaker professes to desire. The earlier work in attitudes towards language variation, and particularly that in the 1982 volume, thus paves the way for an understanding of the contradictory claims made by participants in recent ELF research. (See Chapter 7.)

The 'programme' set out in Ryan and Giles's 1982 collection bears considerable relevance for L2 English language learning and teaching in the light of recent changes in users and uses of English to the extent that EFL is giving way to ELF; in other words, foreign language users and uses of English are giving way to lingua franca users and uses. (See Graddol 2006.) Yet at the time of writing, the vast majority of those engaged in TESOL-related research, be they social psychologists, language planners, or even sociolinguists, have not begun to consider issues such as the role of language variables in determining attitude formation, the complexities and consequences of identification processes, the links between power and linguistic prestige, and so on, in respect of ELF speakers. Nevertheless, much of the social-psychological research into language attitudes conducted in non-TESOL contexts—as reported both in Ryan and Giles (1982) and elsewhere—is able to offer insights into ELF attitudes, even though the researchers themselves do not make the connection.

Despite the move towards the search for organizing principles instigated by Ryan and Giles, much of the language attitudes research of the past twenty-five years continues to form 'a plethora of one-shot studies' (Giles and Billings 2004: 203). None the less, from both this more recent work and—to a lesser extent—the work of the decade or so which preceded the Ryan and Giles volume, other themes and concepts emerge that have particular relevance for ELF research. Because of the 'one-off' nature of the studies involved, however, it is not feasible to organize the discussion into clear themes without distorting the focus of individual studies. Rather than trying to fit square pegs into round holes, I therefore summarize the findings of the key ELF-relevant studies (apart from those relating specifically to accent attitudes, which are discussed in the second main section) in a largely ad hoc manner.[4]

Hierarchy, context, and content

One such ELF-relevant finding is that people tend to evaluate language varieties in a hierarchical manner. As might be expected, standard varieties tend to be more highly evaluated than non-standard. For example, Paltridge and Giles (1984) found that judges evaluated Parisian French more highly than Provençal French, and the latter more highly than Breton that, in turn, was rated more highly than Alsatian French. A little earlier, Ryan *et al.* (1977) demonstrated that judgements of status may be made in a hierarchical fashion both among and within non-standard varieties. Thus, ratings of Spanish-accented English became more negative as the Spanish accent became stronger. As will be seen in Chapter 6, the concept of a hierarchy of NNS English accents is one that emerges strongly from my study of ELF accent attitudes. Accents perceived as more standard, particularly RP and GA, as well as 'nativelike' NNS accents such as Swedish-English, were ranked far higher than those perceived to be less standard.

Another study with particular salience for ELF is that of McKirnan and Hamayan (1980), who found that those Americans who conceived of appropriate norms of standard English more narrowly and restrictively also downgraded the English of non-standard speakers (in this case, Hispanic) correspondingly more. Again, this finding could be applied to ELF speakers to discover whether the same phenomenon occurs in non-immigrant inter-cultural English communication contexts. It would seem self-evident that those NSs and NNSs of English who hold narrow views of 'appropriate' English (which often equates in their minds with 'correct' English), and who admire standard British or American English, would also hold more negative attitudes towards ELF varieties (which they would consider non-standard by definition) than those with more flexible views. But to my knowledge this hypothesis has not actually been tested empirically among either NNSs or NSs.

Not surprisingly, a number of studies have found language attitudes to be sensitive to the context in which those attitudes are evaluated, and that identity plays an important part. For example, Bourhis *et al.* (1973) found that the English of bilingual speakers in South Wales was evaluated more favourably relative to the English of RP-accented speakers than previously, and that this change coincided with a period when the sense of Welsh identity in the area had strengthened. Tong *et al.* (1999) draw a similar link between link language attitudes and identity in their Hong Kong study, by demonstrating how speakers' attitudes have adjusted in relation to their new identities after the hand-back of Hong Kong to the People's Republic of China. Again, Bourhis and Sachdev (1984) investigated the attitudes of Anglo-Canadian secondary school students towards the use of Italian. They found that attitudes were more negative when the proportions of speakers of the two languages (English and Italian) in the school were equal, and more favourable when the Anglo-Canadians were in the majority. They conclude that negative language attitudes are less widespread in contexts where there is a clear in-group and out-group.

Bourhis and Sachdev's conclusion raises an intriguing but fundamental issue for ELF: who is the ELF in-group and who the out-group? ELF communication is, by its very nature, inclusive, whether in its 'pure' form (NNSs from any L1 interacting with other NNSs from any L1) or its more flexible form (NNSs from any L1 interacting with NSs from any inner circle country and with other NNSs from any L1). Because of this diversity of membership, it would be difficult to investigate ELF in respect of in-groups and out-groups with the precision that Bourhis and Sachdev were able to do in Canada. The issue, nevertheless, cannot be avoided, despite its complexity, as it has implications not only for current orientations to ELF, but also, more crucially, for its entire future. We need to know, for example:

- whether acceptance of ELF norms (if and when codified) and of individual ELF varieties will be widespread and mutual among expanding circle groups (in Europe, East Asia, Latin America), or whether new hierarchies of 'correctness' will emerge across these groups;
- whether outer circle groups will also accept ELF norms and varieties; and
- what position inner circle speakers engaged in lingua franca communication will adopt.

These, and many others, are still largely open empirical questions, even though current ELF studies such as those reported in the next chapter as well as my own studies in Chapters 5, 6, and 7, are beginning to indicate some answers.

Yet another ELF-relevant group of language attitudes studies concerns the role of message content. As Giles and Billings point out, this 'has rarely been examined alongside speech-style effects, although it has been shown to bear significant consequences' (2004: 198). Indeed, the earlier matched guise tests were criticized precisely because they ignored altogether the influence of content on evaluations of speech style. The message content research with implications for ELF speakers and listeners concerns evaluations made in instances when speech style and content are judged by the listener to be incongruous. The example of this phenomenon with specific relevance to ELF is that of the incongruity noted by a listener when a speaker has a more standard speech style than is 'implied' by the content of his or her message, or vice versa. For instance, an RP speaker arguing a typically working class position (for example, in favour of trade union power) may be upgraded because his or her accent is assumed (by the listener) to indicate integrity. (See, for example, Powesland and Giles 1975.) By contrast, speakers of standard language varieties may downgrade speakers of non-standard varieties of the language, regardless of the intellectual content of their speech. This is apparently because the speaker's voice patterns lead the listener to assume that the speaker holds dissimilar beliefs. (See, for example, Stewart *et al.* 1985.) On a different but related theme, Giles and Sassoon (1983) found a non-standard speech style to elicit a lower rating on status traits than a standard speech style with RP, regardless of whether the non-standard speaker was known to be middle-class. Such studies provide overwhelming evidence on the one hand of the primacy of language cues, particularly accent cues, in the making of social judgements, and on the other hand of the notion of the 'standard', articulated principally through accent and lexis, as 'legitimate' (Bourdieu 1991).

The implications for ELF speakers are obvious, and relate directly to the question of the possible emergence of ELF 'hierarchies of "correctness"' that was raised in the paragraph before last. At present, many speakers of expanding circle Englishes, even some speakers of (some?) outer circle Englishes, express the view that they are not taken seriously by NS English speakers purely on account of their NNS speech patterns (and, often, their accent in particular). In this regard, two questions need answering. Firstly, will the emergence of ELF norms and expanding circle varieties lead ultimately to a situation in which ELF speakers are judged on *what* they say rather than the (NNS) *way* they say it? Secondly, if and when ELF speakers' message content is no longer evaluated in relation to NS speech styles (rather than to NS message content), will new attitudes-based (ELF) speech-style criteria emerge to replace the old NS criteria? In fact it is difficult to imagine any alternative to the latter. Giles and Billings (2004) point out, citing Billig (1987), that attitudes need to be considered 'in a wider historical context as *positions in an argument* and embedded in particular social controversies', a context in which attitudes embrace not only a 'for' or 'against' position, but also 'an implicit stance *against counter-positions*' (p. 201; emphasis in original). It is inconceivable that more powerful ELF speakers, even in the context of a post-EFL-dominant world, would not very quickly develop and promote certain positions and stances. In this sense, the principal difference from the traditional EFL situation would be that these new positions and new stances against alternative positions would not be *overtly* led by NS ideology. On the other hand, whether NSs would continue to exert a *covert* influence, leading to new ELF hierarchies that were still premised on a position favouring proximity to NS norms, is another matter.[5]

A striking feature of much of the socio-psychological language attitudes research discussed so far in this section is the involvement of Giles and his associates, whether directly or through their influence on others. Their work, particularly with respect to speech/communication accommodation theory (see, for example, Giles 1984) also provided a strong influence on my own earlier research into ELF accents (for example, Jenkins 1996, 1998, 2000), and can thus to some extent be seen as one of the driving forces behind the growth of research into ELF in general. Giles's work is also heavily referenced in what is probably the most recent landmark in the socio-psychological language attitudes research literature: Garrett, Coupland, and Williams (2003). This book, in the words of a reviewer, 'is arguably the most comprehensive attitude study in the British context since Howard Giles's seminal work in the 1970s' (Williams 2005: 411). It provides a systematic survey of the ways in which language attitudes have been researched in recent decades, and then goes on to report the authors' own large-scale attitudes study across Wales, aspects of which have influenced my ELF attitudes research. (See Chapter 6.)

Social-psychological and sociolinguistic overlaps

Preston observes that although socio-psychological research into language attitudes has been productive, it nevertheless leaves two important areas largely unexplored:

1 What linguistic features play the biggest role in triggering attitudes?
2 What beliefs (theories, folk explanations) do people have about language variety, structure, acquisition, and distribution which underlie and support their attitudinal responses and how might we go about finding them out and using them to supplement and even guide future language attitude research?
(2002: 43)[6]

Both questions are relevant to ELF attitudes research. In the case of the first—as Preston himself points out—it is sociolinguists rather than social psychologists who have so far taken the lead in investigating which specific linguistic variables are reflected in social judgements. In fact, he goes so far as to suggest that in this respect, 'much that might go by the name "sociolinguistics" could as well be known as "language attitude study"' (2002: 50). Various (so-called) sociolinguistic studies, beginning with Labov's (1966) study of New York City raters' reactions to the presence or absence of the prestigious non-prevocalic 'r', have explored attitudes towards socially sensitive linguistic variables (for example, Purnell *et al.* 1999; Niedzielski 1999; Trudgill 1972).

Many of the responses given in these sociolinguistic attitudes studies were consciously made. However, this was not always the case. For when misleading information was provided regarding the geographical origin of a particular speaker, as, for example, in Niedzielski's (1999) study, it was found to affect what respondents reported they had actually heard. Such findings echo those of Rubin and Smith in their study of Chinese and Caucasian International Teaching Assistants (ITAs) in US universities, in which listeners were led to expect a foreign accent where none existed (1990). They have important implications for ELF speakers, suggesting, as they do, that some speakers may be evaluated—and comprehended—in relation to their geographical origin rather than their actual speech. The trace of a regional (Japanese-English) accent, for example, in the speech of a Japanese-English-speaking interlocutor, could trigger beliefs about incorrectness and unintelligibility that could, in turn, blind the listener to the degree of correctness and intelligibility of the specific Japanese-English speaker's speech. As Irvine (2001) notes, 'participants in some community of discourse are not entirely objective observers of each other's behaviours. Yet, their own acts are deeply influenced by their perceptions and interpretations of those behaviours' (p. 25). For this reason, she argues, '[l]anguage ideologies are ... to be investigated independently of the distribution of observable sociolinguistics facts, not as a substitute for them' (ibid.). This is a critical point for ELF.

It is evident, then, that socio-psychological and sociolinguistic approaches to language have overlapping interests. As Garrett (2001) points out in a short but crucial discussion on this topic, and one whose concerns resonate loudly with the concerns of ELF research, 'social evaluations of language have rightly been recognised as a central concern in sociolinguistics' (p. 630).

Garrett considers that the study of language attitudes should be 'an essential component of sociolinguistics' and that '[t]he study of socially and geographically distributed linguistic variation goes hand-in-hand with the study of social evaluations and their distributions across social and regional groups' (ibid.). He goes on to argue that:

> ... the systematic patterns that appear in social evaluations provide us with data that is perhaps of even more importance than descriptive distributional data in the explanation of language maintenance and change ... . Language attitudes research in sociolinguistic communities can reveal the dynamic identificational and relational forces at work within them. These include prejudices held against (or in favour of) regional or social varieties, and they include allegiances and affiliative feelings towards one's own or other groups' speech norms, and ... stereotypes of speech styles. So, in addition to sociolinguistic processes at the level of the social group, social evaluative studies can access local processes of interpersonal attraction and distancing and help anticipate the character of social relationships ... within a speech community. And since explanations of sociolinguistic phenomena are most likely to be found in social psychological processes, language attitudes are a key component of sociolinguistic theory building.
> (ibid.)

Social-psychological approaches and folk linguistics

In spite of its potential to enrich sociolinguistics, Garrett (2001) points out that the study of language attitudes has not, in the main, been adequately integrated into sociolinguistic research hitherto. However, one research paradigm where integration of the two approaches is more comprehensive and coherent is that of folk linguistics. Whereas language attitudes research 'proper' reveals the (more unconscious) attitudes that people hold in relation to social structures, folk linguistics research, like most of the 'sociolinguistic attitude studies' mentioned above, reveals people's (more conscious) beliefs[7] about language use. Folk linguistics, however, goes beyond this to investigate 'the cognitive states that govern the comments that people make about [language]' in their meta-language in order to uncover what lies behind these 'reflections and pronouncements' (Preston 2006: 115). It pays attention to 'beliefs concerning the geographical distribution of speech, beliefs about standard and affectively preferred language varieties, the degree of difference perceived in relation to surrounding varieties, imitations of other varieties, and anecdotal accounts of how such beliefs and strategies develop and persist' (Garrett *et al.* 2003: 45). This, then, is the territory of Preston's second question: the attempt to uncover the folk beliefs about language that relate to people's language attitudes.

The major work in this paradigm is Niedzielski and Preston's (2000/2003) book-length study investigating US folk beliefs about, and evaluations of, the different English dialects of their country, by means of map labelling tasks, ratings of US states' English for 'correctness' and 'pleasantness', interviewing, and participant observation. Building on this work, Lindemann (2005) uses folk linguistic methods to explore native US English speakers' perceptions of non-native English varieties such as China English,[8] German English, Italian English, and Spanish English. A number of her findings have important implications for ELF, and are listed here:

- '[a]lthough respondents were initially asked to describe various Englishes, they tended to interpret this as a request to evaluate them' (p. 206);
- 'the most salient non-native speech appeared to be negatively evaluated' (ibid.);
- '[w]hile respondents sometimes describe specific sounds they like, they describe what non-native speakers do 'wrong' in greater detail' (ibid.);
- '[a]reas rated highly on correctness (France, Italy, Germany) as well as less familiar negatively rated areas (India, Russia) garnered fewer and less detailed comments' (ibid.);
- '[t]he largest category within non-native English, and for some respondents perhaps the only category, is a general one of stigmatized non-native English ... . For most respondents, this stigmatized category does not include Western Europe (the English of France and Italy were never described as 'broken'), but for some it appears to apply to the rest of the world with very few distinctions made' (p. 207);
- '[t]he most salient sub-categories of stigmatized non-native English were East Asian or 'Chinese' English and Latin American or 'Mexican' English' (p. 208).

As Lindemann points out, some of her findings, such as the salience and stigmatization of Chinese and Mexican English varieties can be accounted for by the recent US immigrant trends of these groups. On the other hand, she observes, 'reactions to the less salient negatively evaluated groups are probably based on images of these groups in the popular media, since respondents are likely to have fewer first-hand experiences with them' (p. 209).[9] Her findings also point to the likelihood that non-native varieties are not regarded as 'non-standard' in the way that stigmatized native varieties are, but that 'there may be qualitative differences between non-native and non-standard' (p. 210). Familiarity emerges as a potentially important factor in this respect, as respondents tended to be less familiar with non-native varieties than with stigmatized native dialects.

Lindemann concludes that '[w]hile further research is needed into how expectations translate into evaluations of actual speakers, knowledge about the expectations themselves is an important step towards addressing language discrimination' (p. 210). This can be used, she argues, to educate the general public (including, in my view but not necessarily hers, teachers and even linguists) about the links between socio-political factors and expectations about English varieties, in order to reveal the prejudice inherent in such expectations. Although her study differs from mine in so far as it relates to the US context and the respondents are all NSs of English, it has much in common in terms of both methods and goals with my investigation into NNS English teachers' attitudes towards NNS English varieties in ELF contexts.

Preston (2002) notes that much attitudinal data gathered by folk linguistic methods, 'is dominated by the notions of "correctness" (the more powerful) and "pleasantness"' (p. 62), and that these are at the root of much language ideology. The data reveal that '[s]peakers of "correct" dialects do not believe they speak dialects, and educational and even legal repercussions arise from personal and institutional devaluing of "incorrect" varieties' (ibid.). This is implicit in the prejudice that Lindemann (2005) later finds in her data—see my previous paragraph. Further, as Preston points out, in folk theory 'real' language is an idealization, an abstraction, which some people are better (as more 'connected to it') than others at reproducing, and with certain deviations acceptable so as not to sound 'too "prissy"', while others are merely 'error, dialect, or, quite simply, bad language' (p. 64). Such notions of 'correctness' and prejudice against 'incorrectness', I will argue in the light of my own ELF data, play a central role in beliefs about and attitudes towards ELF varieties and especially ELF accents.

In the 'epilogue' to their review of language attitudes research, Giles and Billings (2004) list five aspects of language attitudes that they 'envision that future research will examine' (p. 202). They are:

1 the influence of accent, particularly in regard to content;
2 the heterogeneity of speakers offered as representative of a speech community;
3 the influence of language attitudes on self-presentation, accommodative tactics, and argumentation;
4 the role of friendships in moulding language attitudes;
5 how we talk about language varieties.

All five, to varying degrees, have implications for ELF and ELF research, and the first, the influence of accent, possibly most of all. It is therefore to accent attitudes research that we now turn.

Accent-related research findings

It should be clear from the language attitudes research discussed above, that language attitudes and beliefs are implicated in complex ways in the social judgements that speakers make about other speakers both within and outside their own social groups. Many of these language attitudes and beliefs involve accents specifically. Although the previous section touched on accents from time to time, some language attitudes research is more explicitly connected with accent issues, and in that sense of more particular relevance to my own ELF research than that reported above. This section explores such research and other discussions of accent in more detail.

As mentioned earlier, Giles and Coupland (1991) refer specifically to accent features when they expand on their point that '[m]ost language behaviours are ... socially diagnostic' (p. 32). Citing Huspek (1986), they point out that if two speakers produce an utterance identical in all respects except for the fact that one speaker pronounces a word ending in -ing with [ɪn] rather than [ɪŋ] (for example, 'joggin'' rather than 'jogging'), then the former speaker is likely to be afforded less respect than the latter because of 'the images evoked in response' to the non-standard (i.e. non-RP) form (ibid.). McNamara (2001) likewise opts for accent variables (the vowel sound in the word 'dance' as /æ/ or /ɑː/,[10] the pronunciation of the letter 'h' as /eɪtʃ/ or /heɪtʃ/, and of 'when' as /wen/ or [ʍen]—which sounds like 'hwen') to illustrate his point that '[w]e use language cues to make assessments of people all the time, and use the linguistic evidence to place people into social categories' and 'make social attributions' (p. 17). Giles and Coupland note that '[s]uch slight and inherently trivial details of pronunciation can clearly take on crucial social significance, when they index differences in "standard" versus "non-standard" language use, with their echoes of prestige, class and competence' (ibid.). Lippi-Green (1994) even describes accent as 'a dustbin category', arguing that it is 'the first diagnostic for identification of geographic or social outsiders' (p. 165).

According to Bourdieu, 'the efficacy of an utterance, the power of conviction which is granted to it, depends upon the pronunciation (and secondarily the vocabulary) of the person who utters it' (1991: 70). This is borne out by many language attitudes studies, where a consensus seems to have emerged from much of the research to indicate that accent is the most salient factor in 'evoking images' in response to speech styles and, therefore, that accent exerts the strongest influence on (language-based) attitudes. And as the ELF studies (both other researchers' and my own) reported in this book demonstrate, accents are also highly salient to ELF speaker-hearers, possibly even more so than in communication among NSs of English. Most accent attitudes studies have nevertheless been conducted in either NS–NS or NS–NNS interaction contexts and we will consider some of these in this section before moving on to look specifically at ELF accent attitudes research in the following chapter.

Studies of attitudes towards regional NS accents

A number of studies have focused on regional NS accents. For example, as briefly mentioned earlier (p. 72), Giles and Sassoon (1983) demonstrate that a person's non-standard speech style can override contradictory evidence of their social class. In this study, regardless of whether a speaker was known to be working class or middle class, their non-standard speech style led to lower ratings for status as contrasted with the ratings for middle class RP speakers. Carried over to ELF contexts, this study implies that ELF speakers who are similar in terms of education and class to NSs of English could, nevertheless, find themselves downgraded by both NNSs with near-native accents and NSs, in terms of status merely on the basis of their 'non-standard' (i.e. non-

RP/GA) accent. This is perhaps what Scheuer (2005) means when she claims 'LFC-like approaches' will cause 'foreigners' not to be 'taken seriously in professional exchanges' and to 'come across as unintelligent' (p. 126). The situation even *vis-à-vis* NS accents, however, is not as unambiguous as it is sometimes said to be, and it is possible that attitudes, particularly those relating to RP, are becoming less clear-cut than they were a couple of decades ago. As Giles and Billings (2004: 192) observe, until recently, studies such as Ball (1983) in Australia, Huygens and Vaughn (1984) in New Zealand, and Stewart, Ryan, and Giles (1985) in the US, have consistently shown RP-like accents to be the most favourably-evaluated English accents in inner circle countries. By contrast, Bayard *et al.*'s (2001) study, which investigated evaluations of Australian English, New Zealand English, and American English accents, found the latter to be the most highly evaluated by all three groups. Although RP was not specifically tested in this study, the implication is that GA may be overtaking RP in terms of prestige in Anglophone countries. Such a conclusion, although needing further empirical evidence, is supported by Mugglestone (2003), who argues that in Britain, 'traditional stereotypes of RP are indeed in the process of change' and that it can be 'the loss rather than the acquisition of RP which creates the more positive image, one which significantly also comports those associations of articulacy and intelligence long assumed to be the subjective preserve of the non-localized and ostensibly "educated" accent' (p. 276). She goes on to point out that whereas film heroes and heroines used to have an RP accent, more recently this accent has 'regularly been deployed for those roundly depicted as villains' in, for example, Disney's *Tarzan* and *The Lion King* (ibid.).

However, it is not at all difficult to find precisely the opposite, with broad regional accents being deployed for 'baddies'. For example, in Minette Walter's (2005) psychological thriller, *Devil's Feather*, much is made of the psychopathic villain's broad Glaswegian accent:

> I hated the way he spoke. It was mangled vowels and glottal stops and exploded any myth that 'Glesca patter' was attractive. No printed word can convey the ugliness of his accent or the effect it had on me.
> (p. 243)

And shortly afterwards:

> ... He pronounced 'father' in almost the same way as he pronounced 'feather'—'*fay-ther*'—a rasping, grating sound.
> (p. 245)

The current situation regarding British accents is thus ambivalent, even contradictory. On the one hand it seems that RP may be losing some of its former widespread prestige, and may even be stigmatized in its more marked form, which Gimson calls 'Refined RP' (in Cruttenden 2001: 80). This type of RP, in particular, is sometimes used in films for its 'sinister' connotations (Mugglestone 2003: 276), while at other times its speakers may be treated as figures of fun (Gimson in Cruttenden: 80). On the other hand, many of the regional accents that were stigmatized in the past (for example, Birmingham, Glasgow, Liverpool, and Cockney) seem still to be so. This is demonstrated, for example, by comments in the press, where certain regional accents are regularly singled out and contrasted detrimentally with RP in discussions about accents and employability. For example, Cristina Odone, a columnist on *The Observer* newspaper, recently made the following claim:

> ... there's evidence that we are still prejudiced against regional accents: elocution lessons are a booming business, while a recent survey showed that in the work place, a distinct regional accent is very much a handicap. A received pronunciation (RP), that clipped, cutglass way of talking also known as BBC English, is once again seen as ideal (everywhere that is but at the BBC), more and more Britons are determined to pay good money to shed their gutteral estuary, singsong Liverpudlian, flat Yorkshire accents. To 'talk proper' is not so much a social calling card as a profes-sional necessity, the factor that can make a difference between landing the job with a £20,000 starting salary and stacking shelves at Tesco.
> (January 1, 2006: 21)

Although 'evidence' of this kind is by its nature anecdotal, the popular dis-courses of language found in the press—in columns such as Odone's and in letters to newspaper editors—along with the stigmatizing of certain accents in films and novels, provide useful information about the general public's attitudes towards and beliefs about accent issues. A noticeable feature of the above quotations, for instance, is the readiness to judge certain accents as being intrinsically unpleasant in their overall character and in very specific ways (for example, 'gutteral', 'flat', 'grating') or, as the Australian example above demonstrates, the willingness to judge certain individual sounds as intrinsically unpleasant, such as /æ/ instead of /ɑː/ in a particular set of words (for example, 'dance', 'grass', etc.) even if the stigmatized sound is deemed perfectly acceptable in other words (for example, 'cat', 'flat', 'fact', etc.). In both cases, the evaluations are made confidently but without any phonologi-cal or phonetic evidence, empirical or theoretical, to support them. There is, of course, nothing new here. As early as the 14th century, northern England English accents were being stigmatized in this way by southerners. Here, for example, are the words of the 13th–14th century writer, Ranulph Higden (translated from the original Latin into Middle English by John of Trevissa and into modern English by Crystal):

> All the speech of the Northumbrians, and especially at York, is so harsh, piercing and grating, and formless, that we Southern men can hardly understand such speech.
> (Crystal 2004b: 216)

The best that may be said about British English accent attitudes may be, then, that change is occurring, albeit slowly, in attitudes towards (refined) RP and towards (some) regional accents. Nevertheless, while RP seems to be losing some of its prestige in Britain and other parts of the English native-speaking world, the same does not appear to be true of many parts of the English *non*-native speaking world. In India, for example, as Verma (2002) points out, despite the long history of Indian English, in practice 'it is not universally recognised and accepted, and many educated second language speakers are still classified as 'interlanguage' speakers' (p. 112; and see Jenkins 2006c for a discussion of the notion 'interlanguage' in relation to ELF). This is particularly the case in respect of accents. Here, as Verma goes on to explain, the setting up of call centres in India is playing a part, with Indian call centre employees being trained to 'neutralize' the Indian elements of their accents and move closer to either a British (RP) or American (GA) accent. Indeed, there is probably some truth in the saying that the best place to hear an RP accent nowadays is India. And as will be demonstrated in the next chapter, attitudes towards RP are still largely favourable among NNSs in many parts of the expanding circle, and their desire to 'achieve' a NS accent still strong.

Similar attitudes to those in the UK towards non-standard accents (i.e. non-GA accents) have been documented in the USA (see, for example, Lindemann 2005; Lippi-Green 1997; L. Milroy 1999; Niedzielski and Preston 2000/2003), although Wolfram and Schilling-Estes (2006: 314–15) point out that in practice, 'Regional Standard English' is probably more 'pertinent' to people than the wider-ranging standard GA (which these scholars call 'SAE' or 'Standard American English').[11] Again, though, the main point is the willingness of speakers to stigmatize other speakers on the basis of particular regional and social features of their accents.

Studies of attitudes towards NNS English accents

Not surprisingly, non-native English accents fare still worse than native regional accents in both the US and the UK. Lippi-Green's (1997) concern is the way in which discrimination based on accent is responsible for supporting and perpetuating social inequality in the US. While much of her book (and see also Lippi-Green 1994) concerns African American Vernacular English (AAVE,[12] also known as Ebonics) and other non-prestige native accents (those of 'hillbillies', 'rednecks', and so on), she documents equally powerful evidence of discrimination in respect of those who have non-native accents, 'the stranger[s] within the gates' (p. 217). And in the US, she argues, the repercussions for speakers with a non-native English accent are far greater when their non-nativeness is visible: '[a]ccent, when it acts in part as a marker of race, takes on special power and significance' (p. 228), a theme which also runs through Bonfiglio (2002). Thus, immigrants from a range of Asian and Pacific countries are regularly treated as a homogeneous group and stereotyped *en masse* as having accents that are difficult to understand. In turn, and regardless of the strength (or otherwise) of the 'non-nativeness' of their accents, they experience serious problems in finding employment on account of the supposed communicative difficulties these accents cause for NSs. According to Lippi-Green, there are, by contrast, no documented cases of speakers of West European and Scandinavian L1s being refused jobs on account of *their* accents.

Lippi-Green's claim is supported to some extent by an earlier study of Eisenstein and Verdi (1983) in the US and a later one of Derwing (2003) in Canada. Eisenstein and Verdi found that working class ESL learners who had had considerable exposure to black English nevertheless found this variety more difficult to understand than New Yorkese or standard American English. The authors consider the possibility that negative reactions to black English speakers may have been a factor. Derwing (2003) found differences in NNS immigrants' perceptions of accent-based discrimination depending on whether their immigrant status was visible or non-visible. Her investigation involved interviews with 100 intermediate proficiency ESL students, of which 58 per cent belonged to a visible minority. Slightly over half her participants (53 per cent) believed that their accents caused communication problems and felt that they would receive greater respect and acceptance in Canadian society if their accents were less non-native. Although 60 per cent reported that they were not discriminated against because of their accents, 97 per cent believed that it is important to have good pronunciation,[13] and 95 per cent agreed that they would like an NS English accent. They made comments such as: 'When we have a car accident, the police didn't pay attention what I said. They pay more attention to other women [native speakers] with who we had the accident', and 'I ask a bus driver [a question]. When he hear me in a different accent, he just say "no". He doesn't even look at me or say or explain to me which bus to take. He looked at me in a miserable way and say "No!"' (p. 558).

Of the visible minority accent group in Derwing's study, 37 per cent reported more discrimination because of their accents, whereas in the non-visible minority accent group the figure was 22 per cent. Some participants nevertheless felt more discrimination on account of their accent than their colour, although as Derwing points out, it will probably be impossible to determine the degree to which discrimination against visible minorities can be attributed to accent rather than race. The fact that almost a quarter of the non-visible minority participants felt discriminated against because of their accents, suggests that there is a phenomenon of 'accentism' still firmly in place (to some extent, at least, separate from racism)[14] and qualitatively different in important respects from accent attitudes directed at NSs. It also seems that NNSs are themselves well aware of the accentism directed towards them. One of Derwing's participants actually makes this point: 'They joke. I feel bad very often. *Accent is more important than race*' (p. 557; emphasis in original).[15] This was all borne out by my own research. For example, an Italian participant in my own interview data, whose English is highly proficient, described the recent response she received from a London taxi driver. Her 'offence' was that she could not open the taxi door, but she clearly believed her non-native English accent played the more important role:

> It was like two o'clock at night, and there was me struggling and he was telling me things that I didn't understand, and I was really tired so probably my Italian accent was much stronger than it usually is, and he was really bad to me, and *I think he was really treating me badly because of my accent.*

What is evident from these and many similar examples is that non-native accents are discriminated against by NSs, and that the 'accent bar' segregating NSs and NNSs of English that Abercrombie spoke of more than half a century ago (1951: 13) is still firmly in place.

Attitudes towards NNS English and the intelligibility argument

One 'justification' that is often given for negative orientations towards certain accents is their supposed lack of intelligibility. However, while intelligibility is undoubtedly a factor in people's perceptions of others' accents, as was pointed out earlier with reference to Wolff's (1959) study (see p. 67), it needs to be considered in tandem with language attitudes. A considerable body of research over the past decade or so has investigated intelligibility in relation to NS perceptions of NNS accents (for example, Derwing and Munro 1997; Hahn 2004; Munro and Derwing 1995). And more recently, researchers have begun to explore NNSs' perceptions of NNS accents, sometimes alongside NSs' perceptions as a means of comparing and contrasting the two (for example, Field 2005; Major *et al.* 2002; Munro *et al.* 2006; Riney *et al.* 2005). These studies are, in the main, robustly conducted (in the quantitative sense), and their acknowledgement of the need to investigate ELF as well as EFL communication contexts is timely. By contrast, however, the majority fail to consider the role of attitudes in the judgements of intelligibility made by their respondents, along with a number of sociolinguistic and other contextual factors that need to be taken into account in investigations involving ELF communication.

These studies have tended to be published in influential academic journals such as *TESOL Quarterly*, *Applied Linguistics*, and *Studies in Second Language Acquisition*, and are therefore likely to exert considerable influence on English language teaching and testing policy. In particular, I believe that testing organizations will 'pounce' with delight on any findings suggesting that intelligibility problems originate with 'faulty' NNS pronunciation, or that NSs' assessments of the intelligibility of NNSs can be applied unproblematically to assessments of mutual intelligibility between NNSs. They may then use such findings, for example, as a justification to continue penalizing candidates for making pronunciation 'errors' based on NS judgements rather than considering the possibility of acceptable regional L2 variation. For this reason, it is important that their shortcomings at the qualitative level are pointed out.

A feature that a number of these intelligibility studies have in common is that they tend to draw conclusions about the potential intelligibility of NNS accents in real-life communication from findings drawn from experimental situations. For example, Riney *et al.* (2005) make claims about NNS accent intelligibility in ELF communication (they refer to it as 'EIL') on the basis of an experiment in which recordings of intermediate-level Japanese English speakers and NSs of American English were played to Japanese and American listeners. This is doubly problematic as far as ELF research is concerned: on the one hand, the context is non-interactive and artificial, and on the other, the NNS–NNS element involves only speakers from the same L1. Not surprisingly, these researchers come to conclusions that would not necessarily be helpful (and might even threaten intelligibility) in communication between Japanese English speakers and NNSs who do not come from Japan or certain other non-Asian L1s.[16] Similarly, Field (2005) draws conclusions about the relative importance of word stress in teaching programmes ('a medium level of importance', p. 418) on the basis of NS and intermediate level NNS listeners' ability to decode recorded lists of decontextualized single words produced by a single NS. Interestingly whereas Riney *et al.* (2005) find a great deal of difference between their NS and NNS participants' responses to the recorded stimuli they hear, Field finds the responses of the two groups strikingly similar, as do Munro *et al.* (2006). By contrast with such studies, my own research into the mutual intelligibility of NNS accents (Jenkins 2000, 2002) investigated these accents in actual interactions among NNSs (i.e. ELF interactions), not only in classroom settings as is sometimes claimed, but also in a range of social settings. This meant that I was able to take account of communicative behaviours such as accommodation and negotiation for meaning, phenomena which have been shown to apply to all human communication, not only that involving NNSs, and which have crucial effects on mutual intelligibility. As Bamgboṣe pointed out almost a decade ago:

> Preoccupation with intelligibility has often taken an abstract form characterized by decontextualized comparison of varieties. The point is often missed that it is people, not language codes, that understand one another, and people use the varieties they speak for specific functions.
> (1998: 11)

Munro *et al.* (2006) argue that the usefulness of any statements about the intelligibility of NNS speech 'depends on how well they generalize across listeners in the *contexts in which the learner strives to communicate*' (p. 128; emphasis added). This is a position that I agree with entirely. However, possibly unlike Munro *et al.*, I believe it to imply that since non-native speakers and listeners do not normally communicate with recording equipment in laboratories or carry out tasks such as reading word lists or taking dictation, but communicate with other human beings in the 'task' of everyday conversation, then such research contexts should be naturalistic settings in which participants interact with each other (in the case of ELF) or with NSs (in the case of ESL/EFL). The lack of research of this kind, despite calls for more (see Dauer 2005) is surprising. Meanwhile, claims of varying levels of certainty/tentativeness are regularly made about the intelligibility of NNS accents on the basis of experimental research findings.

Because of my misgivings about both the relevance of such findings as a basis from which to generalize about the intelligibility of NNS speech in real-life (particularly ELF) communication and their possible impact on teaching and testing decisions, I will outline some of my main concerns here. For the sake of simplicity, I focus on one recent study (Munro *et al.* 2006), partly as it is the most recent available at the time of writing (March 2006), and partly to avoid the accusation that I have selected a weaker example: this study seems to be outstanding in the rigour of its methodology, execution, and writing-up. The majority of my comments nevertheless apply to most other studies in the 'genre'. Another reason for selecting this particular study is the authors' own observation that 'in diverse communities with significant numbers of L2 speakers … many of the people with whom ESL speakers interact are not NSs themselves' (p. 114). In other words, Munro *et al.* are making an overt link with ELF—in this case, lingua franca interactions that happen to take place in Canada.[17] Any conclusions they reach, then, have the potential to influence not only teachers and learners in the (so-called) ESL context in which the study took place, but also teachers and learners in expanding circle ELF contexts, where (purely because of the number of ELF speakers involved) most ELF research takes place.

Apart from the problem of applying laboratory-based research findings to real-life communication contexts, which I have already discussed, my main concerns with this type of research are the language level of some of the participants and the marginalizing of factors that do not support the case being made. As regards language proficiency, most ELF studies 'proper' involve only participants with a high proficiency level. The participants in my own research (Jenkins 2000, 2002) were a minimum of high intermediate and many were well above this level.[18] On the other hand, many experimental studies use non-native *speakers* of a much lower proficiency level. This means that the researchers are rarely in a position to consider critical ELF issues such as whether some of the features of their participants' accents could, in line with the sociolinguistic reality of English use, be considered *bona fide* non-native variants rather than errors of greater or lesser intelligibility. It also means that we should not be surprised to find that non-native *listeners* from the same L1 who, in these experiments, are often more proficient than the recorded speakers, do not differ substantially from NS English listeners in their understanding of such low level speakers.

However, proficiency level is rarely taken into consideration as a possible confounding factor in such studies. For example, in the Munro *et al.* (2006) study under discussion, the 48 speakers had been recorded for a previous study (Derwing and Munro 1997). In that study, we are told that twelve of the speakers had taken a TOEFL test, and that these twelve 'represented the upper range of proficiency in this sample' (1997: 4). Their scores ranged from 400 to 565 (mean 479), but of the twelve, only one had a score above 540. Given that high intermediate level begins at around 550 and elementary at around 400, the majority of these speakers seem to have been of a very low level indeed.[19] It is not at all clear how the accents of such low level learners can provide useful information about the intelligibility of NNS accents *per se*. The fact that little difference was found between the intelligibility ratings of the NNS and NS listeners does not, in the event, strike me as surprising. The researchers conclude that 'properties of the speech itself were a potent determinant of the listeners' responses' as regards their intelligibility ratings (2006: 125). But if this is so, and, as they themselves point out, there are other possibilities, then we cannot discount the likelihood that these are properties of the speech of low level learner English, and that quite different findings would have emerged had more proficient speakers been listened to. And perhaps proficiency level can help explain why Riney *et al.* (2005) found substantial differences between their NS and NNS listener groups, as in that study, the NNS listeners were of almost identical proficiency (low intermediate) as the NNS speakers—their TOEFL score means were respectively 466 and 467.

As far as other factors are concerned, Munro *et al.* (2006) do at least consider the possibility that other phenomena than speech properties may be implicated in their findings, even though they refer to them only minimally in this article written for a mainstream SLA journal.[20] In this they differ from many experimental researchers, who appear to be less aware of the ways such factors may impinge on intelligibility judgements, or, else to believe that their role is trivial, and ignore them altogether. One such factor that Munro *et al.* do mention is 'the well-known problem of bias against foreign-accented speech' (p. 128). They refer briefly to the possibility that an interlocutor might claim untruthfully they cannot understand a speaker with a particular accent, and (citing Rubin 1992) that even the mere expectation they will not understand an accent is sufficient to reduce their understanding. They go on to argue, however, that while bias may have been involved in their study, it cannot have played a major role in view of the fact that scores were consistent across all four groups of listeners (Cantonese, Japanese, Mandarin and Canadian English). They may well be right, though there could also be other explanations, including the low proficiency of the speakers and the artificial nature of the listening situation that account in part for the similar listener scores. In the latter respect, the authors do at least point out that 'people might be more likely to exhibit prejudice toward or not work as hard at understanding accented speech in real-life encounters than they are under laboratory conditions' (pp. 128–9), a point which is often completely missing in this kind of research.

One further point that Munro *et al.* (2006) might have considered is the link between their findings and the Lingua Franca Core (LFC). The few experimental researchers who refer to the LFC (and most do not), tend to do so chiefly, it seems, as a starting point for some sort of laboratory-based research which is then used to 'disprove' the LFC or to demonstrate its 'flaws'.[21] Although Derwing and Munro do refer to the LFC elsewhere (2005), they do not do so in this study. And yet, despite my reservations about speaker level in their study, I believe that their conclusion regarding the properties of speech being an important determinant of the responses of listeners from diverse backgrounds shares some common ground with the LFC. In my research, I found that the absence of certain pronunciation features (the 'non core' features such as weak forms) had little effect on mutual intelligibility while others (the LFC features such as consonant sounds and nuclear stress) were crucial to mutual intelligibility across NNS interlocutors from a very diverse range of L1s (Jenkins 2000, 2002). It is possible that the properties of the English speech signal that are ultimately proved necessary in ELF communication regardless of the L1 of the NNSs involved,[22] may relate both to properties of English itself—for example, English syllable structure and the results of consonant deletion in different parts of a word—and to properties of the human condition—for example, our ability to cope with extra information versus our inability to cope as well with missing information. Thus, vowel addition and strong (instead of weak) forms did not, in my data, cause intelligibility problems for NNS interlocutors, whereas consonant deletion caused substantial problems. The majority had little difficulty in filtering out extra vowel sounds, but great difficulty in 'filtering in' missing consonant sounds. Munro *et al.* (2006) may, like most others engaged in experimental research, ignore the LFC, but they could at least consider factors such as these, as well as the sociolinguistic principles that underpin it.

Accent attitudes research and sociolinguistic context

In some respects it seems, then, that the sociolinguistic perspective that was found wanting in the earlier socio-psychological approaches to language attitudes research discussed in the previous section is even more wanting in the NNS accent intelligibility research—even more so, in fact, given that attitudes are often left out of the equation altogether. Experimental research into NNS accents has demonstrated that intelligibility *per se* is undoubtedly implicated in perceptions of NNS accents, including the perceptions of other NNSs themselves, and has given some indications of what factors may be involved. But until substantial empirical research carried out in real-life contexts becomes available, we will not be able to say with confidence more precisely what role intelligibility plays in NNS–NNS communication.[23]

On the other hand, as much of the discussion in this section has argued, intelligibility *per se* is by no means the only, or even primary, factor in perceptions of NNS English accents (and the owners of those accents). Derwing and Munro (1997) and Munro *et al.* (2006) themselves report that accentedness was more harshly rated than was comprehensibility in both studies, and that accents which were reported as being heavy were not necessarily reported as being difficult to understand. In other words, something more than ease or difficulty in understanding an accent seems to be involved in perceptions of NNS accents: some sort of attitude bias must be at work. Indeed, merely knowing a person's place of origin (Jarvella *et al.* 2001) or wrongly guessing it (Llurda 2000) may be sufficient to affect the evaluation of their speech (Jarvella *et al.* 2001). Trudgill and Giles (1978) describe an experiment in which listeners sometimes wrongly identified an accent they heard and went on to rate it according to the place they supposed it to come from. In other words, their 'reactions were probably to the social connotations of the supposed rather than of the actual accent' (p. 184). And as Rubin (1992) has demonstrated, merely assuming from visual cues that a person has a particular NNS accent (in this case, Chinese) is sufficient to cause listeners to 'hear' that accent where it does not exist.

Intelligibility itself, then, cannot be simplistically divorced from attitudes: the two are symbiotically linked. As Major *et al.* (2002) point out, negative attitudes caused by the denigrating of their own English may explain the greater comprehensibility of Spanish speakers as contrasted with the lower comprehensibility of Japanese and Chinese speakers for, respectively the Japanese and Chinese listeners in their study. Although exploring their participants' attitudes was beyond the scope of their research, they none the less 'speculate that attitudes played a role in listening comprehension' (p. 187). And research from Wolff (1959) onwards has shown conclusively that there are other factors than basic understandability of the phonetic/phonological properties implicated in perceptions of accents. Many of these factors involve what Derwing (in an article that takes a very different approach from that of Munro *et al.* 2006) calls 'the politics of accent' (2003: 562). In this respect, as I pointed out earlier (pp. 71–2), the context of language use has an important role. Derwing argues that '[i]n a context where an L2 accent is commonplace, people may not feel 'marked', in contrast to a situation where [non-native] accent is the exception rather than the rule' (p. 561). She has bilingual Montreal in mind, but her point is equally relevant to ELF contexts, and raises the question of whether it is only a matter of time before ELF speakers begin to regard their own and each others' English accents as unmarked and perhaps even NS English accents as the marked ones. If, as has been reported in Brazil (El-Dash and Busnardo 2001), 'the symbolic use of English' among adolescents increases and English becomes more widely used among its NNSs internationally for solidarity functions as well as for the status it confers, this seems all the more likely.

Despite the latter possibility for the future, for the time being it is clear that NNSs, too, hold negative attitudes towards NNS accents including and, at least in some cases, particularly, towards those of their own L1 group. For example, Fayer and Krasinski (1987) found that Puerto Rican listeners both gave lower ratings to the linguistic forms of the Spanish English of the Puerto Rican speakers and reported more annoyance and irritation towards them than did the NS listeners. In other words, the NNS judges who shared the speakers' L1 were less tolerant towards non-native speech than were the NS judges. This leads Fayer and Krasinski to consider the possibility that 'nonnatives, no matter what their proficiency level, are embarrassed by their compatriots' struggles in the nonnative language' (p. 321; and see above, p. 88, in relation to Major *et al.*'s (2002) study). This was the conclusion reached more recently by Beinhoff (2005) on the basis of her study into ELF accent attitudes. She argues that while NNSs are, in general, tolerant of other NNSs' accents, they are stricter towards their own L1 group. Unlike Fayer and Kraskinski, however, she suggests that the cause may be greater awareness of L1 transfer in the English accents of their L1 peer group than in the accents of other NNSs. On the other hand, given Beinhoff's other findings that her participants both wanted native-like accents and saw their NNS accents as part of their identity, it seems that much more is involved in their attitudes to their own L1 group's accents than simply awareness of the presence of transferred features. Ambivalence and embarrassment are, perhaps, to be expected given the findings of attitudes research in relation to non-standard and ethnic speech, as was discussed in the first half of this chapter; and further evidence is provided in the chapters that follow.

When I wrote up my LFC research findings in *The Phonology of English as an International Language* I had, perhaps naïvely, assumed that NNSs engaged in ELF communication would, in the main, be relieved by the notion that their own L1-influenced English accents (with a small number of adjustments according to context) were likely to serve them well in ELF interactions. Although this has indeed been the response of some NNS groups, particularly in Spain and Italy and, to a lesser extent, Japan, it has been far from universal. (See Chapter 1.) But I had failed to take into account the persuasiveness of the ubiquitous standard language ideology and 'native speaker' of ELT, and its potential to affect the accent attitudes and the identities of NNSs themselves. Bonny Norton has argued that

> it is through language that a person negotiates a sense of self within and across different sites at different points in time, and it is through language that a person gains access to—or is denied access to—powerful social networks that give learners the opportunity to speak.
> (2000: 5)

As far as ELF communication is concerned, if NNSs of English remain persuaded that their success in '[gaining] access to ... powerful social networks' in their English-using life, albeit with other NNSs rather than with NSs, is intrinsically bound up with the proximity of their English to NS norms, then it is not surprising if there is a reluctance to relinquish the aspiration of 'achieving' these norms. And as the research reported in Chapters 5 and 6 demonstrates, accent attitudes play a major role in the way NNSs perceive their own and others' English accents, and may ultimately be found to override more basic intelligibility considerations, as well as to interact in complex ways with L2 English identity factors, the theme of Chapter 7. But first, in the next chapter, we look at the small amount of previous research that has explored teachers' attitudes towards ELF.

Notes

1 The VGT format is not without its own problems. For example, there is a possibility that variables other than the one under research will influence informants' ratings, for example, the voice quality or speed of individual speakers, or variation in the subject matter of the samples (if a reading text is not used). See Garrett *et al.* 2003 for both a critique of the original method and a critical survey of subsequent developments.

2 Wolff's study is, however, discussed in a section on intelligibility in a pronunciation handbook for teachers: Dalton and Seidlhofer (1994).

3 In fact, as Giles and Niedzielski (1998) point out, studies have shown that when listeners rate a foreign language variety with which they are completely unfamiliar, and therefore which they are unable to categorize in terms of class or status, they do not discriminate among its varieties on the basis of aesthetic criteria, even though native speakers of that language perceive distinctions in the aesthetic quality of different varieties of the language.

4 Readers who would like access to an inclusive account of the language attitudes research of the past 40 years should consult an overview such as Giles and Billings (2004) or Bradac, Cargile, and Hallett (2001).

5 The concept of a global variety of English, to be known as 'World Standard English', 'World Standard Spoken English', or similar, and whose main influence, it is claimed, will be American English, is a case in point. (See the discussion in Chapter 2, and Jenkins 2006a.)

6 Garrett *et al.* (2003), published a year after Preston's comment, is in fact the first major language attitudes study that also explores people's beliefs in this way.

7 Though as Niedzielski and Preston point out in the preface to their (2003) paperback edition (the hardback having appeared in 2000), they feel that they had previously 'characterized too neatly the conscious versus unconscious dichotomy of folk linguistics, particularly as it contrasts with so-called language attitude study' (p. ix).

8 I have used the term 'China English' (rather than 'Chinese English') throughout the book as this seems to be the term preferred by the majority of those who research and write about this English.

9 Thorne nevertheless argues that 'people think a dialect is stigmatized because the media portrays it that way, but the media portrays it that way as it is commonly perceived to be a stigmatized accent' (2000: 302).

10 Though in Australian English, to which McNamara is referring, this sound is often the more fronted /a:/ rather than the British English (RP) /ɑ:/.

11 Although Wolfram and Schilling-Estes clearly include grammar and lexis as well as pronunciation in their definition of SAE, they are speaking here specifically about accent, and make an explicit comparison between the status of SAE in the US and that of the RP accent in the UK.

12 As Lippi-Green (1997) points out, '[i]t is hard to say with any assurance how many African Americans are native speakers or regular users of AAVE because the term AAVE itself is inexactly defined ...' (p. 176).

13 The discrepancy between these two figures leads Derwing to speculate that the number reporting discrimination against accented speech might have been higher had the interviewers not been Canadian mother-tongue English speakers.

14 I read this somewhere but have been unable to locate the reference. My apologies to the scholar who first made the point for the fact that I have not acknowledged them.

15 The notion that accent takes priority over race is supported by a recent experiment using an online e-commerce site (Nass and Brave 2006). Korean-American and Australian participants heard an agent with either Korean accented or Australian accented English and, regardless of which of the two accents they had been assigned, saw a series of randomly selected photographs of either an ethnic Korean or an ethnic Caucasian Australian with each voice. The agents were more positively evaluated when they spoke with an accent that matched the listener's ethnicity. Less positive ratings only occurred where there was a mismatch between appearance and expected accent, but no effects were found for race *per se*. This suggests that racial identification may be a weaker influence than social identification through accent.

16 Though I take their point entirely about the inappropriateness of my earlier specifying of GA /r/. In Jenkins (2000 and 2002) I argued for GA /r/ rather than RP /r/. My point was primarily, however, that rhoticity *per se* was helpful because it is closer to English orthography (of any variety of English). I was not particularly concerned with which type of /r/ (phonetically) was produced, only that one was produced wherever it appeared in the spelling. I agree entirely with Riney *et al.* that speakers should produce whichever variant of /r/ is most natural and comfortable for them. Indeed, in my more recent publications, I have referred only to rhoticity, and not to GA /r/ specifically. On the other hand, I disagree with Riney *et al.* that because speakers of Japanese as well as 'millions of speakers of other Asian languages' have problems with /r/ and /l/, they can be substituted with other sounds (p. 463). In their view, this is a similar

case to that of the interdental fricatives /θ/ and /ð/. But unless it can be demonstrated empirically (as it has been for the latter two sounds but has not for /r/ and /l/) that the selected substitutions were near-enough universally intelligible, then it is probable that they would hinder rather than help ELF communication except among East Asian English speakers. At any rate, such a decision cannot be based on an experimental same-L1 study, especially when the main focus was on the degree of closeness of Japanese English speakers' accents to American English accents.

17 As ELF researchers frequently point out, it is not the geographical context that determines whether or not an interaction is an ELF interaction: it depends entirely on who the interlocutors are, their communication purpose and goals, and their status within the interaction. An ELF interaction can take place in Toronto, London, and New York (inner circle) just as easily as it can in Tokyo, Vienna, or Buenos Aires (expanding circle) or Delhi, Colombo, or Manila (outer circle).

18 A rare example is James (2000, 2005) whose participants were low intermediate.

19 In the 2006 study, these same speakers are described, rather surprisingly, as having been 'enrolled in high-intermediate-level ESL classes'. I can only wonder how they coped in classes where one would expect a TOEFL level of around 550.

20 Both Derwing and Munro have explored the issue of discrimination against non-native accents in other publications, for example, Derwing (2003; and see p. 82 above) and Munro (2003), and they have also together investigated the effects of cross-cultural training and linguistic instruction on NSs' attitudes towards foreign-accented speech (Derwing, Rossiter, and Munro 2002). It is a pity, to my mind, that they give far less emphasis to such issues when they write for SLA publications such as *SSLA*, as the SLA community would benefit from having their awareness raised in these respects. (See Jenkins 2006c.)

21 In fact Field's (2005) findings about lexical stress are, as Levis (2005: 373) points out, 'not so different from Jenkins's (2000)', although Field does not make the point himself.

22 Although I have always said I believe entirely in the principle of accepting the accents of proficient NNSs of English as accent varieties with their own features rather than interlanguage accents with errors, I have also always pointed out that the LFC is not definitive and will need replication and fine-tuning if it is ever to be used as a teaching resource for ELF learners.

23 In fairness to Munro *et al.* (2006), they point out several times that further research is needed. My point here refers to the *kind* of research that is done, and the need for richer qualitative analyses of data collected in appropriate interaction contexts rather than for further experimental studies of the kind I have been describing.

4

Previous research into ELF attitudes

Despite the relative lack of published studies of ELF attitudes, their number has grown during the past decade, particularly during the past five years. It is likely to grow still faster in the near future, as an increasing number of doctoral students researching ELF attitudes publish their findings in journal articles, conference proceedings, and monographs. In this chapter I provide an overview of some the most important ELF attitudes research that has been published in recent years. My main focus is on studies of teachers' (and, to a lesser extent, pre-service teachers') attitudes. However, there have also been important studies of learners' attitudes, and where helpful, I will also refer briefly to some of these. While the majority of ELF attitudes studies deal with all linguistic levels, most tend to focus substantially on pronunciation. Timmis (2002), for example, argues that 'pronunciation ... seems to go to the heart of the native-speaker issue' (p. 241). For this reason, I have not separated the 'general' attitudes studies from those investigating accent attitudes exclusively, but have ordered the studies in the way that seems to me to be the most coherent, moving from early to later studies, and from those focusing on practising teachers to those focusing on prospective teachers and (briefly) on English language learners.

Earlier studies of attitudes to the local non-native variety

As Dalton-Puffer, Kaltenboeck, and Smit (1997) point out in the introduction to their study of Austrian attitudes, the interest in perceptions of different varieties of English had recently been extended not only to NNSs' perceptions of native varieties, but also to their perceptions of the local *non-native* variety. In this regard, they cite Forde's (1995) study of the attitudes of elementary Chinese students of English toward both Hong Kong English and a range of native English accents. Not surprisingly, Forde found that his Chinese respondents rated GA and RP more highly on all parameters tested including the speaker's ability to teach English. Likewise, Dalton-Puffer *et al.* (ibid.) cite Chiba *et al.* (1995), who investigated the attitudes of Japanese students to a range of native and non-native varieties of English. Again, the finding was that British and US English were rated most highly, while Japanese English was perceived negatively overall. In another study of Japanese attitudes, Starks and Paltridge (1994) found that Japanese students studying in New Zealand rated American and British English well above New Zealand English, and had no interest whatsoever in learning Japanese English. By contrast, and somewhat unusually, in an even earlier study of Japanese attitudes (Benson 1991), the second highest preference (after American English) among Japanese university students was for learning English with a Japanese accent.

In their own study, Dalton-Puffer *et al.* (1997) focus specifically on accents, and investigate the accent attitudes of 132 Austrian university students, of whom approximately two-thirds intended to become English teachers. Rather than merely presenting a series of decontextualized English accents, as is often the case in such studies, they argue, citing Giles (1992) and Smit (1994), that as 'attitudes are a social phenomenon it seems paradoxical to obtain evaluations of speech in a social vacuum' because 'people react to speech *in specific situations* and the same voice or speaker may well get different evaluations in different contexts' (p. 117; emphasis in original). Dalton-Puffer *et al.* therefore provided their participants with a context appropriate to the university setting of the study: the purpose of the taping, the participants were told, was to select speakers for a published audio-book on child language development. Five different accents were heard: two with light but recognizably Austrian accents (one closer to GA, the other to RP), two with RP accents (one RP 'proper', the other a slightly regionally-modified RP), and one with a GA accent.

The analysis revealed a consistent attitude pattern across all dimensions measured (likeability, intelligence, and so on), with the NS accents being preferred to the NNS, the RP accent being rated most highly, and the Austrian-RP accent being rated lowest of all. Interestingly, as the authors themselves point out, the least preferred accent is thus the accent of the participants themselves. In other words, like the Japanese participants in two of the studies described above, these speakers (and advanced level learners) of Austrian English 'display negative attitudes towards their own non-native accent of English' (p. 126). The authors go on to observe that there is a mismatch between the attitude patterns revealed in their study and the level of achievement in relation to the accent to which the participants apparently aspire. There must, they conclude, 'be other factors exerting an influence on students' level of achievement' and these may relate to the fact that pronunciation is 'the aspect of language that most obviously expresses social identity and group membership' (ibid.). They call for further studies that explore questions of self and identification with the target language group in greater depth.

Although this earlier study does not investigate ELF attitudes, I have described it in some detail because its findings have considerable relevance for ELF attitude research—and especially ELF accent attitude research. It is surprising, then, that so few of the published studies of NNS attitudes to ELF refer to it at all. Meanwhile, although the other earlier studies described above were primarily concerned with gauging attitudes to learners' own NNS varieties as compared and contrasted with their attitudes to certain NS varieties, they all nevertheless provide useful precedents for the ELF studies which have followed.

Studies of practising teachers' ELF attitudes

We move on now to look at some of the ELF studies, beginning with those studies that involve practising teachers rather than pre-service teachers or English language learners (Decke-Cornill 2003; Grau 2005; Sifakis and Sugari 2005; Timmis 2002; Zacharias 2005). They are discussed in the order in which they were published, beginning with Timmis (2002), one of the first ELF attitudes studies 'proper' to be published, and one that is frequently cited in other studies and discussions. This study investigates both teachers' and learners' attitudes, but for present purposes we will consider its findings purely in relation to the teacher participants.

Like the other studies of this kind, Timmis's starting point is the issue of whether learners should still be expected to conform to NS norms now that NNSs are increasingly using English in international communication contexts, i.e. in ELF communication. He argues that while the issue has been the subject of much recent debate, 'it is not a debate in which the voices of students and classroom teachers have been heard' (p. 240). This is not entirely true, as is clear from the studies reported above (and see the discussion of Friedrich 2000 later in this chapter). But Timmis is right in one sense: the studies that preceded his went largely unnoticed by other researchers in the field (including Timmis himself) and have continued largely to do so ever since. Despite their potential to inform further research into ELF attitudes, the findings of these earlier investigations into expanding circle teachers' and/or learners' attitudes have not been widely acknowledged or disseminated. It is therefore not surprising that none of them is cited in the studies of teachers' attitudes that I am discussing here.

In his study, Timmis collected approximately 180 questionnaire responses from teachers (including NSs of English) in 45 countries.[1] His questionnaire explored attitudes to pronunciation, standard grammar, and informal spoken grammar by eliciting responses to a series of statements such as this pair (p. 242):

Student A   I can pronounce English just like a native speaker now. Sometimes people think I am a native speaker.

Student B   I can pronounce English clearly now. Native speakers and non-native speakers understand me wherever I go, but I still have the accent of my country.

Would you prefer to be like Student A or Student B?

The responses to the questionnaire (both within the teacher group and between the teacher and student groups) expose a degree of ambivalence that remains unexplored in the article. Both teachers and students revealed, unsurprisingly, an overall tendency to prefer to continue to conform to NS norms, although the teachers, particularly the NSs, seemed less attached to these norms for NNS learning and use than the students. Timmis none the less admits 'it would be absurd to suggest that this survey provides a statistically accurate picture of the state of opinion among students and teachers'. I would add that neither does it provide a qualitatively rich picture, given that the evidence, teacher-wise, is entirely drawn from statistical analysis of, in the main, a series of binary choices. In addition, the fact that respondents came from both outer and expanding circle countries makes the data difficult to interpret in terms of ELF, as does the inclusion of questions relating to issues concerning attitudes to both NNS English and informal spoken NS English. It is surprising, then, that this article is frequently cited uncritically as though it provides definitive evidence about what kind of English teachers and learners 'want'.[2] Tomlinson (2006), for example, quotes without comment Timmis's conclusion that '[w]hile it is clearly inappropriate to foist native speaker norms on students who neither want nor need them, it is scarcely more appropriate to offer students a target which manifestly does not meet their aspiration' (p. 134, quoting Timmis p. 249). Despite the pioneering nature of this ELF study—and it is probably the first of its kind to focus specifically on ELF attitudes, its findings do no more than raise awareness of the existence of conflicting ELF attitudes and signal the need for further and more in-depth investigations.

In a study carried out among German teachers of English, and published the following year, Decke-Cornill (2003) explored attitudes towards ELF of teachers in two different types of German school; the Gymnasium (selective) and the Gesamtschule (non-selective). The study investigated their attitudes towards a possible change in the focus of ELT from a concern with the English of its NS countries to a concern with its role as an international lingua franca. Two semi-structured group interviews were conducted, one with teachers from one of each type of school, on the basis of a short set of questions relating to:

- 'the impending shift from a culture-specific to a global focus of English language teaching',
- the manner this does or would affect their own classrooms,
- the existence (or not) of 'lingua-franca-specific elements' in their teaching,
- the possible influence of an ELF focus on their 'identity and motivation as English teachers', and
- their views on how English teacher education should change in respect of ELF (p. 61).

The first half of Decke-Cornill's title, 'We would have to invent the language we are supposed to teach' is indicative of her findings. As in Timmis's study, there was ambivalence, and while the non-selective school teachers were more relaxed than the selective school teachers with the concept of ELF, even they had certain doubts about what standards and models could be used for guidance in teaching ELF. Decke-Cornill herself points out that the interviews focused on 'the *future* of English teaching' (p. 68; emphasis in original), and that, for the time being, it could be expected that teachers will still feel 'very much compelled to teach their classes "proper English"' (ibid.).[3] She nevertheless points to an intriguing difference across her two groups of participants in terms of their readiness to adopt a new approach. The selective school teachers were less able to envisage a shift from the traditional culture-specific, NS-normative focus of their English studies education. On the other hand, the non-selective school teachers were more able to conceive of the possibility of taking their students' future communication needs as the starting point, and to recognize that ELF would be more effective in this respect. Thus, despite their current discomfort with the linguistic aspect (the language they 'would have to invent'), their perspective embraced 'a less normative, more process-oriented view of communication' (ibid.). Insights of this kind into teachers' attitudes to ELF are crucial if we are to achieve a deeper understanding of what underlies responses of the kind elicited by Timmis. However, once again, much more research of this kind is needed to confirm and extend the findings of Decke-Cornill's study.

Murray (2003) is a survey of Swiss teachers' attitudes to 'Euro-English'. (See Jenkins, Modiano, and Seidlhofer 2001.) Like Timmis's (2002) study, Murray's took the form of a questionnaire. It was sent to teachers in private and state schools in the three main language regions of Switzerland (German-, French-, and Italian-speaking), and from whom 253 responses were returned. Of these, 54.6 per cent were NS teachers of English, 41.1 per cent were NNS, and 4.3 per cent described themselves as full bilinguals. The questionnaire aimed both to gauge attitudes to possible changes that might arise from Euro-English and to investigate their views of the acceptability of particular types of Euro-English lexico-grammatical formations. The questionnaire consisted of two parts. The first contained six statements relating to issues of standards and authority in ELT to which respondents had to signal agreement or disagreement on a 5-point scale. The second part contained eleven sentences each containing a grammatical or lexical 'particularity' (p. 154) of Euro-English, and which respondents had to categorize as 'acceptable' or 'unacceptable' English.[4]

Like Timmis, Murray found that her NS respondents revealed less attachment to NS norms (for NNS learners and users), than did her NNS respondents, and accounts for this in terms of NNS teachers' investment of time in developing their competence in ENL. But although some of her respondents were totally against the notion of Euro-English, there was, overall, a tendency among both NS and NNS 'to favour communication over error-correction' (p. 159) in theory, just as was found with the non-selective school teachers in Decke-Cornill's study. On the other hand, like all the teachers in Decke-Cornill's study, Murray's respondents also expressed doubts about including such language as a teaching model. In other words, there was in both studies something of a gap between what the teachers perceived as acceptable when they were considering ELF in the abstract as contrasted with their response when they considered concrete examples of ELF.[5] This was especially so among the NNS teachers—and see the discussion of Grau below, who found a similar contradiction among her pre-service teacher respondents. Murray explains it as follows:

> Swiss English teachers are caught between accepting and even supporting the existence of Euro-English in the abstract, but rejecting it as a class-room target, mainly because they are at a loss as to how to answer all the practical questions that arise in connection with evaluation, syllabus criteria, and the teacher's responsibilities if ENL competence is no longer the ultimate—albeit unattainable—goal.
> (p. 162)

She concludes that a shift away from ENL is still some way away as far as the Swiss are concerned, and that they 'probably need to become more aware of the new functions of English in their midst before they are ready to accept anything other than an ENL target' (ibid.). She also argues that if Euro-English is accepted, it is likely to be a 'sanitized form' characterized by structures which are 'possible, but unusual' in ENL rather than those which are 'violations of taught rules' (p. 160).

Although some of Murray's claims appear to be based on her own beliefs and intuitions rather than arising from the analysis of her data, she, like Decke-Cornill, demonstrates the possibility of gleaning more sophisticated insights into NNS teachers' attitudes to ELF by means of focusing more specifically and including a qualitative element in the research design. Thus, Murray was able to compare responses from teachers from different L1s, while Decke-Cornill was able to distinguish between respondents from two different types of educational institution, while both demonstrated the existence of a theory/practice divide. None of this was possible in Timmis's larger statistical survey.

Sifakis and Sugari's (2005) research into Greek teachers' attitudes to ELF explores two sets of issues: firstly, teachers' beliefs about pronunciation in the light of ELF and, secondly, the extent to which teachers are actually aware of ELF-related issues such as mutual intelligibility among NNSs of English. Their study involved the analysis of responses to closed and open-ended questions, in questionnaires received from 421 teachers of English in Greek schools across three contexts (primary, lower secondary, and upper secondary levels). The closed questions related to three areas of investigation: the respondents' views about accent-related matters, their teaching practices, and their beliefs about the ownership of English. The open-ended questions asked respondents to give reasons for their answers to four of the questions: those which had asked them whether they were proud of their accent, whether they thought it important for their learners to acquire a native-like accent, which accent would, in their view, be best of their learners, and how much pronunciation feedback they gave their learners and when.

The main findings of the study were that the Greek teachers had little awareness of the international spread of English, still identified English with its NSs, and believed that learners should acquire certain specific features of NS English pronunciation. Primary school teachers, in particular, placed value on their learners' acquisition of a native-like accent. This in some respects echoes Murray's (2003) finding that Swiss teachers of children and teenagers were statistically less likely to agree with the proposition that they should spend more time on communication and less on 'trying to eradicate mistakes that are typical of Euro-English' (155–6). Like the previous two studies, this one also demonstrates something of a theory/practice divide. When respondents were asked about their own pronunciation teaching practices, they revealed 'a strongly norm-bound perspective' with a 'focus on teaching standard NS pronunciation models' (p. 481). By contrast, when they were asked to consider NNS–NNS communication, 'they seemed to believe that none of the rules and standards counts as much as the need to create a discourse that is appropriate for the particular communicative situation and comprehensible for all interlocutors' (ibid.). In theory, then, they can conceive of ELF communication with its own demands in respect of appropriateness and intelligibility. In practice, however, they do not consider it in their teaching and prefer to stay close to a traditional RP model.

It is this practice, presumably, that accounts for Hannam's (2004) finding that Greek and British teachers have different attitudes towards a traditional RP accent. Whereas some of Hannam's British participants considered a traditional RP accent to be 'snobby' and out-of-date, her Greek participants felt comfortable with it. They explained this as the result of their familiarity with the accent: they had grown up with it as learners in the classrooms of their schooldays, where it had been used for listening material and where little variation from it was considered acceptable. From the evidence provided by Sifakis and Sugari, little has changed over recent years in this respect for English pronunciation teaching in Greece. However, rather than accept their findings as a reason to continue accepting NS English norms, the authors end by considering the role that teacher education can play in Greece as well as in other expanding circle countries, in raising teachers' awareness of the practical implications of the spread of English and, in turn, the potential for such awareness to impact on their accent attitudes. (See also Sifakis 2004 in this respect.)

Finally, we come to Zacharias (2005). Although in essence an investigation of Indonesian teachers' beliefs about the use of teaching materials produced locally and in English-speaking countries (described as 'internationally-published'), this study none the less casts some light on attitudes towards ELF. The study involved 100 teachers, of whom 94 were NNSs of English, primarily from Indonesia, and all the participants were tertiary level teachers. The research methods were questionnaires for all participants, along with interviews and classroom observations for 13 of them. The questionnaire findings were that for pronunciation and listening, 86 per cent and 87 per cent of the respondents respectively believed that materials produced in NS countries were more suitable. Zacharias summarizes their content-related reasons as follows (p.29):

- they provide 'natural', 'authentic', 'real', 'original', 'realistic', 'accurate', and 'correct' (error-free) exposure to English,
- they provide appropriate cultural background to language teaching,
- the quality is better in terms of content and appearance ...

He goes on to note that the preference for NS-produced materials was matched by 'a general attitude of distrust towards locally-produced materials', although the reasons given related more to practical matters than to content, for example, lack of availability and redundancy in view of the large number of books written by NSs that are easily available.

A slightly different picture emerged from the interviews and classroom observations. Only one of the teachers observed and interviewed used any locally-produced materials (her own), and then only for a course in applied linguistics, whereas she believed NS-produced books should be used in English teaching because only those expose students to the culture of NSs of English, and '[i]f students don't know the culture behind English, they cannot use the language properly' (p. 32). Her comment, Zacharias observes, reflected a belief in NS ownership of English that was shared by the majority of the other respondents, as is revealed in the comments they made in the questionnaires. Regardless of this, however, there were many occasions when teachers modified the materials to suit local needs, primarily—and paradoxically—because of the remoteness of some of the cultural content. The implication, then, is that the preference so widely expressed for NS-produced language teaching materials involved 'a certain amount of prejudicial bias—which teachers themselves may not be aware of' (p. 33). And as the cultural content is the aspect of these materials that they most feel the need to adapt, it seems likely that the real (content-based) reason for preferring NS materials has more to do with the language itself. In effect, it reflects a preference for NS English (which, their questionnaire responses imply, they believe is 'natural, authentic, real, original, realistic, accurate, and correct'), rather than Indonesian-influenced English which, they seem to believe, is none of these things.

Studies of prospective teachers' ELF attitudes

In addition to these studies of practising teachers' attitudes to ELF, there have been some important investigations into the attitudes of pre-service teachers. We will look briefly at three of these: Grau (2005), Seidlhofer and Widdowson (2003), and Shim (2002). Beginning with the earliest, Shim's study investigated the effect on Korean attitudes of learning about world Englishes. This was explored by means of surveys and interviews conducted over a five-year period from 1995 to 2000, during which Shim traced the development of Korean attitudes towards non-native Englishes, from total rejection to the 'sowing of seeds' and, she argues, the next step of 'planting the roots' is in sight. Her first study was of students' attitudes, and this will be discussed later. The participants in her second study were 24 prospective teachers enrolled on a TESOL master's degree at Sungkyunkwan University in Seoul. Despite having been introduced to the concept of 'varieties of English' and the notion of three concentric circles of English, they still exhibited a strong preference for American English and a unanimous unwillingness to participate in a programme that would introduce them to non-native English varieties. By contrast, in a study with another group of 27 teachers a year later, the results were very different. All 27 responded 'yes' to questions asking whether there was a need to understand non-native varieties of English and whether they would be willing to participate in a programme that introduced such varieties. Shim accounts for this change in attitudes as the result of the extensive exposure of Koreans to world Englishes by means of appearances on Korean television of the (non-native English-speaking) IMF Director Michel Camdessus and, shortly after, the televising of an English education programme, *Crossroads Café* that introduced them to several non-native English varieties.⁶

Seidlhofer and Widdowson (2003) is a study of the attitudes towards ELF of 48 third- and fourth-year Austrian students at the University of Vienna who had elected to take the Teacher Education option (Lehramtsstudium) as part of their English degree. The focus of the study is the students' essay responses to an article by House (2002) that seriously challenges traditional NS-normative notions about ELT of the kind that had been presented to the students as received wisdom on their degree programme up to that point.

The authors produced electronic text files of the original version of House (2002) and of the discussion part of the students' essays, and ran the *Wordsmith Tools'* Key Word programme (Scott 1998) over them in order to produce word frequency lists. From these lists they were able to compare the words that were most key, and thus most indicative of content, in House's article and the students' essays, and for this purpose, looked at the first 15 words in each case. These revealed some overlap. (For example, House's first three words were: 1. ELF, 2. discourse, 3. English, while the students' first three were: 1. English, 2. ELF, 3. language.) However, as the authors go on to observe, a closer inspection of all 15 words on the two lists demonstrates clearly that whereas House's primary concern is with how interactants in ELF discourse interact with each other, the students' primary concern is with teaching, and specifically with cultural aspects and pronunciation. They then look more closely at the ways in which the issues were debated in the essays by some of the students. What emerges (among many other things) is both approval for the conceptual shift from ENL to ELF, and concern about what could be seen as a 'reduced' and 'inadequate' model. But perhaps most importantly, the process that is described in this article represents exactly the kind of process that Sifakis and Sugari (2005) call for: awareness raising of ELF in teacher education programmes. This kind of opportunity would enable pre- and in-service teachers to reflect at length on ELF and should, in turn, prevent the kinds of knee-jerk reactions to it that we saw in some of the studies discussed above. And, as was demonstrated by Shim's (2002) study, the process needs to involve more than a basic introduction to the notion of 'varieties of English'.

Grau (2005) reports an investigation that she conducted with 231 first-year university students at the University of Giessen in Germany. The study consisted of two parts: a questionnaire at the beginning of the one-semester 'Introduction to ELT' course, and a follow-up discussion in the final week of the course. The questionnaire, whose purpose was both to provide data and raise the students' awareness, dealt with issues relating to the international status of English, such as which varieties of English they thought should be taught in German schools, and what they believed the objectives of pronunciation teaching should be. Two of the questions asked about certain concrete linguistic features: the acceptability of substitutions of /θ/ and /ð/ and of 'would' in conditional clauses. In each case, the respondents had to select from three alternative answers, of which one always gave them the opportunity to express no preference or to say they were unsure, an improvement on questionnaire designs that force respondents to select a position that might not truly represent their own.

Grau's results reveal the same 'abstract/concrete' divide that has already been commented on. For example, in response to the question 'What should be the objective in German schools concerning pronunciation in English?', 65 per cent opted for 'international intelligibility … it does not matter if [other speakers] can tell by your accent that you are German' (p. 267), while only 33 per cent selected near-nativeness, and 2 per cent indicated that they had no preference. On the other hand, in response to the specific example of sub-stitutions of /θ/ and /ð/, the position was almost reversed, with only 22 per cent agreeing that '[e]veryone will understand a speaker with a 'th-problem' who uses 's' or 'd' in 'thank you', 59 per cent disagreeing, and 19 per cent unsure. This was apparently the most controversial item on the questionnaire and received the most comments in the follow-up discussion. Similarly, 82 per cent disagreed in respect of the other concrete example, the notion that '[g]rammatical mistakes that do not cause problems of understanding should not be emphasised in class (for example, "would" in conditional clauses' (p. 269).

Perhaps there would have been fewer objections to the two specific linguistic examples in Grau's questionnaire had she not referred to them as a 'problem' (in the case of 'th') and a 'mistake' (in the case of 'would'). This must have sent a clear signal to the respondents that (according to the researcher) vari-ations from NS English forms are errors rather than potential ELF variants—a conclusion that may have been reinforced by the fact that the question asking which variety/varieties of English should be taught, specifically named only American and British English. Thus, a study investigating teachers' attitudes towards ELF is, to some extent, more of a study investigating their attitudes towards 'error' resulting from L1 transfer. On the other hand, as with Timmis (2002), it is also possible that the respondents in Grau's study were forced by the questionnaire design into adopting positions that did not exactly match their own, although in Grau's case, the follow-up discussion provided some scope for fine-tuning.

Like Sifakis and Sugari, Grau concludes by indicating the need for teacher education to include a focus on ELF so that prospective teachers are qualified to make informed choices. But unlike Sifakis and Sugari, she is cautious. Whereas they see education as having a responsibility to *challenge* '[Greek teachers'] assumption that NS norms should be central' (2005: 484), Grau sees ELF education as 'an additional focus' on teaching programmes (2005: 271) rather than a challenge to their traditional focus. Perhaps, like her respondents (and along with most of the respondents in the other studies discussed above), she still believes at some level that 'British English and American English are ... a sound basis for learners' (p. 270).

Studies of learners' ELF attitudes

Although my concern in this chapter, as throughout the book, is primarily with teachers, I will briefly mention the findings of five studies of learners' attitudes to ELF/non-native Englishes—Adolphs (2005), Friedrich (2000), Matsuda (2003), Shim (2002), and Timmis (2002)—as these may help cast some light on teachers' attitudes. The studies are discussed in chronological order.

Friedrich's study investigated the attitudes of 190 adult Brazilian learners of English ('EFL') in Brazil towards the target language. She found that despite all respondents acknowledging that 'English is a language of international communication', nearly 60 per cent would learn it even if this were not the case, and 72 per cent considered American or British English to have more prestige (respectively 54 per cent and 18 per cent). Meanwhile, there was a general lack of awareness of the existence of other varieties of English, and a quarter of the respondents wished to acquire native-like English. Friedrich concludes that her Brazilian respondents have 'many stereotypical ideas about English and learning which are not being addressed in the classroom' (p. 222), such as that there are only two varieties, American and British, and that their goal should be native-like English. She also points out that, given their limited exposure to British English, the claim of several respondents that British English is easier to understand must have been 'directed at the stereotype of the speaker' (ibid.).

The student-focused half of Timmis's study involved questions the same as or similar to those in the questionnaire administered to teachers—see above. The student questionnaire was completed by approximately 400 respondents in 14 countries and showed overall, perhaps not surprisingly, that students, including those who anticipate using English with other NNSs, are moving away from their attachment to NS English norms still more slowly than teachers.

Shim's student study was a survey of the attitudes of 57 intermediate level Korean students of English at the Language Research Institute, Seoul University. The survey involved playing recordings of five different speakers (US, Australian, Canadian, Pakistani, and Korean) to the respondents, who were asked if they would like to have the speaker as their English teacher. 100 per cent of the respondents answered 'yes' in respect of the US and Canadian speakers, only 49 per cent 'yes' (and 51 per cent 'no') in respect of the Australian, and none at all the Pakistani and Korean. The reason given for not wanting each of the last three speakers to provide the teaching model was specifically its 'bad' accent. Interestingly, only 9 per cent of these Korean respondents claimed to be able to understand Korean English 'very well' (and 9 per cent 'well', 62 per cent 'okay'), which is reminiscent of Major *et al.*'s (2002) point about the possible link between intelligibility and the denigration of one's own variety of English—see Chapter 3. This was the earliest of Shim's studies, and it is possible that the students' attitudes would have changed if it had been conducted after the events outlined above in respect of her studies of prospective teachers' attitudes. On the other hand, given the results of the other student surveys, and the popularity in Korea of so-called 'English villages', this cannot be a foregone conclusion.

Matsuda's (2003) study of attitudes towards ELF (here called 'English as an international language') involved 33 Japanese students at a private senior high school in Tokyo, and all aged 17 or 18. The data, collected over a period of 2½ months comprised a questionnaire (to identify general attitudes towards English and select students for interviews), in-depth interviews with ten students, and 36 hours of classroom observation. Matsuda also interviewed four teachers of English 'because of the position of power they hold in the classroom and possible influence they have on students' attitudes' (p. 485). The data revealed that on the one hand, the students perceived English as an international language, but on the other hand, they considered the owners of English to be inner circle speakers. In other words, they 'believed that although English is *used* all over the world, it does not *belong* to the world. Rather, English is the property of native English speakers (Americans and British, more specifically), and the closer they follow the native speakers' usage, the better' (p. 493; emphasis in original). Matsuda concludes, like Sifakis and Sugari, that 'much meta-sociolinguistic instruction for English learners and teachers is necessary in order to prepare students adequately for the future uses of English as an international language' (p. 495). As is demonstrated by both Shim (2002) and Seidlhofer and Widdowson (2003), such instruction needs to provide plenty of scope for reflection and probably also the opportunity for contact with ELF speakers with other L1s. (And see Seargeant's (2005) discussion of sources of information other than those found in the classroom that might influence students' views.)

Adolphs (2005) is a longitudinal study of NNS attitudes to NS English, though this inevitably elicits their attitudes towards NNS Englishes as well. Semi-structured interviews were conducted at two-monthly intervals over a six-month period with 24 students, most of who were studying on an intensive pre-sessional English language course at Nottingham University (UK) at the time, and most of whom came from Asian countries. Adolphs analysed 93 of the interviews for use of the terms 'native speaker'/'native speakers' (for example, which adjectives were used in association with them) and for how uses of the terms changed (or did not change) over time. She then analysed extended stretches of selected interview transcript where these terms appeared. She found overall that the students' attitudes shifted over time from a positive to a less positive orientation to NS English, partly, at least because the variety spoken by many of the NSs around them did not match the 'standard' variety, and particularly the accent, of their previous education. At the same time, through interacting with each other, the students became more aware of the need to understand English in international communication. Adolphs concludes that 'exposure to native speaker English makes learners more critical of this [East Midlands] variety and leads them to re-define their language learning goals with a greater focus on mutual intelligibility in an international context' (p. 130). Paradoxically, however, in spite of all the evidence they have received to the contrary, '[t]here seems to be little evidence in the interviews that the students consider native speaker norms to be irrelevant either in the local or in a more global context' (ibid.). Several appear even in the later interviews to want to speak 'standard' NS English with a (non-regional) NS accent.

The attachment to NS English norms revealed in these studies of learners' attitudes may account for some of the resistance to ELF revealed in the teachers' attitudes, in that they may in part be influenced by their students' (and students' parents') attitudes and beliefs concerning non-native and native Englishes. As an aside, ELT seems somewhat bizarrely to be the only educational subject where an important curriculum decision (which kind of English should be taught) is seen as being to some extent the prerogative of the students or their parents. It would be unthinkable in the teaching of other subjects such as mathematics, physics, history, or the like.

Concluding comments on previous studies of ELF attitudes

The studies of teachers' (and prospective teachers' and students') attitudes towards ELF represent an important contribution to both language attitudes research and to ELF research. In many of the studies, the analysis reveals some sort of contradiction, ambivalence, or a possibly deep-seated bias among the participants, although in most such cases it stops short of exploring in depth the reasons for these phenomena. In most cases, too, the respondents' words are taken at face value, whereas we might have gained a deeper understanding from more probing approaches that attempted to uncover the extent to which the words uttered were indeed 'true reflections of their privately held and complex inner cognitions and feelings' (Giles 1998: 431). In both respects, key-word approaches (see Scott and Tribble 2006) such as those used by Adolphs (2005), and Seidlhofer and Widdowson (2003) seem to offer some promise. But a more extensive qualitative analysis of the respondents' discourse including, in the case of spoken data, their prosody and other accent features—may yield still deeper insights, even though, as I pointed out earlier, we can probably never make definitive links between attitude and cause.

Turning to accent specifically, those researching ELF attitudes have not so far taken up the point made by Dalton-Puffer *et al.* (1997) about the need to investigate, from the point of view of accent, the mismatch between aspiration and achievement and, in this regard, the role played by 'self' and identification with the target communication group. This was already an issue in EFL contexts of learning and use. But ELF has the critical added dimension that the target communication group for most expanding circle learners/users is not a native-speaker but a non-native one. And yet, judging by the attitudes expressed towards NNS English in general and NNS accents in particular, the ELF dimension does not seem to be having much effect. Taking up Dalton-Puffer *et al.*'s call for further research into the accent aspiration/achievement mismatch should cast light on attitudes to ELF in general, given the likely centrality of accent in any discussion of ELF.

Rather surprisingly, very few of the ELF attitudes studies discussed above refer to any of the previous language attitudes research that was surveyed in Chapter 3. Although some of the earlier methods used would not necessarily be useful in ELF research, some of the later methods would be, along with some of the phenomena investigated, such as the influence of the research context, issues of group membership, power relations, linguistic insecurity and so on. One gets little sense, in reading the ELF attitudes studies, of the massive body of attitudes research that preceded them and could inform the direction they take. This awareness gap may to an extent be responsible for the failure of some of the ELF studies to distinguish between *attitudes* and *beliefs*. Many use one term to cover both, or use both terms interchangeably without commenting on the fact that attitudes operate below the level of awareness while beliefs refer to 'overt categories and definitions' that people have concerning linguistic matters (Hartley and Preston 1999: 210; and see Giles 1998).

Giles (1998) argues that '[i]n order to accomplish a fuller picture of the language attitudes landscape ... we need, ideally, *simultaneous* data on at least the following, each to be specified and theorized as regards the different sectors of the community studied (viz. parents, teachers, other professionals, majorities, and minorities according to age, socio-economic background, age (*sic*), gender and social identities' (pp. 431–2; emphasis in original), and he goes on to list these items:

1 What are people's attitudes about past and current language policies ...?

2 What are people's attitudes towards their language experiences and aspirations …?

3 What are people's multidimensional views of the relevant language as spoken by themselves and specified others, and who are the models they use … to assess the proficiencies they see in their linguistic ecology?

4 What are people's language needs, motivations, preferences, anxieties, expectations, and aspirations … regarding the status and communicative values of the relevant languages?

5 How do people attribute their own and others' successes and apparent language 'failures' … and what might they consider to be the likely causes of such social attributions …?

6 How do people talk about the multilingual scene and about the kinds of issues catalogued above …?

7 How will different interest groups be seen to respond to the changing political situation …?

(ibid.)

Giles is speaking specifically about Hong Kong at the time of the hand-back to China. However, I believe that the agenda he sets out would also provide much needed insights into language attitudes among the ELF community. While I cannot claim to be fulfilling Giles's requirements, I hope that my own empirical ELF attitude studies go at least some way towards providing 'the fuller picture of the [ELF] language attitudes landscape' to which Giles refers. It is to these studies that we now turn: in Chapter 5 we explore attitudes to ELF that emerge from spoken and written texts, and in Chapter 6 we consider the results of a questionnaire study that elicited ELF speakers' responses to a range of English accents.

Notes

1 The 400 *student* questionnaires were supplemented by 15 interviews with students who were studying in Leeds at the time, but interviews were not conducted with the teacher participants.

2 Some even use Timmis (2002) to condone the teaching of NS (standard or informal spoken) English. See, for example, Scheuer (2005), who quotes the same passage from Timmis (2002) as Tomlinson does, or Kuo (2006), who quotes from another part of Timmis's conclusion. Interestingly, those who argue that learners who dislike the notion of ELF should be taught what they 'want', do not necessarily take the same libertarian position when learners object to cherished EFL practices such as Communicative Language Teaching.

3 Note that Timmis (2002) similarly points out that his results might be very different if the research was repeated ten years later.

4 Murray does not explain on whose authority these items can be described as 'Euro-English', or whether or not the examples are invented. It seems that she may merely have selected items that are normally described as

'errors' made by German, French, and Italian speakers of English rather than selecting them from accounts of the initial findings of ELF corpora, in which potential ELF norms are being identified in accordance with criteria such as frequency, systematic use, and lack of communication problems arising from their use by proficient speakers in ELF contexts. (See, for example, Seidlhofer 2004.)

5 One of the main reasons for these teachers' ambivalence towards ELF forms is, of course, that they have not yet been fully identified and described, let alone codified.

6 There is in fact conflicting evidence as to the effect of incorporating a world Englishes perspective in teacher education programmes. Brown (2002) argues convincingly that it leads to changes in teachers' epistemologies, whereas Shim's study suggests that alone it does not have much effect, and that first-hand experience is also necessary. Clearly the amount and type of input involved must play a part, but even with a substantial world Englishes element, the evidence is not conclusive. For example, Yoshikawa's (2005) study at Chukyo University, Japan, found that while there was a greater willingness to accept Japanese English after a substantial world Englishes course, there was still 'a stronger preference for traditional English varieties and lower tolerance of New Englishes' (p. 360). Another factor is likely to be the sociolinguistic environment. Friedrich (2003), for example, found in her study of the attitudes to English of a group of 100 MBA students at a business school in Buenos Aires, Argentina, that the goal was for 'native-like command of the language' (p. 180). She links their attitudes to the economic crisis in Argentina at the time of her study, and the association they make between 'English and employment opportunities' (p. 182), with native-like English being seen by them as more likely to enhance their prospects.

5

ELF attitudes observed in speech and writing

We saw earlier that there have been up until now relatively few published studies about ELF attitudes, particularly when compared with the large amount of research that explores language attitudes within inner and outer circle contexts of English use. A recent study into the language attitudes of Danish learners of English (Ladegaard and Sachdev 2006) even starts from the assumption that Danes' choice of English accents 'as an international model' (p. 92) is restricted to a range of NS accents, and investigates their attitudes towards RP, GA, Australian English, Scottish English and Cockney accents. Undoubtedly both the lack of ELF attitude research and assumptions of the kind made by Ladegaard and Sachdev are, in great part, because ELF is still a relatively new notion among both linguists and the general population. In addition, many—possibly the majority—of those who are actually aware of ELF in theory do not subscribe to the notion that ELF is a linguistic phenomenon distinct from EFL. And if the NNS Englishes of the expanding circle continue to be classified indiscriminately as 'EFL' by the vast majority, then, the argument presumably goes, there is no point in investigating attitudes towards them: they are simply interlanguages with a range of proficiencies from beginner to advanced, and the lower the proficiency the lower the evaluation of the English by both NS and NNS judges. According to such a perspective, in other words, the relevant (deficit) attitude is already pre-supposed as self-evident, and 'nativelike' competence is all.

This, then, is the first of three chapters that present empirical research into ELF in general and ELF accents in particular, in an attempt to redress the balance. In this chapter and the next, the focus is on attitudes towards ELF—essentially, what do the research participants think about it? Chapter 7 then focuses on ELF identity—essentially, how do the participants see themselves *vis-à-vis* ELF? The previous chapter explored much of the research into teachers' attitudes to ELF and ELF accents that has been carried out by others in the past few years. In this chapter and the next, I present ELF attitude studies of my own. The first, in this chapter, is an examination of textual evidence, both written sources (published articles) and spoken sources (classroom discussion among teachers on a masters programme and conference question-and-answer sessions). The second study, in Chapter 6, a questionnaire-based investigation of ELF accent attitudes, draws on methods used in folk linguistics research and, more specifically, perceptual dialectology (for example, Niedzielski and Preston 2000/2003; Lindemann 2005; and see Chapter 3). These two ELF attitude studies thus extend the existing research into ELF attitudes that was discussed in the previous chapter, as well as adding more generally to the large body of research into language/accent attitudes discussed in Chapter 3.

A crucial point about the study presented in this chapter (and which applies also to the interview study in Chapter 7) involves the manner in which people speak or write. For as Cargile *et al.* (1994: 211) point out, 'language is a powerful social force that does more than convey intended referential information'. This 'more than' importantly includes speakers' attitudes and beliefs. For example, a stated belief may not necessarily represent a speaker's true position, but may be expressed for reasons relating to the context of the research.[1] In such a case, prosodic features may provide evidence of the mismatch. Again, the strength of a stated belief may be evident primarily through the speaker or writer's use of a particular stylistic or prosodic feature. Thus, as I mentioned in the previous chapter, this 'more than' requires thorough investigation in respect of ELF communication contexts, with close attention being paid not only to what people say/write about ELF but also to *how* they say/write it. And as I also pointed out, research into ELF language attitudes has hitherto focused primarily on the 'what', thus missing the opportunity to provide deeper insights into the beliefs and attitudes it uncovers. By contrast, this chapter's study of observed textual data uses tools drawn from discourse analysis, interactional sociolinguistics, and sociolinguistic ethnography in order to include a focus on the manner in which the ELF beliefs and attitudes are expressed, and thus to uncover the underlying attitudes that would not be revealed by a focus purely on their overt expression.

It is important to point out that even with the additional information provided by an analysis of stylistic features, conclusive causal links cannot be made between the attitudes expressed in the observed/elicited data and standard NS ideology, with its deficit[2] view of ELF, except in cases where the research participants themselves make the link. For example, they may refer to the influence on them of an NS bias in teaching materials used during their own English learning or teaching, or to feelings of inadequacy brought about by having to teach alongside NS teachers of English in schemes such as JET (Japanese Exchange Teaching programme) and NET (Native-speaking English Teacher scheme), or to the effects on them of the presence in their country of so-called 'English Villages'—see Chapter 2. Even here, though, one has to be careful about the kinds of claims that can be made about ideological influences. My aim, then, is the more modest one of drawing attention to what people (mainly NNS English teachers) say and to consider this in the light of points made in Chapter 2 about the extent of standard (NS) English ideology, in order to reveal tendencies that are strongly suggestive of links between that and attitudes. Further evidence is provided in Chapter 7, although the focus there is not on attitude *per se*, but on its interaction with identity.

Finally, before I go on to discuss the study itself, it will be helpful to clarify my use of the terms 'attitudes' and 'beliefs', in view of the different ways these terms are used in language evaluation research. As has already been mentioned, in practice many researchers use them interchangeably, whether or not they acknowledge differences between them in theory. Others maintain a consistent distinction, treating language beliefs as cognitive and overt categories, and language attitudes as latent and affective. Some regard beliefs as underlying and supporting attitudes. Preston, for instance, refers to 'underlying beliefs, presuppositions, stereotypes, and the like that lie behind and support the existence of language attitudes' (2002: 51). Others see it more as a (potentially) two-way process. For example, Garrett *et al.* argue 'even if beliefs do not have any affective content, they may trigger and indeed be triggered by strong affective reactions' (2003: 10). It seems, then, that language attitudes and beliefs are not as easy to separate as the simple cognitive/affective, overt/latent dichotomies imply.

The situation is further complicated by the term 'opinion', which many researchers use interchangeably with attitude while others regard it as cognitive, verbalizable, and non-affective (Garrett *et al.*: ibid.; citing Baker 1992 and Perloff 1993), and thus synonymous with belief. Garrett *et al.* come down in favour of the latter, concluding that opinion is 'a more discursive (or 'discursable') entity—a view that can be developed about something, while attitudes may be potentially less easy to formulate'. This, they add, seems 'to leave open the possibility of a distinction in terms of a person's expressed opinion not necessarily reflecting their attitude' (ibid.). In other words, we cannot assume that attitudes and opinions (i.e. beliefs) necessarily represent two sides of the *same* coin: to extend the metaphor, they may sometimes belong to different coins altogether. So, to conclude this discussion, while recognizing the degree of complexity involved, in this study and the Chapter 6 study, I distinguish between attitudes and beliefs (and opinions) as, respectively, affective/latent and cognitive/overt, though like many other researchers, will, on occasions when neither is particularly salient, use 'attitudes' as a blanket term for both.

Perspectives on ELF in the written texts

The written data is drawn from three recently published articles about ELF, of which one is exclusively about ELF accents, while the other two also consider additional linguistic levels. I have selected texts that are widely available so that readers are easily able to refer to the full version if they wish to do so. This means, however, that my choice was restricted to articles in journals and edited collections and, in turn, that the authors of the three texts are not what might be described as 'ordinary' teachers. Nevertheless, the kinds of orientation to ELF (both overt beliefs and latent attitudes) that are expressed in these articles are, in my experience, representative and typical of those currently being expressed by the vast majority of English language teachers and teacher trainers; and my claim is supported by the fact that the findings of the spoken data (presented in the second half of this chapter) are broadly comparable with those of the written.[3]

Text 1 (Kuo 2006) focuses on ELF in general; Text 2 (Sobkowiak 2005) focuses specifically on pronunciation; and Text 3 (Prodromou 2006) looks at ELF in general as well as lexicogrammar specifically. A further difference between them is that the first two overtly oppose the notion of ELF, while the third is an example of a particular type of ELF discourse, one in which writers (or speakers) display an exonormative rather than endonormative orientation to ELF. In other words, although they express support for ELF, they evaluate it against the yardstick of NS English norms (mainly standard British or American) rather than in its own right. (See Seidlhofer, Breiteneder, and Pitzl 2006.)[4] This in turn means that their orientation in reality has more in common with those who oppose ELF in principle than with those who support it.

In the first part of this section, we explore the beliefs about ELF that are articulated overtly in the three articles and consider the extent to which they are based on misunderstood and unwarranted assertions. In the second part, we move on to consider the *manner* in which these beliefs are expressed, looking at the writers' stylistic choices (for example, the use of metaphor, collocation, and repetition) in order to gain deeper insights into the language attitudes that underlie the argument.

Surface-level argument

Common to all three texts is the notion—articulated in various ways within and across the texts—that ELF represents a deficient kind of English character-ized by errors, and ENL the 'proper' and 'correct' English that is appropriate for L2 learners and users. In a sense, all the issues raised about ELF in these texts are variations on this single theme.

The first text, 'Addressing the issue of teaching English as a lingua franca', presents three main arguments against ELF: firstly, that it is incompatible with what is known about second language learning; secondly, that the validity of ELF corpora is questionable; and thirdly, that ELF will not prepare learners for their future needs in international communication and that, in any case, the choice of appropriate model should be made by learners themselves.

The argument concerning second language acquisition centres on Swain and Lapkin's (1995) work on the cognitive processes involved in producing language. The author cites this as evidence that any redundancy *vis-à-vis* NS forms in the output of co-ELF speakers will prevent NNSs from noticing the 'gap' in their own proficiency. Because it does not 'protect the preciseness and completeness of the message', Kuo argues, 'the ELF approach ... would appear to contradict and misinterpret the nature of language learning and second language acquisition' (p. 216). However, she ignores the fact that Swain and Lapkin's work is about 'languaging': in other words, the comprehensible output hypothesis is about getting syntax right, not about production in general, and not about communication. Meanwhile, by focusing exclusively on reduction, she also fails to mention that this is only one ELF phenomenon among many that researchers have described, and that far more interesting in terms of ELF innovation is the phenomenon of addition, i.e. ELF speakers' creativity in adding new forms to the English language.

Turning to the point about ELF corpora, Kuo first compares corpora-based accounts of ELF unfavourably with corpora-based accounts of NS English (for example, Biber, Johansson, Leech, Conrad, and Finegan 1999) because they are supplemented by analyses at the qualitative level involving, for example, 'accounts of interpersonal intention' (p. 217). It is not clear why she makes the assumption that ELF corpora are not able to do the same. She goes on to argue that an ELF corpus 'would inevitably resort to the quantity-related concept of frequency of occurrence' (p. 217) and that just because 'an error' occurs frequently, this does not mean there is a strong case for its standardization. Leaving aside, for the moment, the assumption that an NNS form is, by definition, an 'error', there is a weakness in the frequency argument, as this is precisely the basis on which corpora of NS English such as CANCODE and COBUILD make their claims about what should be taught to learners of English. The author is thus, in this respect, questioning corpus linguistics as a whole.

The final criticism of ELF relates to what the author calls 'learner voice' (ibid.). In this part of the article, using data collected from her own learners, she presents learners' own views of the kind of English they want to learn. Not surprisingly, given the fact that they have travelled to the UK to study English, her informants express a preference for an NS model, along with a belief that the English of their learner peer group provides an inappropriate model because of its 'phonological and grammatical inaccuracy' (p. 218). This, the author argues, supports Timmis's (2002) finding that students still desire to conform to NS English norms—and see the discussion of Timmis's study in Chapter 4. On the other hand, Kuo does not take into account what might have caused the comments her informants make (including, possibly, the perspective she presented as interviewer) about their own 'bad' pronunciation or about the 'mistakes' their peer group make. Their voice, then, is restricted to stereotypical comments about the English of NNSs, with no suggestion that they were encouraged to explore the issues in any depth.

Text 2, 'Why not the LFC?', focuses entirely on pronunciation and, specifically, on the Lingua Franca Core. (See the account of the Lingua Franca Core in Chapter 1.) The main body of the article is divided into five main parts, each of which presents a different argument against the Lingua Franca Core (LFC) as presented in Jenkins (2000). In the first part, the author argues that most supporters of the LFC ignore the point that what can be described in corpora should not automatically become the subject of teaching curricula. This, he believes, is 'one of the fundamental weaknesses of the reasoning of the founder of LFC, Jennifer Jenkins' (p. 134). The assertion, however, is inaccurate. I have not suggested that the LFC should become the automatic subject of teaching. The point is made in Jenkins (2000) and elsewhere that the LFC is not yet definitive, that it is, in any case, inappropriate for learners who wish to acquire a near-native English accent, and that I believe—in line with Widdowson (1991), a source I regularly quote—that the fact something can be described, does not automatically mean it should be taught.

The second part considers some of the arguments that have been made against the use of the RP model and, in particular, the claim in Jenkins (2000) that RP is not widely used, even among L1 speakers of English, and therefore cannot be assumed to be an appropriate goal for L2 learners. Statistics, Sobkowiak observes, cannot be the only criterion used to define a pronunciation error, and he goes on to criticize the claim that 'there is really no justification for doggedly persisting in referring to an item as "an error" if the vast majority of the world's L2 speakers produce and understand it' (Jenkins 2000: 160). However, he ignores the crucial point about intelligibility in this quotation (and the entire LFC research). The case I built was not 'statistics' based but intelligibility based. Intelligibility, Sobkowiak thus seems to be saying, is less important than other criteria that he nevertheless does not actually name.

In the third part, the author turns to issues around the ownership of English, describing as 'highly emotional, even hysterical' (p. 136) Widdowson's claim that '[h]ow English develops in the world is no business whatever of native speakers in England, the United States, or anywhere else. They have no say in the matter, no right to intervene or pass judgement' (1994a: 385). This is the result, Sobkowiak argues, of mixing linguistic and political/ideological issues. He considers this kind of claim to be motivated by political correctness, a kind of 'politically correct self-castigation' (p. 137) that does not provide a basis on which to build new pronunciation standards. This is a curious claim to make given the fact that the vast majority of ELF researchers are, themselves, NNSs of English and therefore have no reason for 'self-castigation' in respect of NS attitudes to NNS English. But again, this counter evidence is sidestepped.

The fourth part turns to what the author describes as '(socio)linguistic arguments' (ibid.). He begins by considering the LFC as an example of an artificial language model such as Esperanto which, he argues, met with limited success. He goes on to discuss the fact that speech does not only serve basic functions of communication but also involves self-image. Learners of English, he points out, have been shown regularly in experimental studies to aspire to near-native English pronunciation. This, he argues, is because the more 'native-like' their pronunciation, the more highly NNSs are evaluated by both NS and NNS listeners. The point is an important one, and one that resonates loudly with the subject of this book. The issue of learners' wishes, however, is more complex than the author of Text 2 suggests. And as I pointed out in Chapter 4, the fact that participants in studies (experimental or otherwise) rate NS English accents more highly than NNS ones, or express a desire to sound 'native-like' is not of itself reason to condone their position.

The final part moves on to teaching matters. Firstly, the author argues that the LFC represents a fall in pronunciation standards, that such a goal would both encourage them to maintain their foreign accents in their English, and be demotivating to learners. In these respects he criticizes the claim made in Jenkins (2000) and elsewhere that some L2 features, including phonological/phonetic items, are unteachable, although he provides no evidence. He goes on to consider the matter of language teachers, and takes issue with the argument, also articulated in Jenkins (2000) as well as many other sources—see above, Chapter 2 endnote 30—that NNSs of English often make better teachers than NSs do. This is not the case, he contends, because '[m]ost researchers believe that teachers' phonetics should be as close as possible to the native ideal' (p. 142). He cites two sources in support of this claim (Hüttner and Kidd (2000), who are language teachers, rather than researchers, and Majer 1997). However, it is their opinions rather than evidence that he presents.

Finally, the author turns to psychological issues, taking us back to the matter of self-image that he had referred to in the fourth part—see above. He points out that many learners regard near-native pronunciation as an asset, and that the belief that it is so motivates learners to try to sound native-like. He mentions an alternative argument, that of learners' fear of loss of identity, though he counters this by saying that he has never come across a Polish learner of English who did not wish to sound like a native speaker. He concludes this fifth part by quoting Seidlhofer's (2001a) claim that from an ELF perspective, NNSs 'will no longer need to think of themselves as something they are not. Rather they will have a positive means of asserting themselves as competent and authoritative speakers of ELF' (Seidlhofer 2001a: 46). This, argues Sobkowiak, 'projects a completely unrealistic picture of effortless and immediate phonetic competence, once the 'international' standard of English is chosen' (p. 144). Seidlhofer is referring, however, not to learning matters but to the issue of identity and her point thus seems to have been misinterpreted. In addition, there is as yet no 'international standard of English', and nor does Seidlhofer refer to the existence of one. Again, then, Sobkowiak is making an unwarranted assumption, both about Seidlhofer's position and about the nature and current status of ELF.

Text 3, 'Defining the "successful bilingual speaker" of English', begins with a critique of two articles, Alptekin (2002) and Timmis (2002). The author, Prodromou, describes their positions as respectively 'centrifugal' and 'centripetal' the first embracing diversity, and the second favouring a standard NS model for all, in so far as this is what learners want. Prodromou describes these as 'two opposing views on EIL' (p. 52), although it would be more accurate to describe Alptekin's position as EIL (or ELF) and Timmis's as EFL. Prodromou criticizes Alptekin for not describing what a successful bilingual English speaker, according to the centrifugal perspective, actually does with the language, and argues that those who share this position should 'come up with an empirically based and coherent alternative to native norms, based on a valid description of the "successful bilingual"' (p. 53). This is, of course, exactly what ELF researchers are engaged in doing.

The author turns to a consideration of what criteria could be used to define a successful bilingual, asking 'how good does one have to be to count as a "near"-native speaker?', thus establishing a link between 'good' and 'near-native', although he appears not to notice this. He then discusses the issue of the successful bilingual in relation to VOICE (the Vienna-Oxford International Corpus of English), a corpus of English as a Lingua Franca. (See Chapter 1.) While he initially agrees with Seidlhofer's (2001a) questioning of the legitimacy of NS English norms, in contrast to his previous linking of 'good' with 'near-native', he goes on to cite five lexicogrammatical examples from VOICE in order to criticize Seidlhofer's position in respect of learners' aspirations. He argues that 'setting the bar of grammatical acceptability low' like this is 'unnecessarily cautious' (p. 56) because non-native teachers have such a strong 'command and knowledge of the grammatical system of English as it is codified in traditional grammar books' (ibid.). Again, then, he is linking correctness and acceptability to native Englishness. He also describes as 'fallacious' Seidlhofer's extension of the work on ELF phonology to lexicogrammar (p. 55), purely on account of the fact that (in his opinion) learners have greater difficulty in acquiring L2 English pronunciation than they do L2 lexicogrammar. Once again, this demonstrates the author's exonormative orientation to ELF—it is not, he believes, a phenomenon to be investigated in its own right, but one to be compared with ENL, where learner ease and difficulty *vis-à-vis* the native language are important criteria, and where, presumably, 'difficulties' (i.e. L2 features) that remain can be characterized as 'fossilized interlanguage features' rather than instances of L2 regional variation.

Finally, in this part of the discussion, the author, like Sobkowiak (see above), states his objection to Widdowson's (1994a) claim that NSs have no say in how English develops outside the inner circle countries. Prodromou, by contrast, argues that NSs are part of EIL (which of course they are, as a small minority), that they are 'speakers of the most codified and widely accepted variety of English we have', and that '[t]his native variety seems to have facilitated "comfortable intelligibility" across a wide variety of Englishes' (p. 58). Here, the reference to NS English as a (single) variety is inaccurate, and it is not clear which particular NS variety the author is referring to. Leaving that aside, no evidence is offered to support the claims that it is 'the most widely accepted' or that it has promoted intelligibility extensively. In fact, research to date involving outer and expanding circle speakers and listeners has demonstrated that for NNS listeners, NS varieties of English may be less intelligible than NNS varieties. (See Jenkins 2000; Kachru and Nelson 2006; Smith and Nelson 2006.) Prodromou nevertheless sees 'native varieties' (this time in the plural) as 'important strands in the pattern of EIL' (ibid.). This takes him straight back to the exonormative position on ELF (Seidlhofer *et al.* 2006) that I referred to above (p. 112), in which ELF is regarded as existing not in its own right, but with reference to ENL norms.

The remainder of the article presents the author's own corpus of English as an international language, although he also refers to the speakers who provided the data as '*proficient* non-native users of English as a foreign language' (p. 59; emphasis in original), again implying an NS English-normative approach. This is also clear from the list of criteria he used in order to decide which 'successful' users of English to include in his corpus. Many of his informants, for example, were 'recognised international or local experts in the teaching of English' (p. 61), all of them 'used English regularly … with native and non-native speakers' (ibid.), and the author 'compared [his] impressions and data of successful users with definitions widely used by international examining bodies (Cambridge Proficiency, Michigan Proficiency, IELTS). As is pointed out in Chapter 8, there is little about such bodies that is international in the endonormative sense: their tests are all predicated on NS English norms to a very great extent. Given that the author selected such speakers to provide his data in the first place, it is not surprising that his corpus reveals findings such as successful users of English 'have a well-nigh flawless command of grammar' (p. 63), where 'flawless' means 'in relation to NS grammar'. (See also Prodromou 2003a, where the word 'flawless' is also used.) On the other hand, he finds little use of, or creativity with, NS idioms. His concept of a successful L2 user of English as an international language thus appears to refer to someone whose English diverges from NS use of idiomatic language, but in all other respects is more or less identical to it. In other words, Prodromou's successful user's English is close to the 'native-like' L2 English favoured by the authors of Texts 1 and 2, and his successful user is someone of whom they would entirely approve, despite the fact that they oppose the concept of ELF whereas Prodromou claims to support it. His position is thus far closer to EFL than to ELF.

These, then, are the main overtly stated arguments directed against ELF (or, in the case of Text 3, against endonormative ELF) in the three articles. As I observed above, they are all in fact variations on a single theme, that of 'ELF = deficient ENL', which acts as a kind of *leitmotif* across all three texts.[5] And while the arguments are at one level perfectly rational, as I have demonstrated above, they are to a large extent grounded in misinterpretations of the kind discussed in Chapter 1 about the nature of ELF and the position of its researchers. The manner in which these arguments are expressed suggests, however, that concerns about ELF exist at a more deep-seated level than is evident from the analysis of content alone. It is crucial not to ignore these more covertly expressed concerns, as exploring them provides access to the deeper-seated ambivalences and anxieties that underlie the conscious objections to ELF and themselves have to do with basic questions of identity (see Chapter 7), not only in these three texts, but wherever similar issues are raised. It is, therefore, to stylistic analysis that we now turn.

Underlying attitudes and concerns

It seems that when people talk about ELF, there is something about it that causes them to react emotionally. As Lippi-Green observes, '[s]ome of the discussion around language standards is so emotional in tone that parallels can be drawn to disagreements between scientists and theologians over the centuries' (1994: 190). Nowhere has this been more so in the field of ELT in recent years than in the discussion of ELF, where some of the language used suggests that underlying the surface-level argument, there are deeply entrenched latent attitudes about the nature of the English language and who its 'owners' are, as well as deep-seated concerns and insecurities about language change. In this section, we therefore look again at some of the arguments that are articulated overtly in the three texts. But this time, we will explore how the manner in which they are made—the language in which they are expressed—reveals some of the covert attitudes that underlie them.

As I mentioned in the previous section, the anti-ELF arguments in the three texts are all, in effect, variations on the theme of ELF as deficient ENL. The manner in which these arguments are expressed indicates the strength of this position and is particularly evident when the authors consider the issue of errors and correctness. What emerges, especially from the first two texts, is an antipathy towards English that does not conform to NS norms in general and towards ELF in particular. For example, the author of Text 1 uses the word 'reduced' five times to characterize ELF, as well as a large number of negative words and phrases such as 'incomplete', 'inaccurate', 'inaccuracy', 'bad', 'not good', and 'mistakes', some repeated several times, to describe NNS English in general—although this seems by definition to be equated with ELF in her mind, without taking any other considerations such as proficiency level into account. By contrast, she uses only positive language to describe ENL, referring, for example, to its 'socio-cultural richness' (p. 220). She also makes use of one particular phrase—'He look very sad' (taken from Seidlhofer's 2001b data)—on five separate occasions in the article as virtually the only illustration of ELF grammar. This particular example was in fact uttered by a proficient speaker of English, although taken out of context in this way, the omission of third person -*s* becomes more noticeable than it was in the conversation in which it originally occurred. The fact that this potential feature of ELF is so salient to the author suggests that it causes her considerable concern. This, however, is not surprising given that third person -*s* is a grammatical item to which immense importance is attached in EFL grammar books. Its absence is likely to have become for the author—as very probably for the majority of English teachers—a strong marker of L2 learner English (i.e. interlanguage). Hence it is inconceivable to her, despite the known facts about language change, that it could ever be accepted as grammatical in non-ENL spoken communication: it is simply wrong.

This same deep-seated attitude towards ELF is revealed by the author of Text 2, this time specifically in relation to pronunciation errors. Beneath the level of the rational argument, emotive language on several occasions points to a less rational prejudice against ELF, and this is evident particularly in the author's use of metaphor. For example, in describing the decline in standards that he believes would ensue if the aim of approximating NS English accents was abandoned, he demonstrates the depth of his dislike of the ELF alternative by saying 'giving up on this high objective [i.e. RP]—and LFC boils down to this exactly—will easily bring the ideal down into the gutter with no checkpoint along the way' (p. 141). Here, the somewhat emotional metaphor of 'the gutter' indicates the strength of the author's feeling. Meanwhile the repetition of 'down' reinforces his sense of a potential decline in standards, and contrasts with the word 'high', which he uses to express his orientation to RP. There is also a suggestion that while 'boil down to' is used with its meaning 'to amount to', this multi-word verb may have been selected subconsciously because of its closeness to 'boil down', with its image of reduction. The two kinds of pronunciation, NS/NNS, ENL/ELF, RP/the LFC, then, are not merely different: for this author, as for many English teaching professionals, they are diametrically opposed. And as in the first text, the author's attitude is further revealed by the choice of words and phrases to describe NS English pronunciation, for example, 'correct native (-like) pronunciation', 'traditional standard', its 'voluminous supporting research', 'the inherent value of [NS] model pronunciation', and the like. On the other hand, there are no instances where *non*native-like (ELF) pronunciation is referred to approvingly. In fact it is described as exhibiting 'pronunciation errors' even if it contains only traces of a regional (NNS) accent.

Another area in which the choice of language illustrates the strength of the underlying prejudice against ELF concerns change: both language and syllabus change. For example, in Text 1 there is a discussion of phonological and grammatical redundancy in ENL, which, the author argues, provides the language with its precision and, in turn, facilitates comprehension and L2 acquisition. (See above for a critique of the argument itself.) What the author actually says is that such redundancy is 'meant to protect the precision and completeness of the message' (p. 216). Here, the use of the word 'protect' suggests an emotional attachment to traditional NS English, and that it needs protecting against the ELF 'invader' that threatens it. Similarly, in Text 2 there is a reference to the speed of the spread of beliefs about NS English pronunciation: 'the belief that English pronunciation is both unteachable and unlearnable[6] because it is too difficult, spreads like wildfire among the supporters of the LFC' (p. 140). This fear seems to have originated from the author's misapprehension that such beliefs are exerting a strong influence on pronunciation syllabuses in schools and universities, and leading to a change in pronunciation goals. Given his attachment to RP it is not at all surprising that he should both feel anxious about and vastly overestimate the influence of the LFC proposals on teaching. However, earlier in the text, he uses a very different metaphor, that of still birth, to refer to the LFC: like artificial languages such as Esperanto, he says, '[i]t is a paradox[7] that LFC supporters realize that creatures of this sort are usually still-born' (p. 138). On the one hand, then, he seems to have an irrational fear that the LFC proposals are spreading 'like wild-fire' among its supporters; on the other hand, he seems confident that these same supporters expect the LFC not to thrive, but to be 'still-born'. Although this is a contradiction at the surface level, the emotive language in which these two conflicting ideas are expressed suggest that, while the earlier image (the still birth) may represent the author's strongest hopes about the future of ELF and the LFC, the later one (the 'wildfire') may represent his deepest fears about change and declining standards in English teaching.

Linked to concerns about syllabus change is a sense of unease that learners will eventually be *forced* to learn ELF rather than have a choice between ELF and standard NS English. ELF researchers regularly point out that this is by no means the case, and argue that it is proponents of standard NS English (and RP/GA) who have, up to now, denied expanding circle English learners a choice of model beyond the narrow confines of standard British and American English. However, the point is often not taken. An example of this occurs in Text 1, where the use of 'should' and the repetition of 'should be allowed' indicates both the author's assumption that ELF precludes any choice and her concern that this is so: learners 'should be allowed ... to follow a native-speaker phonological or grammatical model' (p. 220), 'learners should be allowed to decide which English to learn, including which accent ...' (ibid.). This is reinforced by her (very reasonable) point that 'it is up to ... the learners in each context to decide to what extent they want to approximate that [NS] model' (ibid.). ELF researchers would agree entirely, but the fact is clearly not appreciated. This is demonstrated again in Text 2, whose author quotes my point that '[i]t will be important not to patronize those learners who, having heard the arguments, still wish to work towards the goal of a native speaker accent, by telling them they have no need to do so' (Jenkins 2002: 101). This 'appeal', the author describes as 'utterly paradoxical' (p. 143). Once again, the use of strong language, as well as the irrational nature of the claim, hints at a deep-seated antipathy towards ELF and even, perhaps, at a fear that having heard the arguments, learners may indeed one day choose to aim for ELF-oriented goals.

The final area for discussion in terms of deeper-level attitudes is that of learner aspiration. Text 3, for instance, makes copious use of, and builds links across the text between, the phrases 'successful non-native/bilingual/ user(s)', 'near-native'/'native-like', and 'student(s) aspirations'.[8] The cumulative effect is to suggest that for the author these terms, in effect, amount to much the same thing, and that his overt arguments against ELF represent a deeper-seated prejudice against ELF as a possible pedagogic model for students of the future to aspire to. The language used in his discussion of learner aspirations seems to confirm this. For example, ELF is discussed as a 'problem' (twice), it is described as too low a 'bar' in terms of motivation and self-esteem (p. 56), it is implied that ELF will not 'do justice to our students' needs and aspirations'

(p. 58), or 'empower them' to cope with the Englishes they will encounter in the real world [presumably native and near-native]', and 'it is implausible that most learners and teachers will be enthusiastic about a model of English that legitimizes non-canonical [i.e. non-native] grammatical forms' (p. 62). This is all summed up in one of the author's final comments: 'I have outlined some of the possible *problems* which a model of *ELF* incorporating user *errors* may present, in terms of student *aspirations* and syllabus design ('error', that is, as defined by current *codified [i.e. ENL] forms* of English)' (pp. 67–78; emphasis added). The italicized items make clear that in his mind, ELF is a problem because by definition it contains errors as contrasted with the native language, and that for this reason it may not[9] satisfy learners' aspirations to become successful bilingual speakers of English.

A similar attitude is revealed in this respect by the language used in Text 2. Under the rubric 'native pronunciation as a learner's asset and ambition' (p. 143), the author argues 'research shows that *correct* pronunciation is regarded by many learners as an *asset* all by itself' (ibid.; emphasis added), again treating the phenomena of nativeness (the term used in the heading) and correctness as synonymous, and linking the two with aspiration. Immediately afterwards, he extends the link to motivation, and goes on to contrast the 'inherent value' of native-like pronunciation with 'resentments due to the fear of losing one's identity' (p. 143). This he dismisses as unlikely on the basis that he has never met a Pole 'who *would not like* to sound like a native' and would not like 'to perfect his English accent' (p. 144; emphasis in original). My interviews with two Polish teachers of English (see Chapter 7) indicate that the situation is rather more complex and less clear-cut than the author suggests. But leaving that aside for now, what comes across most strongly from the lexical choices in this section of the text is his own concern that the nativeness/correctness/aspiration/motivation link should remain in place, and his perception of this link as one of 'inherent value', and one that contrasts with the 'resentment' inherent in the alternative (ELF) perception.

Finally, it is not clear whether Sobkowiak intends his point about the 'inherent value' of an NS accent to call to mind the 'inherent value' hypothesis, which 'maintains that some linguistic varieties are inherently more attractive and pleasant than others, and that these varieties have become accepted as standards or have acquired prestige simply because they are the most attractive' (Trudgill and Giles 1978: 174). This view, however, has long been rejected by linguists in favour of the 'social connotations hypothesis', according to which it is strong, pervasive social norms rather than intrinsic qualities that cause people to agree on which languages and varieties of languages are 'better' than others. (See Chapter 6 for further discussion of the social connotations hypothesis.) Sobkowiak's echo, whether intentional or not, thus reinforces the impression that he believes that some English accents (i.e. nativelike) are inherently 'better' than others (i.e. non-nativelike).

Conclusions to the analysis of written texts

Bourdieu argues that 'the field' makes strenuous efforts to defend itself against change 'by rejecting information capable of calling into question its accumulated information [if] exposed to it accidentally or by force, especially by avoiding exposure to such information' (1990: 56). As has been revealed in the analysis, the authors of these texts are strongly oriented against changes in English language goals in general and, in the case of Text 2, in pronunciation in particular. The fact that their arguments are characterized by misinterpretations of ELF and ELF research suggests, in line with Bourdieu, that these authors have either avoided the relevant information or have accessed it but read (or heard) only what they believed to be true in the first place, and it is this information that they then disseminate in their own texts. To this extent, their texts have 'pretexts' in both senses of the word (Widdowson 2004b): an ulterior motive, in this case, to disparage ELF, and assumptions about their readers' prior/shared knowledge, in this case, knowledge about the English language and ELT from a broadly traditional NS-normative perspective.

But it is not merely a question of selective reading (or listening) and misinterpretation. The pejorative way in which the English of NNSs is characterized in these three texts hints at both a subconscious dislike of, and fear of the spread of, the English of (non-native-like) NNSs in general and perhaps, in the case of Texts 1 and 2, that of the mother tongue group in particular (a phenomenon that McNamara 2001 refers to as 'linguistic self-hatred'). There is an inability to separate the notion of ELF from a more general perception of NNS English that is self-evidently inferior to NS English. In this regard, it is significant that the texts all refer to NNSs' aspirations in English and imply, or state directly, a link between 'good' (native-like) English and positive self-image.[10] These authors, like many others who comment on ELF, seem unable to conceive of the possibility of 'feeling good' in English that has NNS-led features.

Graddol observes, however, that 'the postmodern model of English' and 'its new realities … pose a challenge for many non-native speakers, including members of the existing elites for whom English represents an identity marker, and many of those involved in the traditional English teaching business itself' (2006: 20). The 'postmodern model of English' to which he refers is not standard British or American English spoken with an RP or GA accent, but involves the spread of new NNS-led forms such as those being identified in ELF research. It is, then, entirely understandable that those who have invested considerable time and effort in acquiring 'native-like' English may feel threatened by talk of ELF, and this may be responsible for the strength of emotion that emerges from time to time in Texts 1 and 2. Their authors, and countless other NNS ELT professionals like them, have always been given to understand that excellence in English equates with near-nativeness. ELF, by contrast, calls into question not only the wisdom of their having invested their lives in working towards this goal, but also their identities as teachers, which have until now depended on their success in achieving it. Accepting ELF would involve making a huge psychological shift, and while they may see at the rational level that there are good arguments in favour of appropriating English for their own purposes, at the deeper level they still have a deep-seated attachment to ENL, and search for arguments to support it.

It is for this reason that despite the strength of their anti-ELF perspectives, the texts reveal varying kinds and degrees of ambivalence. This is most evident in Text 1, where the ambivalence relates not only to the English language but also to the author herself. She talks with approval, on the one hand, of how the participants in her own study had said they would turn only to an NS teacher for advice on grammar and pronunciation. Yet on the other hand, she describes these same participants' hopes that *she*, an NNS teacher, would correct their grammar and pronunciation 'mistakes' during the interviews. She is at one and the same time an NNS of English and thus (according to her own, but not an ELF, perception) an eternal learner of the language, and a teacher (surrogate NS?) with responsibility for correcting learners' errors. There seems to be an identity conflict involved here, an issue that will be taken up and explored in Chapter 7, where many of the participants in my own interview study reveal a similar conflict.

We move on now to the spoken data in order to explore the extent to which it reveals the same kinds of misconceptions about ELF and the arguments of ELF researchers, as well as the same underlying attachment to ENL that we have observed in the written texts.

Orientations to ELF in the spoken texts

The spoken texts[11] analysed in this section comprise a representative selection of discussions of ELF and the LFC among NNS and NS teachers of English on five occasions between 2001 and 2004. Two took place during a phonology/phonetics course on a masters programme in English Language Teaching and Applied Linguistics at a British university, the third at a pronunciation workshop for English language teachers at another British university, the fourth at a Pronunciation SIG open forum discussion at an IATEFL conference, and the final one in a discussion with the audience following a panel presentation at another conference. In most cases the focus was primarily on ELF pronunciation, although ELF in general was always discussed, and was the main focus of the final session. The second MA session and the two conference discussions were recorded, while in the case of the first MA session and university workshop, field notes were taken and teachers' comments noted verbatim.[12]

The analysis, like that of the texts in the previous section, explores not only what the participants say, but also how they say it. In the case of spoken data, this means not only their lexicogrammatical choices, but also, crucially, their use of prosodic features. While the main analysis of prosody is reserved for the interview data in Chapter 7, where relevant and feasible (not in the case of field notes), this section draws on tools used in interactional sociolinguistics and sociolinguistic ethnography.[13] In particular, the analysis includes some discussion of how certain prosodic features act in the data as contextualization cues and indicators of speaker meaning beyond the content level. These features are primarily rising and falling intonation patterns; stress, primarily extra stress on a nuclear (tonic) syllable; and pausing. Having said that, I have exercised caution in making claims on the basis of prosodic analysis, and used prosody in the main to support rather than to initiate an interpretation. As Cameron points out, 'the same formal feature may not serve the same purpose for every group of speakers or in every context' (2001: 114). This point always needs to be taken into account, often at the individual as well as the group level, and particularly—in my view—with regard to pitch movement.[14] But it is even more of a concern when the research participants are drawn from a range of lingua-cultural backgrounds and who, in the case of L2 English speakers, may use prosodic features in ways that are influenced by their L1 prosody and which differ in various respects from the prosody of L1 varieties of English.

Overview of beliefs and attitudes in the spoken data

The main anti-ELF arguments that emerge from the data are remarkably common to all five settings and to both the NNS and NS participants. As with the written data, there is again a common theme running through the various contributions made by the speakers, i.e. that of ELF as incorrect English (some participants used the term 'interlanguage') and ENL as correct English. The key aspects of this theme as they occur in the spoken texts are all thrown up by the two MA sessions, and I therefore begin with a discussion of these in order to provide an overview of the kinds of overt arguments and covert attitudes that emerge across the spoken data, as well as being typical of numerous teachers' discussions of ELF and/or the LFC in which I have participated elsewhere.

The first MA session

This dataset consists of 'gut reaction' responses to ELF collected (with permission) from a group of masters students, all experienced teachers of English, studying for an MA at London University. The first set of comments is taken from the part-time programme, where the students are both NS and NNS and all live and work in the UK. Their comments were made during a seminar with me, their lecturer, following their pre-reading of Jenkins (1998) and their introduction in the seminar to the details of the Lingua Franca Core and its rationale.

- 'Isn't this a lowering of standards, a watering down to suit non-native speakers?' (NNS)
- 'All English will fragment so that nobody understands each other.' (NNS)

- 'We'll all become the same.' (NS)
- 'Students don't want it.' (NS)
- 'Learners will sound odd if they don't use weak forms.' (NS)
- 'If all students learn from a teacher who has her own L1, then the English people learn will gradually deteriorate.' (NS)

These comments provide examples of some of the typical misinterpretations of ELF and the LFC, and in particular, that what is involved is a 'lowering of standards' rather than an acceptance of regional variation and norms based on what NNSs rather than NSs do. Interestingly, while one teacher, an NNS, felt that ELF would result in 'fragmentation', another, an NS, thought it would lead, pronunciation-wise, to uniformity and sameness. The latter teacher seemed to believe that ELF is a single variety, the equivalent, perhaps, of Crystal's World Standard Spoken English—see Chapter 2. This ignores the fact that it is an insistence on RP and standard NS English that has always led to greater (though not by any means total) uniformity, while ELF and the LFC allow for greater diversity (although not fragmentation). This comment, coupled with those about standards and sounding 'odd' (i.e. to NS listeners) indicate these teachers' attachment to NS English norms and their belief that these alone represent good English and, in the case of pronunciation, sounding 'natural' (i.e. not 'odd').

The next comment was sent to me by email from one of the above students the day after the session:

> ... I feel I can't get my head round some of the issues you raised i.e. the watering down of the pronunciation system as it exists to suit NNS communicating with other NNS. I'm a purist! ... (NS)

This was the same NS teacher who had, the day before, expressed the fear that ELF would lead to everyone sounding 'the same'. The interesting point about her follow-up email is not only the confusion it reveals in terms of 'watering down', but also the way she expresses her beliefs. The words 'to suit NNS ... other NNS' suggest an underlying attitude that regards NSs of English, despite the global spread of the language, still to hold proprietary rights over its use. Meanwhile, the description of herself as 'a purist', indicates a belief that NS English, and in particular, RP is 'pure', and that submerged beneath this, is the attitude that it should not be 'tainted' by NNS influence.

The second MA session

These are arguments made by the corresponding full-time cohort of approximately 25 masters students (this time predominantly NNSs from outside the UK as well as a small number of NSs, most of whom work outside the UK), on being introduced to the concepts of ELF and the LFC by a colleague.[15] These students' perceptions were in the main similar to the first group's, although they also diverged to some extent from the general disapproval of ELF revealed by the part time students. Many of their comments were, nevertheless, equally as negative. For example:

- It is desirable for learners to achieve NS proficiency 'for clarity.' (NS)
- 'I think you have to present the model [i.e. NS model]—not necessarily RP.' (Non-British NS)
- 'I totally disagree' [with the LFC] although he subsequently modified it by saying 'It's a good idea, but in reality it wouldn't work because there's so much exposure to English through American TV, films ... .' (NS)
- 'I think we need to set some standard.' (NNS)
- 'It is desirable to achieve a native-like accent.' (NNS from the outer circle)
- 'Everyone would sound the same.' (NS)
- 'Better teachers in Russia [where this student had taught English] had better pronunciation too.' (NS) [Though when asked by the lecturer to define 'better', he was unable to provide any specific examples.]
- 'What if those learners can't communicate because they haven't acquired standard English?' (NNS)
- 'In international business the Lingua Franca [Core] could cause problems.' (NS)

Here we see the same overt beliefs and underlying attitudes to the concept of NNS-led standards (which one teacher equates with having 'no standard'), the same bias in favour of NS English as somehow better ('desirable') and more communicative, and towards those with more native-like ('better') pronunciation as 'better' teachers. Again there is the belief that an ELF approach means that people would all 'sound the same'. One (NS) teacher believed that the LFC could cause problems in international business, which is an odd argument, given that international business is a context where an ELF approach has particular potential (whereas it may disadvantage NSs of English who do not speak other languages and are less adept at accommodating their English in international communication). Again, this comment implies that 'international' is being seen from a national (NS English) perspective and, in turn, an underlying perception that NSs are the owners of English wherever it is spoken.

On the other hand, whereas the previous group's reactions had been unanimously negative, this time there were also some positive comments. This may have been partly because the students not only read the same article on ELF accents (Jenkins 1998) before the seminar, but were also shown a video of a lecture I had given at the British Council, Osaka in July 2003, in which I had presented the LFC in greater detail than was possible in the part-time group's seminar. The outcome may also have been a reflection of the large number of NNS students in the full-time group—some of whom had experienced ELF communication at first hand. The following are representative of the comments made in favour of ELF accents:

- 'I fully agree.' [with the LFC] (NNS)
- 'I totally agree with these ideas.' (NNS)
- 'There's no "perfect" English.' (Non-British NS)
- [In response to the lecturer's question, 'Do you agree?'] 'Yes. It's a relief.' (NNS)

- 'It's part of a person's identity [i.e. the NNS-English accent]—why should you try to strip them of that? You don't necessarily want to strip them of their accent. A person doesn't necessarily want you to strip them of their accent.' (NNS)

Three points are of particular interest: the awareness of the diversity of English implied in the statement that there is no 'perfect' version, the 'relief' on hearing that there could be other goals than 'native-like' pronunciation, and the link made with identity. While not always opposing ELF themselves (although many did), some members of the second seminar group also seemed to have a more sophisticated awareness of possible obstacles to it. For example, one student (NS) argued 'People will judge your English level according to your accent—people think it's an important element', and there was general agreement (among both NSs and NNSs) that a speaker's pronunciation affects perceptions of his/her grammar, lexis and general competence, and that a nearer-NS accent gives the impression that a person is a 'better' speaker of English. One student (NNS) also pointed out that 'It will take a long time to change people's attitude'.

The day after the second seminar, one of the participants made the following points in a lengthy email to my colleague who had taught the class:[16]

> Some classmates said after knowing the idea, they felt a kind of relief and they won't correct their students' pronunciation any more. But I feel we should correct them at the beginning to let them know what the standard should be (either RP or GA) ... when my boyfriend asked me out at first time, he's Korean, I'm Chinese, he said 'would you like /kopi/?' Exactly the same as Dr Jenkins said on the video. I was just struggling to try to understand what he meant, but I didn't make it. Now I understand everything he says. 'Let's go to see a /pilm/' or 'I'll me (*sic*) you in /trapalgar square/.' (NNS)

The first part of this email implies once again an underlying attitude of NS-normativeness, indicated by the belief that NS pronunciation is 'correct' and 'standard', and that whether or not it is a 'relief' to hear that other goals may be acceptable, this does not mean that they have the potential to be 'correct' or 'standard'. The second part of the email involves a typical misconception about the LFC: the belief that it is condoning an 'anything goes' situation, i.e. the transfer of all pronunciation features from the L1 to English. In fact native-like consonants (with a limited number of exceptions and some phonetic flexibility) are an important core feature, because L1 transfer of consonant sounds has been shown repeatedly to cause intelligibility problems in ELF communication. Indeed, among the data examples shown to the seminar participants the day before, the substitution of /f/ with /p/ had specifically been mentioned as problematic. And yet this student seems not to have heard the point (see Bourdieu's comment on how people avoid exposure to information that challenges their existing beliefs, above p. 122). On the other hand, she makes an important point about familiarity with NNS accents, and the way in which this leads to intelligibility, although she does not herself seem aware of the significance of her words or the way in which they support the LFC proposals.

To sum up, the main surface-level arguments against ELF and the LFC proposals that emerge from the two MA seminars are the following:

1 ELF represents a lowering of standards and will lead to the deterioration of English.
2 ELF pronunciation (as contrasted with RP or GA) will lead to uniformity or fragmentation.
3 Students do not want to learn ELF.
4 NNSs will sound unnatural if they do not acquire native-like pronunciation.
5 Native-like English is more intelligible, and NSs of English are the best judges of the intelligibility of NNSs.

In addition, the following arguments were made (if rather less frequently) in favour of ELF and the LFC proposals:

1 There is no such thing as perfect English.
2 ELF will be a relief to learners and teachers.
3 An ELF accent is part of an L2 speaker's identity, which he or she may not wish to lose.

Most of the anti-ELF arguments were also made in the three written texts discussed in the previous section. Meanwhile, in terms of the larger picture, all five arguments are aspects of the over-arching theme in both the MA discussions and the written texts of ELF as a deficient version of ENL.

The participants in the university workshop also shared with the teachers on the MA courses a number of negative beliefs about ELF. On the other hand, unlike them, and like the authors of the written texts, they made no wholly favourable comments about ELF. Many of the negative arguments at the workshop concerned the belief that NS accents are more intelligible than NNS. For example, one participant argued that the distinction between the dentals and interdentals (i.e. between /θ/ /ð/ and both /t/ /d/ and /s/ /z/) is crucial to intelligible English in international settings because he, a native English speaker, would not understand an NNS who said 'I am sinking' when the speaker meant 'I am thinking'. Thus, the participant demonstrated that he was, indeed, aware of this consonant conflation and probably would understand the speaker. More importantly, he demonstrated both that he had no conception of intelligibility in ELF as opposed to ENL or EFL communication, and that, in any case, intelligibility was unlikely to have been the main reason for his antipathy to this NNS consonant substitution: it was more likely to have been related to an underlying pejorative attitude towards NNS English accents.[17]

The main attitudes underlying the MA students' beliefs about ELF and the LFC, as has already been noted, concerned perceptions of NS ownership of

English, and of the superiority (including 'purity') of NS English, along with an underlying prejudice against NNS English, which the teachers attempted to justify with a range of rational arguments. The first three datasets reveal a number of patterns in the beliefs and attitudes of those who provided them. The same patterns emerge in the final two datasets, though here, the recordings mean that prosodic information is available to provide additional support for the analysis and interpretation.

Further analysis of beliefs and attitudes in the spoken data

Two discussions provided the data for analysis in this section. The first took place at the Pronunciation Special Interest Group's Open Forum at the 2001 IATEFL annual conference in Brighton, England. It was recorded, transcribed, and subsequently published (Vaughan-Rees 2001), though the transcript itself was 'tidied up' and prosodic features were not included.[18] The extracts from the discussion have been re-transcribed from the original recording, and in the process, the 'tidying-up' has been 'un-tidied' (though some punctuation has been retained to make the transcripts easier to follow), and prosodic features have been added where relevant. (See Table 5.1 below for the conventions used in the prosodic analysis of these two datasets.)[19]

Approximately 30 people, all to my knowledge teachers of English, and all expert speakers of English according to Rampton's (1990) definition, were present at this discussion, which lasted for approximately 50 minutes. They were seated in a large circle and used a roving microphone. The focus of the session was my book, *The Phonology of English as an International Language* (2000), in which the LFC had first been published in detail. The stated aim of the session was for participants to ask questions about and make comments on the book's proposals for changes in pronunciation teaching in line with the spread of ELF (referred to as EIL in the session).

The second discussion took place during a workshop at a large international conference.[20] The audience of approximately 300 listened to four presentations on ELF and were then invited to ask questions, make comments, and generally engage in discussion with the presenters and chair of the panel. In each case, having listened carefully several times to the recordings, I identified the main ELF-related points made by the various speakers and transcribed them.

Because the first discussion focuses exclusively on ELF pronunciation issues and the second on ELF more broadly, I have presented my analyses of the two separately, although it should be noted that themes overlap both across and within the two datasets. On the other hand, I have not dealt with overt arguments and covert attitudes in separate sections. This is because the content and prosodic analysis is so closely linked that it did not make sense to separate them in the discussion.

X	incomprehensible word
XX	incomprehensible phrase
(they don't believe)	transcriber doubt, guess at word(s) in question
[ ]	transcriber commentary
(.)	pause of less than a second
(3)	approximate length of pause in seconds
sen-	abrupt cut-off (hyphen attached to item preceding cut-off)
:	length (repeated to show greater length)
CAPS	emphatic stress ('I' and acronyms are underlined)
↗	rising pitch (only where particularly noticeable)
↘	falling pitch (only where particularly noticeable)
@	laughter
</SOFT> text </SOFT>	to indicate other modes of speaking

Table 5.1 Transcription conventions for the spoken texts, adapted from Niedzielski and Preston (2000/2003) and VOICE (2003)

The Open Forum LFC session

As I observed earlier, the main anti-ELF themes that emerge from these two datasets have much in common with those of the other three datasets in this section, and with those of the written texts analysed earlier. In the case of the Open Forum, the main overtly-expressed arguments relate to accent status and prestige, confusions over the LFC proposals, and student preferences and aspirations. There is also evidence of ambivalence. On the other hand, three arguments were made in favour of the LFC: that it empowers NNS teachers of English; that accommodation is more important than approximating an NS accent; and that vowel qualities, whether 'non-standard' NS or NNS do not affect intelligibility. Interestingly, these pro-LFC points were made by an NNS teacher from mainland Europe who had been teaching English in Japan for many years (and thus had first-hand experience of ELF communication), a teacher with an Indian accent, a third with a New Zealand, and a fourth with a Scottish accent. No positive contributions of this kind were made either by NS teachers with RP accents, or by expanding circle teachers who had had little or no exposure to other NNS Englishes. Because of the extent of the overlaps across the extracts in the commentary that follows, all nine extracts are presented first before the start of the analysis.

Extract 1 (NNS)

1 … I have two questions. Er (.) the first on is about the SOCial prestige aspect of a
2 standard. Whenever we have a standard, a model er it becomes a model not
3 because some erm:: great guru concocted this somewhere in his (upper) basement,
4 it's because er many people consider this particular (.) er way of speaking
5 prestigious (.) for some reason, er for example er in the days of er British Empire,
6 RP sort of th- was the (cream) (.) er in- nowadays when the sort of politically and

7 economically one of the strongest countries in the world is the United States ALL
8 my Japanese students want to learn American English <LOW KEY> with a
9 few exceptions </LOW KEY> So er w- is there any social er sort of status support
10 for er what you're talking of (1) er sort of social-wise I'm not quite following
11 whether there is any connection any prestige er connected with this er sort of
12 international standard you're talking of.

Extract 2 (NS)
1 ... (XXX) Erm I, I was just going to say I think there's probably two kinds of
2 students erm one- er the kind of student who who finds pronunciation very easy
3 and natural and would (sooner embrace) erm the native speaker ↗iDEAL and
4 another kind of student who (has) much more, much more problems
5 understanding natives who would, who would much prefer to embrace er the
6 English as an international language (kind).

Extract 3 (NNS)
1 I'm [name] from India. Well, if everything else is alright—(say) the grammar
2 or (.) selection of words is alright then no matter whether native speaker is
3 speaking to another native speaker, a NON-native speaker is speaking to anOTHer
4 non-native speaker or a NON-native speaker is speaking to a native speaker, take
5 whatever permutation or combination you like (.) when you meet (.) your (.) you
6 know listener for the first time, you've got to be a little more careful. It applies to
7 all of ↘US you know when native speakers speak to US here in Brighton we
8 expect ↘THEM to l- to speak- to- to take a little ↘TROUBle, to speak a little more
9 ↘FORMally so that we can understand them (.) almost effortlessly and this would
10 apply to us TOO. Unfortunately as of now (1) it's generally a one-way (.)
11 TRAFFic.

Extract 4 (NS)
1 (XX disingenuous) by setting up RP (.) erm as the- it- it's obviously the MODel
2 which people aim at. But in terms of saying this is something we could move
3 aWAY from (1) just looking down the non-CORE pronunciation features which
4 you had on your handout, six out of seven of them are true of ↘ALL varieties of
5 British regional English. So in a sense I don't feel that erm you know s- the
6 argument saying that RP is spoken by such a small number of people, that doesn't seem
7 to me to be terribly important, I mean if if you want to say that NATive we
8 should- we should stop X features of NATive English that's fine, that's an
9 argument we could make. But just setting (it) up as something that's moving away
10 from RP because it's only two per cent or three per cent of the population.

Extract 5 (NS)
1 What are you going to replace- what ↘TEMplate w- yes [inaudible words of
2 another speaker] Yes but (.) but but but the template SOUNDS, the IPA, how how
3 are we going to help people to reSPOND to one another similarly so that there's
4 some resemblance

Extract 6 (NS)
1 XXX I use my New ZEAland vowels when I s- when I attempt ↘RP I expect my
2 Spanish students will use their ↘SPANish vowels when they attempt an
3 internationally intelligible form of ↘ENGlish, they don't ↘HAVE to make an
4 adjustment. We've ALL got our own sets of l- of of local ↘VOWels which we'll carry
5 around till the day we ↘DIE I mean (.) how- however much we want to ↘CHANGE
6 them. But it doesn't ma- it do- it makes NIL difference in terms of
7 ↘intelligiBILity.

Extract 7 (NS)
 1 XXX originally from [British region]21, a non-RP speaker @@ Erm (3) I teach German
 2 students erm and there are certain points er which would be FUNCTional where
 3 they need to distinguish between /æ/ and /e/ <SOFT> Germans confuse short /æ/
 4 and short /e/ all the time </SOFT> that CAN lead to communication breakdown.
 5 Erm there are OTHer points though where one cannot make out a FUNCTional
 6 argument for emphasizing th- learning that particular point of <SOFT> RP
 7 ENGlish </SOFT>. Er but erm there's a psychological factor there. Er er I think I
 8 could say of most of my advanced students they WOULD NOT WISH to
 9 pronounce English with a German- erm uvular or velar ↘ 'r'. They'd like to get
10 rid of that for psychological <LOW KEY> reasons or whatever </LOW KEY>
11 and certain other erm aspects of pronunciation which you cannot claim to have
12 any ↘FUNCTional value and they will still XXX [demonstrates 'red' with uvular
13 'r'] erm (1) but they would WANT to erm orientate themselves to- towards a 'red'
14 [with RP 'r'] pronunciation just to take one particular example. What would you
15 say to to that? Would you a- (2) s- ↘adMIT to to er there BEing these
16 psychological factors which (one needs) to take into account nevertheless
17 <SOFT> in a LOCal REGional (teaching) situation? </SOFT>

Extract 8 (NNS)22
 1 XX Erm I personally found X very uplifting in er:: professor Jenkins's book erm
 2 the one point (refers to) the non-native teacher. At last I've found some
 3 justification for my OWN ↘exISTence @@ XX Well er it used to be that er: a
 4 non-native teacher can not really teach pronunciation and be a model at least er (if
 5 teaching non-native speakers means playing) the tape as the right model. So it
 6 appears that: if my Japanese students have a touch of Russian accent in their
 7 English <LAUGHING> it won't do them too much harm</LAUGHING> (.) er on
 8 the whole. So er it's not only me, all non er native teachers I think get a real sort
 9 of boost of (reaction of) enthusiasm from this book. And secondly for the students
10 as I mentioned earlier, er: it's very reassuring to them that they don't really HAVE
11 to sound native that they can just take a reasonable er comprehensibility (.) model
12 and er: ↘unLESS: they have a particular interest in sounding native then it's up to
13 them. So er: I'd just like to thank you @ er for this.

Extract 9 (NNS)
 1 Erm I had a discussion- (.) er (1) and my first language is German XX. I had a discussion
 2 with some of my adult students er: before I came HERE about er global English and
 3 (.) they're wondering which model they should follow in the pronunciation. And I
 4 told them well very soon I'll be going to the IATEFL conference, I'll learn more
 5 about ↘THAT [others laugh]. And next ↘WEEK when I'm going to face them er and er
 6 I will give them the good ↗NEWS you don't have to worry so mu- about so
 7 much any more, you have to (tr- you have to trouble yourself) these are the
 8 CORE ↘FEATures, well then I know exACTly what they're going to SAY, almost
 9 ALL of them, er they would say no we want to know ↘exACTly <LOW KEY> how
10 we have to pronounce that </LOW KEY>

Status and prestige

Several participants refer to the status of RP and GA accents. Speaker 1, for example, brings up the issue of the potential 'social prestige' of an ELF accent as compared with RP and GA. The added emphasis on the first syllable of 'SOCial' (l. 1) the first time the word occurs, as well as the repetition of the word (three tokens) and the associated words 'prestige' (l. 11), 'prestigious' (l. 5), 'standard' (l. 2), 'status'(l. 9) suggest she has serious concerns that an

ELF speaker's accent would lack 'status support' (l. 9) and 'prestige ... connected [with it]' (l. 11). In expressing these concerns, she does not distinguish between ELF and EFL, implying that she cannot conceive of an NNS accent as being anything other than 'not an NS accent'. For her, then, the accent prestige issue simply involves a basic NS/NNS distinction.[23]

The same view of NS English accents as prestigious underpins the contribution of speaker 2 in his reference to 'the native speaker ideal'. Although he is presenting what he sees as a student perspective, his words reveal an assumption that an NS accent is indeed the 'ideal'. This interpretation gains support from the extra emphasis on the second syllable of 'iDEAL' (l. 3), although there are various possible interpretations of the rising tone on this syllable, and I am not able to make a strong claim in this respect. (And the same assumption seems to underpin the assertion of speaker 4 that RP is 'obviously the model which people aim at'. Again, the strength of the assumption is reinforced by the extra emphasis on the first syllable of 'MODel' (l. 1).) Speaker 5 similarly regards the sounds of RP as 'template SOUNDS' (l. 2), with the extra stress on the words 'SOUNDS' and 'reSPOND' (l. 3) emphasizing her belief that it is the sounds of RP that enable 'people' to retain sufficient similarity to be able to communicate intelligibly. Given that a previous speaker (4) has just pointed out that few NSs have RP accents, it seems that this speaker (like 4 too) uses the word 'people' to mean NNSs specifically, even though the potential problems she sees with the LFC will affect NSs rather than NNSs. A specific example is then provided by speaker 7, who describes how Germans 'confuse' two RP vowel sounds and 'need to distinguish between them' (l. 3) because this 'CAN lead to communication breakdown' (the extra stress on 'can' presumably intended to contrast with the LFC claim that this is not so). Despite the fact that some NS accents also lack a distinction between these two (and other pairs of) RP vowel sounds, and that the speaker himself does not have an RP accent, his belief is that in the case of NNSs such as his German learners of English, they are errors, and that they cause intelligibility problems for listeners. His repetition of the word 'FUNCTional' l. 2, l. 5) in relation to the distinction between these two vowel sounds, both times with extra stress on the first syllable, suggests that—like the previous speakers—he believes that the vowel sounds of RP play a 'functional' role in preserving intelligibility in all communication contexts including ELF (even though he himself does not make use of all of them).

Confusions over the LFC proposals

Moving on to confusions about the nature of ELF pronunciation, several comments reveal these teachers' misconceptions. For example, speaker 2 contrasts ELF with the 'native speaker ideal' (l. 3), and argues that learners who find pronunciation 'very easy and natural' will probably prefer an EFL (i.e. ENL) goal, while those who have 'more problems understanding natives' (ll. 4–5) will probably prefer an ELF goal. Thus, he demonstrates his belief that an ELF accent is simply an easier option and an NS accent a more difficult one. This links with the belief expressed in Text 1 of the written texts that ELF is 'reduced' and 'incomplete' by contrast with NS English.[24] This speaker's use of the word 'natural', even though attributed to learners, suggests that at a subconscious level, he may himself consider NS English accents natural and NNS English accents unnatural.

Extract 4 demonstrates another misconception about the LFC: that it has been proposed merely because RP is used nowadays by very few NSs of English. The speaker argues that most of the LFC non-core features also occur in all regional British accents (thus missing the point that NS accents of any kind are irrelevant to the LFC), and in doing so, he puts extra emphasis and a falling tone (suggesting certainty) on the word 'ALL' (l. 4). He also emphasizes 'core' in the phrase 'non-CORE pronunciation features' (l. 3). This marked pronunciation, taken together with the previous emphasis on 'all', suggests that the speaker believes the non-core features are in fact core—because for him, core-ness should be assessed in relation to NS accents, whether RP or regional. This interpretation seems on first impression to be contradicted by his next comment, 'if you want to say that ... we should stop X features of NATive English ... that's an argument we could make' (ll. 7–9). However, his use of 'if *you* want to say' (i.e. not *he* himself), and the tentativeness when he includes himself ('an argument we *could* make') suggests a lack of enthusiasm for the idea, and one which may itself have been partly responsible for his failure to realize that this *is* in fact the LFC position.

Finally, the speaker of Extract 5 reveals the belief that there has to be some kind of identical 'template' (l. 1) for all learners of English, and the notion that all NNSs need to speak 'similarly' (l. 3). And although she does not actually state it, the implication in her use of the word 'we' ('how are we going to help people') is that she has in mind an NS 'template' She seems not to have grasped the LFC's distinction between core and non-core, and assumes that because the LFC proposals do not entail providing a complete set of (imposed) pronunciation norms, they will prevent NNSs from maintaining common ground. She refers specifically to the 'SOUNDS' (l. 2), where her emphasis indicates the salience of English sounds to her. And yet she appears not to realize that the LFC includes almost all the consonant sounds as well as all the vowel sounds where length contrasts are involved.

Students' preferences and aspirations

Like the first two written texts discussed in the first half of the chapter, some of these spoken extracts contain references to students' preferences for NS accents—and see extract 5 of the next dataset below. For example, speaker 7 discusses a 'psychological factor'(l. 7), arguing that while some features do not cause communication breakdown, there are still 'psychological factors' involved. He illustrates this by focusing specifically and only on the single most stereotypical and stigmatized feature of German English accents, the uvular 'r', and says 'my most advanced students WOULD NOT WISH' (l. 8) to use this variant in their English. The extra emphasis on these three consecutive words indicates his desire to make the point particularly forcefully. In line with the positions taken in the written texts and in some of the studies of ELF attitudes reported in Chapter 4, speaker 7 thus conveys the belief that teachers should defer to learners' wishes for native-like English, whether this is 'for psychological reasons or whatever' (l. 10). Here, the low key of his words contrast with the emphasis on 'would not wish', and indicate a belief that learners' reasons are themselves of little importance: the fact of their existence is in itself sufficient. Even speaker 8, who takes a more positive view of the LFC than many of the others, still believes that the decision is for learners themselves, and that it is for them to decide whether to opt for 'reasonable … comprehensibility' or 'sounding native' (ll. 11–12). On the other hand, she also says that students will find it 'reassuring … that they don't really HAVE to sound native' (ll. 10–11), the stress on 'have' suggesting that until now there was in reality no choice. After the conference, she emailed me to say that she had shared the LFC proposals with her students and that although they liked the acknowledgement of their human right not to sound like an NS of English, they still wanted to try to acquire an RP accent.

Evidence of ambivalence

Finally, the two expanding circle speakers show some ambivalence in their positions on ELF and NNS accents. Speaker 9, a speaker of German English, confidently states that his learners would not be interested in the LFC and would expect him to teach them native-like English ('exACTly how we have to pronounce that', l. 9). When I suggest that his own German English accent rather than RP would be the best model for his learners, he replies:

<LOW KEY> thanks </LOW KEY> @@ that's what I wanted
to hear @@

The low key of 'thanks' and his loud laughter both before and after 'that's what I wanted to hear', suggest embarrassment. His instant reaction (low key 'thanks'), although probably embarrassed, seems to reflect genuine pleasure in receiving praise for his English accent. However, the embarrassment swiftly takes over, he laughs, and makes what appears to be a joke against himself, whether or not there is an element of truth in what he says.

Extracts 1 and 8 (the same speaker) reveal ambivalence more overtly. In extract 1, the speaker expresses her concerns about the social status of an accent not based on RP, whereas in extract 8, she discusses the LFC in more positive terms. However, even here, her 'enthusiasm' is qualified by her comment that her Russian accent 'won't do them [her students] too much harm' (l. 7). As with the German English speaker, her laughter as she speaks suggests a degree of embarrassment concerning her claim that her Russian English accent is an acceptable classroom model. And like his response to my point about his accent, her comment, too, seems to be part joke and part serious. Again, despite her support for the LFC, her contrasting of 'reasonable … comprehensibility' with 'sounding native' l. 11) suggests a belief that the former is a lower achievement than the latter, and having referred to her own Russian accent, it seems that she does not regard herself as 'sounding native'. So although she sees the LFC as 'very uplifting' (l. 1), she seems to have conflicting attitudes towards it. This may link with the issue of identity. Curiously, this speaker is one of a very small minority of participants who touch on identity, despite its being an important element in the LFC proposals and in ELF theory in general. Referring to the LFC's position *vis-à-vis* 'the non-native teacher' (l. 2) she says 'At last I've found some justification for my OWN ↘exISTence @@' (ll. 2–3). The added emphasis and falling tone on the word 'exISTence' indicate how much of a part her accent plays in her identity as a non-native teacher of English—in her very existence in this role, and how, until now, she has felt that she could not be a pronunciation model for her students.

Pro-LFC perspectives

Some striking differences in perspective emerge in the contributions of three speakers, one from the outer circle (extract 3), one from New Zealand (extract 6), one from the expanding circle (although with a certain amount of ambivalence: see the previous section), and one from Scotland (no extract provided). For example, the speaker of extract 3 shows a good deal more confidence about his 'NNS' English than do the expanding circle speakers. He also demonstrates much greater awareness than almost all the other speakers, NNS or NS, of the fact that successful communication involves all parties and that it is not a 'one-way traffic' (ll. 10–11) in which NNSs should make all the efforts to accommodate and be understood by NSs. The added emphasis on 'US' (twice, l. 7), 'THEM' (l. 8), and 'take a little TROUBle' (l. 8) reinforces his point that NSs have equal responsibility for successful communication, and contrasts strikingly with the way in which other contributors such as speaker 7 make assumptions about the single-handed role of NNSs in communication breakdown.

Extract 6, an English NS from New Zealand, is closer in attitude to the Indian English speaker than to the majority of the other (mainly British English) NSs or expanding circle NNSs. His point concerns vowel quality and his belief that different (NS or NNS) qualities do not affect intelligibility, and that in any case we cannot change them. He reinforces his point by placing extra stress (in most cases accompanied by falling tone) in 'New ZEAland vowels' (l. 1), '↘SPANish vowels' (l. 2), 'don't ↘HAVE to' (l. 3), '↘CHANGE' (l. 5), 'NIL difference' (l. 6), and '↘intelligiBILity' (l. 7). Like speaker 8, he also invokes the issue of identity, using emphasis to highlight the link between identity and vowel quality: 'our own sets of … local ↘VOWels which we'll carry around till the day we ↘DIE' (ll. 4–5). The Scottish participant whose contribution is not included in the extracts above, shares the perspective of the Indian and New Zealand speakers. He argues for the use of NNSs in teaching materials in order to demonstrate to NNSs that they can be 'ˢPERfectly intelligible' without an NS accent, and concludes with the words 'the more accents the merrier'.

The ELF workshop²⁵

This session was a workshop at a large international conference. The audience of approximately 300 listened to four presentations on ELF and were then invited to engage in discussion with the presenters. There were five audience contributions in all.²⁶ The first is not included here because it was a short question asking the panel how they saw the implications of ELF for the testing of English, and revealed nothing of the speaker's own perceptions of ELF. The final contribution was a lengthy one and is presented as two extracts (4 and 5) because one of the panel members responded to the point made in extract 4 before the speaker moved on to the issue presented in extract 5. The first part of extract 4 is omitted partly because it was a lengthy preamble to the speaker's main point, and partly because several parts of it are virtually inaudible on the recording. The five extracts reveal many of the same concerns, beliefs, and attitudes about ELF that have already been discussed in relation to the other datasets, both written and spoken. In particular, they demonstrate the belief that NS English is authentic ('real') English, the misconception that ELF is a monolith and interlanguage, along with a strong attachment to NS English norms. This time, because each extract brings up a different main point and overlap is minimal, my discussion takes each extract together with its analysis in turn, though refers forwards and backwards where speakers' points overlap or contrast in interesting ways.

Extract 1

 1 Erm (2) I was interested in erm (1) the description of er English as a lingua franca
 2 because as I understand it, the original lingua franca <LOW KEY> five hundred years
 3 ago or whatever </LOW KEY> the ˢSPEAKers of the lingua ˢFRANCa (1) erm
 4 obviously were not native speakers of the language but they beLIEVED they
 5 were speaking the ˢREAL language of the people they were comMUNicating
 6 with, so for example in North Afri- a North African would use lingua franca with
 7 a French speaker (think) he was speaking ˢFRENCH (2) Isn't there a sort of er-
 8 is this (.) possibility of this developing where: the speakers of (ENGlish as a lingua
 9 franca ˢbeLIEVE they are speaking the ˢREAL English (.) of international (English).
10 I don't know, I mean (is this) an open question, erm do you- do you think
11 ˢTHEN we should- as as [panel member] said earlier we should perhaps when they come
12 to a point they're going to erm have contact with OTHer groups native speaker
13 groups and so on, they'll learn the norms of those groups (.) shouldn't we be
14 teaching them erm: (.) code switching to learn more than one code, so they can
15 code switch erm:: as naturally as WE can code switch in our OWN language?

Two points of particular interest in extract 1 are the speaker's concern that speakers of ELF will believe that they are speaking real English and that these ELF speakers may have difficulty in communicating with other (i.e. NS) groups. Her conviction that ELF speakers are not speaking real English is emphasized by the extra stress on 'ˢbeLIEVE' (l. 9) and 'ˢREAL English' (l. 9) and the certainty and finality conveyed in the falling tone in each case.

She seems not to have understood the notion of ELF and to share the belief that underpins many of the writings I discussed in Chapters 1 and 2, that only NS English can be considered 'real' English. Her second point reinforces this interpretation. She argues that ELF speakers will have problems communicating 'with OTHer groups' (l. 12), which she immediately qualifies as 'native speaker groups' (ll. 12–13), and that for this purpose they need to be taught code-switching. Again, this demonstrates a lack of understanding of ELF, and presents a curious view of code-switching as something that comes naturally to (predominantly) monolingual NSs of English ('as WE can code switch in our OWN language' l. 15) but that needs teaching to NNSs of English. The evidence, by contrast, suggests that the opposite is the case, and that code-switching (itself part of accommodation) comes naturally to NNSs of English and is the norm in ELF communication, whereas NSs engaging in intercultural communication expect the adjustments to be made by their NNS interlocutors ('a one-way traffic' as speaker 3 in the previous dataset described it).

Extract 2
1 Erm you've been talking about erm English as an international language as if it's
2 one monolithic ↘THING (1) erm I just wanted to ask whether you think what in
3 ↘FACT will happen if we have several erm REGional Englishes like erm ASian
4 English which XX Hong Kong XX and things and African English which XX XX
5 erm I was wan- wanting to know first if (you think that) matters in fact what
6 would happen and secondly erm if it does happen (.) does this mean that those
7 different ↘ENGlishes will be mutually comprehensible or (NOT and if they're
8 ↘NOT do (you in fact) do we in fact need some sort of standard (middle of the
9 road) if you like that EVeryone CAN ↘reFER to (I mean if) an example is erm
10 someone was telling me that in one of the ↘TALKS erm a gentleman from I think
11 Nigeria was asking a question to erm a presenter who was NOT a native speaker
12 of English and this native speaker (told me he had to) interpret, so, I mean do we
13 in fact need some sort of CENTral (.) I don't know, mutually c- you know code
14 that everyone will understand (this is the) question.

Extract 2 conveys a similar attitude to NS and NNS English. The speaker begins by (wrongly) assuming that ELF is 'one monolithic ↘THING' (l. 2), the use of the word 'thing' together with its extra stress and falling tone conveying a somewhat negative orientation towards ELF. She goes on to consider the possibility that ELF will develop into 'mutually incomprehensible' varieties (l. 7), and to ask the panel whether, in this case, there would be a need for 'some sort of standard'. However, from the anecdote she subsequently tells, in which an NS of English interpreted the words of one NNS for an NNS from a different L1 (ll. 10–12), it seems that by a 'standard (middle of the road) ... that EVeryone CAN ↘reFER to (ll. 8–9)', and later 'some sort of CENTral [English]' (l. 13), she has an NS variety in mind. This in turn implies the belief that NS English is more widely intelligible and 'central' than NNS varieties in any communication context. Meanwhile, it ignores the potential for ELF to develop its own systematic similarities as a result of levelling out processes that occur naturally through contact.

Extract 3
1 Just X (off of) my erm Microsoft WORD program on the ↘corRECTion level (.)
2 they HAVE things like Australian English, Hong Kong (English) I've never had
3 time to ↘LOOK at it but I've often thought <HIGH KEY> I WONder what they
4 do DIFFerently </HIGH KEY> [laughter] This- I don't think that they see it as a-
5 you know a definition of lingua franca but it ↘DOES ↘exIST on this ↘WRITTen
6 level which I thought was quite ↘INTeresting. Erm (.) coming back to YESterday
7 erm I was quite FRIGHTened when you said well it doesn't matter about the third
8 person 's' (you can) leave that out, it doesn't affect communication. And I'm
9 (definitely) ↘WORRied and I'm still worried about the ↘WRITTen level whilst
10 acknowledging that probably eighty per cent of all students of English as a foreign
11 language never actually write it <LOW KEY> very much </LOW KEY> but erm
12 I just cannot imagine doing an exam where if you LEAVE off the 's' in the third
13 person you still get a mark [laughter]

Extract 3 is more concerned with written English. The speaker again approaches the issue from a standard NS English perspective. This is implicit in her assumption that developments in English grammar can only be NS-led, and that NNS features such as 'LEAVE[(i)ng] off the 's' in the third person', are by definition ungrammatical and could not conceivably 'still get a mark' in an exam (ll. 12–13). There is no suggestion that this speaker understands the link between contact and language change or between identity and language change. Instead, she expresses a fear that students will stop conforming to NS norms, particularly written: 'I was quite FRIGHTened' (l. 7), 'and I'm (definitely) ↘WORRied and I'm still worried about the ↘WRITTen level' (l. 9)

Extract 4
1 ..... XX to get more to the point though, I think that (.) er what's interesting is that
2 is that no English teacher (.) er in in the history of English language teaching or
3 language teaching in general has ever been anything but an ↘ELFer, I mean
4 obviously er ↘ALL teachers of language caretake, there is a phrase CAREtake
5 which has been used for some time erm and of course one NEVer speaks to one's
6 students in the way that one speaks to one's mates down the ↘PUB, I mean one is
7 ELFing all the time so (.) teachers are teachers are skilled practitioners of of of
8 lingua franca at least XX the student exchanges they're they're using well correct
9 models but they're they are ELFing if you like.

Extract 4 demonstrates the same inability that characterizes the previous three extracts to understand the concept of ELF. In this case, the speaker's misinterpretation centres on his belief that ELF is a question of language grading, or 'caretaking', rather than language variety. This is clear in his claim about teachers as 'ELFers': 'no English teacher ... has ever been anything but an ↘ELFer' (ll. 2–3) because '↘ALL teachers of language caretake' (l. 4), his point being reinforced prosodically by the extra stress and falling tone on '↘ELFer' and '↘ALL'. He goes on to argue that 'teachers are skilled practitioners of ... lingua franca' when they communicate with their students (ll. 7–8). Thus, ELF speakers, according to this view, are NNS students and their NS teachers.[27] The NS teachers, however, are 'using ... correct models' at the same time as 'they are ELFing' (ll. 8–9), whereas the same is not said of the students. In other words, the speaker sees ELF as grounded in NS English, whether 'skilled' and 'correct' when spoken by (NS?) teachers or, presumably, not when spoken by learners. By contrast, he does not consider the possibility that learners can become proficient ELF speakers or, indeed, that such people exist.

Extract 5
 1 what I'm talking about is a continuum I think, a continuum, a sort of modification
 2 of one's language, you're talking about (.) the fact that that ELF is a is a
 3 requirement of communication between between people who who work who
 4 (work in a in a state) of interlanguage. Now I haven't I've not heard anyone talk
 5 about interlanguage yet. What's the difference between ELF and interlanguage?
 6 And that (sort of problem), I know that (we're in a) stage of ELFing but until we
 7 describe clearly the difference between ELF and INTerlanguage, you see I mean
 8 can we send our students off down XX (interlanguage) and pat them on the back
 9 and say (they're all) ELFing and it's all fine. I mean I I I don't- I don't
 10 understand in in the context (that I'VE taught professionally) I don't come across
 11 these students who are who are happy with with what one (can I) call
 12 ↘deFECTive English or defective production, I mean ALL:: production is
 13 defective <SOFT> of course, it's a continuum </SOFT> but I don't find I don't
 14 find a great amount of the students- I find the students want to be correct, erm I'm
 15 not saying that's right or wrong, I find that's what students ↘WANT.

In his second contribution (extract 5), the speaker expands on his original misconception, arguing that ELF as it has been discussed hitherto is no different from interlanguage (although he does not specify whether he means both the type of ELF that he claims is spoken by teachers, or only that spoken by students). The belief is evidently one that he holds strongly as he repeats the word 'interlanguage' four times. On the other hand, his words 'until we describe clearly the difference between ELF and INTerlanguage' (ll. 6–7) suggest that he also believes it may ultimately be possible to distinguish between ELF and interlanguage. However, in view of his comment on correctness in extract 4, along with his firm belief that ELF according to its current definition and descriptions is '↘deFECTive English or defective production' (extract 5, l. 12), it is likely that the only version of ELF that he would find acceptable is the kind spoken by the 'successful users of English' described in written Text 3 above: in other words, barely distinguishable from ENL.

   Like others in this and the previous dataset, this speaker also refers to what students want: 'I don't come across these students who are … happy with … '↘deFECTive English or defective production', by which he means ELF—see above. Instead, he argues, 'I find the students want to be correct … that's what students ↘WANT' (ll. 14–15), the added emphasis and implied certainty/finality of the falling tone on 'want' suggesting that he believes he should defer to his students' wishes in this respect. Although he disassociates himself from his students' putative views ('erm I'm not saying that's right or wrong' ll.14–15), his unqualified use of the word 'correct' again indicates again that, like the students of his description, he holds the view that correct English is ENL. This being so, his comment that 'ALL:: production is defective' (which

I take to mean NS as well as NNS), followed by the much softer 'of course, it's a continuum' brings us back to the speaker's two kinds of ELF in extract 4. On the one hand, he seems to be saying, NS speech—as demonstrated by NS corpora of so-called 'real English'—is ungrammatical in respect of written English. On the other hand, the length and loudness of the word 'ALL::' contrasts strikingly with the softness of 'of course, it's a continuum', and suggests a meaning contrast too: that in his view, the 'defectiveness' of NS English is of a different order from that of NNS English, echoing his belief that the ELF of NS teachers is 'correct' English and the ELF of NNSs is not. In other words, he considers that NSs have the 'right' to depart from the written standard in their speech, but considers such departures by NNSs to be signs of deficiency. Thus, he implies, it is possible to talk, as collectors of ENL corpora often do, of the grammar of spoken NS English, but it is not possible to talk of the grammar of spoken ELF, even though both kinds of spoken English are characterized by regularities.

Concluding comments on the attitudes and beliefs revealed in the spoken data

The various comments that form the spoken texts in this section, like the written texts in the previous section, demonstrate a number of things: how difficult these teachers, both NNS and NS, find the concept of ELF in general and ELF accents (particularly the notions of core and non-core) specifically; how closely and instinctively they identify with an NS norm (usually RP or GA in terms of accents); how reluctant they are to disassociate notions of correctness from 'nativeness' and to assess intelligibility and acceptability from anything but a NS standpoint; and how, intuitively, they regard 'standard' NS English as being more widely understood than other varieties regardless of the context of use. These teachers' responses, like those who wrote the texts analysed in the first half of the chapter, demonstrate the extent to which the ELF proposals are liable to be misinterpreted. They also demonstrate both the complexity of the attitudes involved, their interplay with overt beliefs, and the ways in which identity in English is inextricably bound up with language attitudes.

As I pointed out earlier, it seems that when standard NS English is called into question, what is being questioned, as far as NNS teachers are concerned, is the value of having invested their lifetime in working towards a goal that they have always understood to represent excellence. This in turn means that their identities as teachers, which have always depended on achieving this goal, are threatened. Thus, even if at the rational level they may be able to see the value of an ELF approach in which they appropriate English to serve their own purposes and promote their own identities, at the deeper level, this involves too great a psychological leap of faith. So they avoid arguments that support an ELF perspective, and instead seek arguments that support them in maintaining their positive orientation towards the prevailing ENL status quo, and their negative orientation towards non-native-like English *tout court*.

In Chapter 2, I demonstrated how the prevailing 'ethos' in much of the ELT and applied and sociolinguistic literature[28] is one of misinterpretation of and negativity towards the concept of ELF in theory and towards NNS varieties of English in practice. It would not be at all surprising, then, if the perspective found in the literature should act to reinforce practising English language teachers' generally conservative orientations towards the English language and promote the kinds of misconceptions discussed in Chapter 1 and found in the analysis of the written texts earlier in this chapter. Nor can we ignore the potential for NS teachers' attitudes towards NNS English, such as those revealed above in the ELF workshop, to exert a negative influence on NNS teachers' perceptions of themselves. Further possible influences on NNS teachers' language attitudes and beliefs are discussed in the final chapter, But for now, having established the complexity and deep-seatedness of attitudes towards NNS English and the fact that identity is crucially involved, we move on to the questionnaire study of Chapter 6 and the interview study of Chapter 7. In the first, we explore what it is about NNS accents that promotes such negativity among teachers of English, and in the second, investigate in greater depth the role played by identity.

Notes

1 This point is made by, for example, Derwing (2003), Giles (1998), and Garrett *et al.* (2003).

2 This was originally Kachru's term to label those who, like Quirk, regard the Englishes of the outer circle as fossilized interlanguages. (See Kachru 1991.)

3 The three authors also represent a wide range of ELT experience. Kuo is a secondary school teacher of English in Taiwan, who was studying in the UK at the time she wrote her article. Prodromou, who grew up in the UK and works in Greece, is both an ELT teacher/teacher trainer and an author, primarily of English teaching materials. Sobkowiak is an academic who also publishes phonetics materials for Polish learners and teachers of English.

4 Seidlhofer (personal communication) has more recently begun referring to exonormative and endonormative orientations to ELF as, respectively, 'etic' and 'emic'. Suzuki (2006) calls the former 'sugarcoated EIL'.

5 I also carried out a key word analysis of the three texts using *Wordsmith Tools* (Scott 1998/2003). This revealed that the term 'native' (including 'non-native') was key in all three texts, occurring in second place in Text 1, fourth place in Text 2, and first place in Text 3, and demonstrates the salience of the native/non-native distinction to all three authors.

6 The LFC proposals relegate certain (but by no means all) features of NS English pronunciation (e.g. weak forms and pitch movement) to the status

of 'non-core', not only because they emerged from the empirical research as unnecessary for intelligibility in ELF communication, but also because they seemed to be unteachable in the sense that learning does not result from classroom teaching. However, the point was also made that with sufficient exposure to NS English pronunciation outside the classroom, such features could be acquired. (See Jenkins 2000.)

7 It is not clear why the author believes this to be a paradox, as he does not clarify the point in his text.

8 To be precise, 'successful non-native' occurs 10 times, 'successful user/users' 14 times, 'successful bilingual' 17 times, near native/native-like 15 times, and 'students' aspirations' or similar 7 times.

9 Although the author tones down his point here by using the modal form 'may', note that earlier in the article, he had expressed this more strongly as 'it is implausible that ...', which seems more in keeping with the attitude towards ELF that emerges from the article as a whole.

10 In relation to aspirations, see Kumaravadivelu for a discussion of the phenomenon of 'self-marginalization' and the way in which 'the center ... perpetuates its dominance by exploiting the practice of self-marginalization on the part of the subaltern' (2003: 548).

11 The term 'texts' is used loosely in relation to the spoken data, as two of the datasets were in the form of field notes rather than transcriptions, and a third was partially transcribed.

12 The second masters seminar was recorded by my colleague, and I transcribed selected passages shortly afterwards. However the recording was not available subsequently, which meant that I was unable to add prosodic features to my transcription.

13 Interactional sociolinguistics and the newer discipline of sociolinguistic ethnography overlap considerably in the way they approach the analysis of prosodic features (although not necessarily in their reasons for conducting the analysis in the first place; see Gumperz 1999 and Rampton 2006).

14 It is difficult to make any generalizations about rising and falling tones even within a single NS English speaker for all contexts of use, let alone across diverse groups of NS and NNS English speakers. (See Jenkins 2000.) For this reason, I pay greater attention to emphatic stress (itself signalled variously by extra syllable length, loudness, pitch change of any kind, and a greater degree of articulation) along with pausing, as more reliable indicators of speaker meaning. (See also the comments made in footnote 19 below and in Chapter 7 footnote 13 about the difficulty of interpreting prosodic features.)

15 The students gave my colleague permission to record the session and me to publish their discussion.

16 The student gave her permission for me to read the email and reproduce it in this book.

17 This is reminiscent of the caller to the Oprah Winfrey show who claimed that when Black people pronounce the word 'ask' as 'aks', it gives the sentence an entirely different meaning. To this, Oprah Winfrey replied: 'Why does it give it a different meaning if you know what they're saying?' (quoted in Milroy and Milroy 1999: 152–3).

18 The original published transcript (Vaughan-Rees 2001) provides the names of those participants who were known to the original transcriber. However, I have not included these names in my own transcripts. The reason is that while permission to record and publish a transcript of the session was given to the original transcriber by the participants, it is not feasible for me, five years later, to seek their permission to re-publish. As there is already a transcript in the public domain, there would seem to be no ethical issues involved in republishing parts of it (albeit in an 'untidy' version and with prosodic details added). On the other hand, I did not feel this would extend to republishing the names of those involved, hence, I refer to speakers, as in the previous spoken datasets, as 'NS' and 'NNS'. In this respect, I am well aware that the term 'NNS' is contentious, particularly for those participants who speak outer circle Englishes, who would better be described as NSs of their variety of English. Despite the reality of the 'NS'/'NNS' distinction to many who contributed to my data, I believe it would be preferable to stop using these terms altogether in favour of alternatives such as 'bilingual' or 'expert' speaker. (See Jenkins 2000: 10–11; Rampton 1990.)

19 Although I have included all the most salient rising and falling pitch movements on the transcripts, I am cautious about making interpretative claims about them, and only attempt to interpret those where, having listened repeatedly to the recording and worked at length on the transcript, I am reasonably confident about my interpretation. (See also the more general comment about prosodic analysis in footnote 14 above.)

20 To ensure the anonymity of those who participated in the discussion, I have not provided any details of the conference or the names of the workshop presenters.

21 The region was not named in the original transcript so for ethical reasons I have omitted it from mine.

22 Extracts 1 and 8 are the same speaker.

23 These concerns about the possible lack of prestige of ELF accents expressed by the speaker of Extract 1, while less strongly articulated, are reminiscent of Scheuer's perception that ELF involves teaching NNSs only sufficient pronunciation to be understood, but not to be taken seriously—see p. 13 above.

24 The belief that ELF represents some kind of 'reduced' English was also articulated in the written texts, and continues to be shared by many others who have not understood the notion of ELF, NS, and NNS alike. Recently, for example, Maley has argued in a short article that contains many similarly unwarranted assertions about ELF that it 'presupposes

that learners of English would buy into the idea of a reduced version of English' (2006: 5).

25 See p. 130 above for the prosodic transcription conventions used in these extracts.

26 Although the panel consisted of two NNSs of English and two NSs, and the audience was made up of both NNSs and NSs, all the audience comments came from NSs.

27 Although the speaker does not specifically refer to NS teachers, his point that teachers do not speak to their students in the same way that they speak to their 'mates down the pub' implies that he has NS teachers in mind.

28 See Chapter 2 for a discussion of literature promoting NS English over NNS both overtly and covertly, as well as the first half of this chapter for a close discussion of three selected texts.

6

ELF accent attitudes elicited

In the previous chapter, we saw that the reality of the spread of ELF seems so far not to have led to a change of attitude among ELT professionals towards the English language. Instead, there is a tendency to cling to an older notion of the need for conformity to NS norms, which continue to represent authentic English and self-evidently to bring with them guarantees of intelligibility and correctness. ELF, by contrast, is synonymous with an older notion of non-native English as deficient in so far as it is not 'native-like'. There are thus two sides to the rejection of ELF: on the one hand, a deeply entrenched attachment to NS English (and therefore to traditional EFL, whose ultimate goal is, after all, ENL), and on the other hand, an equally deeply entrenched prejudice against NNS English, represented in this case by ELF. In order to assess the feasibility of ELF, we need, therefore, to find out more about this attachment and prejudice by eliciting the attitudes towards and beliefs about NNS and NS English that underpin them.

To this end, we shift in Chapter 6 from observed to elicited data in order to establish more comprehensive evidence of attitude to ELF among teachers. The questionnaire study described here explores teachers' beliefs about and attitudes towards English, and specifically English accents, on a larger scale than was possible in the study of texts. My aim in conducting the questionnaire study was to find out in what ways and to what extent the kinds of beliefs and attitudes that typically emerge in written and spoken discussions of ELF (as in the two groups of data analysed in the previous chapter) would be replicated when teachers were given the opportunity to voice their thoughts privately and (if they so chose) completely anonymously. I was also particularly interested in exploring the issue of accent stereotypes: whether some NNS English accents were more stigmatized than others, and whether the degree of stigmatization related entirely to an accent's distance from NS English, or whether other factors were involved. The findings of the questionnaire study, I anticipated, would cast further light on the potential for NNS English accents, relative to each other and to NS English accents, to be accepted at some future stage as legitimate ELF norms in international communication and even as role models in English language teaching.

The methods used in the study draw on folk linguistics. In Chapter 3, we explored previous language attitudes research, much of which was grounded in social psychology, and considered the differences between indirect social-psychological approaches such as the MGT, and the direct approaches used by folk linguists. The value of a direct approach is that it looks beyond the attitudinal responses elicited in the social-psychological language attitudes research to 'the overt categories and definitions speakers have of ... linguistic matters' (Hartley and Preston 1999), and to their 'strongly-held positions about language and its repercussions in communities' (Niedzielski and Preston 2000/2003: 323). As Niedzielski and Preston point out, '[e]verybody is a folk, and the nonspecialist views of topics which touch the lives of all citizens are worth knowing for their bearing on public life in general, on education in particular, and, most specifically, on the regard in which the prejudiced against are held' (ibid.). These are precisely the phenomena that need to be investigated *vis-à-vis* ELF if its researchers are to be in a position to understand the responses to it and to attempt to predict its likely trajectory.

Perceptual dialectology, a branch of folk linguistics, aims to reveal people's (the folk's) beliefs about different language varieties by means of exploring how they overtly categorize and judge those varieties. Whereas MGT/VGT procedures require informants to listen to and rate 'anonymous' speech samples, perceptual dialectology typically involves rating the language varieties of specified regions (for, for example, correctness and pleasantness), ranking such language varieties, and labelling maps according to (the respondent's) perceptions of language variety boundaries and/or of the perceived qualities of language varieties spoken in different regions.[1] As Lindemann points out, 'such analysis provides much more information on *why* community members react as they do to different varieties, what aspects of varieties are salient for them and why, and the degree to which beliefs are shared in a community' (2005: 189; emphasis in original). It is for these reasons that I selected perceptual dialectology procedures for my own questionnaire. In addition, I hoped that the kinds of information these procedures elicited would help explain the findings, *vis-à-vis* ELF attitudes and beliefs, of the spoken and written text studies.

Although it may at first sight seem incongruous to use data-gathering procedures that were devised to investigate the language beliefs of non-specialists, 'the folk', teachers of English are not infrequently ill informed about linguistic theory and description. In any case, 'folk', as Preston is at pains to point out, is a relative category, defined as non-specialist in relation to particular areas of knowledge and expertise. In this case, then, English language teachers may well be the folk in relation to linguistics. In addition, language teachers as a profession tend to hold the same kinds of prescriptive views of correctness and acceptability as the general population. That is, their view of 'correct' and 'acceptable' English is often the one that they acquired during their own schooldays and that was further endorsed in their pre-service teacher training.[2] This means that if new evidence is later shown to them, they may hold on to the traditional perspective of their earlier experience and reject the new. And as Niedzielski and Preston point out, even well-known authors of texts on the English language, such as Fromkin and Rodman, write on 'standard' English in a way that is 'much closer to a folk linguistic description of a standard as their own prejudices peek through' (2000/2003: 42). Thus, it seems that only those linguists whose work is at the descriptive end of English can be entirely excluded from 'the folk'.

A further point is that there are, in any case, good reasons for extending perceptual dialectology to the educational domain, and in this respect, I am not the first to do so. In their major investigation of language attitudes in Wales, Garrett *et al.* (2003) used a range of procedures, some drawn from perceptual dialectology, to explore the beliefs and attitudes of both teachers and teenage school students. While teachers are not 'the folk' in the non-specialist sense, as Garrett *et al.* point out, the educational domain needs exploring in these kinds of ways because it is 'a context in which language attitudes can have a considerable impact on life-opportunities' (2003: 19). As far as TESOL is concerned, English language teachers are the obvious starting point to find out more about the kinds of attitudes towards and beliefs about English accents that are being conveyed to the general populations in the education systems of many countries. Insights into teachers' attitudes to language spread and change in general, and to ELF accents in particular, may provide information not only about the stigmatization of NNS English accents and possible discrimination against their users, but also about how these can be addressed through education systems.

Turning to the study itself, I selected a questionnaire format as the most appropriate one because it provided the most efficient means of eliciting the kinds of information I was seeking through perceptual dialectology tasks. On the practical side, it enabled me to collect information from a large number of participants across a wide geographical spread and, by means of enlisting the help of colleagues in various parts of the world, could be administered in my absence. A questionnaire also has the advantage that participants can choose whether or not they remain anonymous, which is an especially important consideration when private and possibly sensitive attitudes and beliefs are being sought. Even in an anonymous 'pencil-and-paper' task, however, we cannot entirely discount the possibility that some respondents may want to present themselves in a particular light to the researcher and, as a result, may not answer honestly. (See Garrett *et al.* 2003: 8.) An MGT format, of course, avoids this risk (in so far as informants genuinely believe that they are rating individual speakers rather than—via their language—the social groups that they represent). Nevertheless, for the reasons discussed in Chapter 3, I prefer a direct perceptual dialectology approach, and consider that with all the safeguards put in place, the risk of non-truthful answers to my questionnaire was minimal. And the fact that the majority of respondents included their name and email address, both of which were optional, indicated that they were happy for me to contact them to follow up their responses,[3] and were therefore likely to have responded honestly in the first place.

The questionnaire design

The questionnaire (see Appendix, pp. 190–3) was designed to enable me to find out how teachers perceived ELF accents relative to NS English accents: whether they regarded ELF accents as inferior, inauthentic, deficient 'NNS' accents, or as legitimate English accents for lingua franca communication. To this end, specific questions asked respondents to select and rank the five English accents that they considered to be the best in the whole world context, to comment on ten specified NNS and NS accents and on any others with which they were familiar, and to rate the ten specified accents for correctness, pleasantness, and international acceptability. A secondary aim was to explore the respondents' willingness to evaluate accents with which they were unfamiliar, hence on the basis of stereotypical beliefs, and for this reason a familiarity scale was included in the rating task.

Six expanding circle countries—Brazil, China, Germany, Japan, Spain, and Sweden—were specifically named in two of the questionnaire tasks. These countries were selected in order to provide a spread across the three main ELF areas—Europe, East Asia, and Latin America—and within these larger areas, a range of mother tongue influences on speakers' English accents. Three inner circle and one outer circle regions were also specified. The inner circle regions were the UK, the USA,[4] and Australia—the first two because they are widely held to provide 'standard' English accent varieties (RP and GA), and the third as an NS country whose accent still tends to be considered non-standard. I was interested not only in finding out whether respondents perceived RP and GA as 'better', more 'correct', and so on, than ELF accents, but also whether the same was true of the non-standard Australian English accent. In other words, was the issue, for the respondents, simply one of native versus non-native? By the same token, the outer circle country was included in order to provide further insight into the question of whether pejorative attitudes towards ELF are part of a more general negative orientation to all NNS Englishes. For this purpose, India was selected because respondents were likely to have some familiarity with this well-established, nativized English.

The first part of the questionnaire asked for personal information, although making clear from the start that all details would be confidential and that the respondents' anonymity would be protected at all times. As mentioned earlier, they were given the option of providing their names and (if they were willing to be contacted for further discussion) their email addresses. Other information required in this part of the questionnaire was their sex, approximate age, country of birth, country of current residence, mother tongue, other languages, total number of years teaching English, and where/how long in each country.

Turning to the questions themselves, questions one and two related to the world map that accompanied the questionnaire. Question 1 asked for comments on the ten pre-selected accents shown on the map (numbered from left to right), while question two required respondents to label and comment on the English accents of any other countries with which they were familiar. These map questions were placed before the rating task 'so that [respondents'] free-response answers would not be influenced by the more overtly evaluative nature of the country-rating task' (Lindemann 2005: 191). The map as a whole was provided not only for the map labelling task (question two), but also to emphasize respondents' complete freedom of choice as to which accents they selected in that question and in their final comments (question five), as well as acting as an *aide memoire* for these questions and for question three, the ranking task.

The map included country boundaries and a key to the ten countries named in question one. Names and regional boundaries are by definition redundant in studies where respondents are required to draw and label perceived speech boundaries within their own country (as in Preston's US studies reported in Niedzielski and Preston 2000/2003). Such a task is not feasible, however, on a world scale where English accents are, in any case, already differentiated from each other on the basis of L1 influence. In this case, it is more useful for ELF research to learn about perceptions of accents according to pre-existing boundaries, i.e. countries. And in this respect, it is unlikely that respondents will have sufficient geographical knowledge to recognize the countries they are being asked specifically about. This was clear in my exploratory study where I provided boundaries but no names, and was asked by the respondents to run through the names with them. Likewise, in a similar type of study, Lindemann (2005) originally provided a world map with country boundaries but not names (in order to leave space for respondents to write comments on the map). After the first thirty questionnaires had been returned, a number with mistakes over country locations, she began distributing a separate political map containing country names with her questionnaire. I chose not to do this, hoping that the key to the ten countries specified in the first question would facilitate the correct identification of other countries in question 2, the map-labelling task. But as an additional safeguard, I asked respondents to include the country name with each label, so that it would not be problematic if they made a geographical error.

Question 3 asked respondents to select and rank the five English accents that in their view are the best. Again, this question was placed before the rating question so that they would not be influenced by the latter's more obviously evaluative nature. They were again asked to refer to the world map, emphasizing their freedom to choose from the full range of the world's English accents. The question itself aimed to explore a number of issues, for example, how clearly respondents were able to identify a hierarchy of English accents at all, whether the highest-ranking were NS English accents, and how far the rankings corresponded with the descriptive comments made in response to questions one and two, and tallied with their subsequent ratings in question four.

The fourth question asked respondents to rate the ten specified accents for correctness, acceptability for international communication, pleasantness, and according to their familiarity with each one. Whereas the earlier questions referred to 'English accents', this question referred to 'the English accent of a competent *speaker*' in an attempt to disassociate the term 'correctness' from notions of learners of English and interlanguage rather than proficient speakers and language variety. Respondents were required to indicate the degree of correctness/incorrectness/etc. on a six-point scale. Some researchers have used ten- or four-point scales in this kind of rating task, while in other kinds of task there is a tendency to prefer an odd number of scale points (for example, when respondents are being asked to indicate their level of agreement or disagreement with a series of statements). However, my preference for an even number was intended to force respondents to evaluate each accent either positively or negatively and prevent them from adopting a neutral position, as had happened frequently in the exploratory study. If respondents were genuinely unable, for whatever reason, to signal a positive or negative judgement for any country, they still had the option of not completing that particular scale.

My choice of precisely six points was motivated by the wish to provide a 'strong', 'medium', and 'slight' category in both the positive and negative 'half' of each scale. In every case, the positive category was on the left-hand side and the negative on the right-hand side. Although researchers often vary the position of the positive and negative poles to avoid the risk of obtaining set responses to all variables under investigation, I decided that the risk of respondents' not noticing that I had done so was greater, particularly as I would not be there in person to point this out. Meanwhile, I chose to go from 1 = positive to 6 = negative rather than the other way round. This was because the informants had just completed the ranking task where number 1 had represented the 'best' English accent, and I was again concerned that some would not notice if I reversed the numerical meanings in the next question. And even if they did not conflate the different numbering systems in the two tasks, there was still a sense in which number 1 might, after the ranking task, have a psychological reality for them as 'best' and distort their responses.

The four scales were selected on the basis of previous research into language attitudes and beliefs, and in this respect, correctness was particularly important. Preston (1996: 54) points out, with reference to some of his own studies of US perceptions of regional US varieties, that 'the notion of language correctness plays a major role in the folk awareness of the identity of regional varieties of US English' and that 'respondents do not hesitate rating areas of the United States for language 'correctness' when asked to do so'. In Preston's view, 'correctness may be the most powerful contributor to awareness in American English' (ibid; and see Preston 2002; Niedzielsky and Preston 2000/2003 for further discussions of the importance of correctness in this respect). There was, then, every reason to assume that correctness would loom large in perceptions of NNS English accents, particularly when the evaluators were themselves teachers.

The aim of the acceptability scale was to find out whether respondents had any concept of ELF accents as more acceptable than NS English accents in international communication contexts. If this was so, then I would expect them to rate UK and US English lower on this scale than on the other scales. On the other hand, if they shared the widespread view that international communication largely involves using British or American English internationally, then they would rate the NNS accents high on this scale too. As far as ELF accents are concerned, the acceptability ratings would demonstrate whether or not respondents were assessing international acceptability as a separate component from correctness. That is, they may perceive ELF accents as acceptable in the sense of 'tolerated' in contexts where such accents are the most frequent, but without regarding them as acceptable in the sense of 'correct'. In other words, they would still perceive ELF as deficient rather than legitimate.

The pleasantness scale was selected because previous research (for example, Trudgill and Giles 1978; Giles and Niedzielski 1998) has demonstrated links between judgements of the intrinsic pleasantness or unpleasantness of accents and social evaluations. That is, it has shown that judgements of pleasantness are socially constructed. I was interested in finding out how far this applies to NNS accents, especially when being evaluated by other NNSs (including the same L1 group), and whether the comments made in question one reflected the scale point judgements in question four.

As mentioned earlier, I included a familiarity scale in order to find out whether or not respondents would be willing to make judgements even if they had little familiarity with an accent, and thus on the basis of preconceptions. I also hoped that the inclusion of this dimension would encourage respondents to 'have a go' at the other three dimensions even if they did not have much experience of an accent, as they would have the 'security' of being able to point out their limited exposure on the familiarity scale.

Finally, I thought long and hard about whether to include an intelligibility scale and decided not to do so. One reason for excluding it was that intelligibility is less amenable to 'general' perceptions than correctness, acceptability and pleasantness. In other words, respondents who had only very limited familiarity with an accent may have a general impression of its correctness, acceptability, and pleasantness. By contrast, because intelligibility is contingent on a specific speech context (be it interaction, a film, or whatever), respondents who had limited familiarity with an accent might rate its intelligibility according to a single 'concrete' experience. Equally importantly, I wanted to see whether the respondents would, without prompting, raise the issue of intelligibility themselves. Giles and Niedzielski point out that research has shown 'a strong link between the perceived pleasantness of a language variety and the apparent intelligibility of what is said in it' (1998: 87), and I was interested in how far this would be true in respect of ELF. In addition, while most of the responses to the Lingua Franca Core proposals did not call the intelligibility findings into question, it was clear from the negative reaction to the concept of legitimate NNS pronunciation norms that intelligibility alone was not perceived as sufficient justification to accept them. (See Chapter 1.) Thus, if the intelligibility of NNS accents turned out to be particularly salient to the questionnaire respondents without my drawing attention to it, this would thus suggest an ambivalent and even irrational orientation to the phenomenon: one in which intelligibility is not perceived as sufficiently important to justify the acceptance of ELF where NNS accents are intelligible but provides a justification for *non*-acceptance of ELF where NNS accents are *un*intelligible. This in turn would imply that intelligibility *per se* is less of an issue than, and may be determined by, attitudes towards particular accents and their speakers, a phenomenon first observed by Wolff (1959; and see Chapter 3).

The questionnaire ended with a blank section headed 'Any other comments?', in which respondents were invited to say anything they wished about NNS English accents in general or about certain NNS English accents in particular. I emphasized in the rubric at this point that they could discuss any aspect of any accent, were free to say whatever they liked, and that their opinions were important to me. Although I knew from experience that many would leave this section blank, I also knew that if I made it clear to respondents that I valued their opinions, some would be encouraged to provide them. The questionnaire concluded with a note thanking respondents, giving them my email address, and saying they were welcome to contact me if they wished to discuss any issues relating to the questionnaire.

Participants and procedure

Before finalizing the questionnaire design, I carried out an exploratory study during a workshop at the annual RELC (Regional English Language Centre) conference in Singapore, in order to find out whether the map and rubric were clear to respondents. Although Singapore itself is an outer rather than expanding circle country, the RELC conference is attended by delegates from a wide range of countries, including several belonging to the expanding circle, and was therefore suitable for my purposes. Following the pilot study, I increased the clarity of the questionnaire rubric in line with comments that had been made by the pilot respondents, added a key to the world map, and expanded the range of questions.

The questionnaires were then sent to twelve countries: Austria, Brazil, China, Finland, Germany, Greece, Japan, Poland, Spain, Sweden, Taiwan, and Canada (in the case of Canada, to expanding circle NNSs staying temporarily in the country). The countries were selected to provide a spread that would enable me to identify trends in the accent attitudes and beliefs of teachers across the expanding circle. I was also keen to explore expanding circle members' attitudes towards their *own* group's English accents. In particular, I wanted to find out whether they would be more harsh or less in judging their own group's accent than other respondents were, and whether they would be more harsh or less in judging their own group's accent relative to their judgements of the accents of other groups. In order to investigate these issues, I sent questionnaires to all six expanding circle countries that were specified on the questionnaire itself (Brazil, China, Germany, Japan, Spain, and Sweden). I sent the questionnaires to the other five expanding circle countries (Austria, Finland, Greece, Poland, and Taiwan) in order to increase the spread of responses from expanding circle members. These countries were chosen partly because potential respondents in these places were likely to have some familiarity with other NNS English accents, through travel, the media, the Internet, and the like, and partly for practical reasons in that they were places where colleagues were willing to distribute the questionnaire on my behalf. In addition to the NNS respondents, questionnaires were sent to NS teachers of English who were studying for an MA at the University of Bristol and for the Cambridge-ESOL DELTA (Diploma in English Language Teaching to Adults) at King's College London.

The instructions that accompanied the questionnaire asked respondents to answer the questions spontaneously. I suggested a maximum of 30 minutes to complete the entire questionnaire, as I did not want them to engage in discussions with each other as they did so, or to 'agonize' over their answers. After the first few sets of questionnaires had been returned with relatively few respondents having completed the map-labelling task (question 2), I asked my colleagues to point out to respondents the importance of this task. Even then, a substantial number still did not attempt it, though in most cases it was not clear whether this was because they were unfamiliar with any other English accents or with the procedure itself.

The questionnaires yielded 326 respondents in all, excluding the 18 who took part in the exploratory study and 19 Japanese respondents who were education undergraduates on a TEFL methodology course with, as yet, no teaching experience.[5] Of the 326, the vast majority (300) were NNSs of English while only 26 were NSs.[6] Two-thirds (229 or 70.25 per cent) of the respondents were female and less than a third (86 or 26.38 per cent) were male. A further 11 declined to provide this information. As for the respondents' age groups (again excluding the exploratory study and the 19 undergraduates), over a third fell into the 20–29 year category (111, or 34.04 per cent), closely followed by 30–39 (104, or 31.90 per cent), and then a sharp drop to the remaining groups: 40–49 (66, or 20.25 per cent), 50–59 (33, or 10.12 per cent), and 60+ (10, or 3.07 per cent). Only two respondents failed to indicate their age group at all.

Attitudes and beliefs revealed in the responses

The responses to all five parts of the questionnaire reveal striking similarities in terms of overt beliefs about and covert biases towards NS and against NNS English accents. In this section we will consider the responses to each part of the questionnaire in turn, and then go on in the next section to explore the wider issues that they throw up. The analysis begins with questions three and four (the accent ranking and accent rating tasks). As mentioned earlier, these questions were placed after the qualitative tasks so that they would not influence respondents' answers to the latter. For the purpose of analysis, however, it makes better sense to see how respondents ranked and rated the various accents numerically, and then go on to look at how they actually described the accents. We begin with the accent ranking.

Ranking of English accents (Question 3)

The purpose of the ranking task was to find out the extent to which the respondents perceived English accents as belonging to some kind of hierarchy in terms of quality, and if so, whether they would only consider NS accents in terms of 'bestness'. Some of the 326 respondents left the question blank, a subset of these indicating that they did not believe it was possible to rank accents in this way. However, the majority attempted the question, even though some did not go beyond the first one, two, or three ranks. As will be clear in the discussion below, the respondents overwhelmingly believed that UK and US accents are better than other NS accents which, in turn, are better than more closely related NNS accents, which are better than more distantly related NNS accents. I begin by presenting the overall trends in more detail, and go on to point out the main differences across respondent groupings, as well as to look at some individual responses, primarily those that 'complained' about the nature of the task itself.

UK and US English accents were ranked first and second 'best' by a very large majority of respondents, with UK[7] accents being first-ranked 167 times, and US accents 100 times. There was then a massive drop to the other three top first-ranked accents, which again were all NS accents (Australian and Canadian English each 5, and Irish English 4). The remaining five accents shown in Figure 6.1 (below) were first-ranked by only a tiny number of respondents (three in the case of Dutch and two in the case of French, Indian, Japanese and Swedish). Because of the massive gap between the two first-ranked accents, i.e. UK and US, and all the rest, the only conclusions that can be drawn about the latter is that these eight were less non-preferred as 'the best' English accent than all other accents. There are probably many different reasons for their selection. For example, it was two Japanese respondents themselves who ranked Japanese English as first 'best'. Meanwhile, the over-whelming favouring of UK and US English accents is further demonstrated by the fact that a number of respondents did not fill in the third, fourth, and fifth places, as if they could not conceive of a 'best' accent being anything other than UK or US English.

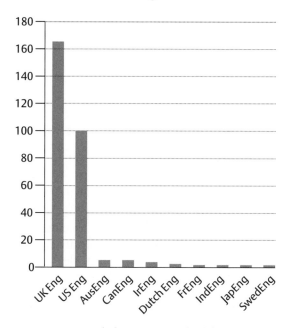

Figure 6.1 English accents ranked first

Moving on to the second ranked accents (see Figure 6.2 below), this time the first and second positions are reversed, with US accents ranked second 'best' by 98 respondents and UK accents by 92. The drop to the next three is less dramatic than for the first-ranked accents with, respectively, Canadian English (36), Australian English (18), and Irish English (10) times. Of the remaining seven accents shown on the bar chart, five are from the expanding circle and of these, the two with the highest scores are German English with eight, and Swedish English with four: in other words, two accents that are often perceived as close to RP. Again, then, the gap between the top (NS) accents and all the others is vast, and US and UK accents emerge as the only possible second 'best' English accents for the majority of respondents, with the choice being dictated in the main by which of the two they had already ranked first best.

The figures for the other three rankings continue the NS/NNS divide. However, now that most respondents have already ranked UK and US English accents, they turn to other NS accents. Third place (see Figure 6.3) goes almost equally to Canadian accents (62) and Australian accents (59), while UK and US English fall some way behind with, respectively, 35 and 34. They are followed by a large drop to a range of accents from all three circles: Swedish (13), China (7), Dutch and German (each 6), Irish and S. African (each 5), and Danish (4) and New Zealand (appearing for the first time, also

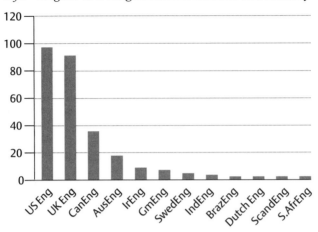

Figure 6.2 English accents ranked second

4). Meanwhile, although not shown in Figure 6.3, a further five accents were each ranked third three times (all but India from the expanding circle). The implications of this finding must not be exaggerated given the wide numerical gap between the higher and lower placed accents in the third rank, as well as the likely psychological gap separating the first two ranks from the other three. But it is interesting, nevertheless, to note that expanding circle accents start at this point to gain a little ground over some inner circle accents: Swedish, China, Dutch, and German English accents are all placed higher than Irish, S. African, and New Zealand for third rank place. Also of interest is the fact that the China English accent is in sixth place after Swedish, with all seven nominations coming from East Asian respondents (mainly Chinese), whereas those for the Swedish English accent came from a broad range of expanding circle members as well as two NSs. This suggests that whereas the Swedish English accent is widely perceived as near-native and thus by definition 'good', the China English accent is placed high on account of group identity and solidarity. (See below and Chapter 7.)

Turning to the fourth-ranked accents (see Figure 6.4 below), Australia takes a very strong first place, with exactly half of its 74 nominations coming from respondents in Japan, Taiwan, and China. These same groups had also nominated it very highly as third-ranked accent, suggesting that in East Asia, an NS Australian accent is the most preferred accent after a UK or US accent, but that to date, it is nowhere near replacing either of them. As far as the other fourth-ranked accents are concerned, there is little to choose between them. Of the other 11 that appear in Figure 6.4, five are NS accents and six are NNS (including Indian English). The figures range from 20 (Swedish English accents) to 7 (Irish English accents). There is also a large tail, with 16 other accents being nominated between once and 6 times. Again, a large number of the (18) Chinese 'votes' were from East Asians, and particularly from the Chinese respondents themselves, once again suggesting that solidarity and identity were playing a part in their perceptions of China English accents.

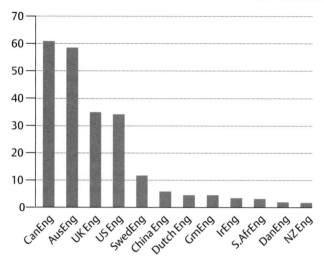

Figure 6.3 English accents ranked third

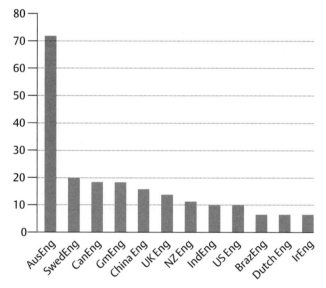

Figure 6.4 English accents ranked fourth

The situation relating to fifth-ranked accents is far less polarized. In terms of the spread of nominations, as Figure 6.5 (below) demonstrates, it is much closer to the situation for third-ranked accents than to any of the other three sets, although with gentler gradations. The most striking point is the position of the New Zealand English accent, which was not mentioned at all until the rankings for third place, and in both third and fourth rank had relatively few nominations (4 and 12 respectively), but has now increased to 31, putting it marginally ahead of the Australian accent at 30. Again, there was an East

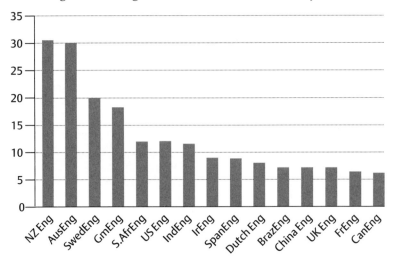

Figure 6.5 English accents ranked fifth

Asian effect, with 23 of New Zealand's 31 coming from respondents in China, Japan, and Taiwan, who gave the New Zealand accent substantially more nominations than they gave any other accents for fifth rank. The European and Brazilian respondents, by contrast, gave far higher percentages of their nominations to Australian, Swedish, German, UK, and US English accents. Of the other thirteen accents shown on the bar chart, the range is from 20 (Swedish English) to 6 (Canadian English). And again, there is a lengthy tail, with 26 accents being nominated fifth best just once, twice, or three times.[8]

Looking at the findings of the ranking task overall, as a very large rule the majority of these respondents ranked NS accents above NNS. For the first- and second-ranked accents, this was true of the five most frequently named accents. For the third-ranked accents it was still true of the top four. It is only with the fourth best rank that the Swedish English accent comes second (after a very large drop from Australian English in first place), and that two other NNS accents, German and China English, enter the top five accents. And although the fifth-ranked accents include a large number of NNS accents, the top two are still NS accents (New Zealand and Australian English). Despite the current widespread international use of English among expanding circle speakers, and the likelihood that they will communicate in English with other NNSs rather than with its NSs, their attachment to NS accents (primarily UK and US) seems to have shifted hardly at all.

On the other hand, a small number of respondents complained about the nature of the task itself, implying that they felt uncomfortable 'judging' English accents in this way. In some cases they left question 3 blank, while in others, they still completed the ranking task. Some of those who left the question unanswered nevertheless went on to complete the rating task (question 4). In other words, they were willing to rate accents in terms of correctness, acceptability, and pleasantness, but not 'bestness'. It seemed that such respondents felt more comfortable with a task that was broken down into components and which did not require them to make direct comparisons between accents. The most common complaint was that there is no such thing as a best accent, for example, 'the word "best" doesn't seem to be appropriate', or 'I don't think there are good or worse English accents and definitely there is no "best English accent"'. A few respondents explained this to me at length, revealing in the process a good deal of sociolinguistic awareness (though, perhaps, a lack of awareness of the fact that my aim was to find out whether they, the respondents, believed there was such a thing). Others did not do the ranking but instead commented that all accents are equal, for example, 'I accept all of them as long as they are consistent', or 'all accents are the same'.

Finally, we turn to the question of how the speakers from the participating expanding circle countries ranked their own English accents. As I pointed out earlier, while the vast majority of respondents did not consider their own accents to be candidates for 'best', some respondents did nominate their own group:

- One Taiwanese and two Japanese respondents each ranked their group's English accent as first best.
- One Greek and two German respondents each ranked their group's English accent as second best.
- One Japanese, two Chinese, two Germans, and two Taiwanese each ranked their group's English accent as third best.
- One Spanish, one Swedish, two German, four Brazilian, five Taiwanese, and nine Chinese each ranked their group's English accent as fourth best.
- One Japanese, one Taiwanese, two Spanish, three German and four Brazilians each ranked their group's English accent as fifth best.

These numbers are very small as contrasted with the total number of NNS respondents. However, the fact that even a small number had the confidence to nominate their own NNS accent as, in their opinion, one of the five best English accents cannot be overlooked, particularly in terms of the number of East Asian English speakers who did so. It is possible that this is the start of a trend, and that in the next few years, increasing numbers of expanding circle speakers, following in the path of outer circle groups, will resist the pressure to 'aspire' to NS English accents, and instead will demand recognition for their own accents. In this sense, they will be engaging in acts of resistance of the kind that Canagarajah (1999) documented in his classroom in Sri Lanka.

The rankings nevertheless demonstrate clearly that most respondents in the sample currently perceive English accents as belonging to a hierarchy, with UK and US accents at the very top,[9] followed by certain other NS accents (particularly Canadian and Australian), and then a few NNS accents that they perceive to be near-native. Most respondents, by contrast, reveal no sense at all of perceiving that non-nativelike English accents could be considered among the 'best' of the world's English accents. Linguistic insecurity seems to be implicated in this. The vast majority of the expanding circle respondents did not rank their own accents anywhere among the best. Nor, for the most part, did they rank each others' NNS accents among them either, and even when they did, tended to focus on the few that are closest to RP, primarily Dutch, Swedish, and German. We return to the part played in this by linguistic insecurity in Chapter 8, but turn now to the rating task, in order to learn about the respondents' accent attitudes in greater detail.

Rating of English accents (Question 4)

With the rating task, we move on to look at more specific perceptions of NNS accents. The respondents were asked to rate each of the ten specified accents on four dimensions (correctness, acceptability for international communication, pleasantness, and their own familiarity with the accent) on a scale of 1 to 6, where 1 represented 'very correct', 'very acceptable', etc. and 6 the exact opposite. The rating scales yield some interesting responses from the informants in respect of both their own accents and those of other groups. For example, certain 'group perspectives' emerge among the NNS groups, and there are also some striking contrasts between the NNS and NS ratings.

The overall NNS means (i.e. for the combined NNS groups) and the NS group means can be seen in Table 6.1 below.[10]

	Accent	Raters	Correctness	Acceptability	Pleasantness	Familiarity
1	US	All NNS	1.812 (N = 262)	1.550 (N = 267)	2.086 (N = 265)	1.548 (N = 267)
	Eng	NS	1.816 (N = 21)	1.714 (N = 21)	2.666 (N = 21)	1.333 (N = 21)
2	Braz	All NNS	3.594 (N = 202)	3.348 (N = 202)	3.348 (N = 204)	3.917 (N = 206)
	Eng	NS	3.315 (N = 19)	2.473 (N = 19)	2.210 (N = 19)	3.210 (N = 19)
3	SpEng	All NNS	3.504 (N = 226)	3.311 (N = 225)	3.405 (N = 227)	3.526 (N = 226)
		NS	3.800 (N = 20)	3.000 (N = 20)	2.750 (N = 20)	2.350 (N = 20)
4	UK	All NNS	1.471 (N = 263)	1.558 (N = 263)	1.781 (N = 265)	1.762 (N = 265)
	Eng	NS	1.600 (N = 20)	1.300 (N = 20)	1.950 (N = 19)	1.550 (N = 20)
5	Gm	All NNS	3.188 (N = 228)	2.860 (N = 230)	3.360 (N = 230)	3.286 (N = 230)
	Eng	NS	2.210 (N = 19)	2.052 (N = 19)	3.263 (N = 19)	2.263 (N = 19)
6	Swed	All NNS	2.698 (N = 194)	2.620 (N = 199)	2.854 (N = 196)	3.650 (N = 196)
	Eng	NS	1.750 (N = 16)	1.625 (N = 16)	2.176 (N = 17)	2.647 (N = 17)
7	Ind	All NNS	3.373 (N = 230)	3.413 (N = 232)	3.797 (N = 234)	3.740 (N = 235)
	Eng	NS	2.736 (N = 19)	2.421 (N = 19)	2.650 (N = 20)	1.900 (N = 20)
8	China	All NNS	3.583 (N = 236)	3.342 (N = 238)	3.719 (N = 241)	3.162 (N = 240)
	Eng	NS	3.947 (N = 19)	3.315 (N = 19)	3.900 (N = 20)	2.450 (N = 20)
9	Jap	All NNS	4.055 (N = 245)	3.836 (N = 245)	4.110 (N = 248)	3.508 (N = 248)
	Eng	NS	3.473 (N = 19)	3.105 (N = 19)	3.000 (N = 20)	2.600 (N = 20)
10	Aus	All NNS	2.137 (N = 251)	2.161 (N = 254)	2.482 (N = 254)	2.789 (N = 257)
	Eng	NS	1.947 (N = 19)	1.578 (N = 19)	2.350 (N = 19)	1.950 (N = 19)

Table 6.1 Means for the rating task

While descriptive statistics cannot be used to generalize beyond the specific sample, the means in Table 6.1 are indicative of certain of the tendencies that also emerge from the ranking task and first map-labelling task. (See the discussion of question 1 below.) As regards the ranking task, some clear similarities can be observed once the rating means are reorganized into descending order for each of the four dimensions—see Table 6.2 below. The most obvious similarity to the ranking task is the appearance of the three NS accents in the first three places in the rating task. Interestingly, while UK English accents were rated better than US for correctness and pleasantness, US English accents did marginally better than UK accents on acceptability, and substantially better on familiarity, despite the fact that over half the respondent groups would originally have learnt English based on an RP model. This suggests that they had had substantial exposure to US English through American films, media, and the like. As in the ranking task, Australian accents did less well than both UK and US accents in the rating task, where it was separated from them by a substantial gap on all dimensions.

Correctness		Acceptability		Pleasantness		Familiarity	
UK Eng	1.471	US Eng	1.550	UK Eng	1.781	US Eng	1.548
US Eng	1.812	UK Eng	1.558	US Eng	2.086	UK Eng	1.762
AusEng	2.137	AusEng	2.161	AusEng	2.482	AusEng	2.789
SwedEng	2.698	SwedEng	2.620	SwedEng	2.854	China Eng	3.162
GmEng	3.188	GmEng	2.860	BrazEng	3.348	GmEng	3.286
IndEng	3.373	SpEng	3.311	GmEng	3.360	JapEng	3.508
SpEng	3.504	China Eng	3.342	SpEng	3.405	SpEng	3.526
China Eng	3.583	BrazEng	3.348	China Eng	3.719	SwedEng	3.650
BrazEng	3.594	IndEng	3.413	IndEng	3.797	IndEng	3.740
JapEng	4.055	JapEng	3.836	JapEng	4.110	BrazEng	3.917

Table 6.2 Rank ordering of NNS respondents' accent rating means

After the three NS accents, the picture becomes fuzzy and comparisons with the ranking task more difficult to make, especially in view of the low numbers of nominations for NNS accents in the ranking task. In the rating task, Swedish and German English accents were nevertheless consistently rated best of the remaining seven accents, with Swedish fourth on all but the familiarity dimension and German fifth on all but pleasantness, and very close indeed to Swedish, but a long way behind US and UK accents on acceptability. The main point, then, is that in terms of correctness, acceptability for *international* communication, and pleasantness, the accents rated most highly (i.e. with the lowest scores) were consistently NS followed at some distance by the closest (i.e. German/Swedish) NNS accents. This confirms the finding of the ranking task that the best English accents by far are perceived by the respondents to be those of its NSs. And it further demonstrates that 'bestness' relates not only to correctness as one might have predicted, but also to the pleasantness of the accents and even to their acceptability for international communication.

As regards the remaining five accents, one notable feature is the poor rating of Indian English relative to all the other accents bar one (Japanese English) on the acceptability and pleasantness dimensions. This is surprising given the status of Indian English as an established institutionalized variety. It also contrasts with the position of Indian English in the ranking task, where it was often the NNS English accent to be nominated next after Swedish and German. The fact that in the *rating* task this was only the case *vis-à-vis* correctness suggests that correctness may have been the aspect of 'bestness' that had been uppermost in respondents' minds in the earlier ranking task, and that they had been less concerned with other measures of quality. This interpretation is strengthened by the fact that in the rating task, all three NS accents as well as the two most positively rated NNS accents (Swedish and German) were rated more positively for correctness than they were for pleasantness (albeit only slightly). On the other hand, apart from German for pleasantness, they were all still rated more positively on both pleasantness and acceptability scales than the other five NNS English accents were, particularly so in the case of US and UK accents. It seems that the majority of NNS raters were unable to conceive of NNS English accents as being better than or even as good as NS English accents in any of these ways.

The NS raters' position on acceptability for international communication and for pleasantness differed in some respects from those of the NNS respondents. As regards acceptability, the NSs' top-rated accent was UK English, followed by Australian, Swedish, and only then, US English. For pleasantness, UK English again received their best rating, while their next best-rated accents were, respectively, Swedish, Brazilian, Australian, Indian, and only then, US English. It is perhaps not surprising that these NSs, most of whom were from the UK, should rate UK English in this way, and it may well be that the UK and US accent evaluations would be reversed if the exercise were repeated with NS raters in the US. Clearly, further research into NS teachers' attitudes is needed, and in a range of geographical contexts, if we are to be able to do any more than speculate on the extent of NS–NNS differences, let alone reasons for them. Nevertheless, the indications so far are that there may indeed be some differences in the ways that NSs and NNSs of English evaluate English accents, and that while both groups tend to evaluate NS English accents more highly than NNS accents, NS teachers may have more flexible attitudes towards NNS English accents (or at least may want researchers to think that they do).

In addition to differences between the NNS and NS responses, there were variations across the individual NNS respondent groups. For example, the Japanese respondents' means for the correctness, acceptability, and pleasantness of China English accents were 3.45, 3.27, and 3.666, whereas the corresponding Chinese respondents' means for Japanese English were considerably worse at 4.482, 4.655, and 4.833. Nevertheless, both these East Asian accents tended to be more negatively rated than the other accents by the western and Brazilian respondents on all three scales, and to be more positively rated by the eastern respondents than the western. While the Japanese English accent was the lowest rated overall, some individual respondent groups judged the China English accent to be the worst on some dimensions (for example, the Brazilian respondents *vis-à-vis* pleasantness) or all (for example, the German and Spanish respondents, as well as the NS group).

The self ratings also reveal differences from the overall NNS ratings, in that five out of the six NNS groups rated their own English accents better, some substantially so, on all dimensions than the ratings they received in their aggregate NNS means. Only the Spanish respondents rated their accents worse, and then by only a small amount. (See Table 6.3 below, where the aggregate means appear in parentheses.) The Chinese respondents were particularly positive about their own English accents relative to their overall ratings. In fact apart from their rating of German English on correctness (mean 2.692), they rated their own accent as better than all the other NNS accents on all dimensions, thus demonstrating the same confidence that had been revealed in the ranking task, where several Chinese respondents had nominated China English as one of the five best English accents. On the other hand, whereas the Swedish respondents had been reticent in respect of their own accent in the ranking task, they were less so in the rating task, improving on the already very positive ratings of the aggregate means (although not rating their own accents nearly as positively as they rated the NS accents (UK 1.4, 1.4, and 1; US 1.6, 1.4, and 2.2; Australian 1.6, 1.4, and 1.8)).

Respondents/accent	Correctness	Acceptability	Pleasantness
2 BrazEng	3.000 (3.594)	2.814 (3.348)	3.037 (3.348)
3 SpEng	3.894 (3.504)	3.388 (3.311)	3.944 (3.405)
5 GmEng	2.960 (3.188)	2.720 (2.860)	3.000 (3.360)
6 SwedEng	2.400 (2.698)	2.400 (2.620)	2.600 (2.854)
8 China Eng	2.733 (3.583)	2.533 (3.342)	2.677 (3.719)
9 JapEng	3.767 (4.055)	3.089 (3.836)	3.403 (4.110)

Table 6.3 Means of self-ratings

The familiarity scale was included in order to discover whether and how the respondents' familiarity with an accent affected their perceptions of its correctness, acceptability for international communication, and its pleasantness, and here there are some interesting discrepancies. For example, US English was rated more familiar than UK English, but also less correct and pleasant. On the other hand, Swedish English was rated more unfamiliar than all the NNS accents except Brazilian and Indian English, and yet more correct, acceptable, and pleasant than any other NNS accent. This implies that some respondents were not evaluating the Swedish English accent in accordance with any experience of the accent, but because they had heard that Swedish English is 'nativelike'. Brazilian English was rated the most unfamiliar accent of all ten, but not by any means the most incorrect, unacceptable, or unpleasant, while the opposite was true of Japanese English. Clearly the relationship between familiarity and perceptions of the quality of English accents is a complex one that requires extensive research, especially in the light of research reported in Chapter 3, demonstrating that people may 'hear' the accent that they expect to.

I was also interested in finding out whether respondents would attempt to evaluate accents with which they had limited familiarity. In a number of cases, respondents left the scales for certain accents blank, sometimes adding a comment to indicate that they had not heard the accent concerned. On the other hand, as in Lindemann's (2005) study, a substantial number of my respondents were willing to evaluate accents that they did not know at all well. This does not show up clearly in the aggregate NNS means, where even the least familiar accent (Brazilian English) was rated 3.917, i.e. 'slightly unfamiliar'. However, it could be that in some cases, respondents who had completed the other three scales for an accent then felt uncomfortable about evaluating accents that they did not know, and over-reported their familiarity. (See above p. 149 on the phenomenon of presenting oneself in a good light even in anonymous reporting.)

The main conclusion to be drawn from the rating task, then, is that for this sample of NNS teachers at least, NS English accents, and especially UK and US accents, are overwhelmingly the best in terms not only of correctness, but also of pleasantness and acceptability in *international* communication. The concept of ELF and the appropriateness of NNS accents for communication in lingua franca contexts seem not to have occurred to the vast majority of them. Instead, their assumptions, like those of the writers and speakers in Chapter 5, appear in the main to be identical with those that underpin EFL, whose norms are dictated by NS English use and whose models are those of ENL. In terms of NNS English accents, the rating task results also confirm the findings of the ranking task in respect of a hierarchy of NNS English accents. Again, the respondents perceive certain European accents as being higher up the accent 'ladder' than all other NNS accents on all three dimensions, and Asian English accents as being lower down on all three. This perception appears to be true even of the East Asian respondents themselves, with the one exception of the Chinese respondents' positive rating of their own accent, which supports the observation I made in the previous section about the role of solidarity, identity, and resistance.

Having established that the respondents hold these polarized beliefs about NNS and NS English accents, we move on to the map-labelling tasks where we find out what they actually have to say about the accents.

The map-labelling tasks (Questions 1 and 2)

The qualitative data analysed in the remainder of the chapter provides insights into the attitudes that were identified by the numerical data. Even if I had used inferential rather than descriptive statistics to analyse the ranking and rating tasks, and therefore been in a position to generalize beyond the sample, the statistics thus generated would still have told us little about the actual attitudes and beliefs of the respondents and their peer groups beyond the fact that these attitudes and beliefs exist in the first place. This takes us back to the issue of 'what' versus 'how' that I discussed in the previous chapter. The numerical data demonstrate, for example, that the majority of the NNS respondents find NS accents the most acceptable for international communication, that they evaluate NS English accents, particularly UK and US, far more highly than NNS accents on various dimensions, that they consider Asian English accents to be the 'worst', and that they have little or no awareness of the concept of legitimate ELF accents. But in order to find out what their beliefs about and attitudes towards these accents actually are, it is important to examine what the respondents say *in their own words*. This is the purpose of the map-labelling tasks, which enable us to discover more precisely how NNS and NS English accents are evaluated and categorized by (expanding circle) NNS teachers of English, which accent areas and which aspects of the various accents are salient to them, and the extent to which their perceptions agree or differ at a qualitative level.[11]

Overall, the respondents' descriptions range widely. At the overt level, the majority of respondents demonstrated that they held firm beliefs about particular accents, whether they articulated these in a more general or more detailed manner. At the deeper level, covert attitudes emerged particularly in some of the more abstract pejorative and at times emotional words and expressions they used to describe certain NNS English accents. Among the types of comment that occurred most frequently, many were general descriptors such as 'good', 'bad', 'nice', and 'unpleasant'. Others were more specific: some referred, for instance, to the perceived (in)correctness of an accent (for example, 'proper', 'standard', 'mispronounced', or 'they don't ... / should ... '), some to the degree of L_1 influence, and some to an accent's intelligibility or clarity of articulation—there was a tendency to conflate the two. Others focused on speed of delivery, rhythm, fluency, volume, or tone quality, or on salient phonetic features, while still others described accents in terms of personal characteristics (for example, 'snobbish', 'arrogant', 'impetuous', and 'friendly').

In the following sub-section, I consider in turn the respondents' comments on the ten accents specified on the map in question 1, summarizing the descriptions of each, and illustrating them with verbatim examples.

Descriptions of the ten specified accents (Question 1)

1 US English accent

Comments describing the US English accent tended to occur in complementary distribution with those describing UK English. That is, those respondents who liked the former tended to make pejorative comments about the latter, and vice versa. Surprisingly, in this respect no strong group patterns emerge. Instead, the preference for one or other so-called 'standard' English accent varies within rather than across the respondent groups. Meanwhile, a substantial number of respondents described both accents in favourable terms.

The aspect of the US English accent that received most comment was its perceived intelligibility, with the most frequent positive description being 'easy to understand' (many times). Other intelligibility-related descriptors include 'clear', 'clear to me', 'easy for me', 'close to spelling', and 'comfortable'. On the other hand, a small minority of respondents described the accent as 'hard to understand' or similar. Further relatively frequent comments concern its perceived 'casual' quality, for example, 'laid back', 'informal', 'relaxed', and 'casual', although those who had a preference for UK English tended to interpret this quality as 'careless' or 'sloppy'. Several referred to the rhoticity of US English in either neutral comments, for example, 'r's above all' or, less often, pejoratively, for example, 'too much r-coloring'. Most of those who did not favour US over UK English, described the perceived lack of pleasantness of the former, for example, 'unpleasant', 'doesn't sound nice', or similar, whereas those who did favour it used terms such as 'pleasant' or even 'beautiful'. Even among those who disliked US English, however, there was no suggestion in the respondents' descriptions that they considered it to be in any way incorrect, while some specifically described it as 'correct'.

2 Brazilian(-Portuguese) English accent

Many respondents did not comment on the Brazilian English accent at all because of their lack of familiarity with it (which contrasts with their willingness, in several cases, to rate the accent in question 4). Of those that did comment, their descriptions most frequently concern the accent's tuneful quality. A number described it as 'melodious' or similar (for example, 'like a song', 'smooth', or 'sweet') and in one case ambiguously as 'melodious but off tune'. A smaller number, by contrast, described the accent as, for example, 'harsh', 'hard', 'flat', or 'lacking both rhythm and intonation'. Interestingly, the Brazilian respondents themselves were divided in this respect, some finding their own accent tuneful, others the opposite. Several respondents also referred to the accent as 'strong', although this was not necessarily intended negatively, as it collocates with favourable as well as unfavourable adjectives (for example, with both 'sweet' and 'harsh').

The majority of other descriptions follow no clearly discernible pattern (for example, 'rolling', 'borrowed', 'pleasant'), though a number are pejorative (for example, 'difficult to understand', 'not precise', 'not serious'), and again, some present contradictory perceptions (for example, its rhythm is described as both 'smooth' and 'broken'). There are also several idiosyncratic descriptions, such as 'like a bouncing ball', 'speak with an egg inside the mouth', 'some sounds pronounced in the teeth'. The almost complete lack of reference to specific phonetic features suggests that most respondents did not have a clear idea of what a Brazilian English accent sounds like. (This is corroborated by its familiarity score in the rating task.) And perhaps because of this, the accent's perceived degree of correctness was rarely mentioned, despite the fact that it was subsequently judged in the rating task to be among the worst of the ten accents for correctness.

3 Spanish English accent

The most frequent comments about the Spanish English accent concern its tone/intonation and speed of delivery. A large number described it as 'melodious', although in one case, this is ambiguous: 'melodious, "Spanish-spoilt"'. Otherwise, very few respondents commented negatively in this respect, with only a handful describing the accent as, for example, 'very harsh' or 'harsh'. Many respondents described it as 'fast', 'quick', 'speedy', and the like. Despite the accent's perceived speed, a substantial number of respondents focused positively on its intelligibility, describing it as, for example, 'easy to understand', 'clear', 'understandable'. Fewer took the opposite view, with comments such as 'not very clear', 'not clear pronunciation', and 'melodious rhythm and pitch interferes with understanding' (the latter comment, like the ambiguous Brazilian example above, being made by a respondent from the accent group itself).

The aspect of the Spanish English accent that was most consistently described in negative terms is its 'Spanishness' (for example, 'Spanish-like', 'they sound Spanish when they speak', 'like Spanglish'). Some made explicit links between its Spanish quality and incorrectness (for example, 'interference', 'lack of precision', 'not precise', 'Spanish do not speak English very well'). A few were more specific about what is 'wrong' (for example, 'wrong vowels, wrong pitch'; the rhythm is 'halty', 'chopped', 'broken'; 'nasal sound', ''r' very distinct'). The fact that many more such comments were made about the Spanish than the Brazilian English accent is probably a function of the respondents' greater familiarity with the former. By contrast, when it comes to the rating scales, the two accents' means on all dimensions except familiarity are reasonably similar, with SpEng being slightly better rated for correctness and acceptability, and BrazEng for pleasantness.

4 UK English accent

Many respondents referred to the accent's perceived 'authenticity', commenting that it is 'normal', 'traditional', 'authentic', 'proper', 'classical', and the like. Many also referred to its intelligibility (for example, 'clear', '(very) easy to understand'), and some linked its authenticity and intelligibility, in one case contrasting it with US English: 'traditional accent, normal, easier to listen to than US accents'. Interestingly, whereas correctness is not mentioned specifically in the descriptions of US English, it occurs many times and in various ways with reference to UK English (for example, 'good', 'correct', 'perfect', 'exact', 'precise', 'proper', 'standard', 'RP standard', 'well-articulated'). A large number also described the accent positively in aesthetic terms (for example, 'beautiful', 'pleasant', 'elegant', 'lovely to listen to', 'absolutely pleasant to the ear'). Others, though fewer, perceived it as, for example, 'harsh, unpleasant', 'too fast, somewhat artificial', or having 'broken words', while one commented 'British English sounds too complicated. It is like listening to an opera'. In most of these cases, though, the latter nevertheless went on to rank the accent second best (after US English) in question 3 and to rate it positively in question 4.

Some respondents described UK English, as they also did US English, in terms of perceived personal qualities, both positively (for example, 'competent', 'authoritative', '(polite and) formal', 'slow, gentleman-like', 'royal') and negatively (for example, 'snobbish', 'posh', 'arrogant'), as well as ambivalently ('somewhat snobbish, but beautiful in its way'). Others focused on specific aspects of the accent's articulation, for example, 'sounds blur', 'words connected closely', 'fast and front of the mouth', or its non-phonetic nature ('pronunciation different from spelling'). A few referred to its non-rhotic quality, most taking a neutral or positive stance, but one commenting 'they should pronounce /r/'. Overall, then, the descriptors for the UK English accent bear out the quantitative findings, in which it was ranked by a sizeable majority as the best English accent, and also best-rated in terms of correctness and pleasantness, with US English coming second in each case.

5 German English accent

Comments on the German English accent focused primarily on its perceived inferior aesthetic qualities and its correctness. Many respondents described the accent as 'harsh' or 'hard' (also 'super hard', 'very harsh', 'harsh and growly', 'harsh, difficult to focus on', 'harsh—low pitch', as well as providing idiosyncratic descriptions such as 'harsh/guilty', 'anger'), and one respondent is more explicit about his/her orientation: 'harsh, personally not very pleasant to listen to'. Others referred to the accent's strength (for example, 'robust/ strong', 'strong, not pleasant to hear', 'funny strong accent', 'has strong accent'). Some of these singled out specific German sounds. For example, 'the Germans pronounce /w/ as /v/, /ð/ as /z/', 'the 'w' sound', 'German has funny accent with 'w' → vat? for what', 'problems with pronunciation ('th')', and 'problems with 'th' pronunciation', or just 'German sounds evident in their English', while two referred to the sounds being produced in the throat, and a number commented pejoratively on prosodic features (for example, 'wrong rhythm, wrong pitch, lacks melody', and 'irritating especially in terms of intonation').

In addition to its harshness and strength, the accent was perceived as 'rigid', 'stiff', 'strict', 'cold', 'distant', and 'precise'. On the other hand, it is this very precision that was also positively evaluated in respect of correctness (for example, 'good, correct, easy to understand', 'only minor errors', 'formally correct', 'sounds no different from British accent to me', 'good speakers, sound British' and, more ambivalently, 'correct but boring a bit'). In a similar vein, many respondents also described the accent as clear and thus easy to understand.

The conflicting comments about the German English accent seem to result from the fact that many respondents found the 'stereotypical German' features of the accent very salient and unpleasant. This led in turn to their impression that the accent is 'strong'. On the other hand, they also perceived the accent as having much in common with a British English accent, which implied to them that in this respect it is 'correct'. Surprisingly, this ambivalence did not appear to be reflected in the rating task, where correctness (3.188) was rated only slightly better than pleasantness (3.360). A possible explanation is that the respondents' negative perception of the German English accent's pleasantness had a negative 'pull' on their correctness rating, while their positive perception of its correctness had a positive 'pull' on their pleasantness rating.

6 Swedish English accent

One of the most frequent types of comment about the Swedish English accent concerns its perceived proximity to an NS accent, for example, 'fluent, almost mother tongue-like', 'nativelike', 'sound like a native speaker', 'quite natural like native speakers' ('natural' being equated here, as so often, with 'native-like'). Some specified a British English accent (for example, 'near British accent', 'people in Sweden speak English with a British accent', 'sounds no different from a British accent to me'—the same point as was also made about German English), while others comment specifically on its correctness/accu-racy (for example, 'precise, clear', 'well mastered', 'fluent/accurate', 'well articulated', 'often nearly perfect') or its high quality in general (for example, 'most speak very well', 'very good accent', 'fluent, good accent', 'excellent pronunciation'). Even a respondent who had limited familiarity with the accent nevertheless assumed that it is close to RP: 'I'm not familiar with this accent, but I reckon very much British-like'.

Judging from the number of these kinds of comments, it seems that the respondents believed the Swedish English accent to be more 'nativelike' than German English. This may in part account for the lack of negative comments *vis-à-vis* its aesthetic qualities relative to those made about German English. Many described the Swedish English accent as pleasant (for example, 'pleasant to listen to') and easy to understand. Two hinted at its international accept-ability ('approaches General Standard at international level' and 'precise, standard European'). By contrast, only a very small number of respondents, mainly Finnish and Polish, said anything negative in any of these respects (for example, a handful used terms such as 'harsh', 'rough', and 'gutteral'), while one of the Swedish respondents themselves described the accent as 'formal, hypercorrect'. Given the relatively low familiarity rating of the accent, it is not surprising that on the rare occasion a pronunciation feature was singled out, it was described in fairly general terms (for example, 'the English vowel sounds are formed in the front part of the mouth, intonation doesn't match'). It is also not surprising, given the stereotype of Swedish English as being close to British English, that so many respondents described it very positively despite lack of familiarity with it.

7 Indian English accent

The most frequent comment about the Indian English accent concerns respondents' difficulty in understanding it. Several made a general point about this (for example, 'difficult to follow', 'hard to understand, similar to mum-bling', 'mumbled-like, difficult to understand', 'takes some time to follow the accent', 'very difficult to understand = pron', 'difficult to understand unless specific features are known'). Many others identified specific phonological or phonetic causes of the problem, usually in a judgemental way. For example, several referred to the Indian English production of particular sounds (for example, 'the /r/ is mispronounced', 'enerving 'r'-sound', 'needs a lot of energy to listen to ('r' sound)', 'India 'r' sound', 'retroflex', 'cannot distinguish 'b' and 'p' sound'). Some referred to prosodic features (for example, 'intonation sometimes makes it difficult to understand', 'difficult intonation', 'intonation and stress confusing', 'its rhythm broken', 'not clear, no rhythm', 'sounds choppy and fast', 'staccato') or mentioned both segmental and prosodic items, for example, 'sometimes hard to understand because of rhythm and [r] sound'. A small minority, by contrast, considered the accent to be easy to understand, and described it as 'fluent', while two compared it with singing and chanting, implying a more positive evaluation of its rhythm ('quick, a little bit like singing', 'as chanting Buddhist songs').

There was general agreement that the accent is strongly influenced by the L1 (for example, 'very much affected by native accent', 'native, personalized, nationalistic', 'has some accents, strong', 'strong accent'), although there was some disagreement as to whether or not it is pleasant. A few described it as 'melodious', one as 'melodious, clear, explosive' and one as 'strong accent, it sounds sweet and friendly', while many others considered it to be 'harsh'. It was also perceived to be an exotic accent, although this was not necessarily seen in a negative light (for example, 'exotic', 'strange', 'a little bit strange', 'funny and nice', 'peculiar'). Correctness, although mentioned less often *per se*, was described in negative terms (for example, 'the accent is 'far away from standard', 'not very correct', and see above for comments on the 'incorrectness' of specific features of the accent). One respondent somewhat ambiguously said 'well-pronounced in spite of the accent'.

Only one respondent mentioned the link with British English. This is sur-prising and perhaps demonstrates that these respondents had a fairly limited knowledge of Indian English and its background. It seemed to belong, in many respondents' perceptions, with China English and Japanese English in an 'Asian' category. Meanwhile, its outer circle status as a long-established, codified variety was largely overlooked in their comments, which sometimes appeared to be based on media stereotypes rather than direct experience. Indeed, in this respect, one respondent actually said: '[the accent] reminds me of the "Party" with Peter Sellers'.

8 China English accent

The most frequent type of comment made about the China English accent related to the fact that it is a tone rather than intonation language. There were many references to the perceived effect of this on rhythm and intonation (for example, 'choppy', 'chopped', 'sort of chopped, tone-like', 'spiky', 'broken', 'broken, not fluent', 'staccato effect', 'short and abrupt (ping-pong)', 'see-saw', 'no stress or intonation, choppy', 'difficulties with rhythm', and so on). The outcome was frequently described in terms of lack of intelligibility (for example, 'hard to understand', 'difficult to understand', 'unintelligible', 'incomprehensible', 'in general almost incomprehensible', 'impossible to understand = pron', 'unclear, imprecise', and the like). Other pronunciation features that were often mentioned as problematic are high pitch, lack of word stress (for example, 'no proper word accent'), dropping of sounds (for example, 'they eat sounds/letters'), lack of long vowel sounds, and the production of certain consonants. Several respondents singled out the /r/ phoneme (for example, 'some sounds not correct ('r' sound)', while one provides a stereotypical example to illustrate the point: 'the "r" especially when Chinese say "fried rice" = "flied lice"'. Not surprisingly, given the number and range of the accent's 'problem' features, several also referred to its perceived strength (for example, 'strong accent', 'strong interference', 'foreign', 'far away from standard'), and others to its strangeness (for example, 'strange pronunciation', 'funny', 'ambiguous'). In terms of aesthetic qualities, some described it as 'harsh' or 'unpleasant', while one called it 'quarrel-like', and another simply said 'appalling'.

While the Chinese respondents, too, described their own accent in negative terms, when they did so it was mainly to comment on words being articulated over-clearly and the lack of connection between them (for example, 'too clear, no connection'). On the other hand, they described the China English accent favourably in ways that contrast strikingly with the pejorative descriptions of respondents in the other L1 groups (for example, 'nice', 'beautiful in pronunciation', 'good', 'quite good and correct', 'very clear', 'understandable'). Of the few positive comments made by others, most were from Japanese respondents, some contrasting the accent favourably with their own (for example, 'better than Japanese'), while a Taiwanese respondent described the accent as 'clear but snobbish (personal opinion)'. Thus, except for the comments of its own speakers and those of a few other (mainly Japanese) respondents, the China English accent fared considerably worse in the map-labelling than it did in the rating task, and appeared to be more heavily stigmatized by most other respondent groups than its ratings suggest.

9 Japanese English accent

An interesting feature of the descriptions of Japanese English is the greater number and length of comments relating to it as compared with those relating to the other nine accents. Given that Japanese English was by far the worst rated of the ten for correctness, this observation concurs with Lindemann's finding that 'respondents had more to say about the countries that were negatively evaluated on correctness' (2005: 199). Even the Japanese respondents themselves were largely negative about the quality of their accent (for example, 'flat and no pitch', 'not confident', 'broken', 'katakana sounds', 'we add a vowel to a consonant'), although they also described it as easy to understand.

The most frequent type of comment about the Japanese English accent, as with China English, concerns intelligibility problems (for example, 'almost incomprehensible', 'hard to understand what they say', 'unless specific pronunciation features are known, in general almost incomprehensible', 'hardly intelligible', 'very very difficult to understand = pron', 'hard to understand if you don't speak Japanese'). Apart from comments made by the Japanese respondents themselves, the data contains very few instances of positive descriptions in respect of the intelligibility of the Japanese English accent. Related to the perception of Japanese English as lacking intelligibility, is that of its strength. A number of respondents made this link (for example, 'strong accent (not understandable)', 'strong Japanese accent', 'difficult to understand, strong interference').

Large numbers of respondents linked the accent's perceived lack of intelligibility with specific aspects of its phonology/phonetics (for example, 'problems understanding accent due to pronunciation of sounds', 'they eat or add sounds/letters', 'unclear, imprecise, no strongly pronounced consonants'). Several were very specific about which sounds are the 'problem' (for example, 'a lot of [wu], as in [pɪkunɪku]', ' hard to understand /f/', 'not very comprehensible, have trouble with "l"', 'difficult to understand, funny, no "r" sound'). Others focused on prosody (for example, 'difficult to understand/without stress or rhythm', 'rather high pitched', 'weird pitch', 'flat', 'the tone seems like they feel surprised all the time'). Interestingly, some of these comments were made by respondents whose own group's English accent tends to be characterized by the very feature they criticized in Japanese English (for example, China English and /l/–/r/ conflation, Brazilian English and elision).

Respondents also commented on what they believed to be the general incorrectness of Japanese English, describing it as, for example, 'bad', 'mispronounced', 'imprecise', and 'limited'. Others referred to its perceived strangeness (for example, 'weird pitch', 'like a strange melody', 'incredible pronunciation, like something missing'), and unpleasantness (for example, 'tough', 'hard, never fluent', 'menacing', or simply 'torture'). In addition, whereas some of the Japanese respondents made positive comments about China English, the Chinese respondents were almost entirely negative about Japanese English, some comparing it unfavourably to their own accent (for example, 'not very good, difficult to understand', 'bad', 'almost incomprehensible', 'strong accent', 'not so good as the Chinese'). A very few respondents had something positive to say about the Japanese English accent. A Brazilian respondent, for example, described it as 'good', while a German respondent, in a double-edged compliment, commented 'far away from standard but easy to understand as well'. It is curious that the Japanese English accent fared even worse than China English and that lack of intelligibility was so often presented as the cause, when the theory of recoverability (Weinberger 1987) as well as my own NNS–NNS interaction data (Jenkins 2000) suggest that as far as intelligibility is concerned, it should be the other way round. On the other hand, as Wolff (1959) has demonstrated, judgements of intelligibility are complex, and 'linguistic comparability ... is not a decisive factor' as contrasted with 'cultural factors' (p. 39; and see Chapter 3).

10 Australian English accent

One particularly salient aspect of the Australian English accent was its perceived 'half-way' point between US and UK English accents (for example, 'sounds like the combination of British and American accents', 'lovely, a perfect compromise between US and UK English', 'their accent is like between: American English and England English'). Not surprisingly, then, it was often described as intelligible (for example, 'clear, easy to understand', 'understandable'). On the other hand, a smaller number said the opposite (for example, 'difficult to understand, too regional', 'accent is not easy to understand for British like English', 'strong, obscure at times'). In this respect, several respondents mentioned one particular Australian English sound, the use of the diphthong /aɪ/ where US and UK accents have /eɪ/, as being problematic for intelligibility. Some described this 'problem' at length, providing examples to illustrate it (for example, 'might cause misunderstanding (as in 'did you come here to<u>day</u>?' to die)', 'some vowels are difficult to understand because they are different from those in American English (for example, <u>A</u>pril)'. This diphthong was the only specific pronunciation feature mentioned, and was evidently highly salient to some respondents. The fact that they were so aware of its difference from the 'standard' UK and US equivalent suggests, though, that it did not in fact cause intelligibility problems for them, but that (perhaps) like the vowel addition of Japanese English, it was stigmatized by those who orient negatively to the accent overall.

Many respondents referred to the accent's perceived aesthetic qualities, both favourably (for example, 'singing sounds', singing/melodious', 'beautiful', 'pleasant'), and pejoratively, for example, 'harsh', 'unpleasant, too weird', 'odd', 'strange/open', or mixed, for example, 'musical but vowel sounds are too "open"' and, rather strangely, 'English crow'), while one likened it to 'Cockney'. As with US English (but even more so) a number of respondents commented either neutrally or positively on the accent's perceived casual nature and impression of solidarity (for example, 'laid back, broad', 'oblivious, easygoing', 'relaxed', 'broad accent, easily approachable people (friendly)', 'happy, positive'). Others were more ambivalent in this respect, with statements such as 'peasant', 'link all the words together, for example, 'G'day! Hawya?', 'sounds a bit funny but makes me in a good humour').

It seems, then, that there was a certain amount of ambivalence about the Australian English accent—far more so than there was in respect of UK and US accents, but less than in respect of most of the NNS English accents. They favoured it over the latter presumably because, despite its 'shortcomings', it is still an NS English accent. But many nevertheless perceived it as inferior to 'authentic' NS accents (i.e. UK and US), sometimes in quite major ways.

The comments made about the ten specified accents reveal a number of recurring themes that relate particularly to correctness, authenticity, and intelligibility, as well as a good deal of ambivalence and ambiguity in respect of all three and a sense that identity is playing an important role. There are also strong indications that as far as correctness and authenticity are concerned, regardless of whether they come from the expanding or outer circle, the NNS accents were being described wholly in terms of their proximity to or distance from one or other of the two favoured NS accent varieties. On the other hand, it is clear that at the aesthetic level some accents were liked in spite of their 'flaws' in terms of correctness and their perceived lack of authenticity. And as far as intelligibility is concerned, there is a good deal of ambiguity. We return to all these issues below, but first consider the findings of the second map-labelling task, where respondents were asked to describe any other English accents with which they were familiar.

Descriptions of other English accents (Question 2)

The first map task was designed to ensure a spread of expanding circle accents as well as to enable comparisons with perceptions of inner and outer circle accents. The purpose of the open-ended map-labelling task, on the other hand, was to provide respondents with the opportunity to single out any other accents that they wished to, my expectation being that they would select those about which they had particularly strong feelings one way or the other. We begin by considering which other English accents turned out to be most salient to the respondents, i.e. those that they mentioned the most frequently. We then consider the different types of comments made about each of the five most frequently mentioned accents, along with examples of respondents' verbatim descriptions.

The most commonly described accents are shown in Table 6.4 below, along with the number of respondents that referred to each. Looking at the types of comment made about the first five accents, the most noticeable thing is that those for Canadian English are almost exclusively favourable, those for

Russian English exclusively pejorative, while those for the other three are mixed to varying degrees.

Comments about the French English accent focused primarily on its strength and unintelligibility. There were references to it as a strong accent that sounds 'too much like French'. There was even a suggestion that this is deliberate: 'refuse to speak English, French penetrates strongly in sounds'. Some referred to the uvular /r/, for example, 'funny because of incorrect /r/-sound', while one, presumably intentionally, mis-spelt the word 'hard' as 'harrd'. Another said 'French has funny accent with "h"'. Others linked the Frenchness of the accent to their perceptions of it as difficult to understand, for example, 'difficult to understand ("French pronunciation")'. On the other hand, there were several positive comments, with descriptions of it as 'elegant', 'charming', and 'melodious', as well as 'melodious, charming', although some also combined 'melodious' with a pejorative comment, for example, 'melodious, funny' or 'melodious, annoying at times'.

Accent	Number
1 French English	30
2 Canadian English	27
3 Korean English	22
4 Italian English	21
5 Russian English	14
6 Irish English	10
7 New Zealand English	9
8 Finnish English	8
S.African English	8
9 Taiwanese English	7
10 Argentine English	6
Mexican English	6
Philippine English	6
Singapore English	6

Table 6.4 Most commonly described accents in world map-labelling task

The descriptions of Canadian English were a different matter. The only negative comment was 'pompous', and there were also a few neutral descriptions concerning the closeness of Canadian English to US English. Even here, the comments tended to favour Canada (for example, 'easier than USA', 'a little clearer than the US'), although one comment, 'the (more) country cousin of American English' was perhaps intended to imply something of the 'peasant' that was used to describe Australian English in the first map task. Otherwise, the comments all referred positively to the perceived clarity and intelligibility of Canadian English, to its pleasantness (for example, 'nice on the ear', 'melodious') and to its correctness (for example, 'very standard'), while one respondent stated simply: 'great, I like hearing them speak'.

The descriptions of the Korean English accent were the exact opposite. Although there were both negative and positive comments, the proportion of negative comments was a lot higher than that relating to the French English accent. In fact, apart from a few descriptions of Korean English as easy to understand, the commentary was almost entirely negative. Several described it in various ways as difficult to understand, one as 'strange', two as 'harsh', one as 'nasal', and one as 'quarrel like'. Some singled out specific pronunciation features, for example, 'pronounce final consonant with a vowel /hʌsbəndo/ for husband', and 'pronunciation [f] vs. [θ]. They sometimes say 'I fink' instead of 'I think', while one merely stated 'some consonants aren't pronounced correctly'. Surprisingly, only one respondent commented on a sound substitution that has been shown to cause a lot of intelligibility problems, i.e. /p/ for /f/: 'Korean people pronounce good "l" sound, but their "f" sounds like "p" sound, for example, where are you from?'

The positives and negatives were far more balanced in respect of Italian English. Two referred to the accent's 'Italian' quality: 'very Italian' and, more stereotypically, 'speak English like they speak Italian—fast and hands swinging in the air'. Others described the accent as 'careless', 'ugly', 'irritating', 'flat/blunt', and 'fast and sticky'. As regards specific pronunciation items, one pointed out a phonemic 'error', i.e. 'think /tɪnk/', another commented 'fast, lots of ch's', and a third that 'rhythm interferes with understanding'. On the other hand, several referred to the accent's melody (for example, 'singing', 'they sing a lot', 'clear and melodic', 'melodious', 'sweet sounding').

Russian English, on the other hand, was described in unremittingly negative terms. Most of the comments concerned the accent's perceived inferior aesthetic qualities, with some describing it as 'harsh', one noting 'harsh, especially about [r] sound', and another, 'harsh, unfriendly'. Others described it as 'strong', 'strange', 'heavy', 'sharp', and aggressive'. There were no comments on correctness, while only one person commented (pejoratively) on intelligibility, which suggests that very few respondents had actually experienced Russian English first-hand, and that their comments may have been based on stereotypes presented in the media and films.

The open map-labelling task thus produces very similar results to those of the earlier closed map task, with the NS accent highly favourably perceived, the western European accents less so, and the Asian English accent, this time along with the Russian, at the receiving end of the most pejorative comments. The results of the open map task are also very similar to those of Lindemann's (2005) study that I referred to earlier in the chapter, despite the fact that her respondents were all NSs of English (from the US), and mine all NNSs. Not only did the two groups find many of the same countries' accents the most salient,[12] but they also shared similar perceptions of NS, European, Asian, and Russian English accents. Another factor that emerges from both sets of results (and this also includes the results of my first map task) is a strongly NS-normative belief about the correctness and pleasantness of NS English accents. It is perhaps only to be expected that NSs of English would demonstrate a strong preference for NS English accents in these respects. The fact that NNSs of English share this preference with them suggests, once again, the influence of the prevailing standard NS English ideology that was discussed in Chapter 2, and to which we return in the final chapter.

Concluding comments on the map tasks

The findings of the map-labelling tasks thus support, extend, and provide insights into those of the ranking and rating tasks. At the overt level, many of the respondents articulated firm beliefs about English accents: their correctness, pleasantness, intelligibility, authenticity and so on. At the covert level, both the emotional language in which these beliefs were at times expressed (labels such as 'quarrel-like', 'menacing', 'aggressive', and the like),[13] and the ambivalences that sometimes emerged, point to the existence of more deeply entrenched and ideologically influenced attitudes which, in turn, may explain the respondents' generally negative perceptions of ELF—and possibly all NNS English—accents.

Beliefs about the correctness and authenticity of two NS English accents, UK and US, emerge as unshakable. Even if some respondents did not find one or other accent pleasant or intelligible, and commented negatively in these respects, they did not question its correctness or status as authentic English. Meanwhile, they labelled other accents, whether inner, outer or expanding circle, in terms of similarities to and differences from one or both of these two 'marker' accents. And even if they occasionally responded positively to an accent's differences from UK/US accents at the aesthetic level, this was not sufficient to challenge their perceptions of that accent's subordinate status.

In terms of intelligibility, the variable that I had deliberately chosen not to mention by name (see p. 153), many respondents described particular accents as being in some way difficult to understand. As a rule, however, these turned out also to be accents that the respondents appeared not to like, as demonstrated by the types of comment they made about unpleasantness in particular, thus confirming Giles and Niedzielski's (1998) point—see above, p. 153. In addition, respondents often cited specific features of an accent that they considered to be unintelligible, and yet the very fact that they were aware of a feature implies that it did not present an intelligibility problem for them. This takes us back to the point I made in Chapter 5 in relation to the teacher who believed that he would not understand an NNS of English who pronounced the word 'thinking' as 'sinking'. It suggests, in turn, that something else is involved below the surface, and that this 'something else' has to do with language attitudes, which, as Wolff (1959) points out, are closely linked with issues of power—see Chapter 3. In many of the respondents' minds, it seemed, the power effect meant that intelligibility could not be disassociated from intelligibility for communication with or between NSs of English (respectively EFL and ENL). And as with the common assumption that British and American English are the only kinds of English that can be used as the yardstick for testing English internationally, while all other Englishes have only local relevance (see the analysis of publications in Chapter 2), so there was an assumption that only NS or near-NS English is internationally intelligible. Although some respondents' comments, especially in the final section of the questionnaire (see below) indicated that this was not universally the case, there was an almost total lack of awareness of the possibly greater intelligibility of ELF accents for international communication shown in the comments they made in the map labelling task.

We return to these issues and others in the conclusion to the study, but first explore the comments provided at the end of the questionnaire by a large number of the respondents.

Any other comments?

The issues that the questionnaire raised for the respondents were such that almost half added a comment where invited to do so, some at considerable length. While these comments range widely, some very detailed, others very general, some providing a highly personal perspective, others taking a more holistic view, a number of common themes emerge from what they say. On examining the key points in each comment, I was able to identify six main (although sometimes overlapping) categories or themes, all of which are outlined in turn below together with copious verbatim examples to provide a strong sense of the 'flavour' of the original.[14]

Reservations

One group of comments falls into a category that can loosely be called 'reservations'. A number of respondents in this group object to the nature of the tasks they have been asked to carry out, in some cases commenting perceptively on the difficulty and/or inappropriateness, in the light of the spread of English, of ranking English accents for 'bestness' or rating them for correctness and pleasantness. For example:

> I don't think there is a so-called 'good' accent of English. English is supposed to be a language for communication, not to be compared for values because of its different accents. People are just familiar with specific accents. It's the familiarity that matters.

> The words 'correct' and 'incorrect' in the questionnaire surprised me, especially when the euro-centric world is getting 'decentered'. I suppose 'British and 'non-British' might be better words to use.

> I can't grade English accents because English is becoming a common language in the world and various Englishes have been accepted.

On the other hand, some argue this point only in relation to NS (mainly US and UK) English accents, and most frequently in terms of correctness, imply-ing a belief that these NS accents are, by definition, 'correct'. Others point out that there are many different varieties of all accents, and that it is therefore not possible to talk, for instance, of a 'US', 'UK, or 'China' English accent. Some go on to argue that intelligibility is the most important factor, although those that try to pin it down, tend to resort to NS norms (for example, 'Wouldn't it be more natural and practical to use the patterns that original native speakers already have …?'). Still others point out that they have limited experience of some of the specified English accents and ask, for example, 'how can I make judgements (let alone make generalisations) from such a few speech samples?' Almost all respondents in the 'reservations' category nevertheless attempt the less overtly evaluative map-labelling tasks in the first part of the questionnaire, while some, despite their objections, nevertheless go ahead and complete the rating and (to a lesser extent) the ranking tasks.

Prejudice

The second, and much smaller category concerns prejudice. Some respondents discuss what they see as the inevitability of prejudice and bias, even in their own individual cases, for example:

> Prejudice is never good, especially when talking about intercultural relationships and communication. But it is impossible not to have certain attachments to this or that group of people, society, etc. and the way they speak, due to our individual experience with all our feelings involved. It wouldn't be honest to deny it.

> I've tried to be honest when providing these answers but my honesty sometimes scares me. I am probably as biased towards certain accents of English as I encourage my students not to be!

> It was difficult to deal with the concept of 'correctness' as it is already filled with prejudice, to say the least. Applying it to the ever-called 'native speakers' of English felt very odd and uncomfortable, which in my opinion, served to show me how much I'm still attached to the idea that the English spoken by its native-users still is the model to be followed.

Another argues that the whole issue needs politicizing:

> I also feel that the issue should be viewed in political terms since accent can be, and very often is used to discriminate. Funny thing is that language, instead of being used as a means to communicate becomes the very thing to discriminate for example, social class, race (in general terms what constitutes the 'other' in S. de Beauvoir's terms).

Intelligibility

A third theme, though one that overlaps with the first, is intelligibility. Like some of those who object to the questions themselves, other respondents believe that intelligibility should be the main criterion for evaluating English accents:

'Best' means 'intelligible' in my judgement ... To me, accents which are intelligible are pleasant and acceptable. Accents which are difficult to comprehend ... are obviously not pleasant.

Again, as with some in the 'reservations' group, some of this third group link intelligibility with the spread of English and equate it with the 'acceptability for international communication' dimension on the questionnaire:

I think it's all right that there are a variety of accents of English language. What is important is 'intelligibility' because the language is the tool of 'international communication'.

[Japanese people] think the pronunciation of native speaker is the norm and any other type of pronunciation is wrong. They should pay much more attention to the 'acceptability' of their pronunciation, in the context of globalization and World Englishes.

Others approach intelligibility from a much more NS-normative perspective, arguing that NS accents should be taught and used because they are the most universally understood. For example:

Non-native English accents are not problems in communication. However, we still try to teach them with a so-called standard one like American accent. Because in teaching, its important to teach students to speak language (English) that could be understood by most of people in the world.

From my experience, Canadian accent seems clear and easy to understand. It's not fast, and the accent does not seem to have a peculiar characteristic. I think the acceptable English accent for international communication should not be noticeable and peculiar, but be clear plain, and normal in speed.

Various other comments of this sort indicate that many of the teachers believe North American or British English accents to be the most intelligible and therefore internationally acceptable because they are the most 'normal', and 'correct'.

Familiarity

Connected to the previous category is the 'familiarity' theme, in which a number of respondents argue that experience of an accent leads to ease of understanding. The following is a typical example:

When we get used to each accent of languages and understand the aspects and differences, we get to understand especially in listening to that accented English.

Some start from the premise that unfamiliar NNS accents are difficult to understand, and identify what they believe to be the phonological or phonetic causes:

> Non-native English accents are very hard to understand for non-native speakers, especially if the language they speak is not familiar to you. It very often depends on how they <u>stress</u> the words if you do not understand them. (emphasis in original)

On the other hand, several refer to NS accents, often drawing a link between familiarity and perceptions of authenticity and standardness. For example:

> Japanese people are so accustomed to American English that any other accents including even British accent sound 'unfamiliar' or 'not mainstream'. They are keen to acquire so-to-speak 'authentic' English though it's gradually recognised that there are a variety of accents in the world, which should be accepted.

> In my country, many people seem to regard American pronunciation as standard, because in English class, almost all of the model speakers of CDs and tapes are American. Although I say to myself that I must accept every variety, I sometimes feel unfamiliar accents to be a little uncomfortable (especially if they are far from GA or RP).

One respondent does not make the NS link specifically. However, given that she ranks UK, US, and Canadian English accents (in that order) as the three 'best' in question 3, and rates UK and US accents as far better than the other eight in question 4, 'good' presumably equates with 'NS':

> I think that less familiar accents tend to sound worse to our ears. Why is it so difficult to teach our students a good English accent?

Personal preferences

Another theme can broadly be described as 'personal preferences'. Several respondents use the comments section to explain which accent(s) they or their L1 group particularly like or consider to be particularly good, and why. Not surprisingly, the majority of these are NS accents.

> I like the Australian accent. I'm also familiar with it. Like to hear and listen to them. I even try to imitate it, mix it up with my German accent.

> American accent is very popular among Finnish school children and very much copied and imitated. British RP is considered funny and pompous.

> Originally I did think US accent is the very correct, mainstream one. However, when I contacted the British-like accent, I came to realize that British one has its speciality and uniqueness that cannot be 'conquered' or overthrown ('replaced') by North American, to be honest. Gradually, the most correct accent could be British one in my mind.

A few respondents express a preference for NNS accents. For example:

> Why I like the German accent is because I'm so familiar with it and can understand it best. English and German are similar languages and for that it is easy to learn English for German students.

> I just would like to say that I've always been surprised by the quality of the English accent of people from Eastern Europe and Scandinavia; it's even more pleasant than the accent of native speakers sometimes!!!

In other cases, though, an NNS accent is preferred merely because the NS accent used for comparison is a 'non-standard' one such as Cockney, or because the NNS accent has a reputation for being 'good'. For example:

> Personally, I would prefer the accent of non-native speakers to the group of native English speakers who swallow the words and letters, for example, 'better' becomes 'be'er', 'them' becomes ''em', 'have' becomes ''ave'. Simply horrible! At least the non-native speakers try to pronounce the words properly, though their accent is influenced by their native language.

> I remember, when living in England, that my teacher of English used to compliment my Swedish classmates on their accent by saying how good or correct it was.

Accent 'problems'

The last, but by far the largest, category comprises comments on the accent 'problems' of NNSs in general and specific L1 groups in particular. In almost every case, the respondent appears to be working on the basis of NS norms as 'correct' and differences from them as indicative of 'problems'. The following examples arc typical:

> All non-native accents suffer strong interference from its mother tongue. So impressions and evaluation will vary a lot. English-speaking people from Asian countries <u>do</u> have trouble with pronunciation. It's really hard to understand what they say. The more educated they are the better their English sounds. (emphasis added)

> In my opinion, when a non-native English speaker speaks English, she/he does not pay attention to the correct way of how to pronounce a word or his/her mouth shape. And also the effect of their native accent. To be a good speaker in English, imitating is the first thing.

> Non-native speakers generally receive great influences from their mother tongue. Take Japanese for example. In Japan, every sound ends in vowels, so Japanese people are liable to voice every sound in English, even a voiceless consonant. They tend to add a vowel automatically to each sound. For instance, they may pronounce apartment as apartomento.

Also, I find many Spanish speakers have the habit to pronounce a [e]
sound when they pause to think during a conversation.

Actually, most of the non-native English learners are trying to pronounce
English like native speakers. But it's very difficult because the accents and
pronunciation would relate to the movements of the tongue and lips,
velum and so on. Korean people often pronounce /f/ sounds as
/p/ sounds, and for Japanese learners, /r/ and /l/ sounds are very difficult.

One respondent argues that all NNSs have the potential to speak with good
(i.e. nativelike) English accents, but that this is less likely in the case of speakers
of Asian Englishes as compared with speakers of European Englishes because
of the greater distance between their mother tongues and English:

In my experience <u>competent</u> speakers from all countries speak very well.
<u>Perhaps</u> there are relatively fewer competent speakers in countries like
Japan and China, since for many Chinese and Japanese people English is
not a second language. In addition, Chinese and Japanese as well as the
many Indian languages are further away from English than the European
languages are. This means that those speakers have to work a lot harder
to achieve a good level. The Chinese stress seems to be very different from
the English one, for example. (emphasis in original)

Few respondents discuss the possibility that NNS accents may be acceptable
in international communication, while several refer to the perceived risk that
the range of NNS accents will lead to mutual international unintelligibility.
For example:

Accents of mother tongue always exert great influence on non-native
English accents. Actually, each part of the world has its English accent
which will set obstacles to the understanding of each other. So we have an
embarrassment now: we may all speak English but we can't understand
each other.

On the other hand, a small number go on to point out that the NNS
pronunciation features they have described as problematic may in fact be
internationally intelligible:

I don't really know why, but the fact that Spanish speakers have a difficult
time distinguishing between /s/ and /z/ in words like 'cosy', for example,
really bothers me. What's interesting is that it doesn't hinder communication, usually.

Thus, while some of the respondents' comments reveal an acute awareness of
the issues involved in the spread of English and, in particular, its growing role
as an international lingua franca, this is not so for the majority. It appears that
many of these NNS teachers of English believe they should still be operating
within a framework of NS-normativeness that in essence is no different from
English as a foreign language. It also appears that the majority are unaware

of possible links between their social and accent evaluations. While a small number refer to accent-based prejudice, only one, an NS respondent, makes an explicit link with social evaluations in admitting that the process of completing the questionnaire has led him to realize that his social evaluations of different groups of NNS English speakers affect his evaluations of their accents:

> I realised doing this how my opinions of the nationality/people quite influenced my attitude to their accents. Particularly with regard to how pleasant I find them to listen to/be with (perhaps the two categories are practically one and the same in my mind!)

Conclusions to the questionnaire study

In one sense, the patterns revealed in the questionnaire study are straightforward: NS English accents, and particularly UK and US accents, are preferred in all respects by this large group of expanding circle respondents, when evaluated overtly in the rating and ranking tasks. They are also highly valued for their perceived correctness and intelligibility in the qualitative map-labelling tasks and commentaries, although not necessarily quite as much in terms of their aesthetic qualities.

Meanwhile, all NNS accents are non-preferred in the ranking and rating tasks, but in a hierarchical fashion, with those closest to NS accents being least non-preferred (apart from German English on the pleasantness scale), and those furthest from them, i.e. East Asian English accents, being most non-preferred. With a few notable exceptions, this trend again emerges in the commentaries. On the other hand, in the map-labelling tasks, some NNS accents are perceived rather more positively in terms of their pleasantness and (less often) their intelligibility, while others are heavily stigmatized. Despite the perceived pleasantness and intelligibility of some NNS English accents, this was never sufficient for an NNS accent to challenge the pole position of UK and US English accents in the ranking and rating tasks. In this respect, then, for some of these NNS respondents, as for some of Lindemann's NS respondents, it seems that 'the largest category within non-native English, and for some respondents perhaps the only category, is a general one of stigmatized non-native English' (2005: 207).

Many of the respondents thus reveal strongly held positions about the correctness, pleasantness, and international acceptability of English accents (sometimes on the basis of limited familiarity), and firm linguistic beliefs about the locus of the 'best' English accents (i.e. the US and UK). They also appear to regard correctness as the single most important criterion in evaluating English accents. Although this could be attributed to the fact that the respondents in my study are all teachers of English, prescriptivism has also been found highly salient among non-teaching folk (for example, Niedzielski and Preston 2000/2003). Thus, while some 'teacher folk' may have a more sophisticated knowledge of phonology and phonetics than the 'non-teacher folk', with few exceptions they all (NS as well as NNS) seem to share with non-teachers the 'common sense' view of correctness that links with, and suggests the possible influence of, the standard language ideology that was discussed earlier. (See Chapter 2.)

In some respects, the respondents' beliefs about NS and NNS English accents can be explained by the 'social connotations hypothesis' (Trudgill and Giles 1978). According to this hypothesis, reactions to accents are reactions to their social connotations rather than to their intrinsic features, and involve, according to Trudgill and Giles (1978: 186) 'a complex of social, cultural, regional, political and personal associations and prejudices' that 'have no basis in objective linguistic fact'. Uniform stereotypical views of accents, the authors argue citing the findings of early matched-guise tests, 'could suggest that the subjects in these experiments have been 'brain-washed' to an extent that renders objective responses on their part very unlikely' (op. cit.: 175). Trudgill and Giles go on to point out that even those who 'themselves use very varied varieties of language ... nevertheless often appear to share as a community as a whole, a common set of norms as to what is 'good' and 'bad' in the language' (ibid.). If we consider ELF attitudes in light of the social connotations hypothesis, we must consider the possibility that the NNS teachers who took part in the study (along with most of their peer group) have, at least to some extent, been so strongly influenced ('brainwashed' even) by the prevailing standard NS English ideology that they, like the subjects to whom Trudgill and Giles refer, are unable to make 'objective responses' based on linguistic fact. And they, too, share a 'common set of norms as to what is 'good' and 'bad' in the language', even though they themselves speak varieties of the language that they would classify as 'bad'. For as Lin, Wang, Akamaatsu, and Riazi point out, '[t]hese dichotic, essentialized catgegories are so pervasive in our [NNS] consciousness that we even reproduce them in our own stories' (2005: 214).

In other respects, however, all is not quite so straightforward as there seems to be a rather complex dynamic operating across the correctness–pleasantness–acceptability spectrum that suggests a degree of ambivalence. In particular, as I pointed out earlier, in some cases and most noticeably German English and Australian English, an evaluation of the accent on one dimension seems to exert an upward or downward pull on its evaluation on another dimension, although much more research is needed to explore exactly how this works. The point for now, though, is that these NNS respondents' apparent liking for the aesthetic qualities of some NNS accents, as well as their belief that some are easily intelligible internationally, represents an encouraging first step in the legitimizing of ELF accents. It is also refreshing, in this respect, to observe the beginnings of an ELF perspective emerging and replacing that of EFL among a minority of respondents in the comments they make about NNS English accents in the map labelling tasks and, especially, in their commentaries at the end of the questionnaire. While many still seem to subscribe to the view often found in the literature that as far as international acceptability is concerned, 'US English = international English', there are signs that things may be slowly changing at the 'chalk face'.

Again, while linguistic insecurity is certainly in evidence (and see Chapter 8), it is also encouraging that some respondents appear to feel reasonably positive about their own accent, and the Chinese respondents particularly so. Giles and Niedzielski (1998) point out that 'language "facts" can sometimes swiftly change' (p. 89), and that '[w]hen subordinate groups in society come to question the legitimacy of their inferior roles in society and attribute these to oppressive and discriminatory measures of an "elite" group, they can redefine the beauty and importance of their language, accordingly, and sometimes vociferously' (pp. 89–90). The accent attitudes study discussed in this chapter has shown that such a redefinition may just be beginning to take place. And there are indications that identity is playing a part in it—an issue that is explored in detail in the next chapter. Perhaps globalization also has something to do with it. As Coupland (2003: 469) points out with reference to Blommaert (2003), Blommaert 'reminds us ... that the values of styles and varieties can easily shift as they are scrutinised in different localities'. Although Blommaert's reference is to the way in which 'globalisation can be a powerful source of new language-centred inequalities' (Coupland ibid.), there seems to be no reason why this cannot work in the opposite direction, and that globalization cannot be a powerful source of new language-centred *equalities*. As English, the language of globalization, spreads around the world and is appropriated by an ever-increasing range and number of NNSs, it is perhaps inevitable that their sense of inferiority in the language will one day begin to diminish and that they, the majority speakers of the language, will eventually start to see themselves as at least equals alongside NSs in the global lingua franca English context.

The studies in this chapter and the last have approached ELF and ELF accent attitudes in various ways, both qualitative (in the analysis of the spoken texts, some aspects of the written texts, and some parts of the questionnaire) and quantitative (in the analysis of other aspects of the written texts and other parts of the questionnaire). In so far as these studies as a whole are at all representative, they share one 'big' (if unsurprising) finding, that despite the massive shift in the use and users of English over recent decades, many and perhaps the majority of teachers of English in expanding circle countries continue to believe that 'proper' English resides in certain of its 'ancestral homes', principally the UK and US.[15] This, along with some of these studies' other findings about teachers' attitudes and beliefs, raises a number of issues concerning, for example, linguistic insecurity, language myths, response to change, and, of course, the relationship between language attitudes and socio-political attitudes, issues to which we return in the final chapter. It also raises important issues about teachers' identities in English in terms of how they see themselves both as successful English teachers and as members of their own L1 groups, and of the ambivalence that may be generated by the clash between the two. It is to such identity issues that we turn in the following chapter.

Appendix: English accents questionnaire

Personal information

If you provide your name and/or your email address, these will remain entirely confidential and your anonymity will be protected at all times.

Name (optional) _____

Male / female (*circle as appropriate*)

Age (circle as appropriate)   20–29   30–39   40–49   50–59   60+

Country of birth _____

Country where you live now/for how long? _____

Mother tongue _____

Other languages you speak _____
_____

Your total number of years of English teaching _____

In which country/countries? _____
_____

How long have you taught in each country? _____
_____

Email address (if you are happy for me to contact you) _____

Map questions

Please refer to this map when you answer the questions that follow.

1 Write in the spaces below a word or phrase that represents for you the English accent of each numbered country on the map. You can refer to *any* aspect of the accent, such as its speed, its quality of tone (e.g. 'harsh', 'melodious'), its pitch, its rhythm (e.g. 'like a machine gun'), its precision, its strength, how easy it is to understand etc. etc. There is no correct answer. Please say what you think—I am interested in your views

1 _____   6 _____
2 _____   7 _____
3 _____   8 _____
4 _____   9 _____
5 _____   10 _____

2 Look again at the map. Draw an arrow towards any *non-numbered* countries with whose English accents you are familiar, and label each arrow with a word or phrase that represents for you the English accent of that country. Each time write the name of the country next to your word or phrase.

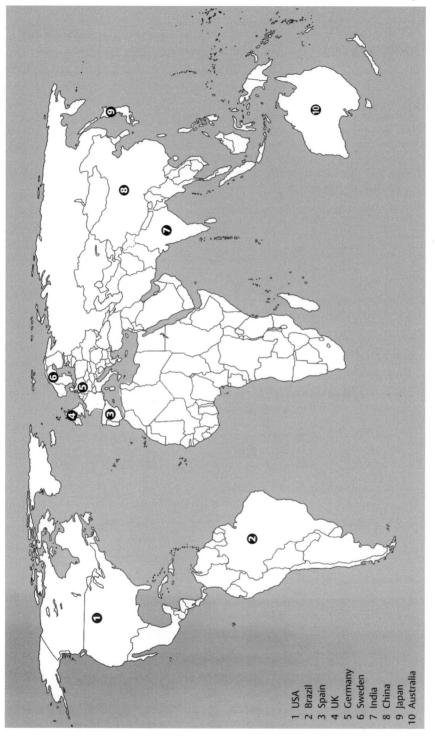

1 USA
2 Brazil
3 Spain
4 UK
5 Germany
6 Sweden
7 India
8 China
9 Japan
10 Australia

3 Now list below the *five* English accents that you think are the best (with the best English accent in the world as no.1, the second best as no. 2 and so on). Choose from *all* the countries in the world, not only the ten numbered countries on the map.

1 _____   4 _____

2 _____   5 _____

3 _____

4 Put the English accent of a competent speaker of English from each of the ten numbered countries on the map on page 2 onto the following scales for (a) *correctness* (b) *acceptability for international communication* (c) *pleasantness* (d) *your familiarity with the accent*. In each case, put a circle round the number that you have chosen.

Accent of speakers from country number **1**

a	very correct	1 2 3 4 5 6	very incorrect
b	very acceptable	1 2 3 4 5 6	very unacceptable
c	very pleasant	1 2 3 4 5 6	very unpleasant
d	very familiar	1 2 3 4 5 6	very unfamiliar

Accent of speakers from country number **2**

a	very correct	1 2 3 4 5 6	very incorrect
b	very acceptable	1 2 3 4 5 6	very unacceptable
c	very pleasant	1 2 3 4 5 6	very unpleasant
d	very familiar	1 2 3 4 5 6	very unfamiliar

Accent of speakers from country number **3**

a	very correct	1 2 3 4 5 6	very incorrect
b	very acceptable	1 2 3 4 5 6	very unacceptable
c	very pleasant	1 2 3 4 5 6	very unpleasant
d	very familiar	1 2 3 4 5 6	very unfamiliar

Accent of speakers from country number **4**

a	very correct	1 2 3 4 5 6	very incorrect
b	very acceptable	1 2 3 4 5 6	very unacceptable
c	very pleasant	1 2 3 4 5 6	very unpleasant
d	very familiar	1 2 3 4 5 6	very unfamiliar

Accent of speakers from country number **5**

a	very correct	1 2 3 4 5 6	very incorrect
b	very acceptable	1 2 3 4 5 6	very unacceptable
c	very pleasant	1 2 3 4 5 6	very unpleasant
d	very familiar	1 2 3 4 5 6	very unfamiliar

Accent of speakers from country number **6**

a	very correct	1 2 3 4 5 6	very incorrect
b	very acceptable	1 2 3 4 5 6	very unacceptable
c	very pleasant	1 2 3 4 5 6	very unpleasant
d	very familiar	1 2 3 4 5 6	very unfamiliar

Accent of speakers from country number 7

a very correct	1	2	3	4	5	6	very incorrect
b very acceptable	1	2	3	4	5	6	very unacceptable
c very pleasant	1	2	3	4	5	6	very unpleasant
d very familiar	1	2	3	4	5	6	very unfamiliar

Accent of speakers from country number 8

a very correct	1	2	3	4	5	6	very incorrect
b very acceptable	1	2	3	4	5	6	very unacceptable
c very pleasant	1	2	3	4	5	6	very unpleasant
d very familiar	1	2	3	4	5	6	very unfamiliar

Accent of speakers from country number 9

a very correct	1	2	3	4	5	6	very incorrect
b very acceptable	1	2	3	4	5	6	very unacceptable
c very pleasant	1	2	3	4	5	6	very unpleasant
d very familiar	1	2	3	4	5	6	very unfamiliar

Accent of speakers from country number 10

a very correct	1	2	3	4	5	6	very incorrect
b very acceptable	1	2	3	4	5	6	very unacceptable
c very pleasant	1	2	3	4	5	6	very unpleasant
d very familiar	1	2	3	4	5	6	very unfamiliar

Any other comments?

Please use the rest of this page for any comments you would like to make about non-native English accents in general or about specific non-native English accents. You can refer to the English accent of any country/countries whether or not they are numbered on the map, and to any aspect of English accents. Feel free to say whatever you like—your opinions are important to me.

_____

_____

_____

_____

_____

_____

_____

_____

Thank you very much for completing this questionnaire. I am very grateful. You are welcome to email me at jennifer.jenkins@kcl.ac.uk if you would like to discuss any issues relating to the questions.

Notes

1 Within the field of folk linguistics as a whole, researchers may also make use of ethnographic interviews and participant observation in order to explore people's language beliefs in greater detail and depth.

2 This seems to be the case even when the theoretical study of World Englishes is included in the curriculum. Seidlhofer (2001b), for example, points out that students in her department at the University of Vienna who are studying to be English teachers are familiarized with research into indigenized Englishes, linguistic imperialism, the future of English and the like on their applied linguistics course. Then they go to their English language class, where they are presented with a standard British or American native speaker model, which they are expected to approximate and against which their performance will be assessed.

3 The final item in the section on personal information was 'Email address (if you are happy for me to contact you)'.

4 I deliberately did not specify GA for the US and RP for the UK, partly because some respondents may not have known these terms, but mainly because I was interested in finding our how the respondents *themselves* would define US and UK English accents.

5 Most of the German respondents were also studying to become teachers, but they already had some English teaching experience, for example, as teaching assistants and private tutors, a few over a period of several years.

6 Although 26 is a very small sample as compared with the aggregate NNS sample, the NS responses were included purely for comparison with the NNS. In other words, I was not interested in the NS responses in themselves, but only in terms of any particularly noticeable differences and similarities to the NNS responses that they might reveal in terms of accent attitudes and beliefs.

7 As I pointed out earlier, the questionnaire did not distinguish between different UK and US accents, but left it to individual respondents to refer to them if they so wished. A few respondents complained about this, rightly pointing out that 'UK' and 'US' each include a wide range of English accents. For the purposes of presenting the results of the ranking task, all UK accents have been classified as 'UK' even if, for example, 'Scottish' or 'Cornish' was actually specified, and US accents have been classified according to the same principle. (But see below for comments on some of the more detailed choices that respondents made.)

8 Several of those ranked fifth just once were ranked thus by the NS group, who seemed to use the slot to mention the accent of a country where they had taught (for example, Mexico, Poland, Turkey) or had had some other form of contact, and whose English accent they perhaps simply liked rather than thought of as fifth 'best'.

9 Although the majority did not comment on the subject, some respondents made very specific choices in respect of UK and US English. As far as UK accents are concerned, the following accents were all specified: English-English, RP, BBC English, Oxford English, Cambridge English, South England, Queen's English, London English, Estuary English, and Scottish English, while a small number chose 'smaller' regional accents such as Cornish and Leeds. Within the larger US category, a few specified a New York accent (one NNS adding that 'New York has an international English'). Several referred to an American Standard accent, to GA, or to specific regions such as East, Midwest, North West, and 'Southern drawl', or even mentioned accents that they excluded, for example, 'US, not southern or very broad', or 'not Southern states'.

10 In some cases respondents left an entire set of scales blank, often indicating that they had no experience of that particular accent (for example, 'no idea', 'don't know'). In other cases, they completed all ten sets of scales for all but one or two of the dimensions, sometimes indicating that they did not consider it possible to rate an accent for, for example, correctness. A number also left the entire question blank. In some cases the reason was not clear, while in others, respondents commented on not being able to judge accents in this way. Some of them nevertheless completed the map-labelling tasks. Hence the number (N) in brackets after each mean varies from item to item, and is always below the potential total of 300 NNS and 26 NS responses.

11 The 26 NS responses were not included in the analysis of the map labelling tasks as my interest was primarily in examining NNS English teachers' accent attitudes and beliefs as a prelude to considering the ways in which they interact with the NNS teacher identity issues explored in Chapter 7.

12 The ten most frequently mentioned countries in Lindemann's study were, in descending order, China, Australia, Mexico, Russia, UK, Canada, France, India, Germany, and Italy. Of these, five (China, Australia, UK, India, and Germany) had already been specified in my first map task, so were not available in the second task. Of Lindemann's other five, four were among the five most commonly described in my second map task, i.e. Russia, Canada, France, and Italy.

13 Comments such as these were made by respondents who also demonstrated (in the rating task) that they had little or no familiarity with the accent concerned. In other words, they were responding to stereotypes. And regardless of whether their speakers belong to the outer or expanding circle, and had East or South Asian accents, Asian English accents received by far the most derogatory emotive language, with the exception of Russian. Because of this, we cannot discount the possibility that there was an element of racism involved. (See Chapter 3.)

14 Unless otherwise stated, as with the map-labelling tasks, the comments that I report are all drawn from the NNS responses.

15 A rather different picture has emerged in recent unpublished studies of secondary school students' preferences, in which around a third opt for an international kind of English rather than a British or American variety (Anna Mauranen, personal communication; and see the ELFA website for references). Although this is a different issue from that of 'proper' or 'best' English, and it is not clear exactly what such students mean by 'international', it is an interesting development, and opens up the possibility that younger English speakers may at some future stage start to resist ENL regardless of what they are taught. If some of them went on to become teachers of English themselves, ELF might then become the focus of English teaching by default.

7

ELF and identity

As we saw in the previous two chapters, there seems to be a good deal of ambiguity in English teachers' perceptions of ELF in general and ELF accents in particular. On the one hand, the majority involved in the studies in Chapters 5 and 6 revealed an unquestioning certainty that NS English (British or American) is the most desirable and most appropriate kind of English for international communication. On the other hand, it is evident that beneath the surface-level argument used to justify ENL and disparage ELF, lie deeply entrenched attitudes and, at times, an emotional and even irrational attachment to British and American English. These attitudes, I suggested, have to do with identity, whether that of the 'NS English-aspiring' NNS teacher of English or of the 'NS English-owning' NS teacher. In this chapter, we focus on ELF identity issues as they affect NNS teachers, exploring in particular the extent to which any ambivalence towards ELF may be the result of some kind of conflict between their identities as successful teachers and as members of their own L1 groups and a wider ELF community.

Language and identity

It is not at all surprising that identity is crucially involved in attitudes towards ELF given that, as Joseph points out, it 'is at the very heart of what language is about, how it operates, why and how it came into existence and evolved as it did, how it is learned and how it is used, every day, by every user, every time it is used' (2004a: 224). This holds true for L2 speakers as much as for L1 speakers, a point frequently made by those who take a sociocultural approach to second language learning—for example, Donato 2000; Pavlenko and Lantolf 2000; Pavlenko 2002—as well as others—such as Norton (2000) and V. Cook (2002b)—who regard learners first and foremost as social beings and users of their L2 in their own right rather than 'disembodied brains' (Thorne 2000: 220). It is a point that is echoed, too, in Preston's concern that learners should be 'allowed to develop their personal selves as they learn a new language' (2005: 56).

Linguistic identity, as the fast-growing literature on the subject makes clear, is a complex phenomenon that cannot be divorced from other phenomena such as language attitudes and ideologies, and linguistic power, while the relationships among them are becoming ever more complex in postmodern societies. Pavlenko and Blackledge point out in their discussion of identity in multilingual contexts that 'language choice and attitudes are inseparable from political arrangements, relations of power, language ideologies, and that interlocutors' views of their own and others' identities' (2004b: 1). ELF is not immune from this, and it is inconceivable that the NS English language ideology discussed in Chapter 2 and the attitudes to NNS accents revealed in the previous two chapters do not play important roles in ELF speakers' identities,[1] as well as in how they ascribe identities to others.

Globalization and identity

One of the main reasons for the increased complexity of identity in recent times is the phenomenon of globalization and, with it, shifts in 'the range of identities available to individuals' (Pavlenko and Blackledge op. cit.: 2). In terms of the English language specifically, its rapidly-growing dominance as the world's main lingua franca is leading both to an increasing diversity in the way the language is spoken, and to corresponding attempts to limit this diversity by the continued 'distribution' of NS norms to an ever-larger number of English speakers. (See above, p. 6, on Widdowson's distinction between language 'distribution' and 'spread'.) However, the current situation in the expanding circle is potentially rather different from typical situations in which powerful NS groups impose their linguistic norms on less powerful, often minority, NNS groups. In particular, many groups of English speakers in parts of Europe, Latin America, and East Asia (especially China) are both economically powerful and numerically large, and this may ultimately prove to be decisive in the 'fight' for the recognition of ELF. In turn, it may affect the ELF identity 'landscape' in ways that are at present only dimly discernible.

Dörnyei *et al.* (2006: 9) make a similar point *vis-à-vis* the related notion of motivation. Having argued that 'English is rapidly losing its national cultural base and is becoming associated with a global culture', they go on to point out the 'major consequences on L2 motivation research because the lack of a well-specified target language community undermines the attitudinal base of Gardner's (1985) integrative motivation'. In other words, many L2 English learners and users may in future no longer perceive themselves as wishing to integrate into an NS English culture, but into what Dörnyei *et al.* (ibid.) refer to as 'the world at large'. This, in turn, is bound to influence the extent to which, and the ways in which, L2 English speakers identify with the English language and its users, and their sense of how they see themselves and how they want to see themselves in English. And this has implications for the relationship between ELF speakers' personal identities, which up to now have tended to be affected by mainstream SLA's emphasis on interlanguage and individual differences (see Jenkins 2006c), and the various group identities to which they might wish to claim allegiance.[2] In this respect, the ELF interview data presented later in this chapter suggests that while some speakers may currently wish as individuals to identify themselves linguistically (but rarely in other ways) with NSs of English, they may at the same time feel more 'at home' in English as part of their own linguacultural community or even an international NNS community, and wish also to signal their affiliation to these groups linguistically. We return to these issues after a brief consideration of the literature on language and identity.

Growing interest in language and identity

In the past few years, there has been an increase in research into language and identity on a scale approaching the explosion of research into language attitudes in the later decades of the twentieth century. (See Chapter 3.) It is becoming the norm for books on discourse, sociolinguistics, language variation, and the like to include a chapter on linguistic identity. (See for example, Blommaert 2005; Chambers *et al.* 2002; Coulmas 1997; and Thomas *et al.* 2004.) Meanwhile a growing number of monographs and edited collections devoted exclusively to the subject and approaching it from a wide range of perspectives began to appear in the late 1990s and have been appearing at an ever-growing rate ever since (for example, Antaki and Widdecombe 1998, Benwell and Stockoe 2006, De Fina 2006, Joseph 2004a, Norton 2000, Omoniyi and White 2006a, and Pavlenko and Blackledge 2004a, among many others), while the *Journal of Language, Identity and Education* was launched in 2002, and a special issue of *TESOL Quarterly* (Norton Peirce 1997) has been devoted to the topic. There are many possible ways to categorize the language and identity literature, but for the purposes of the discussion below, I have chosen in the main to follow Pavlenko and Blackledge (2004a), who divide it into socio-psychological/interactional approaches and poststructural approaches. (For other accounts see for example, Blommaert 2005, Mendoza-Denton 2002, and Tabouret-Keller 1997.)

Earlier approaches

The earliest approaches to researching linguistic identity were social-psychological inter-group approaches drawing on Tajfel's (1974) theory of social identity (for example, Giles and Byrne's 1982 theory of ethnolinguistic identity). Such approaches were subsequently challenged for their assumption of a one-to-one correlation between language and ethnic identity, for the way they essentialized identities, and for a monolingual, monocultural underpinning that 'conceives of individuals as members of homogeneous, uniform, and bounded ethnolinguistic communities and obscures hybrid identities and complex linguistic repertoires of bi- and multilinguals living in a contemporary global world' (Pavlenko and Blackledge 2004b: 5). Also problematic, as far as ELF is concerned, is the fact that inter-group approaches ignored the way in which a world language may be appropriated in order to express new social identities (op. cit.: 5–6). On the other hand, as Block (2006: 37) argues in line with May (2001), 'it is probably wrong to take concepts such as hybridity, third places and choice to the extreme of arguing that social phenomena such as ethnic affiliation cease to have any meaning'. This is an important point to bear in mind for ELF in view of the ethnic affiliations that emerge in the interview data reported later in this chapter.

Early interactional approaches to linguistic identity, such as those of Gumperz (1982) and Le Page and Tabouret-Keller (1985) focused on code-switching, accommodation, and language choice. Instead of seeing identities as fixed, they moved towards a view of them as fluid and locally-constructed in interactions. Le Page and Tabouret-Keller (1985), for instance, showed how a multilingual speaker may perform 'acts of identity' as he 'creates for himself the patterns of his linguistic behaviour so as to resemble those of the group or groups with which from time to time he wishes to be identified, or so as to be unlike those from whom he wishes to be distinguished' (1985: 181).

These early interactional approaches have been criticized for their use of an untheorized concept of identity to explain language practices, for their failure to account for the possibility of speakers' identity construction using language resources that do not 'belong' to them, i.e. the notion of 'crossing' (see Rampton 1995), and for ignoring the fact that identity is not the only reason for code-switching. Interactional sociolinguistic approaches nonetheless acted as an important stimulus to further research into linguistic identity. Indeed, as Omoniyi and White (2006b: 14) argue, Le Page and Tabouret-Keller (1985) 'may be said to have triggered the wave of sociolinguistic research that began to view identity as produced within social interaction rather than as pre-existing categories to which people and things are assigned'. Meanwhile the notion of identities as locally-negotiated and co-constructed, and the emphasis of interactional approaches on practices such as code-switching and accommodation, are particularly relevant to ELF.

Poststructuralist approaches

Poststructuralist perspectives on identity have introduced into the equation a number of previously ignored concepts of which the most important as far as ELF is concerned is probably the effect of power relations on the negotiation of linguistic identity (for example, Heller 1982, 1992, 1995). According to Heller's (1992, 1995) framework, language is seen as a way in which people influence others in social interaction and as a symbolic resource linked to power. As Pavlenko and Blackledge (2004b) point out, 'any analysis of language practices needs to examine how conventions of language choice and use are created, maintained, and changed, to see how language ideologies legitimize and validate particular practices, and to understand real-world consequences these practices have in people's lives' (p. 12). They go on to consider how power relationships may shift and 'game rules' be renegotiated, so that 'new identity options come into play and new values are assigned to identity options which have previously been legitimized or devalued by dominant discourses of identity' (pp. 12–13).

The issue of shifting power relationships and 'new identity options' is likely to be a crucial one in terms of the future of ELF communication. For the past two decades or so, a paradoxical situation has existed according to which linguistic power in *lingua franca English* communication (i.e. overwhelmingly NNS–NNS) has tended to be wielded by absent *NSs of English*: in other words, by an NS norm, the idea (itself idealized) of how an NS would say something were he or she present in the interaction. This is not to say that linguistic power is being wielded in the expanding circle in the sense that it was in the past in outer circle countries such as Kenya (or, for that matter, inner circle countries such as Wales), i.e. by brute force, including physical punishment for those who 'erred' from the standard British English path. The power to which I refer is less overt, more subtle, and can perhaps better be described as an ideological undercurrent that quietly pervades most aspects of ELT (see Chapter 2), acts as a constraint on learner/teacher choice, and is realized in practice as (often) voluntary deference to a supposedly superior NS linguistic competence. It also seems plausible to argue, given the findings of the study reported in Chapter 6, that there is a second tier of power relations in ELF interactions, i.e. among ELF speakers themselves, to the extent that they see ELF varieties not as equals but as hierarchical. Thus, power is, at present, likely to be a major influence in the way many ELF speakers both categorize/affiliate themselves and ascribe identities to each other. On the other hand, as the studies in both this chapter and the last indicate, it does appear that new identity options may slowly be starting to come into play for at least some ELF speakers, an issue to which we return later in the chapter (and see the point made about ELF power relations on p. 198 above).

I turn briefly, for the sake of comparison, to the issue of power relations in the Englishes of outer circle countries. Here, the existence of a local identity in L2 English (although 'L2' is usually a misnomer) tends to be taken for granted in much of the literature. However, the situation is rather more complex than this would suggest. For in terms of the hold that the standard language ideology of the latterly absent NS speech community still maintains (see for example, Verma 2002 in respect of India, and Wee 2005 in respect of Singapore), it seems that substantial numbers of speakers of indigenized Englishes share common ground with English speakers in the expanding circle in their orientations to 'good' English and in their self-categorizations in relation to the L1 and 'L2'. Hong Kong is a particularly strong case in point.[3] As Joseph's (2004a) study reveals, speakers of Hong Kong English, a variety whose very existence many of its speakers themselves deny, regard differences between their English and standard British English as errors, no matter how widespread and easily intelligible among themselves these

Cantonese-influenced features are. It seems, then, that on one level they reject the notion of a local identity in their English. And yet, on another level, it is not implausible that—as with many of the expanding circle participants in my interview study—there is a desire (perhaps subconscious) to maintain and project that identity by means of a locally-influenced English accent. (See pp. 204–5 below for further discussion of Hong Kong.)

Power relations are by no means the only aspect of poststructuralist language and identity research relevant to ELF. Omoniyi and White (2006b: 2) present six 'common positions' currently taken on linguistic identity:

1 that identity is not fixed;
2 that identity is constructed within established contexts and may vary from one context to another;
3 that these contexts are moderated and defined by intervening social variables and expressed through language(s);
4 that identity is a salient factor in every communicative context whether given prominence or not;
5 that identity informs social relationships and therefore also informs the communicative exchanges that characterize them;
6 that more than one identity may be articulated in a given context, in which case there will be a dynamic of identities management.

Each of these positions resonates as much with ELF as with any other kind of English-medium communication context[4] and ELF could fruitfully be researched in respect of all of them. The various papers in Omoniyi and White's (2006a) edited collection themselves throw up a number of issues relating to these six positions that are particularly relevant to ELF. One such issue is the existence of multiple identities. Omoniyi (2006) proposes a 'hierarchies of identities' model according to which, 'a cluster of identity options … are … distributed on a hierarchy based on ratings from least salient to most salient' (p. 30). At any given point in an interaction, '[i]dentity options are always co-present' (ibid.) and the language *not* chosen at that point represents 'alternative identities that are backgrounded' (p. 20). This offers an alternative and far more appropriate perspective on ELF than the traditional SLA one in which differences from NS English norms are automatically regarded as deficiencies. Instead, the hierarchy of identities model opens up the possibility of approaching such differences as identity-driven, with speakers being aware of what an NS of English would do at a given point, but choosing to do something else, perhaps in order to signal a shared identity with a particular NNS interlocutor. This interpretation is supported by work already in progress (for example, Dewey 2005).

Other ELF-relevant papers in the collection demonstrate how identities can change over time. This is the case, for example, in Llamas's study of shifting identities in the northern English border town of Middlesbrough, and in Sallabank's study of language shift on the Channel Island of Guernsey. Some authors in the volume, such as Block and Sallabank, observe that identity is not purely a matter of choice, but that it may also be shaped or even constrained by social context, a phenomenon that currently holds very true for ELF. Meanwhile, in her study of Irish identity, White demonstrates the need, given Ireland's position in the globalized economy, 'to re-evaluate the historical roles played by standard British English and Irish' as markers of Irish identity (p. 228). She argues that identity might now be more effectively expressed in a standard Irish English, which, as the volume's editors point out, would allow 'speakers to express Irish identity while at the same time permitting international communication' (p. 7). This is precisely the same argument that I have made for ELF accents, to which we now turn.

Background to the investigation of ELF identity

As I pointed out in Chapter 1, responses to the Lingua Franca Core proposals have been mixed. The ELF intelligibility principle *per se*, i.e. the notion of prioritizing mutual pronunciation intelligibility for NNSs in ELF communication, has proved fairly uncontroversial except among those who have not grasped the conceptual difference between ELF and traditional EFL. (See Chapters 1 and 4 on misconceptions about ELF and the LFC.) In addition, a small number of scholars and practitioners have questioned certain of the LFC's exemptions, i.e. the non-core items. However, in most cases to date, their objections have been based on classroom anecdote, evidence drawn from experimental studies such as word recognition tests, and even intuition, rather than evidence drawn from empirical studies of ELF interactions. This is not to claim that the LFC in its current form is definitive. As I pointed out in my 2000 book and in many subsequent publications, intelligibility in NNS–NNS communication has not been sufficiently researched, because of a preoccupation with the intelligibility needs of NS listeners to NNSs. For this reason, the LFC proposals need to be supported (or not) by replications similar to the empirical studies of the original research. On the other hand, while I entirely accept the possibility that some of the LFC and non-core features may need adjusting (although no solid evidence to my knowledge has so far proved this), I believe that the principle underpinning the original research of providing a more internationally-relevant alternative to EFL and of legitimizing ELF accents remains firmly intact.

As was demonstrated in some of the responses to ELF and the LFC in the spoken and written texts in Chapter 5, however, it is the underlying ELF principle itself that is often contested, and by NNSs of English themselves. There is still, among many, and possibly most, NNS English teachers (NSs too), a staunch belief in the primacy of NS English and the need to approximate it as closely as possible. Many NNS teachers do not accept the legitimacy of NNS regional accents. Hüttner and Kidd (2000: 76) probably speak for many when they argue that teaching ELF pronunciation would mean that their Austrian learners would acquire 'Austrian English' and that this 'would defeat the purpose of foreign language instruction'. Despite all the socio-political changes affecting English over the last few years, the attachment to a native-like English accent, at least above the level of consciousness, appears not to have shifted noticeably. In my 2000 book, I quoted Andreasson (1994), who had contrasted 'the idea of identity' in the outer circle, where a speaker 'will be careful to speak in a way that will make his or her identity clear', with that in the expanding circle, where 'the ideal goal is to imitate the native speaker of the standard language as closely as possible'. She went on to say that '[i]t would, therefore, be far from a compliment to tell a Spanish person that his or her variety is Spanish English. It would imply that his or her acquisition of the language left something to be desired' (pp. 401–2). Six years later, and twelve years after Andreasson made her point, there is little evidence of a change from this deficit perception of NNS accents among expanding circle teachers, teacher trainers, and ELT testing institutions.

On the other hand, as Chapter 4 demonstrated, despite their apparent support for native-like accents, learners' and even teachers' 'achievement' rarely matches the NS ideal of their attitudes. As Dalton-Puffer *et al.* (1997) have observed, this suggests that there are other more deeply seated identity factors involved, which Kramsch (2006: 102) describes as 'a deep desire to preserve what is theirs'. In particular, it seems possible that while below the level of consciousness there may be a desire to express aspects of L1 group membership by retaining some aspects of the L1 accent in L2, there may be a tension between this desire and the conscious belief that a nativelike English accent is somehow better—a belief that was widely confirmed in the questionnaire study reported in Chapter 6. The situation is further complicated by the fact that the issue of affiliation to a wider ELF community also enters the equation and needs to be thoroughly explored.

In his case study of the linguistic situation in Hong Kong, Joseph (2004a) makes a number of points that have direct relevance to the situation regarding ELF. As I mentioned earlier, Joseph notes the anxiety of its ethnic Chinese over Hong Kong English: '[w]ith few exceptions, it is linguists who talk about this language. Its speakers scoff at the notion that there is anything other than "good English" (represented by the overseas standard) and the "bad English" of their compatriots' (p. 139). Luk and Lin make a similar point in observing that although the general public in Hong Kong are aware of a distinct Hong Kong English accent, it is not the variety to which they aspire. Rather, they 'still look up to … the norms provided by native-speaking countries, particularly Britain' (2006: 9). Joseph links the prevailing attitude with the emergence of distinctive Hong Kong features (see for example, Hung 2002 on the phonology of Hong Kong English), and argues that its success as a separate variety will depend in part on the desire of its speakers for the variety to be recognized. The problem is that 'the "emergence of Hong Kong English" and the "decline of English standards in Hong Kong" are *one and the same thing*, looked at from two different points of view' (p. 147; emphasis in original). Thus, ethnic Chinese speakers of English in Hong Kong are both producers of Hong Kong English and deniers of its existence. A similar contradiction obtains for ELF and, in particular, for ELF accents, as the interview data below demonstrate.

Joseph hints at prestige and status as being implicated in the ethnic Chinese response to the existence of a distinctive Hong Kong English. In a similar vein, Miller (2004) discusses the notion of a 'politics of speaking which implicates speaker and hearer in ways that are ideologically loaded, and which may be the basis of empowerment or discrimination' (p. 291). She appeals to the notion of 'audibility' in order to explain the way in which speakers are positioned or—more importantly for the present ELF context—position themselves through the use of a second language. Miller defines audibility as 'the degree to which speakers sound like, and are legitimated by, users of the dominant discourse', and cites the work of both Lippi-Green (1997) and Bourdieu (1977) in support of her argument. According to Lippi-Green, for example, there are rewards for speakers who lose their L1 accent in their L2 English and sound more like the dominant NS majority. Miller concludes that being understood in the L2 is not sufficient: 'sounding right' is also important. Although she is referring specifically to migrant students in Australian schools, her argument has direct relevance to ELF contexts. For as was indicated in the introduction to this chapter, even in expanding circle contexts of use, where NSs form a very small minority, legitimate English is still widely considered by native and non-native speaker alike to be that which adheres to the norms of educated NSs. By contrast, as Bourdieu (ibid.) points out, there may be negative consequences for speakers who speak the L2 with a non-native accent, to the extent that they may be negatively evaluated in terms not only of their accent but also of their social identity.

Joseph (2004a: 160) warns linguists that we 'risk having only a very partial understanding of the linguistic situation if we dismiss the popular perception outright because it is contradicted by our '"scientific" data'. We cannot ignore, for example, that at present in Hong Kong, the use of the term 'Hong Kong English' is interpreted as derogatory, and as referring to L2 speakers' mistakes in respect of the standard NS language. The same could equally be said of attitudes to ELF varieties (Spanish English, Japanese English, and the like). The key to the recognition of the linguistic distinctiveness of Hong Kong English, Joseph argues, is English teachers themselves:

> … only if and when teachers come to recognise that the 'errors' in Hong Kong students' English (at least the regularly occurring ones) are precisely the points at which a distinct Hong Kong identity is expressed in the language, will a Hong Kong English genuinely begin to emerge and to be taken as a version of Standard English rather than as a departure from it. (p. 160)

Again, precisely the same obtains for ELF varieties.

In pursuing my original ELF accent research, I had assumed that if the intelligibility and legitimacy arguments were well made, teachers would wish to incorporate the research findings into their pronunciation teaching.

Meanwhile, I had taken the existence of some kind of ELF speech community and the desire for ELF group membership as givens rather than empirical questions. From the responses, however, it is evident that many NNSs do not regard themselves in this way, at least in any straightforward sense, and that had self-categorization been considered, the conclusions drawn from the original research may have borne some identity-related caveats. Intelligibility alone, it seems, is an insufficient basis on which to legitimize ELF accents. The subsequent in-depth interview study reported in this chapter which complements the attitudes/beliefs study in Chapter 6,[5] is an attempt to assess the feasibility of the ELF pronunciation proposals by exploring teachers' perceptions of NNS and NS English accents and the ways in which these perceptions are interwoven with their linguistic identities.

Researching teachers' ELF identity

The interview study was carried out in parallel with the attitudes research discussed in the previous chapter in order to provide a fuller picture. I anticipated both that the attitudes and beliefs revealed in the responses to the questionnaire would provide insights into the identity positions expressed in the interviews, and that the interview data would cast light on the questionnaire responses. I opted for in-depth semi-structured interviews as a means of gaining 'empathic access to the world of the interviewee' (Kvale 1996: 125), and because in such interviews 'the interviewee's lived meanings may be immediately accessible in the situation, communicated not only by words, but by tone of voice, expressions, and gestures in the natural flow of conversation' (ibid.). Indeed, it has been argued that in-depth interviews are 'the *only* way to collect data where it is important to set the perspectives heard within the context of personal history or experience; where delicate or complex issues need to be explored at a detailed level, or where it is important to relate different issues to individual personal circumstances' (Lewis 2003: 58; emphasis added).[6]

By such means, I hoped to gain an understanding of how the 17 participants' past and present experiences were influencing their identity choices in English in relation to ELF and ENL, along with further insights into the sources of the deeply entrenched and sometimes contradictory attitudes and beliefs revealed in the studies presented in Chapters 5 and 6, and the impact these might have on non-native English speakers' identities. More specifically, the aims of the study were to investigate:

- the extent to which the participants desired to signal some kind of L1 lingua-cultural identity in their L2 English (as had been assumed in my earlier research);
- the extent to which they desired to signal some kind of native-like English identity in their L2 English (which, earlier, I had assumed they would prefer not to do); and

- whether they considered themselves to be members of some kind of ELF speech community and desire to project some kind of common ELF identity (cf. Pölzl 2004; Pölzl and Seidlhofer 2006) or some other hybrid NNS identity grounded in a view of themselves as 'fully-fledged participants ... in their second self-chosen world' (Pavlenko and Lantolf 2000: 169), that they 'transform' rather than 'merely conform to' (Donato 2000: 46).

My approach, like that of Llamas (2006) draws on the concepts of both language ideology (for example, Woolard 1992) and social identity (for example, Turner 1999; and see the reference to Tajfel's work above). As Llamas points out, '[w]ithin a language ideology framework, speakers' comments about language and other social phenomena are used as a means of interpreting and understanding linguistic variation, thus allowing insight into social psychological motivations for linguistic variation which may otherwise be inaccessible to the analyst' (p. 94). Meanwhile, as she notes in respect of social identity, '[i]nvestigation of the accent or dialect groups to which speakers perceive themselves to belong and those to which they compare themselves may allow insight into speakers' self-categorization in terms of language and social or community identity' (op. cit.: 95). This is not to suggest an older essentialized view of social identity, but a poststructuralist approach that is entirely in keeping with the six common positions outlined above (p. 202), in which it is seen as fluid, multiple, co-constructed in context, and so on.

The interviews

Each interview lasted approximately 60 minutes, although the precise length was determined by the participants' desire to speak, and two were considerably longer while three were only around 30 minutes. The final part consisted of my more detailed explanation to the participant of the purpose of the interview as a prelude to seeking consent to use the recorded data for academic study and publication. In the first round of interviews (participants A to H), I stopped the recording at this point. However, the explanation often elicited further, and sometimes substantial, commentary from some participants, and because of this, I left the recording equipment running to the very end of each session for the remaining nine interviews.

The seventeen NNS teachers who participated were all female, were aged between 25 and 43 at the time of the interviews, and came from China (L, M, P), Italy (E, G), Japan (A, H), Korea (R, S), Malaysia[7] (B), Poland (C, F), Spain (D), Taiwan (I, K, Q), and Ukraine (N).[8] They were all proficient speakers of English, and all had bachelor degrees. Their teaching experience ranged then from pre-service in one case (A) to 17 years in another (H). The interviews all took place in London, at my own institution and at another institution where some of the participants were studying. Some were attending a two-week teacher-training course at the time, others were at various stages of a one-year masters programme, and three were doctoral students. Some knew nothing at all about ELF (or EIL) until I explained it, many knew a little, while the doctoral students and a few of the masters students knew considerably more. It has been suggested to me that any negative views about ELF and positive orientations towards NS English that were expressed by these participants could be explained by the fact that they were currently in the UK. In order to demonstrate the inaccuracy of this suggestion, in the results below, I compare the views expressed by the participants in my study with those collected by Christopher Tribble in conjunction with the British Council (Tribble 2003) in a range of L2 English contexts outside the UK. One particularly noteworthy point is that it is the participants in Tribble's study who turn out to be the more staunchly pro-NS English norms, and who in most cases do not even acknowledge the possibility that some NNS English features might belong to a category distinct from errors. It seems, then, that the fact of being in the UK, learning even a little about ELF and most importantly, directly *experiencing* ELF communication (as did all my interview participants in their multilingual teacher training/education classrooms), may encourage positive attitudes about and beliefs towards it rather than the opposite (and see Chapter 4 above on previous ELF research that has demonstrated the importance of direct experience).

The interviews followed a rough pattern, with unscripted prompts being used flexibly to cover a range of issues relating to English accents and the ELF[9] pronunciation proposals. (See Jenkins 2005b for examples of question types.) These issues included the participants' attitudes to NNS and NS English accents, their own English accent aspirations, their perceptions of others' attitudes and aspirations, any negative experiences they had had where they felt their accent was involved, and their position on ELF accents. In addition, participants were encouraged to elaborate at length on and introduce topics that were particularly salient to them. My aim was to understand the situation from the participants' perspective and, in the process, to gain insights into the reasons for their attitudes, beliefs, aspirations, and identifications, and any areas of conflict. Because of this, I often returned to a topic several times with differently worded prompts, which also had the effect of highlighting any contradictions that were emerging. One further factor that I bore in mind was that it was important for the participants to gain some benefit from participating in a study that had such direct relevance to their own lives. And from various comments at the end of the interview, this seems to have been the case for the majority. For example, participant H volunteered 'I recognized before this interview I still have the native-like model [i.e. as goal], but now further recognition about the contradiction in terms of my view ... . So yeah, that's a good interview, and I can reflect on my idea in terms of EIL, yeah'.

I transcribed the interviews, coded the transcripts according to the recurring themes that emerged, organized these into main themes and categorized them in greater detail, then refined the themes, taking care in the process not to lose sight of each 'originally lived face-to-face conversation' in 'butchered

... fragmented quotes' (Kvale 1996: 182).[10] Finally, I returned to the selected data (in context), looking for further patterns and explanations.

Results and discussion

From the first eight interviews, three larger themes had emerged: the participants' accent attitudes, the perceived effects of 'accent experiences' on their attitudes/identities, and their perspective on teaching ELF accents—see Jenkins 2005b. After the other nine interviews (I to S) had been recorded and transcribed, however, I adjusted the main themes and detailed categories in order to take account of the increased salience of some points in the newer data. This primarily involved dividing the original theme of 'accent attitudes' into 'accent attitudes' and 'accent beliefs'. My reason for doing so was that the distinction between the two had been less noticeable in the earlier analysis, whereas 'accent beliefs' emerged more conspicuously in the re-analysis as a separate factor that seemed to impact in important ways on the participants' identities. And once I had added 'accent beliefs' as a main theme, it made better sense to deal with hierarchies/status issues within the context of beliefs rather than attitudes. Likewise, a category 'attitudes towards other NNS groups' English accents' that had also been included in the original 'accent attitudes' theme is now subsumed within 'beliefs about "good"/"bad" accents' within the 'accent beliefs' theme. Again this seemed more logical in that the perceptions expressed in respect of other NNS English accents were generally overt beliefs in the sense discussed in Chapter 5. The final framework for analysis is presented in Table 7.1 below.

1 Accent attitudes
   a attitudes towards own English accent/own L1 group's English accent
   b desire or not for a (more) 'native-like' English accent

2 Accent beliefs
   a beliefs about 'good'/'bad' English accents
   b beliefs about English accent hierarchies and status
   c beliefs about suitable English accents for selves as teachers

3 (Perceived) effects of accent-related experiences (specific and general)
   a on self
   b on others

4 Teaching ELF accents
   a own desire or not to teach
   b perceptions of colleagues' desire or not to teach
   c perceptions of future possibilities for teaching

Table 7.1 Interview analysis framework

I mentioned in Chapter 5 the importance of supporting any discussion of the referential content of what people say with an analysis of the forms in which they say it. As Cameron (2001: 154) points out, 'important contextualising information may be carried by small details that are easily overlooked because they have little or no referential content'. These details include formulaic expressions, discourse markers such as 'well', and prosodic features such as pauses, laughter, emphatic stress, and strong pitch movements, all of which may provide insights that are unlikely to be provided by an analysis of content. For example, pauses may indicate that a particular issue is problematic for the participant, laughter may signal embarrassment, while speakers may use various prosodic means to distance themselves from what they are saying.[11] Hammersley and Atkinson (1995: 131) observe that there is no such thing as 'pure' data that is completely free from bias, and it is not absolute 'truth' that is sought in in-depth interviews, but 'what the informant's statements reveal about his or her feelings and perceptions'. Likewise, Kvale (1996: 226) notes '[a] postmodern approach forgoes the search of true fixed meanings and emphasizes descriptive nuances, differences, and paradoxes'. In these respects prosodic features and other aspects of form may provide richer insights than the referential content alone into the identities that participants are constructing and the kinds of people they want to present to the interviewer at different points in the interview. In addition, the analysis of prosodic cues may help to identify any influence of the interviewer on what the participants say.[12] For all these reasons, the extracts from the interviews that are presented in the following discussion include prosodic features. These are indicated in the text by means of the conventions in Table 7.2 below.

There is, nevertheless, a logistical problem relating to analysing prosodic features in these participants' speech. It is the now well-known fact that prosodic features differ across cultures, and that the way they function in the L1[13] is likely to affect their use in the L2. (See for example, Gumperz 1982, Roberts *et al.* 1992.) This means that unless the researcher has a thorough understanding of prosody in the participants' L1s—unlikely when the participants come from many different L1s—he or she will not able to assess the extent of the influence of their L1 prosody on their L2 English. This, in turn, means that caution must be exercised in making claims based on interpretations of prosodic cues, and that they should often be regarded as suggestive rather than indicative of what the participant 'really means'.

We turn now to the data itself. In the rest of this section, I take each of the four main themes in turn, and consider the patterns that emerge across the seventeen interviews. Although the discussion follows the four themes outlined in Table 7.1, there is a substantial amount of overlap, and to avoid repetition, each extract from the data is presented and discussed only once but cross-referenced to other relevant themes. For the same reason, within each main theme the sub-themes are not discussed separately except in those few cases where there is no overlap between them.

X	incomprehensible word
XX	incomprehensible phrase
( )	transcriber doubt
(they don't believe)	guess at the word(s) in question
(they don't)	guess at some of the word(s) in question
(dr-)	
([ ])	uncertain phonetic transcription
[ ]	both phonetic transcription and any commentary
(.)	pause of less than a second
(7)	approximate length of pause in seconds
sen-	abrupt cut-off (hyphen attached to item preceding cut-off)
:	length (repeated to show greater length)
CAPS	emphatic or contrastive stress ('I' is underlined)
↗	rising tone beginning on stressed syllable (only if particularly noticeable)
↘	falling tone beginning on stressed syllable (only if particularly noticeable)
over[lapping [talk	overlapping talk
-	interruption: hyphen attached to beginning of interrupter's turn
full stop.	to indicate termination
@	laughter
<SOFT> text </SOFT>	other modes of speaking
J	interviewer
A, B, C, etc.	interviewee (except J)
...	author's gaps

Table 7.2 Prosodic transcription conventions for interviews (adapted from Eggins and Slade (1997), Niedzielski and Preston (2003), and VOICE (2003); and see VOICE website)

Accent attitudes

All the participants revealed ambivalent attitudes towards their own English accents. These often emerged in apparent contradictions in responses to questions asking them whether they liked their own English accents, whether they were concerned if their accent was recognizable to others as being influenced by their L1 (for example, Spanish English, Korean English), and which English accent they would most like to have if they were able to choose. In response to being asked whether they liked their accent, around half were very or reasonably positive. In some cases, however, the use of prosodic features such as pauses, low key, rising pitch (often associated with tentativeness), and laughter, and of the word 'quite' suggests that they had reservations or, in the case of participant P, may have felt that 'loving' their NNS English accent is something that should not be admitted too loudly:

Yeah I like (.) yeah (.) actually I'm quite happy with my pronunciation. (A)

Well I (.) I recorded some er well erm I think last week or two weeks ago I recorded my voice on the voice recorder er I quite liked it (.) and I'm still working on it. (C)

I like my accent. (I)

Erm (.) I don't mind my accent. (L)

Yeah (.) quite good @@@ (M)

Yeah, <SOFT, LOW KEY> I love it </SOFT, LOW KEY> (P)

I think it's ↗oKAY … I mean th- no problem … I don't mind (R)

Others were much less certain, or even negative towards their English accent:

Well (.) I think er it's for me I don't really know if I like it (1) I always try to do my best I think that I'm erm always learning (.) actually I wouldn't say I'm satisfied with my ENGlish because I'm always open to keep on learning … (D)

Erm:: mm: no (1) I think there are some problems that I have to solve … (E)

↗No@ … I don't er (.) I don't (.) well it's it it DOES sound to me like it's something wrong because when I speak everybody asks me straightaway <HIGH KEY> are you from Eastern EURope </HIGH KEY> … (N)

I don't know but actually I HOPE I can speak like a native speaker … No I don't like it … (Q)

No @ (1) my accent (2) it's too strong and then has as I told you before it's no intonation- proper intonation, so like (.) yeah no proper intonation <SOFT> I think </SOFT> (S)

All is not as straightforward as this like/dislike dichotomy implies, however, as many participants' attitudes changed when they moved on to consider how they would feel if they were mistaken for a native speaker of English, and which English accent they would most like to have if they could choose. In almost all cases, those who had been positive about their English accent nevertheless expressed a strong desire for an NS English accent, either British or North American, with participant Q specifying 'old RP' of the kind spoken by the actor Hugh Grant. This was even true of the participant who had said that she loved her English accent. An NS English accent would, P said, make her feel 'very good', 'superior', and would give her 'a lot of confidence'. In fact accent-related confidence is a theme that recurred throughout almost all the interviews, and we will return to it later in the discussion. Similarly, participant I, who had originally said that she liked her China English accent, expressed pleasure at the thought of her accent being mistaken for that of an NS of English:

J Supposing somebody made a mistake and thought you had a native speaker accent (.) how would [you feel?

I   [I'm SO HAPpy (.) I'm very happy (.) you know what (.) because erm well there is one time I was in Covent Garden and I wanted to buy a cup of coffee and er the waiter he said are you from America (.) because you have American accent (1) I'm SO happy (.) but I told him I'm Chinese @@

J @@

I I'm very happy

By contrast, later in the conversation, when I asked her which English accent she would choose if she could have any, after a long pause, and unlike most of the others who had initially said they liked their accents, she chose her own:

I ... [5] I think my ↗OWN accent @ yeah (.) because er: because first of all I am Chinese (.) I don't have to speak like n- American or British (1) it's like identity, because I want to keep my identity @ yeah.

J But it's curious isn't it (.) because just now you said you would be SO pleased if someone thought you had a native speaker accent and yet you want to keep your own accent.

I Because (.) ah yeah y- after these questions I feel that it's quite con-flicted- conflict for me because I feel HAPpy when they say okay you have a native accent (.) but erm if they cannot recognize from my pronunciation (and they think that) okay you are definitely American erm I don't feel that comfortable because I am ↘inDEED a Chinese

The conflict to which participant I directly referred seemed also to be signalled prosodically: in the lengthy pause before she made her choice; in the rising tone on the word 'own', which sounded to me as though she was asking herself a question in the act of answering mine, and then going on to justify her answer to herself ('because ...'); in the short laugh immediately after she had made her choice; and in the extra emphasis and intonational finality on the contrasting 'happy' (to be mistaken for an NS of English) and 'indeed' (she is Chinese). For this participant, then, it seems that her identity as a *Chinese* speaker of English was far more salient to her at this point in the interview than her identity as a *teacher* of the language—see the fourth theme below. Likewise, participant R, who had said her Korean accent was 'okay', also preferred to keep it because 'it's part of identity [...] I'm Korean so it's natural to speak Korean accent'. She nevertheless said that she would be very pleased if her accent was mistaken for an NS English accent, as she would feel it was 'better', a point made by many of the participants—see 'accent beliefs' below.

Another participant, F, initially said that she had no particular attitude towards her English accent, and neither liked nor disliked it. Later in the conversation, in keeping with her earlier comment, she was lukewarm about the idea of her accent being mistaken for a native English accent, saying only that she would find it 'a little bit pleasing ... because that's what I've been taught for so many years and years on and on back in Poland', and added:

> ... and maybe it's not even erm the thing that you SOUND like a native speaker (.) it's- it's the it's the PLAY because you become a different person so erm you've got a different identity but this is as if funny (.) you become like an actor in a way because people think you're from a different country ...

So not only did the idea of having an NS English accent hold no great attraction for her, but she would also find it strange because it would not represent her Polish identity. Still later in the interview, when comparing her own accent attitudes to those of 'most Polish people' for whom perfection is 'to sound like a native speaker', she shifted from her original noncommittal orientation to her own accent, to declare (without having been asked about this): 'I'm happy with my English (.) I'm PROUD of my English'. However, at the very end of the interview, she suddenly became much less sure of her position:

> F   ... I've still got this probably a little bit of linguistic schizophrenia although (3) erm I
>
> J   -what do you mean by linguistic schizophrenia
>
> F   erm (.) the thing that (.) well I know that I don't need to speak like a British person (1) but because I've been taught for so many years that I SHOULD do it (.) when I hear let's say someone speaking erm British English like a nice RP pronunciation (.) I LIKE it.

It seems from this extract, then, that F was in some ways as conflicted as participant L: she was proud of her English accent, would find it strange to sound (or be thought to sound) like a native English speaker, and felt no obligation to do so despite years of education during which she had been told she should. But in spite of all this, she still liked the NS English RP accent and at the end of the interview her attitude towards it and towards her own accent was ambivalent—a point she herself recognized in using the term 'linguistic schizophrenia'. Again, prosodic features provide further information. In particular, the emphatic stress on both 'should' and 'like' and the almost poetic repetition of 'I should do it.... I like it' suggest that her own attitude had more in common with the traditional Polish perspective than she had previously been aware. Lexically, too, her use of the adjective 'nice' to describe RP is somewhat at odds with her previous 'neutrality' towards the accent.

Turning to those participants who had initially said they disliked their English accents, some, like I, said that if they could choose any English accent they would nevertheless keep their own accent. Participant E, for example, responded without any hesitation, 'oh, mine, mine', and went on to explain:

Because I don't want to (1) how do you say (.) I don't want to be what I am not (1) I am ⟶ ITALian (.) I have my own culture my original- my roots are Italian so I like if people tell me yes (.) my origin (.) I ⟶ LIKE it.

She nevertheless thought it would be 'a good thing' if her accent was mistaken for that of an NS of English because 'it's part of learning a new language (or it's thought to be) erm:: to sound as much as the model'. Here, she articulated a belief that was shared by most of the other participants: that having a 'native-like' English accent equates with competence in the language although unlike most of the other participants, this did not mean that she would choose, even in 'teacher mode', to foreground an NS rather than Italian English identity through her accent.

Finally, one participant, K, who had recently learnt about ELF and who, earlier in the interview had described her accent as 'Chinese English', contrasted her present and past feelings about her English accent:

K NOW (.) I will be very- I will feel more er reLAXED and er (1) I think it's- everybody will have it (.) I think er every nationality speak English in (1) in some er- have some accent (.) will be like erm (1) natural thing.

J An accent from their first language (.) you mean

K Yeah

J Okay (.) why have you changed your mind then

K Erm (.) I think it's- that's er (1) beneath- underneath world Englishes (.) EIL (.) I think there's some tolerance and acceptance of the diversity so I REALly think it has changed my mind and my personality sometimes.

Taken at face value, K's words suggest that she was reasonably happy with her accent now that she had learnt about EIL. However, she chose her words carefully. Although she was asked whether she *liked* her accent she did not answer the question directly, but referred instead to feeling 'more relaxed' about it. The extra stress on the word 'relaxed' suggests that she was using the word contrastively, that is, to contrast with 'liking'. Her change of mind, then, does not appear to indicate a change in terms of liking, but simply of 'tolerance' and 'acceptance'—two words that she went on to use herself.

At this point in the interview, K's references to 'everybody', 'every nationality', 'world Englishes', and 'diversity' suggest that she was foregrounding her identity as an ELF speaker. In other words, she may not actually have *liked* her accent, but felt that it was 'natural' as an ELF speaker to have L1 influence in her English pronunciation, and that her accent was accepted in this respect. Later in the interview, however, when asked which English accent she would choose if she could have any accent, including her own, she took a full eight seconds before replying 'British or Chinese', and when pressed to select just one, after a further four-second pause, answered 'British'. She went on to explain her choice as follows:

K   it is 'because when I come BACK I will be regarded as a very (1) successful English teacher' (1) I know they may- I (.) I @@

J   So to be a successful English teacher you need to have a native speaker English [accent

K   [its not-it's not my point (.) but I think it's still (.) it's still strongly held in China

J   So this is the opinion in China

K   Yeah

J   Is it ↗your opinion

K   No (.) and I er I am confident that th- the situation will be changed because when I chat with my flatmate who is from Ger- German- Germany and he he's quite open to any oth- any other variety of English though himself speaks British English very well and (1) he erm I didn't talk- say anything about world Englishes but he seems to have accepted all kinds of Englishes. So I think maybe because of the global interaction many people have been aware and have been erm (1) confident to- er tolerant to accept any (kind of) English.

The long silences before K finally settled for the choice of a British English accent suggest that she was finding it very difficult to resolve the issue in her mind, and that as with participant I (but even more so) there was a degree of conflict involved. Her eventual selection of a British accent, and her emphasis on the word 'back' imply that the salient part of her identity at that point was no longer that of EIL speaker in the 'world at large' but that of successful English teacher in China. To fulfil this role, she said, she needed to conform to 'strongly held' Chinese accent attitudes and sound like an NS of English. However, she hurriedly distanced herself from these attitudes by turning the subject away from her accent choice to how she saw the future, supporting her point with information about the 'open' attitude of her German flatmate. Again, though, the emphasis was on accepting and tolerating rather than liking, while her description of her flatmate as speaking British English 'very well' seems to some extent to contradict her pro-EIL stance, and to be more in line with her choice of a native-like British accent for herself.

The overall picture of the participants' attitudes towards their own English accents, then, is one of ambivalence. Even A, who liked her accent and wanted to keep it, felt 'really mixed' at the thought of it being mistaken for an NS English accent. It is also a picture in which their accent attitudes and their identities-in-English seemed to be closely bound up with each other, and to shift in tandem at different points of the interview. Underpinning these attitudes, too, were various beliefs about NS and NNS English accents, to which we now turn.

Accent beliefs

One of the most prevalent beliefs, and one that was articulated by every one of the participants in one way or another was that an NS English accent is 'good' and an NNS 'bad'. A wide range of adjectives was used to describe NS English accents favourably, for example, 'good', 'proper', 'perfect', 'competent', 'proficient', 'fluent', 'standard', 'accurate', 'correct' and the like, while no such words were used in respect of NNS English accents. By contrast, when the latter were described, it was with pejorative adjectives such as 'not good', 'wrong', 'incorrect', 'deficient', and in two cases even 'horrible'. One participant, N, articulated this dichotomy explicitly, saying that in her view, there was only one distinction between English accents: native and non-native. In this, she echoed my questionnaire respondents as well as those of Lindemann (2005), for some of whom the largest and even the only category of NNS English was 'stigmatized non-native English'. (See Lindeman 2005: 207; and Chapter 6, p. 186 above.) Meanwhile, participant E thought there was a general assumption that NNSs can only speak 'good English' if they 'can imitate a native speaker'.

Not only did the interview participants believe in the existence of a major qualitative distinction between NS and NNS English accents, like the informants in the map task (see Chapter 6), many were also easily able to cite specific pronunciation features of other NNS accents that they believed to be 'bad', and often volunteered these features unprompted. Similarly, when they described distinctive features of their own group's English accent, they did so by problematizing the accent and focusing on stigmatized features and 'difficulties'. Not surprisingly, the features that they mentioned in both cases were always referenced to NS English forms (which they assumed to be 'correct' by definition), and all involved L1 transfer. For example, participant I described how 'one Japanese student said 'shart' but should be shirt', and added 'Japanese people always say shart'. Meanwhile, one of the Japanese participants (H) stated that Korean English speakers replace this same sound /ɜː/ so that 'they tend to pronounce poopose not purpose' adding that 'purpose is er standard accent'. Participant F discussed the Polish influence in her pronunciation of the sound /r/ as well as the Polish 'confusion' of the sounds /ɪ/ and /iː/ 'because we don't have them, we've got the, the one in the middle'. Participant L went into detail about pronunciation distinctions between Taiwanese and mainland China English accents, saying that speakers of Taiwanese English have difficulty with the sounds /f/ and /v/ and substitute them with something like /h/, while speakers of China English have a problem pronouncing final voiceless consonants and say, for example, 'sto' instead of 'stop'. Finally, several participants referred to 'problems' with the sounds /θ/ and /ð/. In none of these (or most other) cases is there any suggestion that some of these features might be acceptable variants of the respective L2 English.

Inevitably, given the participants' unanimous stance on 'good' and 'bad' English accents, another very frequently expressed belief was that an NS English accent is a sign of pronunciation proficiency and an NNS accent a sign of a lack of it. For example, N stated categorically that having an L2 accent in her English was 'not good', and that if someone recognized her accent as East European she would be displeased:

> ... because I presume it's something wrong (like) you know it's er (2) it just you know sounds subconsciously it means: (.) well that I'm not good ↗eNOUGH (.) I will never reach a level of BEing good enough.

Similarly, participant C explained that she 'would like to sound like erm English person' and, in particular, would like to have an RP accent 'because it's for me it's just erm (1) it just shows that well I'm quite proficient'.

Other participants did not share this belief, but were aware that it existed, and even believed that some people assess NNS English proficiency at all linguistic levels on the basis of pronunciation. In L's opinion, for instance, 'if you are speaking English (.) people will judge your English level er maybe through the accent through the pronunciation'. Some even believed an NNS English accent to be interpreted by others, particularly NSs, as a sign of lack of intelligence or education. For example, G said that when NSs of English heard her Italian accent, they formed 'presuppositions' about her:

> ... sometimes for some people (.) especially people who are not maybe linguists (.) who haven't got a linguistic background (.) that maybe has some presuppositions about even the cultural erm knowledge of the person (.) erm sometimes they think that you don't know so many things (.)

Many participants expressed the belief that NS English is best because it is authentic English—several described NS English, particularly British English, as 'original' or 'real', and NNS Englishes as 'not real' or 'fake'. Participant D, for instance, stated:

> I would really try to speak as close as I can to a NATive speaker (.) that's for sure (.) but er because I think that all of us tried to do things in a REAL way [...] get through to get the REAL thing. I mean if you are learning English (.) I WANT to- or I'd like to speak English the way an English person would do.

She went on to say later in the interview that the native speaker reference point was crucial because NSs 'are out of human race let's say (.) those who have come closest to the language'. Participant G did not share the view herself, but attributed the widespread belief among NNS English teachers that the RP accent is 'perfect English' to the fact that 'they think because English (1) because English was originally HERE [...] has to be back to the origin [...] that's where English was born', and that people did not consider the use of English elsewhere in the world. N likewise argued that NS English was 'created historically' and had 'years of development'. Participant Q compared English to jazz, opera, and wine, saying that in all these cases, she would want the 'real thing'.

Bound up with the participants' accent belief of 'NS good, NNS bad' was their belief in an accent hierarchy, with NS English accents at the top and NNS accents lower down (but with European accents placed above East Asian). The interview participants' beliefs in this respect bear a striking resemblance to the findings of the questionnaire study in Chapter 6, particularly the ranking task, and resonate with Blommaert's distinction between 'central' and 'peripheral' (i.e. respectively NS and NNS) English accents, which are defined by 'place', and whose differences may be 'rather trivial linguistically, but huge in terms of social value and purchase in the world' (2005: 223).

As is clear from the comments reported in the previous section on 'good' and 'bad' English accents, all the participants believed at least to some extent that NS English accents were superior to NNS. Even those who liked their own accents, and claimed not to value NS English accents over NNS, still used favourable adjectives such as 'good', 'nice', and 'perfect' to describe the former (not necessarily realizing that they had done so) but not the latter. And as with the questionnaire ranking task, it was specifically 'standard' UK and US accents that they had in mind (i.e. RP and GA) and not, for example, Australian or New Zealand English accents, or even other accents of the UK, such as Scottish- or Irish-English, or of the US, such as a Texan accent. (One participant even referred to not wanting an accent like that of George Bush.)

Several participants mentioned what they saw as the different positions of European and East Asian English accents on the accent hierarchy. This often emerged when I asked them how they would feel if their accent was mistaken for that of another NNS of English. H, for example, said 'I think I have more positive idea of Italian accent French accent'. Participant I echoed this in saying that she would be reasonably happy if her accent was mistaken for a European rather than an Asian accent:

> I think European language is similar to English so if THEY say I have European accent or French accent I'll be happy because that means erm my accent is closer [...] it's better than other Asian students because Asian language how to say (.) I think for example Chinese is very very different with erm English so if they say I have Chinese accent that means I am similar with other Chinese students. But if they say I have French accent probably there is something which is common among English speaking country or European coun- country in my English so I will feel better because I feel closer

Even within East Asian English accents, participant I placed the accents at different points in the hierarchy, and as in the questionnaire study, Japanese English accents were in her view the worst:

> For example, okay, if they say oh you have Japanese accent I'm not happy because from Chinese point of view we believe that Chinese- erm Japanese

students have lower individual ability than us @@ because we always criticize Japanese pronunciation.

Participant B said much the same in respect of the beliefs of Malaysian teachers of English: 'I think they had this view you know that if you speak like a Japanese speaking English and things like that you know that it was a lower ranking kind of English'. Meanwhile, participant S, herself Korean, said that she did not like Japanese or Chinese English accents, and that 'they're as bad as Korean accents', although she added that she thought Chinese English accents were better than Japanese. Within Europe, too, participants had hierarchical beliefs about English accents. Participant C, for example, said of Spanish speakers of English 'they have a strong Spanish accent', but of a Swedish teacher on her course 'she really, well she sounds like a native'. Thus, in terms of an accent hierarchy, the interview participants echoed the findings of the questionnaire study respondents, who ranked and rated NS accents followed by European accents, particularly Swedish-English, most favourably, and Asian accents, particularly Japanese-English, least favourably.

Some participants also believed certain NS English accents to be the most widely intelligible and clear. D, for example, argued that an RP accent would make it 'easier to communicate or to speak with people from many different countries s- English speaking countries', while H believed that an NS accent was more intelligible for 'everybody', both NS and NNS, provided it was not a 'dialect' (by which, it subsequently emerged, she meant any accent other than RP and GA). Meanwhile, N argued that 'people should learn English to talk to native speakers' as they would then be understood by all NNSs too.

There is probably a good deal of truth in the notion that NS accents are easier to understand not only for for NSs themselves, but also for NNSs for whom NS accents were the sole teaching models and who have subsequently had little exposure to NNS English accents. On the other hand, plentiful research has shown that it is by no means the case that NS English accents are *universally* more intelligible (see Jenkins 2000). The interview participants were, themselves, familiar with a range of NNS accents, and by their own admission found it easy to understand them as a result of that familiarity. The belief of some in the universal intelligibility and clarity of RP and GA may thus have had more to do with cultural and socio-political factors of the kind revealed by Wolff's (1959) study, in which the language of a group seen as more powerful was considered intelligible by a group seen as less powerful, but not vice versa—see Chapter 3. This would be consistent with the participants' unanimous placing of NS accents at the top of the English accent hierarchy, although their case differs from the Wolff study in that it is the less (linguistically) powerful group itself that is making the non-intelligibility claim about some of its own members.

It appears, then, that the interview participants' beliefs about NS and NNS English accents, like those of the questionnaire respondents, can to some extent be explained by the 'social connotations hypothesis', i.e. that reactions to accents are reactions to their social connotations rather than to their intrinsic features—see above, Chapter 6, p. 187. But while the participants in the interview study, like the respondents in the questionnaire study, may to some extent have been 'brain-washed' (Trudgill and Giles 1978: 175; Chapter 6: ibid.) by the prevailing standard NS English ideology (a word that one of my interview participants actually used), there are signs in what they say, as well as in the literature, that change is in sight—see below, this chapter, and Chapter 8. For the time being, however, it is not surprising that while they did not necessarily approve of the situation, many of the interview participants believed an NS English accent to be necessary for them as teachers of English. In this respect, they seemed to share the beliefs of the participants in Friedrich's (2003) study that a native-like English accent would enhance their career success. (See p. 108 above). Participant K, for example, argued that in China 'you will be regarded (1) as a successful teacher if your pronunciation is like a native speaker'. H was more specific:

> Er:: (2) for example (1) er s-when (1) teachers' meeting er Japanese- in Japanese school English department teachers' meeting er (1) I- if I have- I have Japanese accent and another teacher who brought up who was- who brought up in English speaking country and for example she s- can speak like native speakers er like BBC presenter if you like (.) in that case maybe she got good job rather than ME.

We return to the issue of teachers' accents and the impact of NNS English accents on these participants' identities as legitimate teachers of English in the section on 'Teaching ELF accents'. But first we consider the part played by their accent-related experiences in developing the accent beliefs and attitudes that inform their identities in English.

(Perceived) effects of accent-related experiences

Every single one of the participants referred to at least one negative accent-related experience or situation. In some cases, participants initially said they had not had any such experiences, but subsequently recalled one or more. In other cases, the experiences were of a more general nature that emerged during the general discussion and involved, for instance, the effect on them of being a learner of English in a particular situation. Some also referred to the experiences of friends and colleagues. In this section, I provide a few examples of the kinds of experiences that the participants described. Given the very idiosyncratic nature of most of these accounts, I cannot claim that those I have selected are 'typical' of all the others. Rather, they provide a range of both specific and general experiences that the participants described.

I begin with a more general experience. In the course of explaining why she was attracted by what she saw as EIL's tolerant approach to English, participant K described her the English learning situation in China as follows:

[…] when we were taught in school, it's it's quite strict if you pronounce-
you didn't pronounce, pronounce well enough or it's not British style. So
we will- many people can't er dare not to talk in class because (.) because
they- we were afraid that we will be laughed at if w- we have Chinese
accent or we didn't IMitate exactly British English and some teachers
might punish us as well (.) gave students er homework like you go back
you record your own er English (.) you read it then record it and compare
with the- because the students have er cassette er they er which is- which
which was from er British- the British people er read it then the students
will compare er how far I should go or what correctness I should make.

The way in which K switched from first to third person and from present
to past tense suggests that although she believed herself to be describing
a general situation, she was also recalling her personal childhood English
learning experience. The large number of non-fluency features (particularly
fillers, false starts, and blends), give the impression that her attention was
focused heavily on the substance rather than the form of her account, and,
in turn, that there was a high degree of emotional involvement. This, along
with the emphatic stress on 'imitate', and the choice of lexis ('strict', 'can't
dare', 'punish', 'correctness') suggests, in turn, that the memory of her days
as a learner of English may have had a lasting effect on her sense of self as an
English speaker.

Participant F recalled a similar type of situation from her days of learning
English as a university student in Poland:

[…] we have many more British teachers than American teachers so if the
school has got British teachers they do British English or er erm […] we
had a lot of training and erm sitting in a language lab with the teacher er
stopping us every word and correcting and hours and hours wasted @ a
very very traditional I guess sort of way of teaching as well.

Like K, participant F presented her account as though it referred to the
general situation in her country rather than her personal learning experience.
However, the effect of some of her lexical choices (for example, 'stopping us
every word', 'hours and hours wasted', 'very very traditional') as well as her
laugh after 'wasted', suggests that she had her own experience in mind. H
likewise referred to her general experience as a learner and how she was made
to feel that her English accent was poor by comparison with the accents of
those of her fellow students who had spent time in the US:

[…] it's not directly but I f- when I was a student for instance high school
student or college student I felt that that intention from teachers er for
instance er my class- some of my classmates erm studied at English
speaking p- countries for instance in USA or somewhere and they have a
good accent and a good Am-for instance (American speak)

Many more participants recounted specific experiences, some saying themselves that they felt these had affected them in the longer term. Participant I, for example, described an incident when she made a mistake and was corrected by one of her students:

> [...] I pronounced some vocabulary not quite accurately and some students recognized it (1) and they tried- and er they- after class they criticized me and said miss [I] you pronounced this word (.) and it makes me SO sad because my students can find my mistake. That means because in our culture erm teachers shouldn't have mistakes in front of the students [...] you are English TEACHer and you are kind of authority in the class how can you have ↘pronunciATion mistakes (.) right (.) yeah (.) so especially for those kids they just begin go learn English (.) if I @ and they recognize my mistakes so that makes me feel very bad but erm that is only one time makes me feel bad about my pronunciation and then er:: after all- after that time I began to look at my dictionary every time @@

Another participant, A, without any prompting, described a particularly traumatic classroom experience from her days as a young English language learner:

> [...] mm- the I NEVer forgot this (1) yeah (.) this story so I have started to learn English (.) when I was age (.) yeah eLEVen and from the st- very start of (1) th- junior high school education and it's (.) yes school term from: April (.) probably it was er May or (.) June and my (.) first English (.) TEACHer forced me to pronounce one particular word in front of other students but I COULDn't (.) because er: i- that that word is actually tree T-R-E-E tree and I pronounce like teree or something like that I think it was quite okay (.) but he forced me to pronounce so ↘MANy times (1) actually this was the- (.) yeah I was a child and er I have just started to learn (.) English. I lost motivation actually and er many student started to laugh at ME. It was ↘QUITE a bad experience so in- so but I'm still learning (.) English and I'm still (1) yeah learning about English teaching or something like ↘THAT so it's a kind of my reSIStance to the such kind of (1) mm (2) yeah such kind of TEACHers and er yeah so

As with K's account above, the non-fluency features in A's description of her childhood experience suggest that she was focusing far more on content than on form. Even more suggestive of the depth of the effect of this experience is the emphatic stress on certain key words in her story, i.e. 'never', 'eleven', 'couldn't', 'many', 'teacher(s)', and 'resistance', as well as a noticeable falling tone on others ('many', 'quite', 'that'). Later in the interview, this interpretation was reinforced by the participant's comparison of making comments on someone's pronunciation with commenting on their physical appearance: 'your eyes are small or something like that (.) it's quite a similar thing I think'.

Although I did not ask participants about positive accent-related experiences, a small number volunteered them. One example is shown above on page 213, where participant I described her pleasure when her accent was mistaken for that of an NS of American English. In fact the few other positive experiences that were recounted also concerned being thought a native speaker, whereas the negative experiences related to the participant's English accent not being sufficiently native-like. The fact that these participants were able to recall such experiences, often from long ago, and often in great detail, suggests that the events and situations they described may have played a substantial role in the development of their accent attitudes, beliefs, and identities, not only as speakers but also as teachers of English and, in turn, can be expected to have influenced their orientations towards the teaching of ELF accents, the theme to which we now turn.

Teaching ELF accents[14]

Regardless of whether or not the participants had heard of ELF (or EIL) prior to their interview, with just two exceptions (D and N), they responded to it positively at a theoretical level. By contrast, they did not think it would at present be feasible to implement the teaching of ELF accents in classrooms in their own countries or even, in most cases, to use their own proficient NNS English accents as pronunciation models. Most put this down to pressure from governments, schools, and parents to teach British or American English accents. In this respect, a commitment to do their best for their students seemed to be an important element in their personal identities as teachers. (See Golombek and Jordan 2005 for a similar finding.) They saw it as their role to fulfil their students' needs, usually in a test-driven, NS English-oriented education system, and often referred to using tapes of NS speakers as pronunciation models despite any personal loss of face this might involve. The need to help their students become 'native-like' was, in fact, a regularly recurring theme in the interviews once the discussion had turned to teaching ELF accents. The following exchange is a typical example:

L   you know erm sometimes you have to meet the parents' needs and you can't really think of your own s- I mean (.) your OWN way so [erm

J   [what are the parents' needs

L   they they if they send the kids to your school they want them to pass the exam they want them to- because we got a speaking test you know Taiwanese there there is English proficiency test in Taiwan we call it G-E-P-T general English proficiency test and then they- this is a four skill test so (.) they don't want th- they don't really want their kids to make some kind of pronunciation prob- er mistakes

L went on to explain that the students who achieved the highest marks were those whose English was closest to that of an NS, and vice versa. When I asked her whether she thought this was a good thing, after a second's hesitation, she replied 'actually I don't- I don't think this IS a good thing because like what I say I REALly (want) English is it's just like an international language and you have m- you have to be more open to all the people'.

Various tensions seemed to be at play here in relation to L's identity as an English teacher. On the one hand, she saw herself, and wanted to be seen, as a competent and committed English teacher. This involved both aspiring to NS English for herself (she had earlier referred to the need to 'polish' her English, and said that an NS accent would make her feel more 'confident'), and trying to teach it to her students: 'I will try my best because that's my JOB'. On the other hand, she did not believe it *should* be necessary to teach native-like English given that English is an international language, though she was willing to compromise her 'own way' for her students' sake. But on yet another level, at various points in the interview she revealed, like all the other participants, that she did in fact believe that NS English was 'better' (her word) and that NNS differences from it were 'mistakes'. In other words, L, like most other participants, supported the abstract notion of an international lingua franca, but deep down did not accept ELF varieties as legitimate. For this reason, although she did not consider it problematic if other Taiwanese people spoke English with a local accent, she did not as a teacher want to do so herself:

L   actually I don't mind people speak Taiwanese accents

J   but would you call it standard

L   erm:: I would call it standard as well but to me I say it's personal standard (.) I have double standard @ <LAUGHING> double standard (.) I- I'm very open to others but not so open to myself </LAUGHING>

Many other participants expressed this kind of 'double standard', as L put it, in that they thought a local NNS accent was acceptable for others but not for themselves. P, for example, said that having learnt a little about EIL, she did not believe an NS accent was necessary, but that she needed one for herself because of the 'pressure from society' that she felt as a teacher. H, like L, referred to her personal standard and the way this contradicted her theoretical position on ELF:

@@ yes that's the- lots of contra- contradiction in the view (.) so in theory I can understand- I can understand er varieties of English and non-native accent it's good it's accepted as far as intelligibility exists (.) but pers- at a personal level still I'm aiming at native-like speaking

It seems, then, that there was a tension between these teachers' commitment to their students' NS-dependent success in *practice* and their positive views of NNS English accents and ELF in *theory*; and this was further complicated by their underlying and sometimes subconscious acceptance of standard NS English ideology. Like the participants in Golombek and Jordan's study, their 'identities as legitimate English language speakers and teachers were fraught with ambivalence and contradictions' (2005: 527).

None the less, when the interviews turned to discussion of the future, many participants were vociferous in expressing their views about both what needed to change so that ELF would be accepted, and the positive effect its acceptance would have on their confidence as teachers. Only two of the seventeen were entirely against the notion of ELF, with N describing it as 'an excuse for bad English'. Others saw serious obstacles to ELF in their own countries at present, and thought that it would not be easy to change teachers' opinions. For example, F said that ELF would be difficult to implement in Poland because of university teachers' traditional attachment to NS English and the influence of the British Council on English teaching policy:

> [...] with the erm teachers we've got in the universities (.) most of them
> are erm rather er past their middle age and @ and they've been taught a
> different way and they don't really want to revise it (.) they don't want to
> learn the new thing 'cause it's- they are set in their sort of roots of erm and
> ways and they don't want to revise them too much. [...] it's also the case
> because we've got the strong British Council work and they started in
> 1990 more or less just after Solidarity and so most of the teacher training
> colleges or English (philologists) at different universities they are strongly-
> really strongly connected with BRITish English and with BRITain.

Several participants thought that teachers needed to have personal experience of ELF communication in order to be able to appreciate that native-like English and especially RP and GA accents were not necessary for international communication, and that these accents did not prepare students to understand most of the English accents they heard, or help them make themselves understood internationally. In this, they shared Canagarajah's view that a single standard variety of English 'fails to equip our students for real-world needs' (2005: xxv). Besides the need for teachers to have direct experience of ELF communication, several participants argued that changes were needed in two other respects before ELF could be accepted: in the ubiquitous use of NS models in teaching and testing materials, and, in the case of East Asia particularly, in the importing of NS English teachers. As regards the former, they pointed out that it would not be possible to teach ELF accents until appropriate NNS-based materials were available. As participant G observed:

> the materials they have (.) it's mainly videos or tapes it's all native speak-
> ers' accents so that's what- that's the only model they have (2) maybe if
> more materials around was with different accents and non-native speaker
> accents then if (you say) then it's like recognizing- it's like codifying (.) it's
> like accepting it (1) worldwide and why all the erm phonetics dictionaries
> and er it's all like written there like RP

In her view, the effect of the prevailing focus on NSs in English teaching materials was to make teachers and learners believe that NS English accents were more educated. In the follow-up discussion to the interview, G went on to say that in her opinion, classroom materials were a problem for NNS teachers' identities, because they 'show competent native speakers but not competent non-native speakers'. She described this as a kind of 'brainwashing'. Participant S felt similarly negative towards NS-based materials, particularly tapes. She pointed out that her students noticed the difference between the NS accents on the tapes, which they thought were 'absolutely right because they are native speakers' and her own Korean English accent, and as a result 'they think I'm wrong'. Thus, her competence was diminished in her students' eyes and therefore her own, and her identity as a teacher was compromised.

For many of the East Asian participants, however, the import of NS teachers was seen as the more serious problem in terms of its impact on NNS teachers' feelings of self-worth. Participant P, for instance, said the following:

> in Taiwan we EVen want to hire the (1) the teachers from from the English speaking countries to come to Taiwan and teach i- in the elementary schools (2) yeah @ er er t- to tell you the truth I don't really understand why- why they need to do it because- just because the the NATive speakers got better er- more er got the native ACCent (.) yeah because er (.) as (for) teacher I I thi:nk ONly the local teachers can ⬊KNOW the (1) the NEED of the students and what kind of ERRor they will have

P had initially referred to NS accents as 'better', but immediately corrected herself. When I drew her attention to this, she at first replied 'this is what the government think', but when asked if it was also her personal view, she admitted that there was 'a conflict in my mind' and said:

> I REALly WANT to accept the idea that people can get their own accent (1) yeah but (.) in reALity in the tea- er in the education system in my country now […] you know I just- when I'm teaching I wi- I will think er I wi- I USually I think I USually compromise with the reality of the the situation

She added, 'I think for now f- for (1) hh NOW (1) IF they can speak more like native speakers that will be better for them if they want to get a job (outside X)', and said that her students, in any case, found an NS English accent highly desirable: they 'really love it'. Thus, her identity as a competent teacher who understood her students' needs and the causes of their errors seemed to have been compromised by the presence of NS English teachers, by her own belief that NS accents were 'better', and by the knowledge that her students thought the same—and, by extension, that they preferred to be taught by NS teachers. As the discussion drew to a close, she explained how difficult she found the current situation:

I- I I really feel bad about THIS you know (I think) whe- when when your own English has- I FEEL like I have to lose my identity (1) you know [..] I really think that I'm a Taiwanese people- I'm a Taiwanese person and I should feel comfortable about THIS okay erm an- and and I just feel that when I'm speaking English I REALly WANT to- I will want to be like a native SPEAKer and it's really (1) it's really HARD you know (1) y- you feel comfortable living here and you just er: every- you just w- er in your daily life you just- you communicate with the local people in TaiWAN but how come I- whe- when it is- it is- when speaking English I HAVE to speak like a native ⬎SPEAKer

Thus, a discussion that started with the effect of the presence of NS teachers in her country threw up perceptions of conflict, compromise, and loss of identity. Such feelings were expressed by several of the other East Asian teachers who had been directly affected by schemes to import NS teachers into their countries.

On the positive side, while none of the participants would teach ELF accents at present, all but two said they would do so if ELF was accepted, even though some were less optimistic about their colleagues, and one (E) said she would only do so because 'there's no way to make them [students] speak as an English [person]'. As far as their identities as teachers of English were concerned, the general consensus was that in order for them to feel competent at present, their accents needed to be as native-like as possible. However, if ELF was accepted in future, they thought this would no longer be the case, which, as one participant put it, would come as 'a relief', because teaching ELF rather than NS English would enable them to feel more confident about their own accents and hence their identities as teachers. On the other hand, most of them also said that while they would teach ELF accents, they would continue to regard NS English as 'correct', and would still aspire to an NS accent for themselves. The fact that they believed they would still see ENL as their *personal* goal suggests that even if and when ELF is established, it may take some time for NNS teachers' sense of ambivalence towards their own and NS English accents to fade.

Contrasting findings in an EFL context: Tribble's interview study

It seems, then, that there is cause for guarded optimism in many of the participants' perspectives on teaching ELF accents. Despite the fact that most of them still seemed, like most of the questionnaire respondents in Chapter 6, to accept the prevailing ideology of 'NS is best', there were stronger rumblings of dissatisfaction with it among the interview participants. And while they clearly felt ambivalent towards ELF, the very fact that they had conflicting feelings could be interpreted as a sign that they were taking the notion seriously, and beginning to question the prevailing deficit model of NNS Englishes. This contrasts with the untroubled orientations to English of the expanding circle interviewees (from China, Georgia, Poland, and Tunisia) in Tribble's study.[15] (See p. 53 above.) While the two sets of interviewees shared a number of perceptions about 'good' English, Tribble's participants seem neither to have heard of ELF/EIL, nor to have had any concept of English that is not grounded in NS norms. Each participant in Tribble's study was asked what kind of pronunciation model he or she used, the interviewer being careful to include a reference to EIL in his question. Most, however, did not appear to realize the significance of the word 'international', and if they referred to it at all, interpreted it as meaning British or American English. The following are typical responses to the question about pronunciation models:[16]

G2   We always try, old generation teachers and nowadays young genera-
      tions at our schools, we must teach British English, pure British
      English, which we have taught before. [...] if you know British
      English, classical, not old English, then it is easier to understand
      other people too ...

G3   ... They [the students] think America is powerful, you know, now.
      When they think about English, I feel they think about America. But
      I made them to think that the homeland of English is England. No?

CT   What is your opinion of RP as a model?
P3   Well, it is a model! Everybody follows it. I don't think it can be
      changed. We should treat it as a model. There should be one model,
      because I guess it's fairly universal.

T1   ... We are trying, all over Tunisia, to teach international English,
      which is British English. I know there is American English and
      Canadian English and I don't know what else, but we are trying to
      talk and to give British English, which is international and which is
      understood by everybody.

T2   I try to follow the British model of pronunciation, because I think it's
      a standard. I try to work with CDs of pronunciation for my pronun-
      ciation. I try to help the students to pronounce better. Sometimes it
      does not work very much because they have three languages and
      French is also influencing their pronunciation. So it's sometimes
      difficult to have what you want.

T3   I've always tried to ask people who are native speakers to assess the
      way I pronounce English, because I have no clear idea as to whether
      my pronunciation is good or bad or acceptable, in terms of native
      speaker judgement. [...] I think that if we teach a language like
      English, we should reflect to some extent the culture of, basically,
      England and America, because these are the leading users of this
      language. I'm aware of the fact that there are other areas in this
      world that use probably different Englishes, but I think that we are

> naturally driven towards the UK and America, as being the most representative entities of English use.

A small number of interviewees showed a more flexible view of pronunciation models in that they exposed their students to a range of accents, although in most cases this seemed to mean only other NS accents. In addition, a few teachers, such as C2 and T3, referred to pronunciation in terms of its communicative value. Even here, however, the first articulated a personal preference for British English, while the second implied that his stance was borne of necessity in that he believed, like participant E in my study (see page 228), that it is impossible to 'achieve' native-like English:

C2   Well, I like to study British pronunciation, but now I don't care what they use, what kind of language, because if you can speak English, that's okay. I think it's a tool. You can communicate with others.

T3   … I believe that as non-native speakers of English, we will always try to approximate a native speaker-like pronunciation, but we'll never be able to be like a native speaker. So I don't think that … communication and mutual understanding is more important.

I surmised earlier (p. 208) that the certainty of Tribble's interviewees as contrasted with the ambivalent and even conflicted perspectives of my participants was largely a function of their differential knowledge and experience of ELF communication. Tribble's interviewees showed very limited, if any, knowledge of ELF/EIL, and almost none of them referred to any experience of speaking English with NNSs from other L1s. Instead, the majority seemed to take it for granted that they should teach traditional EFL, saw the choice of target variety as a straightforward one between British and American English, and seemed to regard exposure to other Englishes as meaning other NS Englishes. They thus seem to fit into two of the categories in Pavlenko and Blackledge's identity framework (2004b: 21–2), i.e. 'imposed' and 'assumed'. In other words, their identities as NNSs of English have been imposed on them, but they are comfortable with this and will do their best to achieve a high standard within the accepted constraints.

Most of my interview participants, on the other hand, seem to fit better into Pavlenko and Blackledge's third category of 'negotiable identities' (ibid.). They seemed aware that they were at some kind of transition point between the old EFL of the twentieth century and the new, but as yet not widely known or accepted, ELF of the twenty-first, and were finding its potential impact on their identities as teachers unsettling and ambiguous. One even described herself as 'going in between'. They were nevertheless well aware that ELF would also be to their advantage, in that it would help them to 'overcome the profoundly pernicious deficit model of their own professional competence' that they had previously 'come to accept and silently learned to live with' (Rajagopalan 2005: 287), and convince themselves that 'they are successful multicompetent speakers, not failed native speakers' (V. Cook 1999: 204).

Most importantly, it would mean that they would 'no longer need to think of themselves as something they are not', but rather 'have a positive means of asserting their professional roles as competent and authoritative speakers and instructors of EIL, not with a borrowed identity but with an identity of their own as international users of an international language' (Seidlhofer 2003a: 23).

Some final thoughts on ELF and identity

The similarities in attitudes and beliefs about NS and NNS English accents among the seventeen participants, despite their differences in L1, teaching context, and teaching experience, combined with the findings of the questionnaire study, lead me to conclude that at least for the time being, NNS teachers may have very mixed feelings about expressing their membership of an international (ELF) community or even an L1 identity in their L2 English. Past experiences, combined with factors in their present situation, and judgements about the effect of their accent on their teaching careers, seemed to exert a strong influence on the interview participants' attitudes to their accents and, in turn, on their choice of accent identity. In most cases there was a strong sense that they desired a native-like English identity as signalled by a native-like accent, especially in their role as teachers. Many perceived an almost immutable link between a native-like English accent and their chances of success in their teaching careers. And yet most also expressed an attachment to their mother tongue and nationality, projected through their English accent, that they seemed reluctant to relinquish. This pull in opposite directions led, in turn, to the ambivalence revealed in their seemingly contradictory statements about both themselves and ELF. Some even noticed the contradiction and used terms such as 'linguistic schizophrenia', 'double standard', and 'conflicted'.

The indications are that identity will continue to play a critical role in NNS English speakers' orientations towards their L2 English accents and thus towards ELF in the future. Norton (2000: 5) argues that one aspect of identity in language learning is 'how the person understands possibilities for the future'. It seems that whether or not ELF accents will be taken up in years to come by NNS teachers (and thence passed on to their learners) will depend in large part on how they believe ELF is perceived in the wider English-speaking context, and within that context, the extent to which they believe such accents will enhance their success rather than discriminate against them. Inbar-Lourie (2005: 269, citing Paikeday 1985) points out that accent 'is the most evident indicator of group membership both within and outside of the speech community', while Nero observes that 'the motivation to maintain affiliation with our ascribed language group(s) is contingent upon the benefits derived therefrom' and 'is often weighed against the perception of the group's language (and by extension, of the group itself) by the society at large' (2005: 195). Decisions about ELF accents may thus involve difficult group membership choices, and substantial tensions between 'deep personal identity' and 'the various group identities' to which people may wish to 'stake a claim' (Joseph 2004a: 5). Given that identities are widely seen as 'multiple and potentially conflictual' (Meinhof and Galasinski 2005: 2), however, it would be surprising if this was not so in the case of ELF. Indeed, the very existence of conflict indicates that ELF is being taken seriously by the NNS teachers who know about it.

For the time being, there is nevertheless some positive evidence that the interview participants in my study shared a sense of a community and commonality that calls to mind the notion of a 'community of practice' (for example, Wenger 1998), with its 'mutual engagement', 'jointly negotiated enterprise', and 'shared repertoire' (Meyerhoff 2002: 528–9; Wenger 1998: 72ff.).[17] Some participants referred to feeling more comfortable in the company of ELF speakers, in the sense of 'we're all in the same boat'. One participant (G) commented that she 'instinctively' liked ELF accents because they signalled to her that she and the other speaker(s) had 'already got something in common'. Another (L) made a similar comment about English speakers who shared her L1, adding 'they're like YOU […] so they will have more in common'.

All things considered, however, it is not surprising that expanding circle speakers of English—even those who in theory support ELF and who, through their accent, reveal a desire to promote an ELF and/or L1 identity in their L2 English—are nevertheless subject to tensions. This is what Bamgboṣe (1998) seems to mean when he talks of NNS English speakers' 'love-hate relationship' with NS English, and especially with the RP accent. Correctness, prestige, and authenticity are still linked to NS English by traditional phoneticians, grammarians, mainstream SLA researchers, and many corpus linguists. NNS English is still stigmatized as 'interlanguage', 'broken English', 'intermediate English', and so on. (See, for example, Görlach 1999, 2002; Medgyes 1999; and Jenkins 2006c for a discussion of the phenomenon.) Meanwhile, some accent attitudes reveal undercurrents of racism (see for example, Bonfiglio 2002; Lippi-Green 1997), and literary, and journalistic sources continue to make derogatory references to NNS English as they have done over the centuries. (See Bailey 1991; Pennycook 1998.)

Luk and Lin (2006: 12) argue in respect of Hong Kong English, that it may be local forces rather than imperialism that are 'sustaining the local hegemony of English'. This may be true also of several expanding circle regions. (For example, it is almost certainly the case in Poland.) Where it is so—and it is, of course, a matter of local choice—then I run the risk of being labelled patronizing in arguing that it is not necessary or even relevant to 'aspire' to speak ENL in international communication, all the more so because of the fact (sometimes described as an irony) that I am, myself, a native speaker of English. But this is not a simple case of an NS of English 'telling' expanding circle NNSs what is best for them. As V. Cook points out, while it may be 'L2 users themselves who want to be native speakers … their attitudes are the product of the many pressures on them to regard L2 users as failed natives', and 'this acceptance of the native speaker model does not mean these attitudes are right' (1999: 196). Whatever 'circle' we come from, we all—NSs and NNSs of English—need to think about *why* we make our linguistic choices and what attitudes and beliefs (and myths) inform the identities we accept for ourselves and ascribe to others. In light of the spread of English and what is known about the links between accent and identity, all English speakers need to (re)visit these issues and decide for themselves whether or not they truly believe that Anglo accent norms are the most appropriate for lingua franca English communication. And as Luk and Lin (op. cit.: 19) point out, this process may involve some 'reverse training' for inner circle English speakers.

Notes

1 Joseph (2004a: 10) observes, citing Ivanič 1998, that '[i]t has recently become fashionable to eschew "identity" in favour of the verb "identify" and its nominalization "identification", on the grounds that these refer to a process rather than a "fixed condition"'. Like Joseph, I nevertheless use the term 'identity' much of the time, given that it is 'the everyday word for people's sense of who they are' and hope not to be misinterpreted as implying that identities are 'inherent and unitary' (ibid.).

2 This is not to suggest that there is a simple or generally accepted relationship between personal (or individual) and group (or social) identities. As Meyerhoff (2002: 531) points out, intergroup theory has postulated different relationships between them at different times. For example, while Tajfel (for example, 1978) sees them as belonging to a single continuum, Giles and Coupland (1991) see them as orthogonally-related, and Turner (1999) as distinct.

3 Hong Kong is sometimes considered to belong to the expanding rather than outer circle.

4 House (for example, 1999, 2002, 2006) takes a rather different view of ELF from most other researchers in arguing that it is 'a repertoire of different communicative instruments or registers an individual has at her disposal, a useful and versatile tool, in short a "language for communication"' and that '[a]s such it can be distinguished from those other parts of the individual's repertoire which serve as "language(s) for identification"' (2006: 90).

5 See Jenkins (2005a) for an early report of the first phase of the interview study.

6 Interviews are certainly likely to prove more effective than ethnographic observation as far as teachers' perceptions of ELF are concerned. This is because any positive orientations that they might have towards ELF are unlikely to be revealed in classrooms, whose curricula, syllabuses and teaching practices are in the main dictated from above. It is still current practice in certain English language schools, for example, to bug classrooms in order to ensure that teachers do not use the students' L1. Any lack of visible ELF orientation in classroom teaching situations therefore could not be assumed to reflect the teacher's position on ELF.

7 Although Malaysia is not in the expanding circle, it has only recently (2003) returned to an English-medium education policy, so in this important respect the Malaysian participant shared common ground with the other sixteen participants.

8 J is the interviewer.

9 In the interviews themselves I used the term EIL (English as an International Language) rather than ELF as those participants who had any familiarity with the concept tended to know it as EIL.

10 This is particularly important when the individual categories overlap substantially, as is the case with my data. For this reason, I coded the data manually and returned frequently to the full transcripts and even the recordings when I was working on individual quotations, rather than focusing primarily on a series of extracts. This was a much more time-consuming process, but provided me, I believe, with a more complete sense of what was 'going on'.

11 This is not to suggest that there is a one-to-one relationship between any prosodic feature and speaker meaning. The interaction context and the individual speaker play a crucial role, particularly in respect of pitch movement, and for this reason, prosodic cues have to be interpreted within the specific interaction and not only according to any 'known' generalizations about the workings of prosody. (See Dalton and Seidlhofer 1994, Jenkins 2000; also above, Chapter 5, footnote 13.)

12 See, for example, Mendoza-Denton 2002: 479, on the researcher's identity and its influence on the data; Hammersley and Atkinson 1995: 130–1, on the effects of the researcher's presence and how this may shape the data; and Cameron 2001: 176, on the role of the interviewer in the co-construction of the participant's 'self'.

13 Again, this is not to suggest (in the case of intonation, as opposed to tone, languages) the existence of a one-to-one relationship between the use of a prosodic feature by a particular speaker in the context of a specific interaction, and that speaker's meaning. The picture is further complicated by the fact that participants in ELF communication may transfer their L1 communication norms, and/or use '"[a] mixed form" resulting from accommodation and negotiation processes' (Meierkord 2002: 120).

14 By 'teaching ELF accents' I am referring to the teaching of a local standard NNS accent adjusted as necessary for the specific ELF interaction.

15 The interviews were carried out in conjunction with the British Council and were published in 2003 in a CD-ROM, *Looking at ELT*, by the British Council. There were also interviews with outer and inner circle members, but I have not included examples of these. (See above, Chapter 2, p. 53, for further details.)

16 G1, G2, etc. refers to the interviewee (Georgia interviewee 1, Georgia interviewee 2, etc.) and CT, where used, to the interviewer. Note that the responses provided here represent only a very small proportion of Tribble's expanding circle data.

17 House (2003: 572) makes this very point in arguing that '[i]nstead of basing ELF research on the notion of the speech community, we may therefore consider another sociolinguistic concept, the concept of "community of practice"...' Wenger's (1998: 76) 'three dimensions characterizing a community of practice ... may indeed be applicable to ELF interactions'. Graddol (2006: 115) also makes the point indirectly, in arguing that 'few native speakers [of English] belong to the community of practice which is developing amongst lingua franca users', and that NSs as a result, 'may be a hindrance' in international communication in English (ibid.).

8

Attitude, identity, and the future of ELF

In 1998, the British government launched the so-called 'Blair initiative', allocating five million pounds to promoting English as the global lingua franca abroad. Two years later, the Education and Employment Secretary of the time, David Blunkett, recognizing the value of English language teaching to the British economy, advised a meeting of business leaders 'to capitalise on their advantage as native speakers' (*The Observer* 29 October 2000: 1). Going forward almost four years to early 2005, the Chancellor of the Exchequer, Gordon Brown, took a trip to China. *The Observer*, in reporting his visit, noted that Brown 'hopes to exploit the fact that English is a global language' (*Business Supplement* 27 February 2005: 3), with education being one of the two areas he had singled out (along with financial services) 'in which … "Global Britain" could make progress in the Chinese market' (ibid.). In this respect, he was reported elsewhere as having 'stressed the importance of exporting the English language and its learning methods to China, citing the country as a "key market"' (*EL Gazette* May 2005: 1).

However, it seems that the British brand of English that is being so energetically promoted is not always what the world actually wants. By a somewhat amusing coincidence, shortly after Brown's visit to China, another article in *The Observer* (24 July 2005), discussing the downside for Britain of the spread of English, described the case of Korean Airlines, 'which reportedly chose a French supplier for its flight simulators because its "offshore" international English was more comprehensible and clearer than that of the UK competitor' (*Business Supplement*: 10). Thus, on the one hand, we have a situation in which the British government and business sector (among others) believe they should 'capitalise on', 'exploit', and 'export' their own 'brand' of English; and on the other hand, the possibility that the English spoken by its British (or, for that matter, North American) NSs is not the most internationally intelligible. And given that Korean Airlines is by no means the first to notice this, the future may turn out to be more problematic for many English NSs—unable to speak other languages or to adapt their English for international communication—than for many NNSs.[1] Clearly, this is not what might be considered an 'advantage', even if the fact is not yet widely appreciated by either monolingual or bilingual English speakers, let alone their governments.

This book, however, is not about NSs of English, but about its NNSs, and in particular, its NNS teachers. I cite these examples merely to demonstrate how far attitudes and beliefs fall short of reality when it comes to English being spoken as a lingua franca. And in this chapter, it is time to take stock. When I originally conceived this book, I had expected to find that in the years since the publication of *The Phonology of English as an International Language*, years in which so much has been said and written about ELF, there would have been a substantial shift in attitudes towards NS and NNS Englishes, and in particular, towards the Englishes of the expanding circle, from where the majority of English speakers now come. As the previous three chapters have demonstrated, however, things are moving rather more slowly.

I have used this chapter, then, to consider the future of ELF in the light of my attitudes and identity research findings and the various gatekeeping practices that still hamper its acceptance as legitimate English. It is, of course, too early to talk of 'teaching ELF' as such. Before this can happen, we need comprehensive, reliable descriptions of the ways in which proficient ELF users speak among themselves, as the basis for codification. Only after that can discussions about teaching ELF for production begin. For, as I pointed out in Chapter 1, unlike many compilers of NS corpora, ELF corpus linguists do not believe in an automatic transfer from sociolinguistic description to pedagogic prescription. This means that commentators such as Mukherjee and Rohrbach are as pedagogically wrong to describe ELF as a 'teaching model' as they are conceptually wrong (like many of my interview participants) to think of ELF as an attempt to 'dissociate the English language … from its sociocultural context' (2006: 210): ELF *is* a sociocultural context of the English language every bit as much as ENL is.

The fact that it is not yet possible to teach ELF does not mean, however, that there should not be a change in mindset in the meantime. It should be (but often is not) manifestly clear to all who communicate internationally in English that ELF exists, and that its speakers can no longer be assumed to be deficient where their English use departs from ENL. It should also be clear that in international communication, the ability to accommodate to interlocutors with other first languages than one's own (regardless of whether the result is an 'error' in ENL) is a far more important skill than the ability to imitate the English of a native speaker. These factors alone should by now have generated at least some changes in orientation in the policies of government education departments, examination boards, ELT publishers and the like. But so far, this is not the case. For as will be demonstrated below, while there are indications that ELF is gradually becoming more accepted in theory among (some) ELT practitioners and applied linguists, and there are even very occasional examples of good ELF-oriented practice, nothing has changed at the 'top'.

We turn now first to consider gatekeeping practices, in which the focus is on mainstream SLA, English language testing, ELT materials, and teacher education; and second, teacher insecurity, in which the focus is on linguistic insecurity related to NS English language ideology, and pedagogic insecurity related to language innovation and change. Finally, we look at some positive signs, and consider what these might mean for the future of ELF.

Gatekeeping

The word 'gatekeeping', to my surprise, does not appear in any of my English dictionaries. By contrast, they all include an entry 'gatekeeper', and provide a literal meaning (for example, 'one who tends or guards a gate', *Longman Dictionary of the English Language*) and, in some cases, also a metaphorical one (for example, 'an individual or group that controls access to sb or sth', *Encarta World English Dictionary*). Gatekeeping, by extension, then, refers in its metaphorical sense to the control exerted by an individual or group over access to somebody or something, and in the context of the present discussion, is used specifically to describe control of access to decision-making processes about legitimate English. It is thus closely bound up with language ideology of the type discussed in Chapter 2: in other words, gatekeeping is informed by language ideology in that the gatekeepers of English (government institutions, examination boards, universities, publishers, the British Council, English Only and the like) in the main grant access to decision-making only to those whose orientation to English they approve of.[2] And in something of a vicious circle, their language policy decisions (what is 'good' and 'bad' English, what is 'correct' and what is an 'error', and so on) seem, as the previous three chapters have shown, to impact on the attitudes and beliefs of non-gatekeepers around the world who, in turn, generally 'choose' to conform to these policy decisions.[3]

Gatekeeping can also operate in less obvious (and perhaps less conscious) ways, as is the case in mainstream SLA research, with its tenacious attachment to the idealized native speaker. It is implicit in most SLA researchers' assumptions that the ultimate goal of English language learning is NS English proficiency, and that anything that 'falls short' should be designated interlanguage (if learning continues) or fossilization (if it has ended). Thus, no concessions are made to the fact that English differs from other foreign language learning in so far as the majority of learners will speak it as a lingua franca with other 'NNSs' rather than as a foreign language with NSs. It is an irony that, as Littlewood (2004: 504) points out, SLA researchers 'have far more information about English than other languages' and therefore tend to use English—as he does himself—to provide most of their specific language examples. This means that English is regularly used as the prime instantiation of L2 acquisition, despite the fact that it is the prime example of an L2 that does not fit the general pattern. Rather than being foregrounded, then, it should be excluded from any SLA research where the goal of learning cannot be demonstrated as NNS–NS communication.

Aspects of mainstream SLA, and interlanguage theory in particular, have been challenged in recent years by, among several others, Bhatt (2002), Norton (2000), and Y. Kachru (2005), while Firth and Wagner (1997) refer specifically to English as a special case because of its widespread international use as a lingua franca, and argue for the study of ELF within an SLA framework. Meanwhile, other perspectives on SLA have emerged, such as that of the sociocultural theorists (for example, Lantolf 2000), who consider L2 learners as people who 'actively transform their world and do not merely conform to it' (Donato 2000: 46), and the 'L2 user group', who regard L2 speakers as users within their own right rather than failed NSs (V. Cook 2002a). And both Norton (for example, 2000) and Miller (for example, 2004; and see p. 205 and above) offer alternative approaches to SLA, by reconceptualizing motivation as investment and linking it with issues of power and identity.

Such scholars are questioning traditional SLA beliefs and addressing issues crucial to ELF, such as the role of identity and social realism. Thus, like ELF researchers such as Pölzl (2004; see also Pölzl and Seidlhofer 2006), they are providing alternatives to older, interlanguage-based views of L2 identity and speech community (for example, Tarone 1988; Zuengler 1989) by offering L2 variety-based views of identity and group membership. However, for the time being at least, it seems that mainstream cognitive SLA and alternative sociolinguistic approaches inhabit 'two parallel SLA worlds' (Zuengler and Miller 2006: 35). This is problematic for ELF, because it is largely mainstream SLA researchers who appear to be considered by many ELT gatekeepers the best authorities on English language learning, and whose work therefore continues to inform English language teaching in methods/approaches such as task-based learning and teaching, and communicative language teaching. (See the critique of CLT in Leung 2005.)

In turn, for English as much as for any other language, the concepts of interlanguage and fossilization remain very much in vogue. They are regularly recycled on ELT teacher training/education courses and publications for teachers. For example, in an article entitled 'Beat the fossils to it', the author likens fossilization to 'bad habits' such as smoking and drinking, and advises readers on how to 'nip it in the bud' (McCulloch 2003: 12). Similarly, Han and Selinker (2005) discuss fossilization with little change from the way it was originally conceived by Selinker (for example, 1972, 1992). It is undoubtedly true that some users of English in expanding circle contexts may need English for communication with its NSs, and for them, interlanguage and fossilization may be valid concepts. But because SLA is, in effect, closed to researchers who do not subscribe to the mainstream position,[4] a far larger number of users seem to have been convinced by the prevailing native speaker ideology into believing that their English is interlanguage or fossilized if it is not 'native-like'. And as was clear in the interview data in Chapter 7, some teachers have been persuaded that 'native-like' English is what they need to achieve success in their careers.

Gatekeeping inevitably operates in a less subtle manner when it comes to language testing. It is self-evident to ELF researchers that the recent and dramatic changes in users and uses of English demand some kind of a rethink of English language teaching in terms of the language that is taught. And while it is also self-evident that any curricular changes will first require an overhaul of English language testing,[5] the various English language testing boards (of which the most internationally powerful are sited in the US and UK) seem reluctant to make concessions in order to keep pace with sociolinguistic developments.

As an example, I argued recently (Jenkins 2006a) that although we do not yet have definitive descriptions of ELF, examination boards could still make their practices more relevant to the ways in which most English is spoken in the expanding circle, by prioritizing accommodation skills and not penalizing forms that are already emerging as frequent, systematic, and intelligible among proficient ELF speakers, regardless of the fact that they differ from the way in which NSs of English speak to each other. Responding to my article, Taylor (2006) explained current Cambridge-ESOL policy and practice, largely without reference to the issues I had raised. However, when she did address my argument, she conflated ELF variety with language competence by referring to the fact that Cambridge-ESOL do not penalize the heavy influence of L1 pronunciation features in elementary level candidates. What she failed to mention was that at advanced level, candidates are indeed expected to use 'native-like' pronunciation features and are assessed on their 'inaccuracies' and 'inappropriacies' in this respect. (See also Levis 2006 for discussion of such issues in the testing of pronunciation.)

To give another example, this time from the US, TOEFL (Test of English as a Foreign Language) has recently introduced an Internet-based test (TOEFL IBT). In a glowing review of the new test, Fulcher (2005: 6) praises its integration of skills as follows:

> In the speaking tasks, learners are asked to read-listen-speak in two tasks, and listen-speak in a further two. These tasks tap new constructs that are not just about 'speaking' in the traditional sense, but about the ability to integrate information from different sources, summarise that information, find a solution to a problem, or explain how examples relate to arguments.

Through such 'Evidence Centred Design', it will be possible, says Fulcher, 'to predict ability to operate in a "real" academic environment', and the test, he concludes, 'is the best product for assessing English for academic purposes' (ibid.).

What is completely missing here is any consideration of what 'real' academic environments actually are for the target test community and what kinds of English are spoken in them. The majority of university students using English in academic environments in expanding circle countries are speakers of ELF varieties, while even in universities in inner circle countries they form very sizeable minorities. This means that for much of the time both inside and outside the classroom, the communication context is ELF rather than EFL or ENL. And either way, after their university studies, most NNSs of English who go on to have academic careers, do not operate within an NS English university environment in today's 'globalized' world. Thus, there seems to be no good reason why, even for study in inner circle countries, they should be expected to defer to ENL academic norms or to be tested on them in order to be admitted to their studies. Indeed, it might be more useful if their NS university peer groups and teachers were to become familiar with other ways of speaking (and even writing) than those exclusive to NS academic contexts.[6]

For the new TOEFL IBT to be widely relevant, then, it needs to focus less on the academic skills of proficient ENL users and more on those of proficient ELF users as described, for example, by Mauranen (for example, 2003, 2006) in respect of her ELFA (English as a Lingua Franca in Academic Settings) corpus. And the same is true of IELTS (International English language Testing System).[7] A new set of practice tests to prepare learners for IELTS (Gould and Clutterbuck 2004) contains three CDs that simulate the test itself. The accompanying book describes these recordings as providing a range of 'international dialects and accents' (p. 2). However, the accents for the four listening tests all turn out to be those of NSs, primarily cultivated Australian English, North American English (GA and Mid-Atlantic) and, in a few cases, British English (RP). The only time an NNS features on these recordings is in the sample speaking test, where a (not particularly proficient) Turkish speaker of English is heard being interviewed by an Australian NS English speaker. Thus, all the proficient speakers and all those in positions of authority are NSs of English, while the single NNS is both a less proficient English speaker and in a subordinate social role.

Leaving aside the washback effects of such test approaches on students' feelings of self-worth in English, the fact that there is such an exclusive focus on NS English varieties means inevitably that these are the varieties students will want to learn and teachers to teach. As Canagarajah (2006: 236) argues, 'given the reality of washback effect, tests based on inner circle norms will prevent the development of pedagogical material and methods for local varieties, and stultify the expansion of local varieties altogether'. This applies as much to ELF as to the outer circle varieties with which Canagarajah is primarily concerned and, as was seen in Chapter 6, affects teachers' attitudes towards and beliefs about NNS English varieties. And for NNS teachers, unable to 'match' the voices on NS-biased recorded material, it means, in turn, the kinds of identity conflict described in Chapter 7 and the linguistic insecurity that we consider in the next section.

Many of the more traditionally-oriented applied linguists (for example, Davies 2003, 2004), like the examination boards themselves, continue to see the NS of English as the only possible yardstick for English language tests, and to respond to criticism by arguing, for example, that the bias claim is speculative, lacking in empirical evidence, and 'takes the form of polemic rather than discussion of data' (Davies *et al.* 2003: 573).[8] Just how blinkered and fixed such ideas about NS English are, even among those who claim academic authority, is evident in other of Davies's pronouncements. For example, in his *Glossary of Applied Linguistics* (2005), he defines ELF (which he calls 'ELiF') as follows:

> A concept related to English as an international language, the idea of ELiF is based on a corpus of EFL (sic) uses. The rationale is that most English use in the world today is between non-native speakers and that what they are using is ELiF. This needs to be described and promoted. Like English as an international language, it represents an attack on the native speaker and suffers just as much from the consequent loss of a definable model.
> (p. 42)

And in an article on assessing ELF (Elder and Davies 2006), we find the extraordinary statement that researchers in ELF adopt a deficit position.

By contrast, others have strong reservations about the current nature of English language tests, and many of these reservations resonate with ELF. (See, for example, McNamara 2004 on language tests and identity; McNamara 2005 on 'shibboleth-like tests'; Roever and McNamara 2006 on the social dimension in language testing; and Shohamy 2001 on the issue of power in testing practices.) And as Canagarajah (op. cit.: 233) argues, proficiency in the postmodern world is a matter of measuring not how closely the English of certain inner circle English speakers is imitated, but 'the ability to shuttle between different varieties of English and different speech communities' (see also Canagarajah 2005), in examinations such as Cambridge-ESOL First Certificate of English and TOEFL. Leung and Lewkowicz (2006), meanwhile, address ELF directly in their state-of-the-art paper on language testing, arguing that 'the growing knowledge of English as a Lingua Franca (ELF) in the past few years is beginning to make this self-imposed normative insulation untenable' (p. 228) and that '[t]he progressive establishment of a stable body of knowledge of ELF features and the use of ELF in a wide range of contexts will no doubt generate new momentum for a renewed debate on language norms and the nature of language proficiency for teaching and assessment of English' (p. 229). Likewise, Coleman (2006: 11), in an article on English-medium teaching in higher education in Europe observes:

> There is already evidence that students in English-speaking countries on SOCRATES-ERASMUS exchanges socialize more with other foreign students than with native speakers, and can better understand other non-native speakers than local students. ... As ELF diverges further from standard varieties in the UK, the US, Ireland or Australia, these countries

too could become diglossic, and native speaker English become a sociolinguistically marked variety, no longer automatically acceptable in
international contexts. Then the predominance of international academics with a range of native tongues other than English may well diversify
even academic discourse away from today's ubiquitously delocalized
Anglo-American standard. And the world may see the emergence of a
more democratic model of English as a lingua franca ...

This perspective is the exact opposite of that of the examination boards
discussed above. It seems unlikely, however, that the examination board
gatekeepers will develop a more internationally relevant frame of mind in the
near future,[9]

I have already mentioned the washback effect of ENL-biased testing on
ELT materials. Having said that, as I pointed out earlier, it would be unreason-
able to expect either tests or materials to focus for production on ELF forms
before ELF has been fully described, codified, and considered from a range
of pedagogic perspectives. But this does not mean that testers and publishers
should continue to promote a strong NS bias: there is sufficient evidence
available of how English is used around the world—and by whom—for them
to be able to include other users and uses of English than those of the inner
circle. And yet existing ELT tests and, in turn, materials (coursebooks, recordings, grammar references, and dictionaries) persist with a heavy, and often
almost exclusive, focus on ENL and its speakers' formal and informal uses of
English. They thus miss important opportunities to expose learners to other
ways in which the language is used, and to develop learners' accommodation
skills—arguably far more useful for international communication than the
ability to approximate the English of a native speaker.

The problem lies not only in the general lack of non-ENL-oriented published materials, but also in the fact that ENL is almost always presented as
the only 'real' English, and its speakers as the only 'experts'. This is made
very clear by the blurbs in the 'big' publishers' advertisements. To take just
a sample of those I have recently collected: Pearson Longman's advertisement for the *Longman Dictionary of Contemporary English* claims to be
'your link to the living language'; Collins Cobuild's advertisement describes
the *English Dictionary for Advanced Learners* as 'helping learners with <u>real</u>
English' (emphasis in original); and a Cambridge University Press advert for
Carter and McCarthy's *Cambridge Grammar of English* calls it 'the ultimate
authority on English as it's really used'.

This state of affairs is, inevitably, repeated inside the materials themselves.
Most have a strong NS bias in their subtexts by showing competent NSs but
rarely competent NNSs (Matsuda 2003). And as Matsuda (2002b) points
out in relation to her study of ELT coursebooks in Japan, '[t]he large number
of inner circle characters ... gives the impression that they are the dominant
users of English' whereas Japanese characters 'do not come across as regular
and extensive users of English but rather as prototypical examples of EFL

learners' (pp. 189–90). This, she argues, 'sends a message that English is most closely associated with the inner circle' (p. 193). Meanwhile, the 'overwhelming majority of the chapters present international use between one or more native speakers and one or more nonnative speakers of English', and this 'may give the impression that nonnative speakers learn English in order to communicate with those from the inner circle' (pp. 194–5). She concludes that 'the representation of English in EFL textbooks may be *an important source of influence in the construction of students' attitudes and perceptions* towards the target language' (p. 196; emphasis added), precisely the point made by several of the interview participants in Chapter 7. Not surprisingly, then, Matsuda (2002a: 438) finds that '[s]tudents may be shocked by varieties of English that deviate from Inner Circle English, view them as deficient (rather than different), or grow disrespectful to such varieties and users'.

A few of the mainstream 'global' ELT coursebook publishers do make small concessions to outer and (to a lesser extent) expanding circle Englishes in their ELT materials. For example, in designing their coursebook, the authors of *Natural English* (Gairns and Redman 2002) recorded proficient NNSs rather than NSs (whose speech, they felt, was too idiomatic) carrying out tasks in order to provide the basis of the syllabus. While still heavily NS English-based, the outcome is a focus more on regularly-occurring speech patterns than on finicky grammar rules, and leaves more to the learner's discretion in the various free activities than is usual. *Cutting Edge* (Cunningham and Moor 2003) even has a unit on 'global English', which includes a section on 'Changing English in a changing world' (p. 10) and an authentic interview on the subject.[10] Students are then asked to consider their views on the arguments put forward in the interview. Examples such as these, nevertheless, constitute little more than a few nods in the direction of lingua franca English use, or at least non-ENL-centric use. And although there have been other very recent developments in this respect, (see the final section of the chapter), little has changed in practice.[11] Indeed, one of the best-selling English coursebooks in China at present, and one which has apparently sold one hundred million copies, is Stannard's *New Standard English* (published by Macmillan and the Chinese publisher FLTRP) in which the author 'describes aspects of British culture such as our love affair with curries and coffee bars and the custom of buying a hamburger at half-time at a Sunday football match' (*Times Higher Education Supplement* 12 May 2006).

There is at present, then, a major problem in the kinds of English presented to learners in coursebooks, grammar reference books (whether prescriptive or corpus-based), and dictionaries. Even dictionaries that describe themselves as 'international' are only international in the sense of the so-called 'international' tests described above: in other words, they are heavily based on a range of inner circle English varieties.[12] The single small, but significant, development in this regard is the seventh edition of *OALDCE* (*Oxford Advanced Learners' Dictionary of Current English*), which has a page explaining ELF (p. R92) written by Seidlhofer.

Finally, in this discussion of gatekeeping practices, is the issue of teacher education and training. In Jenkins (2000), I discussed weaknesses in pre- and in-service teacher training with regard to ELF. I referred, for example, to the fact that at diploma level (specifically the UCLES DELTA),[13] there had been 'few concessions in terms of internationalization' in respect of phonology teaching, and 'no principled discussion (if any discussion at all) of the selection of internationally appropriate pronunciation models' (2000: 200). Slightly more attention is paid to such matters in more recent versions of the syllabus guidelines. In 2003, two new components were added to the CELTA syllabus, ('Varieties of English', and 'Multilingualism and the role of first languages'), and two to DELTA ('Designing teaching programmes to meet the needs of adult learners in different contexts', and 'Implementing teaching programmes to meet the needs of adult learners in different contexts').[14] However, it is not clear exactly what is included in either case, or even whether the varieties in question extend beyond the confines of the inner circle.

The overall impression, then, is that these two teacher training programmes are still heavily prescriptive, and that when trainees are asked to be descriptive, they are expected to do so within firm constraints. It is no surprise, then, that many teacher trainers themselves seem to be unaware that the two syllabuses have changed in any way (Martin Dewey, personal communication). And judging by what I hear from DELTA trainers, and by the evidence of my own ears when post-diploma students arrive at my institution to start a masters programme, it seems that there is not a great deal of change taking place in practice.

Even when teachers do have an opportunity to learn about ELF and NNS English varieties, as is sometimes the case on masters (and occasionally bachelors) programmes around the world (see the final section below), there is still a massive gap between theory and practice. Teachers who attend courses on varieties of English or world Englishes may respond positively to the notion of ELF. However, when these same students begin or resume work as English language teachers, the institutional constraints imposed on them to teach 'standard' NS English by traditional communicative methods prevent them from making links between what they know in theory and what they do in their classrooms. Thus, despite the value of teacher education in raising awareness of the existence of ELF, and in providing teachers with the opportunity to engage with its principles, much institutional practice, with its attachment to 'nativelike' communicative competence and standardized NS norms 'circumscribes learner and teacher autonomy' in this respect (Alptekin 2002: 61).

All these gatekeeping activities conspire (some literally, some metaphorically) to promote a particular view of 'good' English and 'good' English speakers, and to have a malign influence on teachers' (both NNS and NS) as well as expanding circle learners' attitudes towards the English language. In turn, they lead to linguistic insecurity among NNS English teachers as well as linguistic over-security among NS English teachers.

Linguistic insecurity

The kinds of gatekeeping practices described in the previous section inevitably have an effect on the way teachers feel about themselves. Although causal links cannot necessarily be made between the NS bias in English language testing and teaching materials, it was clear in the interviews in Chapter 7, that several of the participating teachers attributed their lack of confidence at least in part to such phenomena. Some South East Asian participants also mentioned the displacing or undermining of NNS English teachers by NS teachers in countries such as China, Japan, Korea, and Taiwan, where 'real native speakers' are imported in substantial numbers. If there was a major shift in policy in this respect, as well as in the kinds of teaching materials that were published, I suspect that NNS teachers of English, such as several of those participating in my interviews, might begin to feel more confident in themselves as authoritative English speakers and teachers, particularly in terms of their English accents. They would in turn (apart, perhaps, from a relatively small number of mainly older English speakers in Central/Eastern Europe) find that their identities as speakers of ELF varieties of English would overlap more closely with their identities as successful, competent teachers and confident English speakers rather than conflicting with them.

However, neither development seems likely to happen in the near future, judging by the many adverts for NS teachers that I have spotted recently. These include:

- an advert by Chinese State University, South China, where one of the three minimum qualifications is 'Native English Speaker';
- an advert for Portugal's largest language school asking for 'English Native Speakers standard only';
- another for an ALT[15] post at one of Japan's 'Big three language schools' offering work as 'Expatriate teachers' to recent university graduates in the UK; and
- several for the NET[16] scheme in Hong Kong.

Meanwhile, two recent articles in *EL Gazette* refer to the fact that 'Seoul city hunts 900 native speakers [of English]' for its primary and junior high schools (June 2005: 3), and that Taiwan's Ministry of Education is considering lowering recruitment standards 'to meet its goal of introducing 1,000 qualified native English teachers into the country' (September 2005: 3). And Qiang and Wolff (2005: 57) refer to the situation in China as 'the current invasion of EFL teachers', while Kirkpatrick (2006: 4) notes an advert for a teaching post in Japan where no teaching experience or qualifications are needed; the applicant simply needs to be an NS English graduate and like children.[17]

It would not be at all surprising if such offers to NS but not NNS English teachers were to generate linguistic insecurity in the latter and linguistic over-security in the former. In fact, it would be surprising if this was not the case. Taken to its extreme, it seems to result in NNSs of English being 'co-opted into linguicism' (Joseph 2004b: 360), in what Kumaravadivelu (2003:

547–8) refers to as 'self-marginalisation', and in what Lippi-Green (1997: 242) describes as being 'complicit in the process' of their own subordination by, for example, downgrading their own accents. For, as Lippi-Green points out, 'no-one can make you feel inferior without your consent' (op. cit.: 240). McNamara (2001: 18) even talks of 'linguistic self hatred'. This would probably be overstating the case for most NNS English teachers, but it nevertheless resonates with some of the comments made by my interview participants, and by other NNS teachers quoted in the literature. For example, Braine (1999: xviii) quotes a teacher 'who is also an accomplished author' as having 'self-doubt' because of 'my deficiency in the language'. The teacher/author goes on to say that he has confidence in his English because 'I know I write better than average native speakers … and my accent is better than most NNSs, but that does not necessarily qualify me for the teaching of the language I have not completely mastered'. His high proficiency in written English (better than that of average NSs) and his good teaching skills apparently did not compensate in his mind for his 'less than idiomatic' English and his NNS accent—presumably as measured against an NS yardstick.

Turning to the issue of ELF-generated insecurity specifically, and this currently applies as much to NS teachers of English as to NNSs, it is a well-documented fact that teachers tend to find curriculum change and innovation unsettling, and that a number of issues and concerns need to be fully considered if teachers are to view such change positively. For present purposes I mention those that have the most relevance for ELF (many of the key issues are discussed in more detail in Roberts 1998). One of these is the evidence suggesting that planned innovations are only likely to be implemented effectively if the need for change is acknowledged by teachers themselves. (See Fullan 1982.) This is more likely to be the case if teachers have, themselves, been involved in some way in the research that leads to the curriculum development. (See Somekh 1995.) There is also a need for institutional and national support and resources if any educational innovation is to be successful. (See Fullan ibid.; Lamb 1995.) It is also a mistaken assumption that changes in teachers' beliefs and attitudes will lead to changes in classroom practices (Fullan 1982)—something that has already been shown to be the case with ELF. Connected to this is the likelihood that teachers' deeply-held beliefs about the nature of knowledge and teaching will lead them to implement innovations only at the margins of their practice (Cuban 1993). There is also the need to address teachers' concerns about maintaining the esteem of others when they introduce innovations (Olson and Eaton 1987), an issue which could prove particularly sensitive in a case such as ELF, which many teachers regard as an inferior simplified English and may feel that they are being patronized. And for ELF, as with all innovation, there is a need to take into account the fact that the learning process which seems to underlie teacher change is non-linear, situated, and personal in nature (Clarke and Hollingsworth 2002), something which helps to explain some of the differences in response among my interview participants. Training has also been shown to be 'of pivotal importance' and in this respect, the value of training, or, preferably, educating teachers about ELF cannot be overstated (Lamie 2004: 135; and see the final section on the inclusion of world Englishes and ELF in teacher education programmes). Finally, Roberts (1998: 178) also points out that '[a]ssumptions about the nature of language learning often cluster with assumptions about teaching and learning' and that because learning about English is so important for teachers, a particularly good way to explore their beliefs and assumptions is through language awareness activities.

As far as insecurity about ELF is concerned, its researchers may to some extent be part of the 'problem' in that they have taken some of these issues for granted, explained too little,[18] and not involved teachers closely enough in the research process. For one thing, researchers have not always made it sufficiently clear that they are not at this stage talking about teaching (as yet uncodified) ELF forms. Rather, they are suggesting that teachers might take account of some of the premises underlying ELF communication, for example, that it is important for many expanding circle learners to gain familiarity with a range of L2 English accents and to develop accommodation skills, and less important for them to spend a lot of classroom time on NS English features that are widely *not* used by ELF speakers. In this respect, too, as Jennifer Bassett suggested in response to the evident disquiet among teachers at an ELF workshop in 2004, it would be helpful to recommend to teachers that they '[u]se action research and [their] own judgement to replace traditional NS targets with the NNS–NNS criterion'. (See Jenkins 2004: 40.) Even then, it is crucial that researchers do not expect teachers to change their minds and abandon cherished principles and practices overnight. As one of my research participants (H), a teacher with many years of experience, predicted in respect of her own L1 peer group, 'step by step, gradually and gradually, and the Japanese view should be changed'. On the other hand, whether the necessary institutional and national support and resources, including a reorienting of English language testing, will be forthcoming is another matter altogether, and depends on the extent to which the current gatekeeping practices discussed in the previous section continue to prevail.

As is clear from the discussions of gatekeeping and linguistic insecurity, there are a number of major obstacles still facing ELF in terms of attitude and identity. And as was demonstrated in Chapters 5, 6, and 7, there is a tendency for NNS English, and particularly accents, to have negative associations such as low educational level, intelligence, and status among NNSs themselves. A major problem in all these respects is that while sociolinguists dismiss out of hand the 'language is power' arguments of prescriptivists such as Honey (1997) and Quirk (1990) in relation to stigmatized *NS* English varieties, they tend to treat NNS Englishes differently, exhibiting a prejudice that seems at odds with their normal principles. (See, for example, Trudgill 2005.) Meanwhile, the general public and the majority of English language teachers and students remain staunchly in support of the prescriptivist position. This is not to minimize the importance of taking teachers' views of ELF into account and responding to their concerns. As G. Cook points out, '[m]ediation ... is needed between the knowledge of "the experts" and the wishes and wants of individual students and teachers. The latter too, have their own valid ideas about how language learning is best conducted and it is unlikely that the process will be successful if these are not taken into account' (2003: 72). In other words, my point is that knowledge of the advantages and benefits of ELF is not in itself sufficient: it is important to find convincing ways of demonstrating these to teachers. This, too, will involve offering teachers a viable rather than an abstract alternative to traditional EFL for their day-to-day teaching. And until ELF has been fully described and codified, this is obviously not feasible. In the meantime, it is nevertheless possible to offer some broad guidelines, such as recommending that teachers encourage and reward accommodation skills regardless of whether or not they result in forms that would be correct in ENL; or that they do not necessarily make a point of correcting features such as 'informations' and 'discuss about', that are emerging as systematic, frequent, and mutually intelligible in ELF. (See Jenkins 2004: 40–41 for further suggestions.)

The future of ELF: some positive indications

So where does this leave us? In some respects, back with the standard language ideology that I discussed in Chapter 2, and which was found to be heavily implicated in the contents of three widely distributed periodicals for teachers. But I end by moving on from the remaining obstacles to ELF, to look at some of the more positive signs that have recently begun to emerge—even in the time that I have been writing this book.

One very recent positive sign is the emergence of pronunciation materials that take an ELF perspective. The example *par excellence* is Cauldwell's *Streaming Speech* (2002), a CD-ROM which originally presented a range of aspects of spoken British English pronunciation, but which Cauldwell has recently extended on his website to include what he calls *ELF/EIL Voices* (Cauldwell 2006). The recordings feature speakers from Argentina, France, Germany, Japan, Poland, and Sudan, and the accompanying text is as follows:

> English is often thought of as being the property of British and American native speakers, and British and American accents have become the benchmarks for proficiency in pronunciation and speaking. Recently, the appropriacy of these benchmarks has been challenged. The people pictured [on the webpage] speak as well as, or better than, many native speakers while retaining an important part of their personal, social, and cultural identity—their accent. They are all expert communicators in English, with accents from their first language backgrounds—Polish, German, Japanese, etc. All of them use English in their professional lives.

This represents the most major practical advance *vis-à-vis* ELF pronunciation so far, not only because it enables learners (and teachers) to familiarize themselves with a range of ELF accents, but because it legitimizes these accents—and thus these speakers along with all those like them. For the first time, NNSs of English have been presented in materials intended for international use as competent speakers whose accents could serve as models.

Another development pronunciation-wise is Underhill's phonemic chart—see Underhill 1994. Originally this was presented as a means of teaching the RP accent. However, recently Underhill has begun to include in his presentations a discussion of the way in which the chart can be adapted to suit any accent. This could be even to the extent of removing non-core sounds for production altogether (for example, /s/ and /z/ could be used for /θ/ and /ð/ in the German ELF chart), although for reception, learners would still need familiarizing with all the alternatives, both NNS, for example, /t/ and /d/, as well as the NS /θ/ and /ð/. This would help remove the stigma from replacements of NS English 'th' by, in effect, marginalizing the NS variants and prioritizing the NNS. Yet another development has been Walker's work (for example, 2001a, 2001b) in adapting the Lingua Franca Core to make it appropriate for Spanish learners of English. This is an important step, as it provides the same kinds of benefits as are offered by Cauldwell's *ELF/EIL Voices*, and it is to be hoped that pronunciation experts working with learners from other L1s will follow Walker's example. Hung (2002), provides strong arguments for dictionaries to include phonetic transcripts according to the way in which words would be pronounced according to a proficient speaker of the local English (in his case, Hong Kong English) rather than according to the pronunciation of an absent ENL speaker.

The last four years have also seen the publication of a small number of teachers' handbooks and edited volumes that have moved away from traditional monolithic 'how to teach X' advice to approaches that take ELF developments into account. Among the few examples are Burns (2005), Gnutzmann and Intemann (2005), Lee and Azman (2004), and McKay (2002). In addition, an SLA handbook for teachers that has always been firmly attached to the NS yardstick, Lightbown and Spada (2006), in its third edition makes a brief reference to ELF researchers 'who argue for the acceptance of language varieties other than those spoken in the language's "country of origin"', and goes on to point out that '[p]eople increasingly interact with speakers who have learned a different variety of the same language' (p. 106). And Dörnyei *et al.* (2006), a large-scale language attitude/motivation survey, is the first SLA study of its kind to take global issues fully into account, and starts from the premise that the broadening of the ownership of English has 'major consequences on L2 motivation research' (p. 9). Two books on language planning discuss ELF—S. Wright (2004) briefly, and Ferguson (2006) extensively—while ELF is included in two recent books on the history of English (Singh 2005; and Svartik and Leech 2006[19]), and in several recent books on world Englishes (for example, Davies 2005; Jenkins 2003; Kirkpatrick 2007; Melchers and

Shaw 2003). Finally, book-wise, whereas Graddol did not refer to ELF in his 1997 publication, in his 2006 sequel, he allocates it a dedicated section (p. 87).

ELF also features increasingly as the subject of journal articles. For example, it was discussed in two of the articles in a special issue of the journal *World Englishes* on Russian Englishes (Yuzefovich 2005; Proshina 2005), while South East Asian ELF is the subject of an article by Deterding and Kirkpatrick (2006). Particularly welcome in the latter article is the way in which Deterding and Kirkpatrick have taken up from Jenkins (2000) the notion of the importance of accommodation in ELF communication, and applied it to their South East Asian data. Finally, some universities have begun to teach components on ELF (or EIL) on their masters programmes, for example, Chukyo (see Yoshikawa 2005) and Konan (see Nakamura 2002), and see above (p. 108) for further information on the Chukyo course as well as references to other courses of this kind. Such developments provide a welcome if somewhat ironic contrast to the so-called 'English villages' that are sprouting, often in the very same countries. (See Chapter 2, and Seargeant 2005.)[20]

As far as the future is concerned, as I mentioned at the start of the chapter, ELF corpora have a critical role—in fact *the* critical role. For as Coleman (2006: 3) points out, 'Once ELF has been objectively described as a variety and has lost its stigma ... then new and less inequitable conceptions of global English and its learning and teaching become possible'. This was certainly the indication from many of my interview participants, who said they would welcome the opportunity to teach ELF if it was described, codified, and accepted. A good start corpus-wise has been made with corpora such as VOICE (Seidlhofer 2004) and Deterding and Kirkpatrick's corpus of East Asian English (Deterding and Kirkpatrick 2006). But there is still much to be done before there is any possibility of ELF models being offered even on an equal footing with EFL, let alone as the default models. In the meantime, it should not be forgotten both that the changes currently taking place in expanding circle Englishes are part of a natural phenomenon, and that the current anxiety in the face of any language change is a natural response. ELF, however, is likely to continue to evolve of its own accord as long as English remains the principal global lingua franca, regardless of the wishes of those who find it distasteful and independently of the pedagogic considerations and decisions that may follow later.

Widdowson has suggested that TESOL should be known as Teaching English for (rather than to) Speakers of Other Languages (Howatt with Widdowson 2004: 363). This, as Leung (2005: 121) points out, is preferable because it is 'less weighed down with history' and because it 'signal[s] the possibility of defining English from the standpoint of the users/learners'. But if ELF is one day codified and its status as a legitimate means of communication is acknowledged, then we shall be able to talk about Teaching English of Speakers of Other Languages: teaching the ELF of proficient L2 users themselves. If ELF were to be established and recognized in this way, it is reasonable to suppose that the majority of English users in the expanding circle would rethink their attitudes and identities, and choose to learn and use this kind of English because it would be to their advantage to do so. And in so doing, they would be asserting their own claims to the ownership of the language as a genuinely international means of communication.

Notes

1 See Graddol (2006: 114–15) on '[t]he native speaker problem'. Phillipson (2003: 167), likewise, describes '[n]ative speakers as the cause of communication difficulties', arguing that '[i]n many international fora, competent speakers of English as a second language are more comprehensible than native speakers, because they can be better at adjusting their language for people from different cultural and linguistic backgrounds'. See also Jenkins (2000: Chapter 4) on international intelligibility in English.

2 One such example in the publishing context is the refusal by a major publisher of a colleague's proposal for a handbook of ELF accent varieties, despite the enthusiasm of the proposal's anonymous readers. This was because of the perceived risk to the publisher's reputation if it was seen to be promoting 'non-standard' accents. In other words, the publisher was acting as a custodian of conservative NS standards of English.

3 This is not to suggest that there are not pockets of resistance to these English language policies, although so far, these have tended to occur in relation to outer rather than expanding circle contexts. (See, for example, Canagarajah 1999 for a good example.)

4 Firth and Wagner make this very point in responding to the critiques of their 1997 article by a number of SLA researchers. The title of their response is 'SLA property: No trespassing!', and they conclude it by saying '[w]e urge SLA practitioners to open their conceptual and methodological gates and to make 'trespassers' welcome' (1998: 4).

5 As Davidson points out, 'the determination of what is and is not an error is in the hands of the linguistic variety that sets the test' (1993: 116).

6 Aufderhaar (2004) promotes the use of 'authentic' (i.e. NS English) audio materials to improve prospective ITA's (International Teaching Assistants') pronunciation. Again, typical of the current approaches of many pronunciation researchers and materials writers involved in university settings is the lack of any discussion of the listeners' role (in this case, US university students) in negotiating intelligibility, or the part that may be played by accent attitudes. (See, for example, Lippi-Green 1997; Rubin 1992; Rubin and Smith 1990.)

7 IELTS and TOEFL scores are used most frequently to assess whether NNS applicants to inner circle universities meet their English language requirements. Thus, these tests are 'international' only in the 'distribution' sense (i.e. the distribution around the world of NS English norms), rather than in any genuine sense (Widdowson 1997). And see also Lowenberg's

(2002) comments on TOEIC (Test of English for International Communication), another so-called 'international' test that is grounded entirely
in NS English. A recent advert for TOEIC in *The Japan Times* (15
December 2005) described its updated tasks as 'more authentic' because
they expose candidates 'to additional accents, including speakers from
Canada, the US, Britain and Australia', and added that the changes 'will
increase the value of the new TOEIC test to individuals seeking success
in the international business arena'.

8 See also the replies to Davies *et al.* (2003) by Yano (2005), who points
out the need to include ELF in the discussion, and Sridhar (2005), who
argues that Davies *et al.* (ibid.) have omitted from their discussion the
well-attested existence of bias in respect of NNS pronunciation.

9 This is not to suggest that *all* examination boards are *completely* ignoring
the issue. For example, despite the fact that she takes the 'official party
line' (and probably felt obliged to do so) in her 'public' reply to me in her
article in *ELT Journal* (2006), Taylor has elsewhere expressed concerns
about how ELT tests should respond to developments in world Englishes.
(See, for example, Taylor 2002.)

10 I use the word 'authentic' with the utmost confidence, as I was the person
interviewed.

11 There is one major exception to all of this, i.e. Business English. For many
years now, Business English materials writers have adopted a much less
ENL-centred and more truly international approach. For example, in the
international edition of *Business Objectives* (Hollett 2006), the pronunciation exercises focus on pronunciation features that have been shown
to cause problems in international communication rather than mimicking
the minutiae of an NS English accent. Even at the start of the decade,
business English materials were using NNSs of English in listening tasks
in *non*-subordinate roles. For example, in a unit of *Quick Work* (Hollett
2001) called 'Managing discussions', the accompanying listening text
features a capable speaker of German English and an ineffective NS of
British English. This contrasts dramatically with the listening materials
provided with the IELTS course discussed on p. 242 above. Meanwhile,
The New English File (Oxenden and Latham-Koenig 2005), another
business English course, pays particular attention to pronunciation, again
prioritizing features because they are likely to promote international
intelligibility rather than because they conform to an NS accent, and
includes many references to English speakers who do not come from ENL
countries.

12 For example, an advert by Cambridge University Press for *The Cambridge
Guide to English Usage* describes it as 'truly international in its approach'
because 'it differentiates clearly between US, UK, Canadian and Australian usage'.

13 UCLES, University of Cambridge Local Examination Syndicate, is the former name of Cambridge ESOL. DELTA is the Diploma in English Language Teaching to Adults, and CELTA the Certificate in English Language Teaching to Adults, both run by Cambridge ESOL. Trinity College has similar pre- and in-service courses. Both the Cambridge and Trinity schemes are taught widely around the world and (at least in theory) admit both NS and NNS teachers.

14 See *CELTA Syllabus and Assessment guidelines* (Cambridge ESOL 2006: 6) and *DELTA Syllabus and Assessment guidelines* (Cambridge ESOL 2006: 4) for the most up-to-date versions.

15 Assistant Language Teacher.

16 Native-speaking English Teacher.

17 The situation *vis-à-vis* the importing of NS English teachers contrasts starkly with the growing awareness among applied linguists in the same countries that NS Englishes are not the most useful for international communication. See, for example, Chou (2004) in respect of Taiwan, Matsuda (2002a, 2003) in respect of Japan, Shim (1999, 2002) regarding Korea, and Luk and Lin (2006) on Hong Kong.

18 In this respect, the publication of Seidlhofer (forthcoming), an entire book devoted to explaining ELF, will be a major step forward in helping to clarify the many confusions. that surround ELF.

19 Svartik and Leech, however, seem to be rather confused as to what ELF is. On the one hand they describe it as 'a working international variety of [English]' and on the other hand as 'the 'Low' or demotic variety' of Global English in contrast to 'the 'High' variety of WSE [World Standard English]' (2006: 235), They also believe that the emergence of regional varieties of ELF will be a 'problem' (ibid.), although they offer no evidence to support this claim, or explain why they do not see regional varieties of ENL to present a similar 'problem'.

20 Although not directly related to ELF, two other recent changes should be mentioned. The first, the 2005 change in editorship of the journal *TESOL Quarterly*, has already had a positive effect in that the new editor appears to be more receptive to ELF than his predecessors were. The second, TESOL's new 'Position statement against discrimination of nonnative speakers of English in the field of TESOL' (approved by the Board of Directors in March 2006), is likely to impact positively on attitudes to ELF by arguing so publicly against 'an oversimplified either/or classification system that does not actually describe the range of possibilities in a world where English has become a global language'.

Bibliography

Abercrombie, D. 1951. 'RP and local accent' in D. Abercrombie (ed.). 1965. *Studies in Linguistics and Phonetics*. Oxford: Oxford University Press.

Adolphs, S. 2005. '"I don't think I should learn all this"—a longitudinal view of attitudes towards "native speaker" English' in C. Gnutzmann and F. Intemann (eds.). *The Globalisation of English and the English Language Classroom*. Tübingen: Narr.

Alptekin, C. 2002. 'Towards intercultural communicative competence'. *ELT Journal* 56/1: 57–64.

Ammon, U. 2003. 'Global English and the non-native speaker: overcoming disadvantage' in H. Tonkin and T. Reagan (eds.). *Language in the Twenty-first Century*. Amsterdam: John Benjamins.

Andreasson, A-M. 1994. 'Norm as pedagogical paradigm'. *World Englishes* 13/3: 395–409.

Antaki, C. and **S. Widdicombe** (eds.). 1998. *Identities in Talk*. London: Sage Publications.

Aufderhaar, C. 2004. 'Learner views of using authentic audio to aid pronunciation: "You just grab some feelings"'. *TESOL Quarterly* 38/4: 735–46.

Bailey, R. W. 1991. *Images of English. A Cultural History of the Language*. Ann Arbor: University of Michigan Press.

Baker, C. 1992. *Attitudes and Language*. Clevedon: Multilingual Matters.

Ball, P. 1983. 'Stereotypes of Anglo-Saxon accents: some explanatory Australian studies with the matched-guise technique'. *Language Sciences* 5: 163–84.

Bamgboṣe, A. 1998. 'Torn between the norms: innovations in world Englishes'. *World Englishes* 17/1: 1–14.

Baumgardner, R. J. and **K. Brown.** 2003. 'World Englishes: ethics and pedagogy'. *World Englishes* 22/3: 245–51.

Bayard, D., A. Weatherall, C. Gallois, and **J. Pittam.** 2001. 'Pax Americana? Accent attitudinal evaluations in New Zealand, Australia, and America'. *Journal of Sociolinguistics* 5: 22–49.

Beinhoff, B. 2005. 'Non-native speakers' perceptions of their foreign accent of English: attitudes and identity'. Unpublished MPhil research essay. Research Centre for English and Applied Linguistics, Faculty of English, University of Cambridge.

Beneke, J. 1991. 'Englisch als lingua franca oder als Medium interkultureller Kommunikation' in R. Grebing (ed.). *Grenzenloses Sprachenlernen. Festschrift für Richard Freudenstein*. Berlin: Cornelsen.

Benson, M. J. 1991. 'Attitudes and motivation towards English. A survey of Japanese freshmen'. *RELC Journal* 22/1: 34–48.

Benwell, B. and **E. Stokoe.** 2006. *Discourse and Identity*. Edinburgh: Edinburgh University Press.

Berns, M. 1995. 'English in the European Union'. *English Today* 11/3: 3–11.

Bex, T. and **R. J. Watts** (eds.). 1999. *Standard English. The Widening Debate*. London: Routledge.

Bhatt, R. M. 2002. 'Experts, dialects, and discourse'. *International Journal of Applied Linguistics* 12/1: 74–109.

Biber, D., S. Johansson, G. Leech, G. Conrad, and **E. Finegan.** 1999. *Longman Grammar of Spoken and Written English*. Harlow: Longman.

Billig, M. 1987. *Arguing and Thinking: a Rhetorical Approach to Social Psychology.* Cambridge: Cambridge University Press.

Block, D. 2006. 'Identity in applied linguistics' in T. Omoniyi and G. White (eds.). *The Sociolinguistics of Identity.* London: Continuum.

Blommaert, J. (ed.). 1999. *Language Ideological Debates.* Berlin and New York: Mouton de Gruyter.

Blommaert, J. 2003. 'Commentary: a sociolinguistics of globalization'. *Journal of Sociolinguistics* 7/4: 607–23.

Blommaert, J. 2005. *Discourse.* Cambridge: Cambridge University Press.

Bolton, K. 2003. *Chinese Englishes.* Cambridge: Cambridge University Press.

Bonfiglio, T. P. 2002. *Race and the Rise of Standard American.* Berlin and New York: Mouton de Gruyter.

Bourdieu, P. 1977. 'The economics of linguistic exchanges'. *Social Science Information* 16/6: 645–68.

Bourdieu, P. 1990. *The Logic of Practice.* Cambridge: Polity Press.

Bourdieu, P. 1991. *Language and Symbolic Power.* Cambridge: Polity Press.

Bourhis, R. Y., H. Giles, and **H. Tajfel.** 1973. 'Language as a determinant of Welsh identity'. *European Journal of Social Psychology* 3: 447–60.

Bourhis, R. Y. and **I. Sachdev.** 1984. 'Vitality perceptions and language attitudes'. *Journal of Language and Social Psychology* 97–126.

Bradac, J., A. C. Cargile, and **J. S. Hallett.** 2001. 'Language attitudes: respect, conspect and prospect' in W. P. Robinson and H. Giles (eds.). *The New Handbook of Language and Social Psychology.* Chichester: Wiley.

Bragg, M. 2003. *The Adventure of English.* London: Hodder and Stoughton.

Braine, G. (ed.). 1999. *Non-native Educators in English Language Teaching.* Mahwah, N.J.: Lawrence Erlbaum.

Breiteneder, A. 2005. 'The naturalness of English as a European lingua franca: the case of the "third person" -*s*'. *Vienna English Working Papers* 14/2: 3–26.

Brown, K. 2002. 'Ideology and context: world Englishes and EFL teacher training'. *World Englishes* 21/3: 445–8.

Brumfit, C. 2001. *Individual Freedom in Language Teaching.* Oxford: Oxford University Press.

Bruthiaux, P. 2003. 'Squaring the circles: issues in modeling English worldwide'. *International Journal of Applied Linguistics* 13/2: 159–78.

Brutt-Griffler, J. 2002. *World English. A Study of its Development.* Clevedon: Multilingual Matters.

Brutt-Griffler, J. and **K. Samimy.** 2001. 'Transcending the nativeness paradigm'. *World Englishes* 20/1: 99–106.

Burns, A. (ed.). 2005. *Teaching English from a Global Perspective.* Alexandria, Virginia: TESOL.

Butler, S. 1997. 'Corpus of English in Southeast Asia: implications for a regional dictionary' in M. L. S. Bautista (ed.). *English as an Asian Language: The Philippine Context.* Manila: Macquarie Library.

Byram, M. (ed.). 2004. *Routledge Encyclopedia of Language Teaching and Learning.* London: Routledge.

Cameron, D. 1995. *Verbal Hygiene.* London: Routledge.

Cameron, D. 2001. *Working with Spoken Discourse.* London: Sage Publications.

Canagarajah, A. S. 1999. *Resisting Linguistic Imperialism in English Teaching.* Oxford: Oxford University Press.

Canagarajah, A. S. 2005. 'Introduction' in A. S. Canagarajah (ed.). *Reclaiming the Local in Language Policy and Practice.* Mahwah, N.J.: Lawrence Erlbaum.

Canagarajah, A. S. 2006. 'Changing communicative needs, revised assessment objectives'. *Language Assessment Quarterly* 3/3: 229–42.

Cargile, A. C., H. Giles, E. B. Ryan, and J. Bradac. 1994. 'Language attitudes as a social process: a conceptual model and new directions'. *Language and Communication 14*: 211–36.

Carter, R. A. 1998. 'Orders of reality: CANCODE, communication, and culture'. *ELT Journal, 52/1*: 43–56.

Carter, R. A. and M. J. McCarthy. 1996. 'Correspondence'. *ELT Journal 50/4*: 369–71.

Cauldwell, R. T. 2002. *Streaming Speech*. Birmingham: Speechinaction.

Cauldwell, R. T. 2006. *ELF/EIL Voices*, Retrieved 22 August 2006 from http://speechinaction.net/SPARC_ELF.htm.

Chambers, J. K., P. Trudgill, and N. Schilling-Estes (eds.). 2002. *The Handbook of Language Variation and Change*. Oxford: Blackwell.

Chiba, R., H. Matsuura, and A. Yamamoto. 1995. 'Japanese attitudes towards English accents'. *World Englishes 14/1*: 77–86.

Chou, M-C. 2004. 'Teaching EIL to English learners in Taiwan'. *Hwa Kang Journal of English Language and Literature 10*: 72–91.

Clarke, C. and H. Hollingsworth. 2002. 'Elaborating a model of teacher professional growth'. *Teaching and Teacher Education 18*: 947–67.

Coleman, J. A. 2006. 'English-medium teaching in European higher education'. *Language Teaching 39*: 1–14.

Cook, G. 1998. 'The uses of reality: a reply to Ronald Carter'. *ELT Journal 52/1* 57–63.

Cook, G. 2003. *Applied Linguistics*. Oxford: Oxford University Press.

Cook, V. 1999. 'Going beyond the native speaker in language teaching'. *TESOL Quarterly 33/2*: 185–209.

Cook, V. (ed.). 2002a. *Portraits of the L2 User*. Clevedon: Multilingual Matters.

Cook, V. 2002b. 'Background to the L2 user' in V. Cook (ed.). *Portraits of the L2 User*. Clevedon: Multilingual Matters.

Coulmas, F. (ed.). 1997. *The Handbook of Sociolinguistics*. Oxford: Blackwell.

Coupland, N. 2003. 'Introduction: sociolinguistics and globalisation'. *Journal of Sociolinguistics 7/4*: 465–572.

Crowley, T. 2003. *Standard English and the Politics of Language* (second ed.). Houndmills, Basingstoke: Palgrave Macmillan.

Cruttenden, A. 2001. *Gimson's Pronunciation of English* (sixth ed.). London: Arnold.

Crystal, D. 2003. *English as a Global Language* (second ed.). Cambridge: Cambridge University Press.

Crystal, D. 2004a. *The Language Revolution*. Cambridge: Polity Press.

Crystal, D. 2004b. *The Stories of English*. London: Penguin.

Cuban, L. 1993. *How Teachers Taught: Constancy and Change in American Classrooms 1890–1980* (second edn.). New York: Longman.

Cullen, R. 2005. 'ELF: myth and reality'. Paper given at the English as a Lingua Franca seminar. Canterbury Christ Church University College, 16 June 2005.

Cunningham, S. and P. Moor. 2003. *Cutting Edge (Advanced Students' Book)*. Harlow, Essex: Longman.

Dalton, C. and B. Seidlhofer. 1994. *Pronunciation*. (*Scheme for Teacher Education*). Oxford: Oxford University Press.

Dalton-Puffer, C., G. Kaltenboeck, and U. Smit. 1997. 'Learner attitudes and L2 pronunciation in Austria'. *World Englishes 16/1*: 115–28.

Dauer, R. 2005. 'The Lingua Franca Core: a new model for pronunciation instruction?' *TESOL Quarterly 39/3*: 543–50.

Davidson, F. 1993. 'Testing across cultures: summary and comments'. *World Englishes 12/1*: 113–25.

Davies, A. 1999. 'Standard English: discordant voices'. *World Englishes 18/2*: 171–86.

Davies, A. 2003. *The Native Speaker: Myth and Reality*. Clevedon: Multilingual Matters.

Davies, A. 2004. 'The native speaker in applied linguistics' in A. Davies and C. Elder (eds.). *The Handbook of Applied Linguistics*. Oxford: Blackwell.

Davies, A. 2005. *A Glossary of Applied Linguistics*. Edinburgh: Edinburgh University Press.

Davies, A. and C. Elder. (eds.). 2004. *The Handbook of Applied Linguistics*. Oxford: Blackwell.

Davies, A., L. Hamp-Lyons, and C. Kemp. 2003. 'Whose norms? International proficiency tests in English'. *World Englishes* 22/4: 571–84.

Davies, D. 2005. *Varieties of Modern English*. Harlow: Pearson Longman.

De Fina, A. (ed.). 2006. *Discourse and Identity*. Cambridge: Cambridge University Press.

De Swaan, A. 2001. *Words of the World. The Global Language System*. Cambridge: Polity Press.

Decke-Cornill, H. 2003. '"We would have to invent the language we are supposed to teach": The issue of English as a Lingua Franca in language education in Germany' in M. Byram and P. Grundy (eds.). *Context and Culture in Language Teaching*. Clevedon: Multilingual Matters.

Derwing, T. M. 2003. 'What do ESL students say about their accents?' *The Canadian Modern Language Review* 59/4: 547–66.

Derwing, T. M. and M. J. Munro. 1997. 'Accent, intelligibility, and comprehensibility'. *Studies in Second Language Acquisition* 19/1: 1–16.

Denwing, T. M. and M. J. Munro. 2005. 'Second language accent and pronunciation teaching. A research-based approach'. *TESOL* Quarterly 39/3: 379–97.

Derwing, T. M., M. J. Rossiter, and M. J. Munro. 2002. 'Teaching native speakers to listen to foreign-accented speech'. *Journal of Multilingual and Multicultural Development* 23/4: 245–59.

Deterding, D. and A. Kirkpatrick. 2006. 'Emerging South-East Asian Englishes and intelligibility'. *World Englishes* 25/3: 391–409.

Dewey, M. 2005. 'English as a Lingua Franca in a globalized framework'. Paper given at 38th Annual BAAL Meeting: Language, Culture and Identity in Applied Linguistics. Bristol, September 2005.

Donato, R. 2000. 'Sociocultural contributions to understanding the foreign and second language classroom' in J. Lantolf (ed.). *Sociocultural Theory and Second Language Learning*. Oxford: Oxford University Press.

Dörnyei, Z., K. Csizér, and N. Németh. 2006. *Motivation, Language Attitudes and Globalisation*. Clevedon: Multilingual Matters.

Dziubalska-Kołaczyk, K. and J. Przedlacka (eds.). *English Pronunciation Models: A Changing Scene*. Frankfurt am Main: Peter Lang.

Edwards, J. R. (1982). 'Language attitudes and their implications among English speakers' in E. B. Ryan and H. Giles (eds.). *Attitudes Towards Language Variation*. London: Arnold.

Eggins, S. and D. Slade. 1997. *Analysing Casual Conversation*. London: Cassell.

Eisenstein, M. and G. Verdi. 1983. 'The intelligibility of social dialects for working-class adult learners of English'. *Language Learning* 35/2: 287–98.

El-Dash, L. G. and J. Busnardo. 2001. 'Brazilian attitudes toward English: dimensions of status and solidarity'. *International Journal of Applied Linguistics* 11/1: 57–74.

Elder C. and A. Davies. 2006. 'Assessing English as a lingua franca'. *Annual Review of Applied Linguistics* 26: 282–301.

ELFA website (ELF in Academic Settings) www.uta.fi/laitokset/kielet/engf/research/elfa.

Eoyang, E. 1999. 'The worldliness of the English language: a lingua franca past and future'. *ADFL Bulletin* 32/2: 10–15.

Erling, E. 2005. 'The many names of English'. *English Today* 21/1: 40–4.

Escobar, A. 1995. *Encountering Development: The Making and Unmaking of the Third World*. Princeton: Princeton University Press.

Fayer, J. K. and E. Krasinski. 1987. 'Native and nonnative judgments of intelligibility and irritation'. *Language Learning* 37/3: 313–26.

Ferguson, G. 2006. *Language Planning and Education*. Edinburgh: Edinburgh University Press.

Field, J. 2005. 'Intelligibility and the listener: the role of lexical stress'. *TESOL Quarterly*, 39/3: 399–423.

Firth, A. 1990. '"Lingua franca" negotiations: towards an interactional approach'. *World Englishes* 9/3: 269–80.

Firth, A. 1996. 'The discursive accomplishment of normality. On "lingua franca" English and conversational analysis'. *Journal of Pragmatics* 26: 237–59.

Firth, A. and J. Wagner. 1997. 'On discourse, communication and (some) fundamental concepts in SLA research'. *Modern Language Journal* 81: 285–300.

Firth, A. and J. Wagner. 1998. 'SLA property: No trespassing!' *Modern Language Journal* 82/1: 91–4.

Forde, K. 1995. 'A study of learner attitudes towards accents of English'. *Hong Kong Polytechnic University Working Papers in ELT and Applied Linguistics* 1: 59–76.

Friedrich, P. 2000. 'English in Brazil: functions and attitudes'. *World Englishes* 19/2: 215–23.

Friedrich, P. 2003. 'English in Argentina: attitudes of MBA students'. *World Englishes* 22/2: 173–84.

Fulcher, G. 2005. 'Better communications test will silence critics'. *Guardian Weekly: Learning English*. 18 November 2005: 6.

Fullan, M. 1982. *The Meaning of Educational Change*. New York: Teachers College Press.

Gairns, R. and S. Redman. 2002. *Natural English (Intermediate Students' Book)*. Oxford: Oxford University Press.

Gardner, R. C. 1985. *Social Psychology and Second Language Learning: The Role of Attitudes and Motivation*. London: Arnold.

Garrett, P. 2001. 'Language attitudes and sociolinguistics'. *Journal of Sociolinguistics* 5: 626–31.

Garrett, P., N. Coupland, and A. Williams. 2003. *Investigating Language Attitudes. Social Meanings of Dialect, Ethnicity and Performance*. Cardiff: University of Wales Press.

Giles, H. (ed.) 1984. *International Journal of the Sociology of Language. The Dynamics of Speech Accommodation*. Amsterdam: Mouton.

Giles, H. 1992. 'Current and future directions in sociolinguistics: a social psychological contribution' in K. Bolton and H. Kwok (eds.). *Sociolinguistics Today. Current Perspectives*. London: Routledge.

Giles, H. 1998. 'Language attitudes and language cognitions' in M. C. Pennington (ed.). *Language in Hong Kong at Century's End*. Hong Kong: Hong Kong University Press.

Giles, H. and A. C. Billings. 2004. 'Assessing language attitudes: speaker evaluation studies' in A. Davies and C. Elder (eds.). *The Handbook of Applied Linguistics*. Oxford: Blackwell.

Giles, H. and J. Byrne. 1982. 'An intergroup approach to second language acquisition'. *Journal of Multilingual and Multicultural Development* 3/1: 17–41.

Giles, H. and N. Coupland. 1991. *Language: Contexts and Consequences*. Milton Keynes: Open University Press.

Giles, H. and N. A. Niedzielski. 1998. 'Italian is beautiful, German is ugly' in L. Bauer and P. Trudgill (eds.). *Language Myths*. London: Penguin.

Giles, H. and P. F. Powesland. 1975. *Speech Style and Social Evaluation*. London: Academic Press.

Giles, H. and E. B. Ryan. 1982. 'Prolegomena for developing a social psychological theory of language' in E. B. Ryan and H. Giles (eds.). *Attitudes towards Language Variation*. London: Arnold.

Giles, H. and C. Sassoon. 1983. 'The effect of speakers' accent, social class, background and message style on British listeners' social judgements'. *Language and Communication* 3: 305–13.

Gnutzmann, C. 2004. 'English as a Lingua Franca' in M. Byram (ed.). *Routledge Encyclopedia of Language Teaching and Learning*. London: Routledge.

Gnutzmann, C. and F. Intemann. (eds.). 2005. *The Globalisation of English and the English Language Classroom*. Tübingen: Gunter Narr.

Golombek, P. and S. R. Jordan. 2005. 'Becoming "black lambs" not "parrots": a poststructuralist orientation to intelligibility and identity'. *TESOL Quarterly* 39/3: 513–33.

Görlach, M. 1990. *Studies in the History of the English Language*. Heidlberg: Carl Winter.

Görlach, M. 1999. 'Varieties of English and English language teaching' in C. Gnutzmann (ed.). *Teaching and Learning English as a Global Language*. Tubingen: Stauffenburg.

Görlach, M. 2002. *Still More Englishes*. Amsterdam: John Benjamins.

Gould, P. and M. Clutterbuck. 2004. *Focusing on IELTS. Academic Practice Tests*. Sydney: Macquarie University.

Graddol, D. 1997. *The Future of English?* London: British Council.

Graddol, D. 2006. *English Next. Why Global English May Mean the End of 'English as a Foreign Language'*. London: British Council. Also available at www.britishcouncil. org/learning-research.

Grau, M. 2005. 'English as a global language: What do future teachers have to say?' in C. Gnutzmann and F. Intemann (eds.). *The Globalisation of English and the English Language Classroom*. Tübingen: Gunter Narr.

Gumperz, J. J. 1982. *Discourse Strategies*. Cambridge: Cambridge University Press.

Gumperz, J. J. 1999. 'On interactional sociolinguistic method' in S. Sarangi and C. Roberts (eds.). *Talk, Work and Institutional Order*. Berlin: Mouton de Gruyter.

Gupta, A.F. 2006. 'Standard English in the world' in R. Rubdy and M. Saraceni (eds.). *English in the World. Global Rules, Global Roles*. London: Continuum.

Hahn, L.D. 2004. 'Primary stress and intelligibility: research to motivate the teaching of suprasegmentals'. *TESOL Quarterly* 38/2: 201–23.

Hammersley, M. and P. Atkinson. 1983. *Ethnography: Principles in Practice*. London: Tavistock.

Hammersley, M. and P. Atkinson. 1995. *Ethnography: Principles in Practice* (second ed.). London: Routledge.

Han, Z. and L. Selinker. 2005. 'Fossilization in L2 learners' in E. Hinkel (ed.). *Handbook of Research in Second Language Teaching and Learning*. Mahwah, N.J.: Lawrence Erlbaum.

Hannam, S. 2004. 'An investigation into ELT practitioners' views regarding the use of regional British accents in the language classroom'. Unpublished MEd dissertation, University of Sheffield.

Harris, M. 2002. 'Anti-globalisation and ELT'. *IATEFL Issues* 168: 6–7.

Harris, M. 2003. 'Untangling some knots'. *IATEFL Issues* 171: 2.

Hartley, L. C. and D. R. Preston. 1999. 'The names of US English: valley girl, cowboy, yankee, normal, nasal and ignorant' in T. Bex and R. J. Watts (eds.). *Standard English. The Widening Debate*. London: Routledge.

Heller, M. 1982. 'Negotiations of language choices in Montreal' in J. J. Gumperz (ed.). *Language and Social Identity*. Cambridge: Cambridge University Press.

Heller, M. 1992. 'The politics of codeswitching and language choice'. *Journal of Multilingual and Multicultural Development* 13/1: 123–42.

Heller, M. 1995. 'Language choice, social institutions, and symbolic domination'. *Language in Society* 24: 373–405.

Holborow, M. 1999. *The Politics of English*. London: Sage.

Hollett, V. 2001. *Quick Work*. Oxford: Oxford University Press.

Hollett, V. 2006. *Business Objectives*. International edition. Oxford: Oxford University Press.

Holliday, A. 2005. *The Struggle to Teach English as an International Language*. Oxford: Oxford University Press.

Honey, J. 1997. *Language is Power*. London: Faber.

House, J. 1999. 'Misunderstanding in intercultural communication: interactions in English as a Lingua Franca and the myth of mutual intelligibility' in C. Gnutzmann (ed.). *Teaching and Learning English as a Global Language*. Tübingen: Stauffenburg.

House, J. 2002. 'Developing pragmatic competence in English as a Lingua Franca' in K. Knapp and C. Meierkord (eds.). *Lingua Franca Communication*. Frankfurt am Main: Peter Lang.

House, J. 2003. 'English as a lingua franca: a threat to multilingualism?' *Journal of Sociolinguistics* 7/4, 556–78.

House, J. 2005. 'Teaching and learning English as an international lingua franca'. Paper presented at 39th TESOL Convention.

House, J. 2006. 'Unity in diversity: English as a Lingua Franca for Europe' in C. Leung and J. Jenkins (eds.). *Reconfiguring Europe: The Contribution of Applied Linguistics*. London: Equinox.

Howatt, A. P. R. with H. G. Widdowson. 2004. *A History of English Language Teaching* (second edn.). Oxford: Oxford University Press.

Hung, T. 2002. '"New English" words in international English dictionaries'. *English Today* 18/4: 29–34.

Huspek, M. R. 1986. 'Linguistic variation, context and meanings: a case of -ing/in' variation in North American workers' speech'. *Language in Society* 15: 149–64.

Hüttner, J. and S. Kidd. 2000. 'Reconstructing the "Sprechpraktikum". A reply to Daniel Spichtinger "From anglocentrism to TEIL: reflections on our English programme"', *Vienna English Working Papers* 9/2: 75–8.

Huygens, I. and G. M. Vaughn. 1984. 'Language attitudes, ethnicity, and social class in New Zealand'. *Journal of Multilingual and Multicultural Development* 4: 207–24.

Inbar-Lourie, O. 2005. 'Mind the gap: self and perceived native speaker identities of teachers' in E. Llurda (ed.). *Non-native Language Teachers. Perceptions, Challenges and Contributions to the Profession*. New York: Springer.

Irvine, J. T. 2001. '"Style" as distinctiveness: the culture and ideology of linguistic differentiation' in P. Eckert and J. R. Rickford (eds.). *Style and Sociolinguistic Variation*. Cambridge: Cambridge University Press.

Irvine, J. T. and S. Gal. 2000. 'Language ideology and linguistic differentiation' in P. Kroskrity (ed.). *Regimes of Language*. Santa Fe, New Mexico: School of American Research.

Ivanič, R. 1998. *Writing and Identity: The Discoursal Construction of Identity in Academic Writing*. Amsterdam and Philadelphia: John Benjamins.

James, A. 2000. 'English as a European Lingua Franca: current realities and existing dichotomies' in J. Cenoz and U. Jessner (eds.). *English in Europe: The Acquisition of a Third Language*. Clevedon: Multilingual Matters.

James, A. 2005. 'The challenges of the lingua franca: English in the world and types of variety' in C. Gnutzmann and F. Intemann (eds.). *The Globalisation of English and the English Language Classroom*. Tübingen: Gunter Narr.

Jarvella, R. J., E. Bang, A. L. Jakobsen, and I. M. Mees. 2001. 'Of mouths and men: non-native listeners' identification and evaluation of varieties of English'. *International Journal of Applied Linguistics* 11/1: 37–56.

Jenkins, J. 1996. 'Changing pronunciation priorities for successful communication in international contexts'. *Speak Out! Newsletter of the IATEFL Pronunciation Special Interest Group* 17: 15–22.

Jenkins, J. 1998. 'Which pronunciation norms and models for English as an International Language?' *ELT Journal* 52/2: 119–26.

Jenkins, J. 2000. *The Phonology of English as an International Language*. Oxford: Oxford University Press.

Jenkins, J. 2002. 'A sociolinguistically based, empirically researched pronunciation syllabus for English as an International Language'. *Applied Linguistics* 23/1: 83–103.

Jenkins, J. 2003. *World Englishes. A Resource Book for Students*. London: Routledge.

Jenkins, J. 2004. 'ELF at the gate: the position of English as a Lingua Franca' in A. Pulverness (ed.). *IATEFL 2004 Liverpool Conference Selections*. Canterbury: IATEFL.

Jenkins, J. 2005a. 'Implementing an international approach to English pronunciation: the role of teacher attitudes and identity'. *TESOL Quarterly* 38/3: 535–44.

Jenkins, J. 2005b. 'Misinterpretation, bias, and resistance to change: the case of the Lingua Franca Core' in K. Dziubalska-Kołaczyk and J. Przedlacka (eds.). *English Pronunciation Models: A Changing Scene*. Frankfurt am Main: Peter Lang.

Jenkins, J. 2006a. 'The spread of English as an International Language: a testing time for testers'. *ELT Journal* 60/1: 42–50.

Jenkins, J. 2006b. 'Global intelligibility and local diversity: possibility or paradox?' in R. Rubdy and M. Saraceni (eds.). *English in the World: Global Rules, Global Roles*. London: Continuum.

Jenkins, J. 2006c. 'Points of view and blind spots: ELF and SLA'. *International Journal of Applied Linguistics* 16/2: 137–62.

Jenkins, J., M. Modiano, and B. Seidlhofer. 2001. 'Euro-English'. *English Today* 17/4: 13–19.

Joseph, J. 2004a. *Language and Identity*. Houndmills, Basingstoke: Palgrave Macmillan.

Joseph, J. 2004b. 'Language and politics' in A. Davies and C. Elder (eds.). *The Handbook of Applied Linguistics*. Oxford: Blackwell.

Kachru, B. B. 1985. 'Standards, codification and sociolinguistic realism: the English language in the outer circle' in R. Quirk and H. G. Widdowson (eds.). *English in the World: Teaching and Learning the Language and Literatures*. Cambridge: Cambridge University Press.

Kachru, B. B. 1991. 'Liberation linguistics and the Quirk concern'. *English Today* 7/1: 3–13.

Kachru, B. B. 1997a. 'Past imperfect: the other side of English in Asia' in L. E. Smith and M. L. Forman (eds.). *World Englishes 2000*. Honolulu, Hawai'i: University of Hawai'i and the East-West Center.

Kachru, B. B. 1997b. 'World Englishes 2000: resources for research and teaching' in L. E. Smith and M. L. Forman (eds.). *World Englishes 2000*. Honolulu, Hawai'i: University of Hawai'i and the East-West Center.

Kachru, B. B. 2005. *Asian Englishes. Beyond the Canon*. Hong Kong: Hong Kong University Press.

Kachru, Y. 2005. 'Teaching and learning of World Englishes' in E. Hinkel (ed.). *Handbook of Research in Second Language Learning and Teaching*. Mahwah, N.J.: Lawrence Erlbaum.

Kachru, Y. and C. L. Nelson. 2006. *World Englishes in Asian Contexts*. Mahwah, N.J.: Lawrence Erlbaum.

Kamhi-Stein, L. (ed.). 2004. *Learning and Teaching from Experience: Perspectives on Nonnative English-speaking Professionals*. Ann Arbor: University of Michigan Press.

Kellogg, D. 2002. 'A reply to Michael Harris'. *IATEFL Issues* 169: 4.

Kellogg, D. 2003. 'Red-baiting and negotiating'. *IATEFL Issues* 173: 2–3.

Kirkpatrick, A. 2006. 'No experience necessary?' *Guardian Weekly, Learning English*: 4.

Kirkpatrick, A. 2007. *World Englishes: Implications for International Communication and English Language Teaching*. Cambridge: Cambridge University Press.

Knapp, K. and C. Meierkord. (eds.). 2002. *Lingua Franca Communication*. Frankfurt am Main: Peter Lang.

Kramsch, C. 2006. 'The multilingual subject'. *International Journal of Applied Linguistics* 16/1: 97–110.

Kumaravadivelu, B. 2003. 'A postmethod perspective on English language teaching'. *World Englishes* 22/4: 539–50.

Kuo, I-C. 2006. 'Addressing the issue of teaching English as a lingua franca'. *ELT Journal* 60/3: 213–21.

Kvale, S. 1996. *InterViews. An Introduction to Qualitative Research Interviewing*. London: Sage Publications.

Labov, W. 1966. *The Social Stratification of English in New York City*. Washington, D.C.: Center for Applied Linguistics.

Ladegaard, H. J. and I. Sachdev. 2006. '"I like the Americans ... but I certainly don't aim for an American accent": language attitudes, vitality and foreign language learning in Denmark'. *Journal of Multilingual and Multicultural Development* 27/2: 91–108.

Lamb, M. 1995. 'The consequences of INSET'. *ELT Journal* 49/1: 72–80.

Lambert, W. E., R. Hodgson, R. C. Gardner, and S. Fillenbaum. 1960. 'Evaluational reactions to spoken languages'. *Journal of Abnormal and Social Psychology* 60: 44–51.

Lamie, J. M. 2004. 'Presenting a model of change'. *Language Teaching Research* 8/2: 115–42.

Lantolf, J. (ed.). 2000. *Sociocultural Theory and Second Language Learning*. Oxford: Oxford University Press.

Le Page, R. B. and A. Tabouret-Keller. 1985. *Acts of Identity: Creole-based Approaches to Ethnicity and Language*. Cambridge: Cambridge University Press.

Lee, P. and H. Azman. (eds.). 2004. *Global English and Primary Schools*. Melbourne: CAE Press.

Leung, C. 2005. 'Convivial communication: recontextualizing communicative competence'. *International Journal of Applied Linguistics* 15/2: 119–44.

Leung, C. and J. Lewkowicz. 2006. Expanding horizons and unresolved conundrums: language testing and assessment. *TESOL Quarterly* 40/1: 211–34.

Levis, J. 2005. 'Changing contexts and shifting paradigms in pronunciation teaching'. *TESOL Quarterly* 39/3: 369–77.

Levis, J. 2006. 'Pronunciation and the assessment of spoken language' in R. Hughes (ed.). *Spoken English, TESOL and Applied Linguistics* . Houndmills, Basingstoke: Palgrave Macmillan.

Lewis, J. 2003. 'Design issues' in J. Ritchie and J. Lewis (eds.). *Qualitative Research Practice*. London: Sage Publications.

Lewis, M. 1995. 'The Lexical Approach'. Plenary address at the Annual Conference of the International Association of Teachers of English as a Foreign Language, Szombathely, Hungary.

Lightbown, P. M. and N. Spada. 2006. *How Languages are Learned* (third edn.). Oxford: Oxford University Press.

Lin, A., W. Wang, N. Akamatsu, and M. Riazi. 2005. 'International TESOL professionals and teaching English for glocalized communication (TEGCOM)' in A.S. Canagarajah (ed.). *Reclaiming the Local in Language Policy and Practice*. Mahwah, N.J.: Lawrence Erlbaum.

Lindemann, S. 2005. 'Who speaks "broken English"? US undergraduates' perceptions of non-native English'. *International Journal of Applied Linguistics* 15/2: 187–212.

Lippi-Green, R. 1994. 'Accent, standard language ideology, and discriminatory pretext in the courts'. *Language in Society* 23: 163–98.

Lippi-Green, R. 1997. *English with an Accent*. London: Routledge.

Littlewood, W. 2004. 'Second language learning' in A. Davies and C. Elder (eds.). *The Handbook of Applied Linguistics*. Oxford: Blackwell.

Llamas, C. 2006. 'Shifting identities and orientations in a border town' in T. Omoniyi and G. White (eds.). *The Sociolinguistics of Identity*. London: Continuum.

Llamzon, T. A. 1983. 'Essential features of new varieties of English' in R. B. Noss (ed.). *Varieties of English in Southeast Asia*. Singapore: Regional Language Centre.

Llurda, E. 2000. Effects of intelligibility and speaking rate on judgements of non-native speakers' personalities'. *International Review of Applied Linguistics* 38/3: 289–99.

Llurda, E. 2004. 'Non-native speaker teachers and English as an International Language'. *International Journal of Applied Linguistics* 14/3: 314–23.

Lowenberg, P. H. 2000. 'Non-native varieties and the sociopolitics of English proficiency assessment' in J. K. Hall and W. G. Eggington (eds.). *The Sociopolitics of English Language Teaching*. Clevedon: Multilingual Matters.

Lowenberg, P. H. 2002. 'Assessing English proficiency in the expanding circle'. *World Englishes* 21/3: 431–5.

Luk, C. M. and A. M. Y. Lin. 2006. 'Uncovering the sociopolitical situatedness of accents in the World Englishes paradigm' in R. Hughes (ed.). *Spoken English, TESOL and Applied Linguistics*. Houndmills, Basingstoke: Palgrave Macmillan.

MacKenzie, I. 2002. 'Language teaching and the uses of so-called English as a Lingua Franca'. Paper presented at the seminar 'English as a Lingua Franca in Europe', ESSE 6, Strasbourg, 3 September 2002.

Majer, J. 1997. '"Does seek mean eel?" Interlanguage phonology and pronunciation goals for teacher training' in K. Waniek-Klimczak (ed.). *Teaching English Phonetics and Phonology II*. Lodz: Wydawnictwo Uniwersytetu Lodzkiego.

Major, R. C., S. F. Fitzmaurice, F. Bunta, and C. Balasubramanian. 2002. 'The effects of nonnative accents on listening comprehension: implications for ESL assessment'. *TESOL Quarterly* 36/2: 173–90.

Maley, A. 2006. 'Questions of English'. *English Teaching Professional* 46: 4–6.

Matsuda, A. 2002a. '"International understanding" through teaching World Englishes'. *World Englishes* 21/3/: 436–40.

Matsuda, A. 2002b. 'Representation of users and uses of English in beginning Japanese textbooks'. *JALT Journal* 24/2: 182–200.

Matsuda, A. 2003. 'The ownership of English in Japanese secondary schools'. *World Englishes* 22/4: 483–96.

Mauranen, A. 2003. 'The corpus of English as a Lingua Franca in academic settings'. *TESOL Quarterly* 37(3): 513–27.

Mauranen, A. 2006. 'Spoken discourse, academics and global English: a corpus perspective' in R. Hughes (ed.). *Spoken English, TESOL and Applied Linguistics*. Houndmills, Basingstoke: Palgrave Macmillan.

May, D. 2000. 'It just isn't English'. *Times 2 Analysis, The Times*, 24 March 2000: 4.

May, S. 2001. *Language and Minority Rights*. London: Longman.

McArthur, T. 1987. 'The English language'. *English Today* 11: 9–13.

McArthur, T. 1998. *The English Languages*. Cambridge: Cambridge University Press.

McArthur, T. 2002. *The Oxford Guide to World English*. Oxford: Oxford University Press.

McArthur, T. 2004. 'Is it *world* or *international* or *global* English, and does it matter?' *English Today* 20/3: 3–15.

McCarthy, M. J. and R. Carter. 1995. 'Spoken grammar: what is it and how can we teach it?' *ELT Journal* 49/3: 207–18.

McCrum, R., R. McNeil, and W. Cran. 2002. *'The Story of English* (third edn.). London: Faber and Faber.

McCulloch, W. 2003. 'Beat the fossils to it'. *EL Gazette* October: 12.

McKay, S. 2002. *Teaching English as an International Language*. Oxford: Oxford University Press.

McKirnan, D. J. and E. V. Hamayan. 1980. 'Language norms and perceptions of ethno-linguistic group diversity' in H. Giles, W. P. Robinson, and P. M. Smith (eds.). *Language: Social Psychological Perspectives*. Oxford: Pergamon.

McMahon, A. 1994. *Understanding Language Change*. Cambridge: Cambridge University Press.

McNamara, T. 2001. '21st century shibboleth: language tests, identity and intergroup conflict'. Inaugural address, The University of Melbourne.

McNamara, T. 2004. 'Language testing' in A. Davies and C. Elder (eds.). *The Handbook of Applied Linguistics*. Oxford: Blackwell.

McNamara, T. 2005. '21st century Shibboleth: language tests, identity and intergroup conflict'. *Language Policy* 4/4: 1–20.

Medgyes, P. 1999. 'Language training: a neglected area in teacher education' in G. Braine (ed.). *Non-native Educators in English Language Teaching*. Mahwah, N.J.: Lawrence Erlbaum.

Meierkord, C. 1996. *Englisch als Medium der interkulturellen Kommunikation. Untersuchungen zum non-native/non-native speaker Diskurs*. Frankfurt am Main: Peter Lang.

Meierkord, C. 2002. '"Language stripped bare" or "linguistic masala"? Culture in lingua franca conversation' in K. Knapp and C. Meierkord (eds.). *Lingua Franca Communication*. Frankfurt am Main: Peter Lang.

Meinhof, U. and D. Galasinski. 2005. *The Language of Belonging*. Houndmills, Basingstoke: Palgrave Macmillan.

Melchers, G. and P. Shaw. 2003. *World Englishes*. London: Arnold.

Mendoza-Denton, N. 2002. 'Language and identity' in J. K. Chambers, P. Trudgill, and N. Schilling-Estes (eds.). *The Handbook of Language Variation and Change*. Oxford: Blackwell.

Meyerhoff, M. 2002. 'Communities of practice' in J. K. Chambers, P. Trudgill, and N. Schilling-Estes (eds.). *The Handbook of Language Variation and Change*. Oxford: Blackwell.

Miller, J. 2004. 'Identity and language use: the politics of speaking ESL in schools' in A. Pavlenko and A. Blackledge (eds.). *Negotiation of Identities in Multilingual Contexts*. Clevedon: Multilingual Matters.

Milroy, J. 2001. 'Language ideologies and the consequences of standardization'. *Journal of Sociolinguistics* 5/4: 530–55.

Milroy, J. and L. Milroy. 1999. *Authority in Language* (third edn.). London: Routledge.

Milroy, L. 1999. 'Standard English and language ideology in Britain and the United States' in T. Bex and R. J. Watts (eds.). *Standard English. The Widening Debate*. London: Routledge.

Milroy, L. 2004. 'Language ideologies and linguistic change' in C. Fought (ed.). *Sociolinguistic Variation. Critical Reflections*. Oxford: Oxford University Press.

Mufwene, S. 1997. 'The legitimate and illegitimate offspring of English' in L. E. Smith and M. L. Forman (eds.). *World Englishes 2000*. Honolulu, Hawai'i: University of Hawai'i and East-West Center.

Mufwene, S. 2001. *The Ecology of Language Evolution*. Cambridge: Cambridge University Press.

Mugglestone, L. 2003. *'Talking Proper'. The Rise of Accent as Social Symbol*. Oxford: Oxford University Press.

Mukherjee, J. and J-M. Rohrbach. 2006. 'Rethinking applied corpus linguistics from a language-pedagogical perspective: new departures in learner corpus research' in B. Ketteman and G. Marko (eds.). *Planing, Gluing and Painting Corpora: Inside the Applied Corpus Linguist's Workshop*. Frankfurt am Main: Peter Lang.

Munro, M. J. 2003. 'A primer on accent discrimination in the Canadian context'. *TESL Canada Journal* 20: 38–51.

Munro, M. J. and T. M. Derwing. 1995. 'Foreign accent, comprehensibility, and intelligibility in the speech of second language learners'. *Language Learning* 45/1: 73–97.

Munro, M. J., T. M. Derwing, and S. L. Morton. 2006. 'The mutual intelligibility of L2 speech'. *Studies in Second Language Acquisition* 28/1: 111–31.

Murray, H. 2003. 'Swiss English teachers and Euro-English: attitudes to a non-native variety'. *Bulletin suisse de linguistique appliquée* 77: 147–65.

Nakamura, K. 2002. 'Cultivating global literacy through English as an International Language (EIL) education in Japan: a new paradigm for global education'. *International Education Journal* 3/5: 64–74.

Nass, C. and S. Brave. 2006. *Wired for Speech*. Cambridge, Mass.: MIT Press.

Nemtichinova, E. 2005. 'Host teachers' evaluations of nonnative-English-speaking teacher trainees—a perspective from the classroom'. *TESOL Quarterly* 39/2: 235–61.

Niedzielski, N. A. 1999. 'The effect of social information on the perception of sociolinguistic variables'. *Journal of Language and Social Psychology* 18.

Niedzielski, N. A. and D. R. Preston. 2000/2003. *Folk Linguistics*. Berlin and New York: Mouton de Gruyter.

Norton, B. 2000. *Identity and Language Learning*. London: Longman.

Norton Peirce, B. (ed.). 1997. *TESOL Quarterly Special-Topic Issue: Language and Identity.*

Olson, J. K. and S. Eaton. 1987. 'Curriculum change and classroom order' in J. Calderhead (ed.). *Exploring Teachers' Thinking*. London: Cassell.

Omoniyi, T. 2006. 'Hierarchy of identities' in T. Omoniyi and G. White (eds.). *The Sociolinguistics of Identity*. London: Continuum.

Omoniyi, T. and G. White. (eds.). 2006. *The Sociolinguistics of Identity*. London: Continuum.

Oxenden, C. and C. Latham-Koenig. 2005. *New English File (Pre-intermediate Students' Book)*. Oxford: Oxford University Press.

Paikeday, T.M. 1985. *The Native Speaker is Dead!* Toronto and New York: Paikeday.

Paltridge, J. and H. Giles. 1984. 'Attitudes towards speakers of regional accents of French: effects of regionality, age and sex of listeners'. *Linguistische Berichte* 90: 71–85.

Pavlenko, A. 2002. 'Poststructuralist approaches to the study of social factors in second language learning and use' in V. Cook (ed.). *Portraits of the L2 User*. Clevedon: Multilingual Matters.

Pavlenko, A. and A. Blackledge. (eds.). 2004. *Negotiation of Identities in Multilingual Contexts*. Clevedon: Multilingual Matters.

Pavlenko, A. and J. Lantolf. 2000. 'Second language learning as participation and the (re)construction of selves' in J. Lantolf (ed.). *Sociocultural Theory and Second Language Learning*. Oxford: Oxford University Press.

Pear, T.H. 1931. *Voice and Personality*. London: Wiley.

Pennycook, A. 1998. *English and the Discourses of Colonialism*. London: Routledge.

Pennycook, A. 2001. *Critical Applied Linguistics*. Mahway, N.J.: Lawrence Erlbaum.

Perloff, R. 1993. *The Dynamics of Persuasion*. Hillsdale, N.J.: Lawrence Erlbaum Associates.

Phillipson, R. 1999. 'Voice in global English: unheard chords on Crystal loud and clear'. *Applied Linguistics* 20/2: 265–76.

Phillipson, R. 2000a. 'English in the new world order: variations on a theme of linguistic imperialism and "world" English' in T. Ricento (ed.). *Ideology, Politics and Language Policies. Focus on English*. Amsterdam: John Benjamins.

Phillipson, R. 2000b. 'Integrative comment: living with vision and commitment' in R. Phillipson (ed.). *Rights to Language. Equity, Power and Education*. Mahwah, N.J.: Lawrence Erlbaum.

Phillipson, R. 2003. *English-only Europe? Challenging Language Policy*. London: Routledge.

Phillipson, R. In press. 'English, no longer a foreign language in Europe?' in J. Cummins and C. Davison (eds.). *The International Handbook of English Language Teaching*. Vol. 1. Norwell, Mass.: Springer.

Pitzl, M-L. 2005. 'Non-understanding in English as a lingua franca: examples from a business context'. *Vienna English Working Papers* 14/2: 50–71.

Platt, J., H. Weber, and **M. L. Ho.** 1984. *The New Englishes*. London: Routledge and Kegan Paul.

Pölzl, U. 2004. 'Signalling cultural identity in a global language. The use of L1/Ln in ELF'. *Vienna English Working Papers* 12/1: 3–23.

Pölzl, U. and **B. Seidlhofer.** 2006. 'In and on their own terms: the "habitat factor" in English as a lingua franca interaction'. *International Journal of the Sociology of Language* 177: 151–76.

Powesland, P. F. and **H. Giles.** 1975. 'Persuasiveness and accent-message incompatibility'. *Human Relations* 28: 85–93.

Preisler, B. 1999. 'Functions and forms of English in a European EFL country' in T. Bex and R. J. Watts (eds.). *Standard English. The Widening Debate*. London: Routledge.

Preston, D. R. 1996. 'Whaddayaknow? The modes of folk linguistic awareness'. *Language Awareness* 5/1: 40–74.

Preston, D. R. 2002. 'Language with an attitude' in J. K. Chambers, P. Trudgill, and N. Schilling-Estes (eds.). *The Handbook of Language Variation and Change*. Oxford: Blackwell.

Preston, D. R. 2005. 'How can you learn a language that isn't there?' in K. Dziubalska-Kołaczyk and J. Przedlacka (eds.). *English Pronunciation Models: A Changing Scene*. Frankfurt am Main: Peter Lang.

Preston D. R. 2006. 'Response to D. Deterding. 2006. Review of N.A. Niedzielski and D. Preston. 2000. *Folk Linguistics*. Berlin and New York: Mouton de Gruyter'. *International Journal of Applied Linguistics* 16/1: 113–15.

Prodromou, L. 1996a. 'Correspondence'. *ELT Journal* 60/1: 88–9.

Prodromou, L. 1996b. 'Correspondence'. *ELT Journal* 60/4: 371–3.

Prodromou, L. 2003. 'In search of the successful user of English'. *Modern English Teacher* 12/2: 3–14.

Prodromou, L. 2006. 'Defining the "Successful Bilingual Speaker" of English' in R. Rubdy and M. Saraceni (eds.). *English in the World: Global Rules, Global Roles*. London: Continuum.

Proshina, Z. G. 2005. 'Intermediary translation from English as a lingua franca'. *World Englishes* 24/4: 517–22.

Purnell, T., W. Idsardi, and **J. Baugh.** 1999. 'Perceptual and phonetic experiments on American English dialect identification'. *Journal of Language and Social Psychology* 18: 189–209.

Qiang, N. and **M. Wolff.** 2005. 'Is EFL a modern Trojan horse?' *English Today* 21/4: 55–60.

Quirk, R. 1985. 'The English language in global context' in R. Quirk and H. G. Widdowson (eds.). *English in the World: Teaching and Learning the Language and Literatures*. Cambridge: Cambridge University Press.

Quirk, R. 1990. 'Language varieties and standard language'. *English Today* 21: 3–10.

Quirk, R. 1995. *Grammatical and Lexical Variance in English*. London: Longman.

Rajagopalan, K. 2005. 'Non-native speaker teachers of English and their anxieties: ingredients for an experiment in action research' in E. Llurda (ed.). *Non-Native Language Teachers. Perceptions, Challenges and Contributions to the Profession*. New York: Springer.

Rampton, B. 1990. 'Displacing the "native speaker": expertise, affiliation and inheritance'. *ELT Journal* 44/2: 97–101.

Rampton, B. 1995. *Crossing: Language and Ethnicity among Adolescents*. London: Longman.

Rampton, B. 2006. *Language in Late Modernity. Interaction in an Urban School.* Cambridge: Cambridge University Press.

Riney, T. J., N. Takagi, and K. Inutsuka. 2005. 'Phonetic parameters and perceptual judgements of accent in English by American and Japanese listeners'. *TESOL Quarterly* 39/3: 441–88.

Roberts, C., E. Davies, and T. Jupp. 1992. *Language and Discrimination.* London: Longman.

Roberts, J. 1998. *Language Teacher Education.* London: Arnold.

Roever, C. and T. McNamara. 2006. 'Language testing: the social dimension'. *International Journal of Applied Linguistics* 16/2: 242–58.

Rosewarne, D. 2003. 'English as an International Language and the Italian learner and teacher'. *Perspectives* XXX/2: 41–5.

Rubdy, R. and M. Saraceni. (eds.). 2006. *English in the World: Global Rules, Global Roles.* London: Continuum.

Rubin, D. L. 1992. 'Nonlanguage factors affecting undergraduates' judgments of nonnative English-speaking teaching assistants'. *Research in Higher Education* 33/4: 511–31.

Rubin, D. L. and K. A. Smith. 1990. 'Effects of accent, ethnicity, and lecture topic on undergraduates' perceptions of non-native English speaking teaching assistants'. *International Journal of Intercultural Relations* 14: 337–53.

Ryan, E. B. and H. Giles. (eds.). 1982. *Attitudes towards Language Variation.* London: Arnold.

Ryan, E. B., M. A. Carranza, and R. W. Moffie. 1977. 'Reactions to varying degrees of accentedness in the speech of Spanish-English bilinguals'. *Language and Speech* 20: 267–73.

Ryan, E. B., H. Giles, and R. J. Sebastian. 1982. 'An integrative perspective for the study of attitudes towards language' in E. B. Ryan and H. Giles (eds.). *Attitudes towards Language Variation.* London: Arnold.

Sallabank, J. 2006. 'Guernsey French, identity and language endangerment' in T. Omoniyi and G. White (eds.). *The Sociolinguistics of Identity.* London: Continuum.

Samarin, W. 1987. 'Lingua franca' in U. Ammon, N. Dittmar, and K. Mattheier (eds.). *Sociolinguistics: An International Handbook of the Science of Language and Society.* Berlin: Walter de Gruyter.

Savignon, S. J. 2003. 'Response'. *World Englishes* 22/1: 72.

Scheuer, S. 2005. 'Why native speakers are (still) relevant' in K. Dziubalska-Kołaczyk and J. Przedlacka (eds.). *English Pronunciation Models: A Changing Scene.* Frankfurt am Main: Peter Lang.

Scott, M. 1998/2003. *Wordsmith Tools.* Oxford: Oxford University Press.

Scott, M. and C. Tribble. 2006. *Textual Patterns. Key Words and Corpus Analysis in Language Education.* Amsterdam: John Benjamins.

Scovel, T. 1998. *Psycholinguistics.* Oxford: Oxford University Press.

Seargeant, P. 2005. '"More English than England itself": the simulation of authenticity in foreign language practice in Japan'. *International Journal of Applied Linguistics* 15/2: 326–45.

Seidlhofer, B. 1999. 'Double standards: teacher education in the expanding circle'. *World Englishes* 18/2: 233–45.

Seidlhofer, B. 2001a. 'Brave new English'. *The European English Messenger* X/1: 42–8.

Seidlhofer, B. 2001b. 'Closing a conceptual gap: the case for a description of English as a Lingua Franca'. *International Journal of Applied Linguistics* 11/2: 133–58.

Seidlhofer, B. 2002. '*Habeas corpus* and *divide et impera*: "Global English" and applied linguistics' in K. Spelman Miller and P. Thompson (eds.). *Unity and Diversity in Language Use.* London: Continuum.

Seidlhofer, B. 2003a. *A Concept of International English and Related Iissues: From 'Real English' to 'Realistic English'?* Strasbourg: Council of Europe.

Seidlhofer, B. (ed.). 2003b. *Controversies in Applied Linguistics*. Oxford: Oxford University Press.

Seidlhofer, B. 2004. 'Research perspectives on teaching English as a Lingua Franca'. *Annual Review of Applied Linguistics* 24: 209–39.

Seidlhofer, B. 2005a. 'Standard future or half-baked quackery? Descriptive and pedagogic bearings on the globalisation of English' in C. Gnutzmann and F. Intemann (eds.). *The Globalisation of English and the English Language Classroom*. Tübingen: Gunter Narr.

Seidlhofer, B. 2005b. 'Language variation and change: the case of English as a Lingua Franca' in K. Dziubalska-Kołaczyk and J. Przedlacka (eds.). *English Pronunciation Models: A Changing Scene*. Frankfurt am Main: Peter Lang.

Seidlhofer, B. 2006. 'English as a Lingua Franca in the expanding circle: What it isn't' in R. Rubdy and M. Saraceni (eds.). *English in the World: Global Rules, Global Roles*. London: Continuum.

Seidlhofer, B. Forthcoming. *Understanding English as a Lingua Franca*. Oxford: Oxford University Press.

Seidlhofer, B. and J. Jenkins. 2003. 'English as a Lingua Franca and the politics of property' in C. Mair (ed.). *The Politics of English as a World Language: New Horizons in Postcolonial Cultural Studies*. Amsterdam: Rodopi.

Seidlhofer, B. and H. G. Widdowson. 2003. 'House work and student work: a study in cross-cultural understanding' in N. Baumgarten, C. Böttger, M. Motz, and J. Probst (eds.). *Ubersetzen, Interkulturelle Kommunikation, Spracherwerb und Sprachvermittlung— das Leben mit mehreren Sprachen. Festschrift für Juliane House zum 60. Geburtstag. Zeitschrift für Interkulturellen Fremdsprachenunterricht* (Vol. 8: 1–13). Online document: http://www.spz.tu-darmstadt.de/projekt_ejournal/jg-08-2-3/docs/Seidlhofer_ Widdowson.pdf (20 March 04).

Seidlhofer, B., A. Breiteneder, and M-L. Pitzl. 2006. 'English as a lingua franca in Europe: challenges for applied linguistics'. *Annual Review of Applied Linguistics* 26: 3–34.

Selinker, L. 1972. 'Interlanguage'. *International Review of Applied Linguistics* 10: 209–31.

Selinker, L. 1992. *Rediscovering Interlanguage*. London: Longman.

Shim, R. J. 1999. 'Codified Korean English: process, characteristics and consequence. *World Englishes* 18/2: 247–58.

Shim, R. J. 2002. 'Changing attitudes toward teaching English as a world language in Korea'. *Journal of Asian Pacific Communication* 12/1: 143–58.

Shohamy, E. 2001. 'Democratic assessment as an alternative'. *Language Testing* 18:373–91.

Sifakis, N. C. and A-M. Sugari. 2005. 'Pronunciation issues and EIL pedagogy in the periphery: a survey of Greek state school teachers' beliefs'. *TESOL Quarterly* 39/3: 467–88.

Silverman, D. 2001. *Interpreting Qualitative Data. Methods for Analysing Talk, Text and Interaction* (second edn.). London: Sage Publications.

Singh, I. 2005. *The History of English*. London: Hodder Arnold.

Smit, U. 1994. 'Language Attitudes, Language Planning and Education: the Case of English in South Africa'. Unpublished PhD thesis, University of Vienna. Published (1996) as *A New English for a New South Africa? Language Attitudes, Language Planning and Education*. Austrian Studies in English Vol. 83. Vienna: Braumüller.

Smith, L. E. 1992. 'Spread of English and issues of intelligibility' in B. B. Kachru (ed.). *The Other Tongue. English across Cultures*. Urbana, Illinois: University of Illinois Press.

Smith, L. E. and C. L. Nelson, 2006. 'World Englishes and issues of intelligibility' in B. B. Kachru, Y. Kachru, and C. L. Nelson (eds.). *The Handbook of World Englishes*. Oxford: Blackwell.

Sobkowiak, W. 2005. 'Why not LFC?' in K. Dziubalska-Kołaczyk and J. Przedlacka (eds.). *English Pronunciation Models: A Changing Scene*. Frankfurt am Main: Peter Lang.

Somekh, B. 1995. 'The contribution of action research to development in social endeavours: a position paper on action research methodology'. *British Educational Research Journal* 21/3: 339–56.

Sridhar, K. K. 2005. 'Comment 2'. *World Englishes* 24/1: 97–9.

St Clair, R. N. 1982. 'From social history to language attitudes' in E. B. Ryan and H. Giles (eds.). *Attitudes towards Language Variation*. London: Arnold.

Starks, D. and B. Paltridge. 1994. 'Varieties of English and the EFL classroom: a New Zealand case study'. *The TESOLANZ Journal* 2: 69–77.

Stewart, M. A., E. B. Ryan, and H. Giles. 1985. 'Accent and social class effects on status and solidarity evaluations'. *Personality and Social Psychology* 11: 98–105.

Street R. L. and R. Hopper. 1982. 'A model of speech style evaluation' in E. B. Ryan and H. Giles (eds.). *Attitudes towards Language Variation*. London: Arnold.

Suzuki, A. 2006. 'English as an International Language: a case study of student teachers' perceptions of English in Japan'. Unpublished doctoral thesis, King's College London.

Svartik, J. and G. Leech. 2006. *English. One Tongue, Many Voices*. Houndmills, Basingstoke: Palgrave Macmillan.

Swain, M. and S. Lapkin. 1995. 'Problems in output and the cognitive processes they generate: a step towards second language learning'. *Applied Linguistics* 16/3: 371–91.

Szpyra-Kozlowska, J. 2003. 'The lingua franca core and the Polish learner'. *Neofilologia* V: 193–210.

Szpyra-Kozlowska, J. 2005. 'Lingua Franca Core, phonetic universals and the Polish context' in K. Dziubalska-Kołaczyk and J. Przedlacka (eds.). *English Pronunciation Models: A Changing Scene*. Frankfurt am Main: Peter Lang.

Tabouret-Keller, A. 1997. 'Language and identity' in F. Coulmas (ed.). *The Handbook of Sociolinguistics*. Oxford: Blackwell.

Tajfel, H. 1974. 'Social identity and intergroup behavior'. *Social Science Information* 13: 65–93.

Tajfel, H. 1978. 'Interindividual behaviour and intergroup behaviour' in H. Tajfel (ed.). *Differentiation between Social Groups: Studies in the Social Psychology of Intergroup Relations*. London: Academic Press.

Tarone, E. 1988. *Variation in Interlanguage*. London: Edward Arnold.

Taylor L. 2002. 'Assessing learners' English: but whose/which English(es)?' *Research Notes* 10. Cambridge: University of Cambridge ESOL Examinations.

Taylor, L. 2006. 'The changing landscape of English: implications for language assessment'. *ELT Journal* 60/1: 51–60.

Thomas, L., S. Wareing, I. Singh, J. Thornborrow, and J. Jones. 2004. *Language, Society and Power* (second edn.). London: Routledge.

Thorne, S. L. 2000. 'Second language acquisition theory and the truth(s) about relativity' in J. Lantolf (ed.). *Sociocultural Theory and Second Language Learning*. Oxford: Oxford University Press.

Thumboo, E. 2003. 'Closed and open attitudes to globalised English'. *World Englishes* 22/3: 233–43.

Timmis, I. 2002. 'Native speaker norms and international English'. *ELT Journal* 56/3: 240–9.

Tomlinson, B. 2004, September. 'Which English do you want?' *Guardian Weekly, Learning English*: 3.

Tomlinson, B. 2006. 'A multi-dimensional approach to teaching English for the world' in R. Rubdy and M. Saraceni (eds.). *English in the World. Global Rules, Global Roles*. London: Continuum.

Tong, Y-Y., Y-Y. Hong, S-L. Lee, and C-Y. Chiu. 1999. 'Language use as a carrier of social identity'. *International Journal of Intercultural Relations* 23: 281–96.

Tribble, C. 2003. *Looking at ELT*. (CD-ROM). London: British Council.

Trudgill, P. 1972. 'Sex, covert prestige and linguistic change in the urban British English of Norwich'. *Language in Society* 1/2: 179–95.

Trudgill, P. 1999. 'Standard English: what it isn't' on T. Bex and R. J. Watts (eds.). *Standard English. The Widening Debate*. London: Routledge.

Trudgill, P. 2002. *Sociolinguistic Variation and Change*. Edinburgh: Edinburgh University Press.

Trudgill, P. 2005. 'Native-speaker segmental phonological models and the English Lingua Franca Core' in K. Dziubalska-Kołaczyk and J. Przedlacka (eds.). *English Pronunciation Models: A Changing Scene*. Frankfurt am Main: Peter Lang.

Trudgill, P. and H. Giles. 1978. 'Sociolinguistics and linguistic value judgements: correctness, adequacy and aesthetics' in F. Coppieters and D. L. Goyvaerts (eds.). *Functional Studies in Language and Literature*. Ghent: E. Story-Scientia.

Tsuda, Y. 1997. 'Hegemony of English vs ecology of language: Building equality in international communication' in L. E. Smith and M. L. Forman (eds.). *World Englishes 2000*. Honolulu, Hawai'i: University of Hawai'i and the East-West Center.

Tucker, G. R. 2003. 'Language contact and change: summary observations'. *Annual Review of Applied Linguistics* 23: 243–9.

Turner, J. C. 1999. 'Some current issues in research on social identity and self-categorization theories' in R. Spears and B. Doosje (eds.). *Social Identity: Context, Commitment, Content*. Oxford: Blackwell.

Underhill, A. 1994. *Sound Foundations*. London: Heinemann.

Vaughan-Rees, M. 2001. 'Open forum'. *Speak Out! Newsletter of the IATEFL Pronunciation Special Interest Group* 28: 10–15.

Verma, M. 2002. 'English in India: whose English, for whom, and what about Indian languages?' *Indian Journal of Applied Linguistics* 28/2: 101–20.

VOICE (Vienna–Oxford International Corpus of English). Unpublished transcription and mark-up conventions. Version 0.3, June 2003.

VOICE website: www.univie.ac.at/voice.

Walker, R. 2001a. 'Pronunciation priorities, the lingua franca core, and monolingual groups'. *Speak Out! Newsletter of the IATEFL Pronunciation Special Interest Group* 28: 4–9.

Walker, R. 2001b. 'International intelligibility'. *English Teaching Professional* 12: 10–13.

Wee, L. 2005. 'Intra-language discrimination and linguistic human rights: the case of Singlish'. *Applied Linguistics* 26/1: 48–69.

Weinberger, S. H. 1987. 'The influence of linguistic context on syllable simplification' in G. Ioup and S. H. Weinberger (eds.). *Interlanguage Phonology*. Cambridge, Massachusetts: Newbury House.

Wenger, E. 1998. *Communities of Practice. Learning, Meaning, and Identity*. Cambridge: Cambridge University Press.

White, G. 2006. 'Standard Irish English as a marker of Irish identity' in T. Omoniyi and G. White (eds.). *The Sociolinguistics of Identity*. London: Continuum.

Whitney, N. 2005. 'Review of *Defining Issues in English Language Teaching* by H. G. Widdowson'. *ELT Journal* 59/1: 69–72.

Widdowson, H. G. 1991. 'The description and prescription of language' in J. E. Alatis (ed.). *Georgetown University Round Table on Language and Linguistics. Language, Communication and Social Meaning*. Washington D.C.: Georgetown University Press.

Widdowson, H. G. 1994a. 'The ownership of English'. *TESOL Quarterly* 28/2: 377–89.

Widdowson, H. G. 1994b. 'Pragmatics and the pedagogic competence of language teachers' in T. Sebbage and S. Sebbage (eds.). *Proceedings of the 4th International NELLE Conference*. Hamburg: NELLE.

Widdowson, H. G. 1997. 'EIL, ESL, EFL: global issues and local interests'. *World Englishes* 16/1: 135–46.

Widdowson, H. G. 2003. *Defining Issues in English Language Teaching*. Oxford: Oxford University Press.

Widdowson, H. G. 2004a. 'A perspective on recent trends' in A. P. R. Howatt and H. G. Widdowson. *A History of English Language Teaching* (second edn.). Oxford: Oxford University Press.

Widdowson, H. G. 2004b. *Text, Context, Pretext. Critical Issues in Discourse Analysis*. Oxford: Blackwell.

Williams, A. 2005. 'Review of P. Garrett, N. Coupland, and A. Williams. 2003. *Investigating Language Attitudes: Social Meanings of Dialect, Ethnicity and Performance*. Cardiff: University of Wales Press' in *International Journal of Applied Linguistics* 15/3: 411–14.

Wolff, H. 1959. 'Intelligibility and inter-ethnic attitudes'. *Anthropological Linguistics* 1/3: 34–41.

Wolfram, W. and **N. Schilling-Estes.** 2006. *American English* (second ed.). Oxford: Blackwell.

Woolard, K. A. 1992. 'Language ideology: issues and approaches'. *Pragmatics* 2/3: 235–49.

Wright, R. 2004. 'Latin and English as world languages'. *English Today* 20/4: 3–19.

Wright, S. 2004. *Language Policy and Language Planning. From Nationalism to Globalisation*. Houndmills, Basingstoke: Palgrave Macmillan.

Yano, Y. 2003. 'Comment 1'. *World Englishes* 22/1: 67–8.

Yano, Y. 2005. 'Comment 1'. *World Englishes* 24/1: 95–6.

Yoshikawa, H. 2005. 'Recognition of world Englishes: changes in Chukyo University students' attitudes'. *World Englishes* 24/3: 351–60.

Yuzefovich, N. G. 2005. 'English in Russian cultural contexts'. *World Englishes* 24/4: 509–16.

Zacharias, N. T. 2005. 'Teachers' beliefs about internationally-published materials: a survey of tertiary English teachers in Indonesia'. *RELC Journal* 36/1: 23–37.

Zuengler, J. 1989. 'Identity and IL development and use'. *Applied Linguistics* 10/1: 80–96.

Zuengler, J. and **J. Miller.** 2006. 'Cognitive and sociocultural perspectives: two parallel SLA worlds?' *TESOL Quarterly* 40/1: 35–58.

Index